THE SOUND
OF LIGHT

ALSO BY DON CUSIC:

*Cowboys and the Wild West: An A-Z Guide from the
  Chisholm Trail to the Silver Screen*

Eddy Arnold: I'll Hold You In My Heart

Hank Williams: The Complete Lyrics (editor)

Merle Haggard: Poet of the Common Man, The Lyrics (editor)

The Poet as Performer

Randy Travis: Kind of the New Traditionalists

Reba McEntire: Country Music's Queen

Sandi Patti: The Voice of Gospel

Willie Nelson: Lyrics 1959-1994 (editor)

THE SOUND OF LIGHT

A History of Gospel and Christian Music

DON CUSIC

HAL•LEONARD®

7777 W. BLUEMOUND RD. P.O. BOX 13819 MILWAUKEE, WI 53213

All photos courtesy of the Center for Popular Music at Middle Tennessee State University.

Published by Hal Leonard Corporation
7777 West Bluemound Road
P.O. Box 13819
Milwaukee, WI 53213, USA

Trade Book Division Editorial Offices:
151 West 46th Street, 8th Floor
New York, NY 10036

Visit Hal Leonard online at **www.halleonard.com**

Library of Congress Cataloging-in-Publication Data has been applied for.

Printed in the United States of America
First Hal Leonard edition
An earlier version of *The Sound of Light* was published in 1990 by Bowling Green State University Popular Press.

10 9 8 7 6 5 4 3 2 1

CONTENTS

PART 3:

PART 4:

PREFACE

Christianity in America isn't just a faith—it's a gigantic industry that sells over $3 billion worth of music, books, movies, and videos each year.

Christian books account for about $1 billion in revenue, sales of videos about $815 million, and movies are about $17 million. Movies? The highest grossing independent movie in 1999 was *The Omega Code*, which grossed $12 million that first year and $20 million since its release. The *Left Behind* series of novels, written by Tim LaHaye and Jerry B. Jenkins, has sold 28.8 million copies by 2001, and one novel in that series, *The Indwelling,* was number one on the *New York Times* best-seller list. And the *Times* does not count books sold in religious book stores!

Gospel and Christian music accounted for about $747 million in sales of recordings in 2000; however, that doesn't account for money from concerts, which easily makes religious music an over $1 billion annual business.

Although it has entered the mainstream through retailers like Wal Mart, K-Mart, Target and others, the strength of Christian music lies in sales at religious stores—which used to be called Christian book stores—that account for about two-thirds of the sales of Christian music, books, videos, and other assorted products.

The Christian church in America is the most segregated institution in the nation, yet no one really complains. It is a segregation by choice, not law—African-Americans go to churches where the audiences are predominately black while whites go to churches where the congregations are predominately white. A number of people within the white Christian world say they wish it were different—that the blacks are welcome in their churches and they wish more would attend. However, the idea that the problem would be solved more quickly if these whites attended a black church never really occurs to them.

The differences in these audiences are reflected in the music. "Gospel" music has become a term designating the religious music of African-Americans (as well as those in Southern gospel), while "Christian" is the term for religious pop music for predominately white audiences, generally called contemporary Christian music.

The history of religious music goes back to the Bible and also to the Reformation. The story of religious music in America parallels the story of Christianity in America. But the story of contemporary Christian music parallels the combined story of rock 'n' roll and Christianity. That is not to say that these stories are intertwined; many would find their stories diametrically opposed. But the young Baby Boomers who ushered in the rock 'n' roll revolution also ushered in contemporary Christian music. Music was important to this group; it voiced their fears and concerns, and it was the soundtrack to their growing-up years.

The essence of early rock 'n' roll was rebellion—children rebelling again the past, their parents, hypocrisy, dishonesty, and a pressure to conform to the mainstream. In its own way, gospel/Christian music is also a music of rebellion, but it is a rebellion against popular culture, a culture that markets sex, drugs and dysfunctional families as the norm. The messages of rock 'n' roll—stay true to your own soul, don't cave in to pressure to conform, and stand up for your beliefs—are the messages of gospel and Christian music.

The entertainment industry claims it is market-based and that the television shows, movies, and recordings produced reflect a demand from the market. The justification for what is produced is that people watch it and/or buy it, which means that a demand has been satisfied. That's true to some extent—after a movie or recording is released, its success is determined by how many people purchase tickets or recordings. But a relative handful of people decide what is going to get into the market.

This is especially true in Hollywood, where the people who decide which movies and television shows will get produced and released are increasingly further from the mainstream in America.

The Hollywood types refer to middle Americans as "fly-over" people—the idea being that only those in Los Angeles and New York "count." In some ways they're right—because the advertisers, financiers, and producers/writers/directors of television and movies are centered in these two cities. But the people who must watch and purchase what they produce are in middle America. And these are the people who have become increasingly disgusted, upset, shocked, frustrated, and sick of what is being produced and marketed.

Part of it is the aging process. When the Baby Boomers were young, many felt there should be no restrictions on what they saw, heard, or bought—it was an "anything goes" mentality. But as the Baby Boomers had children, the notion that anybody should send into the market whatever they wished—no matter what the language or subject—was gradually replaced with the idea that some things are not appropriate or suitable for public consumption. Some have called this concept "growing up." No doubt the Baby Boomers have grown up—at least they've added numbers to their age—and have generally gotten more conservative as they have aged. Part of this aging process has been a rejection of some of American popular culture.

There is certainly an audience for shows that "push the envelope," which relates to a world saturated with sex and drugs, but there's another world as well, a world that wants to see "clean" entertainment, that doesn't want sex and drugs shoved in their faces, and that wants the media to support and encourage traditional families and old-fashioned values. While L.A. and New York may be agnostic cities, most of America is a faith-based nation. They believe in God and are not ashamed to show it. These "fly-over" people are the backbone of the middle-class and the essential components of the Christian culture.

Gospel and Christian music have grown with the number of "born again" Christians in the United States. It has benefited from demographics (aging Baby Boomers having children), trends (towards family lifestyles and family entertainment), and marketing.

The contemporary Christian music industry is centered in Nashville—the same place that the country music industry is located. In the early 1990s, country music was experiencing unprecedented growth while gospel and Christian were trying to get on their feet. But by the year 2000, sales of country had gone down while Christian music's sales had risen to the point that whenever country music sold ten albums, Christian music sold seven. To put it another way, gospel/Christian music sells about twice as many recordings as Latin music, and more than jazz, classical, and New Age combined.

In *The Sound of Light*, I have attempted to trace the roots of gospel and Christian music, to tell the story of how these musics developed, grew, and evolved into a major segment of American popular culture. And why, even though they are "in" the entertainment industry, Christian musicians are not "of" the entertainment industry. Nor are they "of" popular culture as much as Christianity is a culture all its own, mirroring popular culture while, at the same time, shunning and rejecting it.

A number of people have played a major role in this book appearing; most of them are listed in the "Notes" section at the end of the book. But I would especially like to thank my agent, Jim Fitzgerald, and editor Ben Schafer for nurturing this project along. Also Bill Hearn, who sent me a number of "W.O.W." CDs that helped me "catch up" with the most recent Christian music. Folks I work with—Bob Fisher, Dan McAlexander, Jim Clapper, Pam Browne, Clyde Rolston, James Elliott, Wes Bulla and others—are always supportive. Finally, I would like to thank my family, my wife Jackie and children Delaney, Jesse, Eli, and Alex for always reminding me that there are more important things in life than writing books, but who nonetheless give me support and encouragement when I'm racing against a deadline and spending more time with a computer than with them.

Chapter 1

MUSIC IN THE BIBLE

Throughout the Bible, songs and singing play an important part in life. Music is used in religious services, in secular celebrations, in wars, as private prayer, as a means of offering thanksgiving and praise to God, to record events, in apocalyptic visions of the final days of earth, and in visions of life in heaven where songs will be used as a way to honor God with praise and thanksgiving, expressing awe and wonder.

The 20th and 21st centuries have seen the Bible inspire new Christian revivals and songs have been an integral part of communicating biblical messages, introducing the unbeliever to God, and offering believing Christians new instruments of praise, worship, and thanksgiving for a closer communion with God. Indeed, a whole industry of songs has been born from this tradition of singing songs to, for, and about God.

The first mention of songs in the Bible is in Genesis, Chapter 31, when Jacob leaves Laban. Jacob and Rachel flee early one morning to return to Canaan, the land of his father and grandfather (Issac and Abraham) without telling Laban, whom they had been visiting. However, Laban, learning Jacob has left, pursues him for seven days, finally overtaking him and asking, "What have you done, that you have cheated me, and carried away my daughters like captives of the sword? Why did you flee secretly, and cheat me, and did not tell me, so that I might have sent you away with mirth and songs, with tambourine and lyre?" (v. 26-7). It is clear that even at this early time, music was part of the culture, used in this case for festive occasions.

The first mention of singing in a religious context occurs in Exodus, Chapter 15. Moses has crossed the Red Sea after the sea had been rolled back for the Israelites but then closed on Pharoah's army, assuring the Israelites' safety. Moses and the people of Israel sing a song of thanksgiving to the Lord for their deliverance; the song begins, "I will sing to the Lord, for he has triumphed gloriously; the horse and his rider he has thrown into the sea" and then continues with a description of what happened at the Red Sea and how the Lord had defeated his enemies. This was topical and apparently composed on the spot, probably by Moses who, if this is true, would be the first acknowledged gospel songwriter.

This first biblical song lasts 18 verses and is a celebration of praise and appreciation for what the Lord has done. Although it is not safe to assume that other biblical characters before Moses—Adam, Noah, Abraham, Issac, Jacob, Joseph, etc.—never sang, there is at least no mention of such a thing. It is also significant to note that a song of thanksgiving was established as an important part of the religious life of the new nation forming under the leadership of Moses.

From the earliest establishment of Israel as the nation of God and the Jews as the people of God in the Old Testament, singing has been a vital part of communication with God. When the people were in the wilderness with Moses, without food and water, suffering from their rebellion, they reconciled themselves with God by singing and He provided water.

In establishing the nation of Israel, God commanded Moses to "write this song, and teach it to the people of Israel; put it in their mouths, that this song may be a witness for me against the people of Israel. For when I have brought them into the land flowing with milk and honey, which I swore to give to their fathers, and they have eaten and full and grown fat they will turn to other gods and serve them, and break my covenant. And when many evils and troubles have come upon them, this song shall confront them as a witness (for it will live unforgotten in the mouths of their descendants); for I know the purposes which they are already forming, before I had brought them into the land that I swore to give." Moses writes this song that very same day and teaches it to the people of Israel (Deut. 31: 19-22).

The song itself is Chapter 32 of Deuteronomy and tells the story of the formation of Israel, admonishing the people not to forget that God brought them to Israel to be a special nation, and warning them of the wrath and vengeance of God should they forget their heritage.

After singing the song, Moses commands the people to "Lay to heart all the words which I enjoin upon you this day, that you may command them to your children, that they may be careful to do all the words of this law. For it is no trifle for you, but it is your life, and thereby you shall live long in the land which you are going over the Jordan to possess" (Deut. 32: 45-47).

The Psalms, which are essentially a collection of songs from around the time of David, contain an abundance of references to songs and singing, with the emphasis on communicating with God through singing. Many of the Psalms urge the people of God to sing as an expression of their faith with passages like "Come into his presence with singing" (l00:2), and "I will praise the name of God with a song" (69:30). The Psalms also demonstrate that singing and songs are part of everyday life—not just life in the assembly of worship or churches, but a continuous outpouring of faith and praise. There is also encouragement to compose new songs expressing faith; the passage "Sing to the Lord a new song" is found in several Psalms.

Contemporary Christianity tends to ignore some aspects of the Psalms—the themes of revenge, fear, doubting, frustration, and outrage. Yet these are all part of the Psalms, although modern songwriters prefer to emphasize only the praise and worship aspects of the Psalms. Still, the Psalms show us songs of individual expression, of earthly concerns, of personal cries of pain and help. They also show the roots of Christianity to be strongly based in Judaism—a fact that has been obscured along the way, particularly in the eighteenth and nineteenth centuries when anti-Semitism arose and the Psalms were "Christianized" to fit the doctrines of denominations whose faith was rooted in the New Testament.

There are not a large number of examples of songs in the New Testament; still, it is obvious that singing and songs were considered an important part of the religious life of the early Christian. It was a way of communicating with God as well as of sharing a sense of togetherness among believers.

Perhaps the most significant mention of a song in the New Testament is after the last supper when Jesus and his disciples sing a hymn before retiring to the Mount of Olives where he spends his last free moments with the group that has been the core of his earthly followers. There is no record of what they sang, but the implication is that the song was known by all of them and that they had sung together before, thus implying that singing was a part of the spiritual life of Jesus and his disciples.

A significant example of the power of singing in the New Testament comes in Acts, Chapter 16, where Paul and Silas have been thrown in jail in Philippi after casting an evil spirit from a prophetess. It states, "About midnight, Paul and Silas were praying and singing hymns to God, and the prisoners were listening to them, and suddenly there was a great earthquake, so that the foundations of the prison were shaken; and immediately all the doors were opened and every one's fetters were unfastened" (v 25-26). Clearly, singing was considered part of spiritual life and the New Testament proves this by providing examples of both Jesus and Paul, his chief apostle, singing. Once again, the song Paul sang was not mentioned, but the implication is that it was a known hymn.

Later, in his letters, Paul exhorts new believers to "be filled with the Spirit, addressing one another in psalms, and hymns and spiritual songs, singing and making melody to the Lord with all your heart, always and for everything giving thanks in the name of our Lord Jesus Christ to God the Father" (Ephesians 5:19-20) and to "let the word of Christ dwell in you richly, teach and admonish one another in all wisdom, and sing psalms and hymns and spiritual songs with thankfulness in your hearts to God" (Colossians 3:16).

It is interesting to note that Paul, in these two passages, cites "psalms, hymns, and spiritual songs" as three kinds of songs, but never defines the difference. It may be surmised, however, that the psalms and hymns were known songs, while spiritual songs might have been sung "in the spirit" or extemporaneously and in an improvisational and personal manner, thereby encouraging believers to create their own songs. This implication sets the stage for Christianity to continually produce new songs that fit the changing times and spiritual revivals that have occurred throughout the generations since then.

Not only are songs important in this world, they are also an important and vital part of the next world, according to Revelation. In the apocalyptic vision, a "new song" is sung (Rev. 5:9-10) at the final moment. During the last days, as the scroll of life is opened, a song will be sung about the Savior: "Worthy art thou to take the scroll and to open its seals for thou was slain and by thy blood didst ransom men for God from every tribe and tongue and people and nation, and hast made them a kingdom and priests of our God, and they shall reign on earth." There are also passages (14:3) where Jesus will stand on Mount Zion on the final day and the 144,000 who are chosen to be saved will learn a "new song" which "no one else could learn" (15:3). Also, the song of Moses will be sung during this time as well as the song of the Lamb which says, "Great and wonderful are thy deeds, O Lord God Almighty! Just and true are thy ways, O King of the ages! Who shall not fear and glorify thy name, O Lord? For thou alone are holy. All nations shall come and worship thee, for thy judgments have been revealed" (15:3-5).

Contemporary gospel music is not just songs about the Jesus born two thousand years ago, but about the God of eternity. The Jewish roots have been Christianized and the branches run through the ages, a testament to the timeless spiritual thread that runs through the history of mankind. Contemporary gospel music is really a circle with the Bible as both the starting and ending point. The history of gospel music may be seen as a series of circles that has continually grown larger as the music has become more diverse and encompassed more styles and roles in the lives of believers and non-believers. Thus, the history of gospel music is also the history of Christianity, particularly in the United States where music has played such a vital role in Christian revivals throughout the life of the country.

Chapter 2

THE SIXTEENTH CENTURY:
Roots of Contemporary Christianity

The roots of contemporary American Christianity lie in the 16th century, particularly with three men: Martin Luther, John Calvin, and Henry VIII. The turning point is 1509—the year Henry VIII ascended to the throne of England, John Calvin was born in France, and Martin Luther, then an Augustinian monk in Wittenberg, Germany, read about the "justification of faith" in the epistle to the Romans and became transformed by the concept of "grace." Luther's pilgrimmage would lead to his nailing 95 theses to the door at Wittenberg protesting the selling of plenary indulgences. This act marks the beginning of the Reformation, while Calvin's life would provide Christianity with a book, *The Institutes of Christianity*, which would define and regulate Christianity for centuries. Henry VIII's reign would produce a break with the Catholic church in England, which created a climate for religious dissent—leading to the rise of Protestantism in England. This religious upheaval encompassed a spiritual awakening there, resulting in the settling of America by religious dissenters who viewed the new land as a second Canaan and their mission as akin to Moses leading the chosen people to a chosen land for the creation of a new, God-ordained nation.

Martin Luther gave Christian theology an individualism; John Calvin gave it a legislation that transformed the individualism into a collective force. These twin forces of individualism (the concept of the single soul's spiritual awakening) and collectivism (the concept of the "body" of Christ consisting of all believing Christians) would unite but also pull against each other for centuries. Luther's influence provided an individual liberation that freed the bonds of society on man, setting the soul free to rule the body and serve heavenly purposes in the earthly realm. Calvin preached morality and moralizing, binding the soul to other believers, tying the souls of the elect into a tight bond. Both men believed an individual could communicate with God directly, but Calvin did not trust all individuals to "interpret" this communication correctly. For that reason, the Catholic church's "sin" that both men rebelled against—the autocratic and authoritative directing of the spiritual life of individuals—became the same sin of the Reformed church under Calvin.

The new liberation theology espoused by Luther was quickly adopted by Calvin so that it was in line with living in accordance with the supremacy of the state. It is the state, more than the church, that has dictated the limits of modern Christianity while, at the same time, also assured its success. Most people believe morals are important and should be legislated—specifically and most importantly, other people's morals. The success of Calvinistic Christianity can be attributed to its major goal—the regulation of public morals—being in line with the goals of the state. Certainly the state made use of Christianity, which exacted a trade-off and received protection and certain perquisites (such as tax free income and property) and access to the power holders of the state. It was under Calvinism that the radicalism of Christianity was tamed and the threat to society thwarted and turned into cooperation. The result was that Christianity became, in effect, a social code for being good, law-abiding citizens within the state's definition of good citizenship.

Just as the apostle Paul virtually ignored the physical, earthly Christ and embraced the spiritual Christ so as to establish a code of behavior for Christians, so Calvin took the writings of Paul and further elaborated on this code. Whereas Paul had to fight the state because it was against Christianity, Calvin embraced the state and developed an alliance whereby the state and church co-existed in a theocracy. Luther, too, embraced Paul and the concept of the spiritual Christ, and tethered the Protestant revolt to German nationalism to mute the threat the state posed to Christianity. The net result was a state-sanctioned—or at least tolerated and accepted—religion that worked with the state rather than against it. Henry VIII, in his anti-Catholic revolt, also sought to bring both the state and religion under his thumb by installing himself as the head of the Anglican church. However, because of his lack of spiritual leadership, the two forces could never really co-exist as one.

Paul and Luther used music as a means of communicating with God, singing "psalms and hymns and spiritual songs" as a way of expressing prayer, love, and thanksgiving. Calvin used the laws of the state to carry out the will of God and placed strict limitations on music, insisting it only be used as part of worship. Calvin saw music as a diversion the rest of the time, so music for Christians was limited to congregational singing, with individual expression discouraged. That is why Paul and Luther encouraged music while Calvin frowned on it. The joy of Christianity expressed by Paul and Luther became under Calvin a somber, serious commitment to a code of behavior. Calvin interpreted certain behavior as sinful and placed man in the role of God by judging which behavior was acceptable. It is this emphasis on outward behavior reflecting inner spiritual life that made Calvinism so appealing to the state. For Calvin, the ideal Christian was a well-behaved person; for Luther, he was a rebel. Both were anti-papacy, but Calvin replaced the Catholic hierarchy with one of his own making, giving different names to the offices (elders, deacons, etc. instead of bishops, priests, etc.) but keeping the bureaucracy of belief so that faith would be socially acceptable.

There was religious dissension in Europe before Martin Luther nailed his 95 theses on the Wittenberg door in 1516; however, it was this act—and the subsequent life and trials of Luther—that led to the Protestant Reformation in Europe and to the rise of the Anglican church in England. Meanwhile, the Catholic Church, headed by the Pope in Rome, lost its grip on Europe amidst turmoil that would eventually affect all of Christendom.

Martin Luther was born in Eisleben, Germany, on November 10, 1483, the eldest of seven children, to Hans and Grethe Luther. His father, a peasant and later a miner, was described as "a hard father and strict judge, exacting a joyless virtue, demanding constant propitiation, and finally damning most of mankind to everlasting hell." Luther's father beat him "assiduously" while his mother was a "timid, modest woman much given to prayer."

From early in his life, Luther sang well and played the lute. He disliked the academic life and found scholasticism disagreeable, but managed to obtain a master of arts degree at the University of Erfurt and then began to study law. After two months of study, Luther, aged twenty-two, quit and decided to become a monk. His "conversion" was a road-to-Damascus experience, complete with lightning. It occurred as he was returning from his father's house in Erfurt (July 1505) and encountered a storm. Lightning flashed and struck a nearby tree, which seemed to Luther a warning from God that "unless he gave his thoughts to salvation, death would surprise him unshriven and damned ...[so] he made a vow to St. Anne that if he survived the storm he would become a monk."

According to Luther, "I was a pious monk, and so strictly observed the rules of my order that ... if ever a monk got into heaven by monkery, so should I also have gotten there .... If it had lasted longer I should have tortured myself to death with watching, praying, reading, and other work." He took his vows of poverty, chastity, and obedience in September, 1506, and was ordained a priest in May 1507.

Luther was reading St. Paul's epistle to the Romans c. 1509 when he was struck by the passage in 1:17, "The just shall live by faith." These words eventually led him to a doctrine whereby man can be "justified" and saved from hell only by a complete faith in Christ and his atonement for mankind, and not by good works, which are insufficient to atone for sins against an infinite deity. Luther's religious ideas moved away from the official doctrines of the Catholic church during the years 1512-1517. He began to argue that "the mere acceptance of the merits of Christ assured the believer's salvation" and identified the pope as the Antichrist.

At this time there was an inner turmoil within Germany, an undercurrent of rebellion among the people against the corruption and indulgences (buying your way into Heaven by giving money to the church) as well as a pent-up anticlericalism which found its voice in Luther. The theologian became the leader of the movement because he first articulated this frustration, then stood and fought a battle against Rome.

Pope Leo, an educated, gentle man, tried a reconciliation with Luther and Luther himself seemed to desire to remain part of the church. However, Luther was a fighter and his overtures to Leo were combative and challenged the very acts which accounted for church income. In 1518 Leo summoned Luther to Rome, but the monk did not go.

Around this same time, the Emperor of Germany, Elector Frederick, summoned an Imperial Diet to meet at Augsburg to consider the Pope's request to tax Germany in order to finance a new crusade against the Turks. The Diet refused this request and pointed out money misspent by Rome in the past. Pope Leo requested Luther present himself at Augsburg before Cardinal Cajetan to answer the charges of indiscipline and heresy and "instructed the legate to offer Luther full pardon and future dignities, if he would recant and submit; otherwise the secular authorities should be asked to send him to Rome." The Cardinal apparently "misread his function to be that of judge, not diplomat" and demanded a "retraction and pledge never again to disturb the peace of the Church." Luther refused and then Frederick refused to send Luther to Rome. Luther wrote a "spirited account of the interviews," which was circulated throughout Germany. In a letter at this time to Duke George, Luther stated that "a common reformation should be undertaken of the spiritual and temporal estates," which is the first known use of the term that provided the religious rebellion with its name.

This was not the first effort to "reform" the church, but the other efforts had generally resulted in new orders of monks being formed or the rebellion being quelled by public burnings and hangings. Pope Leo continued his conciliatory efforts and in a papal bull of November 9, 1518, he "repudiated many of the extreme claims for indulgences." Luther, at this time, seemed open to conciliation, feeling "anxious to preserve the unity of western Christendom," but his combative nature and the groundswell of support from the German populus against Rome carried the movement forward.

Luther argued that Germany's clergy should establish a national church under the Archbishop of Mainz and throw off the subjugation of Rome. This plea for nationalism was the key to the Reformation taking over in Germany. Luther, 37 years old, tapped into the German national spirit as well as its spiritual side to foment the revolt. He stuck with his basic doctrine that "faith alone, not good works, makes the true Christian and saves him from hell. For it is faith in Christ that makes a man good; his good works follow from that faith." This made every Christian an independent priest.

When Luther learned that papal envoys were burning his books, he organized his own book burning on December 10, 1520, and cast a papal bull, some canonical decretals and volumes of scholastic theology into the fire. The next day he declared that "no man could be saved unless he renounced the rule of the papacy." Luther thereby excommunicated the pope just as the pope had excommunicated him. It was a marvelous strategy and put him totally on the offensive, no longer answering the threats of Rome.

Meanwhile, in England, the Protestant Reformation was taking hold, but there was no spiritual leader of the magnitude of Luther to lead it. Instead, the anti-papacy movement was led by a political leader, King Henry VIII.

When Henry VIII ascended to the English throne in 1509, he began a thirty-seven year reign that saw him become both a hero and villian during this dramatic time in English history. He was eighteen when he became king and was good at athletics, theology, dancing, and literature. According to Sir Thomas More, the king "has more learning than any English monarch ever possessed before him." However, from this promising beginning there emerged the "incarnation of Machiavelli's Prince" by the end of his reign. During the early part of his reign, Henry VIII protected the papacy; however, by the end he was responsible for the decline of papal influence in England, primarily due to the pope's refusal to grant him a marriage easement.

At the beginning of Henry VIII's reign, Cardinal Wolsey controlled much of foreign policy and the actual governing of England. This close relationship between church and state was as much a result of Wolsey's own power and ambition as it was due to the alliance between Rome and England. When Martin Luther broke from the Catholic Church in Germany, Henry VIII rushed to the papal defense, publishing his *Assertion of the Seven Sacraments* against Martin Luther in 1521, stating in this work that "the whole Church is subject not only to Christ but ... to Christ's only vicar, the pope of Rome." For that, Henry and his successors were given the title of "Defensor Fidei" (Defender of the Faith) by the pope. Luther published his reply in 1525, calling Henry VIII the "King of Lies ... by God's disgrace King of England."

This incensed Henry and he never embraced the German Protestant rebellion and never forgave Luther, despite the latter's later apology. Despite the King's repudiation of the German movement, Luther's influence spread in England through a London group called the "Association of Christian Brothers," which distributed tracts from Luther and others as well as English Bibles. Most clergymen discouraged the reading of the Bible because "special knowledge" was needed for the right interpretation (indeed, excerpts from Scripture were being used to foment sedition.)

There had been English translations of the Bible before this time (c. 1526), including those by Wycliff, but they were in manuscript form. However, the English New Testament printed by Tyndale in 1525-1526 and translated from the original Hebrew and Greek (as opposed to the Latin Vulgate by Wycliff) achieved epochal importance. Tyndale had gone to Wittenberg in 1524 to work under Luther's guidance on the Bible translation and when the Bible was released in England, it was accompanied by a separate volume of notes and aggressive prefaces based on those by Erasmus and Luther. These copies were smuggled into England and "served as fuel to the incipient Protestant fire" despite the efforts of England's clergy to suppress the edition by publicly burning them and trying to silence Tyndale. Cardinal Wolsey ordered Tyndale to appear in court but the translator eluded English officials until he fell into their hands and was imprisoned for sixteen months near Brussels. Tyndale was burned at the stake in 1536, but the influence of his English translation of the Bible remained strong and heavily influenced the Authorized Version (King James) which was published in 1611.

Henry VIII's marital troubles actually began with Cardinal Wolsey's foreign policy. Wolsey had aligned England with Emperor Charles of Italy to fight France. The expense of the campaign hurt Wolsey with Parliament, and the realization that the Continent would soon be under the rule of Charles caused England to align with France against the Emperor in 1528. Compounding this political squabble for the control of Europe was the fact that Charles was the nephew of Catherine of Aragon, Henry's wife, whom Henry wanted to divorce. Pope Clement VII, who could grant the divorce and had granted similar requests in the past, was under the control of Charles so, for reasons of state, the divorce was not granted.

Henry's basic desire was to have a son. Cardinal Wolsey argued for the King, and the papacy had generally acknowledged this national need and had established many precedents of granting annulments for this purpose. However, Emperor Charles, who "controlled" the pope, felt openly hostile toward Henry, so "the Catholic Queen and the Catholic Emperor collaborated with the captive Pope to divorce England from the Church." Historian Will Durant states that "The ultimate cause of the English Reformation was not Henry's suit for annulment so much as the rise of the English monarchy to such strength that it could repudiate the authority of the pope over English affairs and revenues." There were some ideas for reconciliation. The proposal that Henry be allowed to have two wives (a principle that Luther supported later when he addressed the problem of barren wives); but all the appeals failed.

Ironically, Henry attempted to solicit the support of Martin Luther for the divorce. The King sent Robert Barnes, a trusted envoy, to Wittenberg to curry Luther's favor. Henry courted Protestantism so he could "pick and choose, to accept whatever suited his aims to refute the Pope's authority in England and to reject whatever appeared to him an unnecessary and uncongenial doctrinal change." Luther rejected the overture and, in a memorandum written with two other theologians, stated, "They must not think that there could ever be a case when a marriage ought to be dissolved for God's sake, or that they could leave each other because of man-made laws."

The British Parliament and Convocation that convened in 1532 would have a lasting historical and religious importance because of the decision to separate from the papacy. From this "Reformation Parliament" the Church of England was born, growing into an arm and subject of the state. This act would later be of prime importance in the practice of religious tolerance and the separation of church and state when America was settled.

By 1537, Henry was completely divorced from the Catholic church in England and he asked the Irish parliament to acknowledge him as head of the Irish Church as well. They did, but Henry died five years later and Ireland remained Catholic as Mary, a Catholic Queen, ascended the throne and the struggle for Irish nationhood took on religious overtones in the struggle with England.

Since one church no longer dominated religion in Europe, no church could stand united and thus religion was split asunder into factions, often warring against one another. A great amount of disorder prevailed in the church because "in some instances the prayer book was rigidly adhered to, in others psalms in metre were added; in some churches the communion table stood in the middle of the chancel, in others altarwise a yard distant from the wall; some ministers officiated at the sacraments in the surplice, others without it; some used a chalice in the communion service, others were content with a common cup; some favoured unleavened bread, others preferred leavened; some baptized in a font, others in a basin; some made the sign of the cross, others dispensed with it; and so forth." There was a great rise in religious literature as numerous translations of the Bible as well as biblical commentaries appeared. *The Book of Common Prayer* was published in 1549 and "hours" or "primers," long series of books of devotion, became commonplace.

Martin Luther said of Henry VIII, "We should give thanks to God, the Father of Mercy, that He can make such masterly use of such devils and devils' companions towards our and all Christians' salvation and also to the punishment of themselves and of all who do not wish to know God; as He has always done through dreadful tyrants." It was Henry VIII who broke the ties with Rome and allowed the Protestant revolt in England, which set the stage for the settling of America as a "new Canaan."

Chapter 3
JOHN CALVIN AND THE INSTITUTES

John Calvin's mind has been described as "sharp, narrow, devoted, and intense" and his will has been described as "indomitable." It was this mind and this man who used his gifts of administration and organization to give reformation Christianity the laws and order that would come to define the religion. Although he walked in the path cleared by Martin Luther, Calvin's influence would ultimately prove to be greater because his religion was not bound to a single country. Luther had to protect his new church by appealing to German nationalism for its support; Calvin, though a native of France who spent most of his years in French Geneva, was not a nationalist. This enabled him to give Protestantism in many lands the "organization, confidence, and pride that enabled it to survive a thousand trials."

It is both a mystery and an illumination that Calvin's theology caught on and won thousands of converts. During the difficult times of the sixteenth and seventeenth centuries, Calvin imposed on his followers a severity of discipline as well as an optimism stemming from the belief that they were the chosen elect of God. This gave the early Protestants the courage to press on and carry forth their message in a hostile world. Calvin established a theocracy that ruled Geneva—a civil government bound to a religious institution that would be imitated by the early American Puritans—and wrote a book, *Institutes of the Christian Religion*, that would define and guide Christianity for centuries. Although some of Calvin's harsher doctrines (including the concept of predestination) have since been discarded by many churches, his work remains the definitive work on the Christian faith in the secular world as seen by the reformers of the sixteenth century.

Jean Chauvin was born in Noyon, France, on July 10, 1509. His father, Gerard, was secretary to the bishop, proctor in the cathedral chapter, and fiscal procurator of the county. Such an ecclesiastical city, ruled by the clergy, gave the young Calvin an early example of theocracy practiced by religious leaders in the name of God. One of four sons, he registered as Johannes Calvinus at the College de la Marche at the University of Paris and later attended the College de Montaigu, alma mater of Erasmus and of Loyola (who entered as Calvin was leaving). In late 1528, Calvin went to Orleans to study law and, after obtaining a Bachelor of Law degree in 1531, returned to Paris and began to study classical literature. During this time Calvin was dedicated to humanism and admired Erasmus until some of Luther's writings reached him. The Reformation was taking hold in France and many of Calvin's friends were reformers, some of whom would be killed.

Calvin caught the fever of church reform and was scheduled to be arrested when he left Paris for Angouleme in 1534. There, he began to write his *Institutes*. He returned to Noyon, was arrested, freed, and arrested again before being released. He then returned to Paris and joined with Protestant leaders. Francis I, the king of France, undertook a furious persecution at this time and Calvin fled to Basel, Switzerland, where, at the age of twenty-six, he published the first edition of his great work. Originally titled *The Institute of the Christian Religion, Containing almost the Whole Sum of Piety and Whatever It is Necessary to Know in the Doctrine of Salvation. A Work Very Well Worth Reading by All Persons Zealous for Piety and Lately Published. A Preface to the Most Christian King of France, in Which This Book is Presented to Him as a Confession of Faith*, it was later shortened to *Institutes of the Christian Religion*.

The original, published in 1536, contained six chapters with four on topics "familiar to the history of Christian instruction" and used by Luther in his *Catechisms*: the Law, the Creed, the Lord's Prayer, and the sacraments of Baptism and the Lord's Supper. The fifth chapter was an argument against recognizing the rites of confirmation, penance, extreme unction, priestly order, and matrimony as sacraments, and the sixth chapter a "challenging discussion of Christian liberty, involving some elements of political and social teaching."

The first volume contained 520 octavo pages of about six and an eighth inches by four inches and is "about the length of the New

Testament to the end of Ephesians." After repeated expansions and revisions by the author, the book reached its final form in 1559 when it was "about equal in size to the Old Testament plus the Synoptic Gospels." Published in Latin, the book eventually had seventeen chapters of similar length. Calvin later included many references to Augustine, Origen, and other church fathers, along with references to Plato, Aristotle, Cicero, and Seneca, and to some scholarly work so as to lend academic weight to the work. Calvin also added chapters on the knowledge of God and the similarities and differences between the Old and New Testaments, between predestination and providence, and on the Christian life. After the first edition, Calvin increasingly saw the work as a "textbook to be used in the prepartion of candidates in theology for the reading of the divine Word." This explains why the format was changed to make it fit for desk use with the book now comprising 346 pages, measuring thirteen by eight inches and featuring wide margins for student's notes.

The first French translation was done by Calvin in 1541 (based on the Latin edition of 1539) and it is "the earliest work in which the French language is used as a medium for expression of sustained serious thought." In an attempt to reach the common man with the message of Christ, Calvin—as Luther had done for the German lan-guage—gave character to the language of the French nation. The first English translation of Calvin's whole work was published in 1561 in London, although the chapters on the Christian life (Book III, Chapters VI-X) had been circulated in Great Britain before that time. The Latin editions had been circulated in England and Scotland before 1559.

Calvin did not know German and did not know Luther person-ally; however, he did have close personal relationships with those who did know Luther—most notably Melanchthon—and read much of Luther in Latin, including the *Great Catechism*, the *Small Catechism*, *On the Freedom of a Christian*, *The Babylonian Captivity of the Church*, *On the Bondage of the Will*, and *Luther's major sermon on the Eucharist*. In fact, it was Luther's *Small Catechism* which probably served as the model for the first edition of the *Institutes* in 1536.

Calvin and Luther have much in common theologically—partic-ularly in their concept of "justification by faith"—and agree on most major points. The great difference between them was their personalities: Luther was warm, outgoing, and loved life and music, while Calvin was more introverted, cold, and ordered, lacking a sense of humor or a noticeable appreciation for beauty in life or art. While Luther composed hymns and encouraged others to do so, Calvin saw music as a distraction from the gospel and demanded that only passages of Scripture be sung. Unlike Luther, he saw no use for music outside the church. These differences overrode the similarities in thought and tended to give Luther the image of a man who symbolized the love of God while Calvin came to symbolize God's wrath and severity. Still, the two men's faith was extremely similar and they were close theologically and spiritually despite their differences personally.

The *Institutes* is written in much the same style as a sermon: Calvin makes a statement (such as "Human competence in art and science also derives from the Spirit of God") in a brief headline and then elaborates on it. Within the context of his sermons—which generally run 600-800 words—there are biblical quotations to support his thesis. It is from the biblical passages that Calvin draws his conclusions but, although the conclusions are biblically based, they are unmistakably Calvin's own interpretation. It is a technique and style used by contemporary preachers who will take a line of Scripture and then deliver an entire sermon elaborating, explaining, examining, expounding, and interpreting their message.

Calvin believed the church to be built upon Scripture and the Bible to be the cornerstone of Christianity. He believed in a simple and literal interpretation and saw the authority of the Bible as God's Word and as a source of indisputable truth that should never be called into question. He assumed his readers shared these assumptions. Further, Calvin believed the Bible should be read under the direction of the Holy Spirit, the silent voice God uses to speak to his elect. Calvin's pages confront God and view him as a companion in religious struggles. According to John T. McNeill, editor of an edition of Calvin's *Institutes*, Calvin is a "peculiarly articulate and intelligible reporter of religious insights and spiritual promptings that come at least vaguely to consciousness whenever men strive to frame thoughts of the God with whom they have to do."

Calvin wrote from the heart and his book is not so much an intellectual explanation of Christianity as an emotional plea to embrace the faith. According to McNeill, "It is a living, challenging book that makes personal claims upon the reader ... because it presents, with eloquent insistence, that which was laid hold upon the author himself." That "hold" was a fixation on God that sprang from Calvin's conversion. Looking back at his conversion, Calvin wrote, "God subdued my heart to teachableness." From that time on, Calvin was constantly aware of God, intoxicated by God, a God-centered man in a man-centered world. As he noted, "Today all sorts of subjects are eagerly pursued; but the knowledge of God is neglected.... Yet to know God is man's chief end, and justifies his existence. Even if a hundred lives were ours, this one aim would be sufficient for them all."

When Calvin died, on May 27, 1564, he left a work that would haunt Christianity for centuries. Some have tried to live up to the work, others have tried to live it down; some embraced it while others rejected it. Still, it remains a landmark in the history of the Christian religion, while Calvin remains both a guiding light and a dark shadow. Historian Will Durant describes Calvin's book as "the most eloquent, fervent, lucid, logical, influential, and terrible work in all the literature of the religious revolution." Critic Suzanne Selinger presents two views of Calvin: in one, Calvin "imparts to Lutheranism the formal systemization of doctrine, the organization of church life, the discipline, and the dynamism that enabled Reform to spread, survive, take root and flourish," and, in the other, Calvin was the "creative synthesizer who molded ideas and impulses from his predecessors into a coherent whole, a totality greater than the sum of its parts and one that gave direction to both the inner and outer lives of adherents of Reform." Both of these writers summarize the impact and influence of Calvin and the *Institutes*, which is his contribution to the Reformation and his message to Christianity for the ages.

According to Durant, Calvin's "dictatorship was one not of law or force but of will and character. The intensity of his belief in his mission, and the completeness of his devotion to his tasks, gave him a strength that no one could successfully resist." Calvin established an order of pastors, teachers, lay elders, and deacons that is still accepted in Protestant and Presbyterian churches. Although he was strongly anti-Catholic, Calvin set up a church hierarchy much like that of the Catholic church, and though Protestant church leaders did not claim the miraculous powers of Catholic priests, they became a powerful force within the church and state. Calvin insisted the Bible must be the real law of the Christian state and that the clergy are the proper interpreters of the law; since civil governments are subject to that law, they must therefore enforce it as the clergy sees fit.

Like the popes, Calvin rejected individualism of belief. Although the Reformation theology insists on a one-to-one relationship between man and God, Calvin repudiated the principle of private judgment—thus the collectivism of the Catholic church permeated the new Protestant churches. Calvin, an austere and severe man, wanted the conduct of the church to exemplify the Christian belief because good conduct meant the right belief. He insisted that discipline should be the "backbone of personality" and that the clergy should lead by example as well as precept—they may marry and have children but must abstain from "hunting, gambling, feasting, commerce, and secular amusements and must accept ... moral scrutiny by their ecclesiastical superiors."

During his twenty-three years as the leader of the civil government in Geneva, Calvin worked tirelessly as a "preacher, administrator, professor of theology, superintendent of churches and schools, advisor to municipal councils, and regulator of public morals and church liturgy." He also enlarged his *Institutes*, wrote commentaries on the Bible, and maintained a voluminous correspondence. By the time of his death, he had combined his skills of administration and organization with his tireless work habits and self-discipline to establish the Reformed Church with a structure that would dominate Christianity for years to come. He gave a religious sanction and laurel to hard work, sobriety, diligence, frugality, and thrift that "may have shared in developing the industrious temper of the modern Protestant businessman." The self-confidence of being among God's elect gave the followers of Calvin the encouragement to spread the base of education and self-government—if men could choose their own pastors, they could choose their own governors—which led the self-ruled congregation to become the self-ruled state. This concept of divine election later played a major role in the formation of the United States.

Chapter 4

A MIGHTY FORTRESS:
Martin Luther as Songwriter

More people have heard Martin Luther's songs than have read his essays, biblical commentaries, treatises, sermons, his German Bible or even his 95 theses. Although Luther wrote only thirty-seven songs, it is this body of work which has carried Luther's words and thoughts directly to people for over five centuries. The legacy he left in song has lived longer and probably had as great an influence as any of the other works produced by this leader of the Reformation.

Martin Luther's greatest contribution to the music of the church was to return it to the people. For over a millenium—from the Council of Laodicea in the fourth century until the Reformation in the 1520s—congregations had done no singing in church. There were hymns written, but their use was limited to special occasions such as processions, pilgrimmages, and some major festivals, all held outside the sanctuary. Luther put music back into the church and in so doing made the congregation active participants rather than passive onlookers in the church service.

Luther's formal music training began as a boy when he was a soprano in the choir at Mansfield. At the age of 13, in 1497, he attended a cathedral school administered by a religious brotherhood at Madgeburg and studied singing there. Later, at Saint George at Eisencach, he continued his vocal studies. In 1501, Luther entered the University at Erfurt where he studied musical theory and composition and learned to play both the flute and lute. He learned the liturgy and plainchant in the Augustinian monastery he entered in 1501; while there, it is said his chief recreations were playing chess and the lute.

When Luther read in Romans about the "justification by faith" (c. 1509) and embraced the concept of free grace for all believers, it set in motion a chain of events which led to the posting of his 95 theses on the Wittenberg door in protest of the sale of indulgences. This led to a full-scale Protestant revolt, ushering in the Reformation and breaking the stronghold the Catholic church had on Europe. In Luther's desire to bring religion to the people, to convince them they could communicate with God directly—and God with them—without the aid of the church hierarchy, he began writing treatises and giving sermons. Soon, he began his translation of the Latin Vulgate Bible into German to make it accessible for everyone. This work became a landmark in language as well as religion. According to Catherine Winkworth, "In this work, Luther made use of his mother-tongue with such force, purity, and beauty, that his style ... must be considered to have been the germ and laid the basis of the modern high German language." This view of language and the desire to communicate in German for all to understand was the underlying philosophy guiding Luther's songwriting.

Martin Luther had a legendary love for music. He was an accomplished lutenist and could improvise accompaniments for singing. He often played after dinner with his family and guests and composed songs for his children. Throughout his life, he carried his lute with him on his travels and entertained friends and guests after dinner with his singing and playing. Music was not just a recreational tool for Luther—it was an integral part of his life and from it he found a source of strength and comfort. Like Bach, whom he greatly influenced, Luther viewed his music primarily as utilitarian, not as "art for the ages." He stated that we "should praise God with both word and music, namely by proclaiming [the Word of God] through music," and another time said, "He who believes [the gospel] earnestly cannot be quiet about it. But he must gladly and willingly sing and speak about it so that others may come and hear it. And whoever does not want to sing and speak of it shows that he does not believe it." Luther's prophetic statement, "I intend to make ... spiritual songs so that the Word of God even by means of song may live among the people" became a guiding philosophy in his life.

Luther wrote his first hymn, "Out of the Depths I Cry to Thee," in 1523 at the age of 40. He wrote twenty-three hymns that first year and a total of thirty-seven which still survive. They were generally introduced as broadsheets at the church in Wittenberg and later collected into hymnals. He demanded a simple, straightforward German for his songs—-and from those composed by others for the new mass—so that ordinary people could readily understand them. Of the thirty-seven he composed, twelve were translations from Latin hymns, four from German folk songs, and at least five were "completely original hymns." Catherine Winkworth writes that, "They were not so much outpourings of the individual soul, as the voice of the congregation meant for use in public worship, or to give the people a short, clear confession of faith, easily to be remembered. But they are not written from the outside; Luther throws into them all his own fervent faith and deep devotion. The style is plain, often rugged and quaint, but genuinely popular. So, too, was their cheerful trust and noble courage; their clear, vigorous spirit, that sprang from steadfast faith in a Redeemer."

In 1524, Luther invited Conrad Rupf, choirmaster to the Elector of Saxony, and Johann Walther, choirmaster to Frederick the Wise at Jorgau, to live with him and help reform and re-adapt the liturgy for popular use. These men studied the church music and selected tunes which lent themselves to this purpose. They transposed a large number of chorales from old Latin hymns and others from German origin—sacred and secular—and composed a still larger number. In Luther's time, it was customary to change secular into religious songs or older Catholic texts into Protestant ones, retaining the original melody. According to Paul Nettl, "Music was considered a functional art and not merely art for art's sake.... It was not a question of who created the melody. The purpose counted."

The first hymnal from Luther was given to the congregation in 1524 to read while the choir was singing. However, the people were so unused to joining in the public service that "they could not at once adopt the new practice." It took four or five years before Luther taught the people of his own parish church in Wittenberg to sing in church. After this, the custom spread swiftly.

Luther was well aware of the power of music and insisted that its proper use was "to the glorification of God and the edification of man." He said, "We want the beautiful art of music to be properly used to serve her dear Creator and his Christians. He is thereby praised and honored and we are made better and stronger in faith when His holy Word is impressed on our hearts by sweet music." At another time, Luther said of music, "Next to the Word of God, music deserves the highest praise" and "I am quite of the opinion that next to theology, there is no art which can be compared to music; for it alone, after theology, gives us rest and joy."

"A Mighty Fortress is Our God" is considered Luther's greatest song. It was based on Psalm 46 from the Vulgate Bible and has been called "The Battle Hymn of the Reformation." It first appeared in a hymnal in 1529 and by 1900 had over 80 English translations.

A Mighty Fortress is Our God

A mighty fortress is our God,
A bulwark never failing,
Our helper He amid the flood
Of mortal ills prevailing,
For still our ancient foe
Doth seek to work us woe;
His craft and power are great,
And, armed with cruel hate
On earth is not his equal.

Did we in our own strength confide,
Our strength would be losing;
Were not the right Man on our side,
The Man of God's own choosing;
Dost ask Who that may be?
Christ Jesus, it is He;
Lord Saboath His name,
From age to age the same,
And He must win the battle.

And though this world, with devils filled,
Should threaten to undo us;
We will not fear, for God hath willed
His truth to triumph through us;
The Prince of Darkness grim,
We tremble not for him;

His rage we can endure,
For lo! his doom is sure,
One little word shall fell him.

That word above all earthly powers,
No thanks to them, abideth;
The spirit and the gifts are ours
Through Him Who with us sideth;
Let good and kindred go,
This mortal life also;
The body they may kill;
God's truth abideth still,
His kingdom is forever.

In this hymn, called "the greatest hymn of the greatest man in the greatest period of German history," Luther takes a stand against the Catholic church and the German state in the line "And though this world, with devils filled, should threaten to undo us," thus saying that those who opposed the Reformation movement were "devils." He solidifies his own stand with the line, "The spirit and the gifts are ours through Him Who with us sideth," leaving no doubt about whose side God is on. This would become a common tactic of Christians in the Protestant movement throughout the centuries— they were in God's favor and all those who opposed them were instruments of the devil. It is an argument impossible to refute, and though it is also impossible to prove, the Christian refutes the question through the self-assurance of his stand.

Luther's first congregational hymn, "Dear Christians, One and All, Rejoice," summarizes his philosophy and his own conversion experience. It begins,

Dear Christians, one and all, rejoice,
With exultation springing,
And, with united heart and voice
And holy rapture singing,
Proclaim the wonders God hath done,
How his right arm the victory won;
Right dearly it hath cost Him.

This verse would be prophetic as Luther, rejoicing at his own salvation, would "unite heart and voice" and proclaim the gospel with "holy rapture singing." In the lines, "My own good works availed me naught, no merit they attaining," Luther could have been speaking of his life as a monk, where he openly acknowledged that he did all the things a monk should do yet felt no peace with God. This was a classic case of "works" not being enough for salvation. Luther concludes the hymn with the verse:

> *What I have done and taught, teach thou,*
> *My ways forsake thou never;*
> *So shall My kingdom flourish now*
> *And God be praised forever.*
> *Take heed lest men with base alloy*
> *The heavenly treasure should destroy;*
> *This counsel I bequeath thee.*

Luther wrote this from the point of view of Christ, but it is also revealing of Luther's own state of mind as he hopes the things he is doing and teaching will be taken to heart by men.

Luther asserts the supremacy of his version of the gospel in the hymn, "Our Father Thou in Heaven Above," in the line, "Let no false doctrine us pervert; All poor, deluded souls convert," which is an obvious affront to the teachings of the Catholic church of that time. It is also an example of the aggressiveness, assertiveness, and competitiveness which would characterize Protestant Christianity. This was first published as a broadsheet in 1539 and each stanza elaborates on one of the petitions of the Lord's Prayer.

Luther's first missionary hymn was "May God Bestow On Us His Grace" and the lines, "to the heathen show Christ's riches without measure and unto God convert them" and "let all the world praise Him alone, let solemn awe possess us" exemplify the Protestant world view and the missionary zeal the Protestant converts carried into the world—especially America—as European explorers and settlers carried the Protestant Reformation into the 17th century.

Luther's hymn, "From Depths of Woe I Cry to Thee," was sung at the funeral of his friend, Frederick the Wise, and also sung at Halle in 1546 when Luther's body was being brought from Eisleben to

Wittenberg. Luther's Christian philosophy is expressed in the line, "Thy love and grace alone avail to blot out my transgression," while "Though great our sins and sore our woes, His grace much more aboundeth" applies Luther's concept of "grace" and "justification by faith" for all believers. The lines, "Therefore my hope is in the Lord and not in mine own merit; It rests upon His faithful Word to them of contrite spirit" are anti-Catholic statements in that they assert Luther's belief that God communicates to people through the Bible and not through the clergy.

In the hymn, "If God Had Not Been on Our Side," Luther paraphrased Psalm 124 in the Bible but it could easily have been written from the personal experiences of Luther leading the Protestant revolt, facing personal enmity from the church and state and watching others die or be tortured for their Protestant faith. The lyrics are an anthem of positivism and of overcoming adversity, of self-confidence and belief in the Protestant cause.

If God Had Not Been On Our Side

If God had not been on our side
And had not come to aid us
The foes with all their power and pride
Would surely have dismayed us;
For we, His flock, would have to fear
The threat of men both far and near
Who rise in might against us.

Their furious wrath, did God permit,
Would surely have consumed us
And as a deep and yawning pit
With life and limb entombed us,
Like men o'er whom dark waters roll
Their wrath would have engulfed our soul
And, like a flood, o'erwhelmed us.

Blest be the Lord, who foiled their threat
That they could not devour us;
Our souls, like birds, escaped their net,

They could not overpower us.
The snare is broken—we are free!
Our help is ever, Lord, in Thee
Who madest earth and heaven.

Luther's independence and self-assurance asserts itself again in the hymn, "To Shepherds as They Watched by Night," a Christmas hymn composed in 1543, in the line, "Yet shall and must at last prevail; God's own ye are, ye cannot fail" and in the hymn, "In Peace and Joy I Now Depart" with the line "'Tis Christ that wrought this work for me." Both of these examples show Luther to be a strong man, full of assurance about his mission and his life, believing strongly in his God and his cause. It is a confidence that would cause Protestantism to prevail against near-impossible odds in those early years.

"Flung to the Heedless Winds" was written in 1523 to commemorate the martyrdom of two young Augustinian monks who had been condemned to death and burned at the stake in Brussels because of their Lutheran faith. This hymn is interesting because it tells a topical story (like many secular broadside ballads) and concludes that the two men were "penitent and justified, They might go clean to heaven and leave all monkish follies," an anti-Catholic statement that shows Luther's view of his past vocation.

The hymn, "O Lord, Look Down from Heaven, Behold," sums up the Protestant Reformation eloquently and powerfully, pitting the Protestant religion against church and state but on the side of God. It was written in 1523 as a paraphrase of Psalm 12 and published in 1524. The song underlines a key tenant of Luther's faith: he looked to God, not to men for approval and felt that though men were against him, he would prevail because God was on his side. But Luther does not just speak for himself, he speaks for a people and such was Luther's megalomania that he saw himself as not merely an individual, but as a movement.

O Lord, Look Down From Heaven, Behold

Lord, look down from heaven, behold
And let Thy pity waken;
How few are we within Thy fold,
Thy saints by men forsaken!
True faith seems quenched on every hand,
Men suffer not Thy Word to stand;
Dark times have us o'ertaken.

With fraud which they themselves invent
Thy truth they have confounded;
Their hearts are not with one consent
On Thy pure doctrine grounded.
While they parade with outward show,
They lead the people to and fro,
In error's maze astounded.

May God root out all heresy
And of false teachers rid us
Who proudly say: "Now, where is he
That shall our speech forbid us?
By right or might we shall prevail;
What we determine cannot fail;
We own no lord and master."

Therefore saith God, "I must arise,
The poor My help are needing;
To me ascend My people's cries,
And I have heard their pleading.
for them My saving Word shall fight
And fearlessly and sharply smite,
The poor with might defending."

As silver tried by fire is pure
From all adulteration
So through God's Word shall men endure
Each trial and temptation.

Its light beams brighter through the cross,
And, purified from human dross,
It shines through every nation.

The truth defend, O God, and stay
This evil generation;
And from the error of their way
Keep Thine own congregation.
The wicked everywhere abound
And would Thy little flock confound;
But Thou art our Salvation.

Other hymns Luther wrote include: "All Praise to Thee, Eternal God," "From Heaven Above to Earth I Come," "Savior of the Nations, Come," "Now Praise We Christ, the Holy One," "Christ Jesus Lay in Death's Strong Hands," "Come, Holy Ghost, God and Lord," "We Now Implore God, the Holy Ghost," "Isaiah, Mighty Seer in Days of Old," "We All Believe in One True God," "Lord, Keep Us Steadfast in Thy Word," "That Man a Godly Life Might Live," "O Lord We Praise Thee," and "In the Midst of Earthly Life."

Martin Luther had an immense regard for the power of music and for its compatibility with the gospel. He stated, "I should like to see all the arts, and especially music, used in the service of Him who gave and created them." Luther's joy of life was expressed by his love for music and his strong belief was communicated through the songs he composed, songs that have been sung in religious revivals for hundreds of years, carrying the spirit of the Reformation all over Europe and on to other continents as Protestantism spread throughout the world. A major factor in Protestantism's appeal has been the songs it has inspired, while Luther's leadership in giving all people a chance to sing in church has made that religion come alive, infused with joy, for centuries. Because of the songs he composed, Martin Luther is not just an historical figure for Christianity but a continuing presence as well—vibrant, alive, and communicating his timeless message through his songs.

Chapter 5

FIRST SEEDS: GOSPEL MUSIC IN AMERICA

For America, the 17th century was a time of settlement and each group of settlers brought new songs with them. There were songs from churches and songs from the taverns, traditional ballads and new songs composed by people about timeless love or topical news events. A distinctive American voice would not truly emerge until the 19th century, but the musical roots of America were planted in the 17th and 18th centuries.

The settlers in the Jamestown and Plymouth colonies were not the first to come to the New World; in fact, the first Europeans to establish themselves in America were the Spanish explorers who came through Mexico and the southwestern area of what is now the United States. The first gospel songs sung in the New World have been traced to the Roman Catholic church via the inhabitants of southern America and Mexico. Catholic service books were published in Mexico as early as 1556 and the main effect of this Catholic influence was to introduce the Gregorian chant, sung in Latin, to America.

However, the true settling and growth of what became identified as the United States came from the European settlers who peopled the eastern seaboard and then began moving westward. To understand early American music, a knowledge of Europe and European music is necessary since the roots of America are embedded in the European culture these settlers left behind.

The Reformation in Europe brought a new song, sung in the vernacular (not in Latin) by the entire congregation. Two basic forms emerged here, the chorale (associated with the Lutherans and Moravians), and the psalm tune, which developed among the Calvinists. Both the French and the English sang psalms which were paraphrased in meter, to which were added paraphrases of other lyric passages from scriptures. They sang "God's word" from the Bible. The Lutherans also sang "God's word," but welcomed devotional poems written by individuals. The Puritans of New England came from the Calvinist tradition and the transition in America from scriptural to devotional poems—psalms to hymns—was a long and gradual one, hindered by the Puritans' strict adherence to the psalms. Musically, there was a major difference as the Lutherans and Moravians made use of the organ and orchestral instruments in worship while the Calvinists and English dissenters limited their songs to metrical poems sung in unison.

American Hymns Old and New records that psalms were sung at Port Royal, an island near Charleston, South Carolina, in 1562 by a party of Huguenots who landed there and that a short-lived settlement was established in Florida two years later. According to the authors, the Indians there remembered two of the psalms long after the settlement was destroyed. The first English-sung psalms in the new world were noted by Francis Fletcher, the chaplain who sailed with Sir Francis Drake in 1577. He recorded the interest of the Native Americans in singing in the region now known as San Francisco.

When the settlers landed in Jamestown, Virginia in 1607, they brought with them the Este psalter (a psalter is a song book of the Psalms), with some evidence that they also had copies of the Sternhold and Hopkins (The Old Version) psalter. The songbooks brought to the Plymouth colony were the Sternhold and Hopkins psalter, the Scottish psalter, and the psalter by Ainsworth.

The Sternhold and Hopkins psalter began with a group of psalms arranged by Thomas Sternhold and performed with his organ accompaniment. His *Certayne Psalmes* was the earliest version, published before his death in 1549. John Hopkins added seven more in 1551 and by 1562 it included all of the psalms. French tunes entered the English repertory in 1553 when many English refugees fled to Geneva after Mary Tudor became queen. At this time the development of spiritual songs, or hymns, began, primarily due to the French influence on the English refugees.

The Scottish Presbyterians were the last to give up the exclusive use of psalms and the most vigorous in rejecting the inclusion of musical instruments. The earliest Scottish psalter appeared in 1564. The *Ainsworth Psalter* was brought from Holland by the settlers who landed at Plymouth in 1620. This was a collection of psalms with "suitable melodies" by Henry Ainsworth and continued to be used during the early years of colonial America.

The first book published in America was *The Whole Booke of Psalmes Faithfully Translated Into English Metre*, commonly known as *The Bay Psalm Book*. It appeared in 1640 in the Plymouth colony in Massachusetts and contained the first version of psalms made by Americans and used in American churches. The question of whether hymns ("Psalms invented by the gifts of godly men") were to be included in church services was raised in the preface [written by either Richard Mather or John Cotton] with the decision reached to sing only psalms or other paraphrases from passages in the Bible. Some hymns were added to the *Bay Psalm Book* in the 1647 edition.

The success of the *Bay Psalm Book* was immediate, with 1700 copies in the first printing and 2000 copies of a new edition in 1651. In all, there were twenty-seven editions of this book printed in New England and at least twenty in England (the last in 1754), as well as six in Scotland. The ninth edition, published in 1698, was the first to contain music that accompanied the texts. Prior to that, only the words were printed, which were sung to a known melody with a handful of melodies serving a large number of songs. According to Richard Crawford in his essay, "The Birth of Liberty," "singers knowing a mere half-dozen tunes could sing the entire psalter. The evidence is that around the end of the seventeenth century many congregations actually knew no more than that."

Personal, devotional verse was predominant in the 17th century, with Cotton Mather and Jonathan Edwards both writing and singing hymns "unto the Lord." Examples of devotional verse are the poems of Anne Bradstreet, John Wilson's "Song of Deliverance," Michael Wigglesworth's "Day of Doom," and the "Meditations" of Edward Taylor.

In the 18th century, some changes evolved, basically reflecting the changes occurring in England. The Methodists and their Methodism brought the Wesley hymns to New Jersey, and the later comers to New England imported Isaac Watts. Ironically, the initial resistance Watts encountered to his hymns in America was the same he had encountered in England; his "hymns of human composure" were not literal renderings of the psalms but rather from the human heart. The psalm was still the predominant form of gospel music, sung in churches as well as in homes.

The Great Awakening was responsible for a large influx of hymns into church services, altering the traditional view of scriptural songs being the only acceptable music in church. Beginning in Wales under Howell Harris (c. 1730), the "Great Awakening" was a tremendous infusion of religion into society, producing laws that eliminated some of the exploitation and abuse of the poor as well as injecting a genuine spirit of revival into the souls of a great number of people, especially among the lower classes. It grew to epic proportions under George Whitefield (1736-1790) and the Wesleys (1739-1791). In America, the Great Awakening began with Jonathan Edwards in New England (c. 1734) and received an incredible boost under the leadership of George Whitefield, who came to America in 1740, met Edwards in Massachusetts and traveled throughout the colonies preaching.

Hymn singing caught fire in America c. 1740 during Whitefield's visit. According to Hamilton C. MacDougal in *Early New England Psalmody*, "It is easy to understand how welcome the new hymn tunes were, with their pulsating, secular rhythms, their emotional repetitions, the fugal tunes, the iterations of words to cumulative sequences after the 'sleep' of formalism." The author adds that the Methodists with their hymns and singing burst "like heralds of new life." Crowds were drawn to the services by the irresistible charm of the music.

During the 1600s and early 1700s, the New England congregations were noted for singing their psalm tunes at a very slow tempo, known as the "old way." As with most religious customs, its adherents defended it as the "only proper mode" for performing music in church. This was challenged in the early part of the 18th century by advocates of the "new way," who encouraged singing by note instead of rote, briskly in harmony rather than slowly and in unison. The state of singing had sunk badly due to years of having no formal music training for singers and psalm books with texts but no melodies to scan. In *America and Their Songs*, Frank Luther states, "By 1700 things had reached such a point that people could hardly sing together at all. Everybody had his own idea of the tune; and while it might sound well enough when one sang alone, when a hundred people in one room sang a hundred different versions of the same tune at the same time, it sounded like nothing so much as a three-corned dog-fight."

This problem was met with the rise of the singing school, giving instruction and training to members of a church or community in the rudiments of music. The first two manuals written to meet this need, both thin pamphlets, were written by ministers: John Tufts and Thomas Walter. The first edition of Tuft's *An Introduction to the Singing of Psalm-Tunes* probably appeared in 1721, the same year as Walter's treatise. The study of sight singing was taken up by Americans with "enormous zest" and there was a singing school in Boston in 1717. This time was also marked by the rise of the singing master in the 18th and early 19th centuries. These were not only singing classes, they were also social occasions for the youth in the area, a feature that caused many of the church fathers to frown on these gatherings. The impact of the singing master was greatest in the rural areas and small towns; the congregations in the coastal towns retained a closer tie with English tastes. The methods of the singing master are described in *American Hymns Old and New*, which states, "The singing master generally canvassed the neighborhood, assembled a class, and engaged in a large room which might be a schoolhouse, a church, or a tavern. He taught the rudiments of notation, a method of beating time, and solemization. These principles were applied to psalm tunes, and the session terminated with an 'exhibition' in which the class sang the tunes which they had learned to their assembled relatives, friends, and neighbors."

While psalm singing dominated the 17th century and continued to prevail through the introduction of hymns in the 18th century, the nineteenth century was marked by the emergence of the denominational hymn. The order of service was planned to "give the congregational hymn its due place." Although tenors generally sang the melody in earlier years, sopranos sang the melody in the 19th century. The use of the tuning fork or pitch pipe established the key; however, because there was such a prejudice against musical instruments in worship, the pitch pipe was often disguised to resemble a psalm book.

As in the 18th century, the bass viol was often used as an accompanying instrument; it was basically a cello with a short neck and its introduction "caused violent controversies and schisms." In Salem, Massachusetts, the clarinet and violin were first played in church on Christmas Day, 1792, and a flute was played there in 1795. In 1814, in Boston, the singing was accompanied by flute, bassoon and cello. Gradually, the organ was accepted as a proper instrument for the church, with small pipe organs and melodians. Still, the churches proved reluctant to adapt any musical adornment to the plain singing of the congregation during the first 200 years in America.

In the early New England churches, social status was reflected in the seating of the congregation. In the 17th century, one person "set the pitch," then the entire congregation sang the psalm. However, the 18th century saw the emergence of the musical elite—the choir—which changed the seating pattern (and architecture) within the church. A gallery was erected over the entrance vestibule and sometimes on three sides of the church, with the choir sitting apart from the congregation. Wealthy churches with a highly developed liturgy often established professional choirs or choirs with some professional singers. Some of the churches which did not support a choir often hired a professional quartet of singers and an organist.

The influence of England remained strong throughout the 18th century in American churches. This was because English tunes were republished in America and because many American composers were born and trained in England. There were three types of music cultivated by the New England composers—the psalm tune, the fuguing tune, and the anthem. The voices tended to move together with little or no word repetition in the psalm tune; the fuguing tune was in two sections—the first more or less choral in texture and the second beginning with free imitative entires in each of the voices, which were repeated.

During the 18th century, the two most important psalters were by Tate and Brady, and by Isaac Watts. The earliest American edition of Tate and Brady was published in Boston in 1713, although this book, called *The New Version*, was originally published by Nahum Tate and Nicholas Brady in England in 1696. The Episcopal congregations in America adapted an abridged version of Tate and Brady after the Revolution. The Watts psalter first appeared in England in 1719, with the first American edition published in Philadelphia in 1729 and printed by Benjamin Franklin; however, this did not sell well. The major problem with the Watts psalter, according to the American religious establishment, was that Watts did not paraphrase all the psalms, omitting the precatory psalms, and did not repeat himself when the psalms did. Americans were accustomed to reading or singing all of the psalms in numerical order, sung at one standing, regardless of the subject of the sermon.

The second major problem with the Watts psalter was the laudatory lines to Great Britain and her ruler, which became increasingly unacceptable as America moved closer to the Revolution and the break with Great Britain. However, many religious leaders sought to alter Watts' version and adapt it for American use. Before his psalter appeared, Isaac Watts had published *Hymns and Spiritual Songs* in 1707, which soon found its way to the new world. The first American edition of this work was published in Boston in 1739, followed by editions in Philadelphia (1742) and New York (1752) and these hymns were welcomed, imitated, and incorporated into private devotions within Protestant denominations in this country.

American psalters were developed by Thomas Prince, who revised the *Bay Psalm Book* in 1758 with such freedom as to nearly produce an entirely new version; Cotton Mather (1718) and John Barnard (1752) also produced versions of their own, while John Mycall (1775) and Joel Barlow (1785) endeavored to amend the patriotic lines in Watts and fill in the gaps he left. Henry Alline was among the early Baptist hymn writers in America whose *Choice Hymns and Spiritual Songs* was published in 1786. Samuel Holyoke published his *Harmonia American* in 1791, and *Village Hymns of Asahel Nettleton* was published in 1824. *The Divine Hymns or Spiritual Songs* by Joshua Smith was another favorite book with the Baptists, with many of these hymns set to music by Jeremiah Ingalls. The first Catholic hymnal in the United States was published by John Aitkin and titled *A Compilation of the Litanies, Vesper Hymns, and Anthems*, as sung in the Catholic Church. This was published in Philadelphia in 1787. For the Episcopals, collections of hymns included those by William Duke (1790) and Andrew Fowler (1798), titled *A Selection of*

Psalms with Occasional Hymns and published in Charleston in 1792. Hymn writers among the Universalists included John Murray, whose first hymns were published in 1782, Silas Ballouw, whose collection appeared in 1785, and George Richards, whose *Psalms, Hymns, and Spiritual Songs* appeared in 1792.

The development of tune books (books that contained melodies) was due primarily to enterprising individuals who developed these books for singing school classes, church choirs and, eventually, for the organist. There was an obvious convenience to having the music associated with the words, although they were generally on opposite pages. After the mid-19th century, the congregation hymnal with words and music appeared. The words were generally under the tune on the same page and sometimes several texts were given for one tune. The most convenient arrangement was in the books where the words were printed between the staves, in upright form, a form still used today.

Sacred music had long felt the influence of secular music as congregations were exposed to both forms in their lives. According to Richard Crawford in his essay, "The Birth of Liberty," "Americans were used to singing a variety of sacred texts to a small number of psalm tunes. They also were likely to know by heart a stock of secular tunes from the English theatre and from the broadside-ballad tradition, and to be accustomed to singing those tunes to old and new texts." It was not unusual for one melody to be used over and over again with new verses written. This occurred in both religious and secular music, with a handful of tunes functioning as the source of countless songs; writers felt that the familiarity of the tune helped people learn the verses quickly, and there existed a widespread belief that all music was in the public domain.

The 18th century saw a secularization of sacred music occur that would help make that music more appealing to the masses of people as well as carry it outside the church where it would stand alone outside of worship. The churches of New England adopted Calvinist practice by prohibiting musical instruments or choirs in their public worship, thus separating themselves from the professional music traditions of the Roman Catholics, the Lutherans, and the Anglicans. In the latter churches, the emphasis on the music had shifted from the congregation to a designated group of singers singing to a non-participating audience, as in a theatre. The introduction of choirs led to more elaborate songs, with a tendency towards "wide-ranging melodies, word repetitions, 'fuguing' (imitative voice overlapping), fast tempos, and expressive treatment of text," which placed church music in a totally different musical environment and framework than that known to Cotton Mather and his associates. Musicians were increasingly important and powerful in the development of church music in the 18th century. Richard Crawford, in his essay "Joyful Noise," states, "There is a crucial difference ... between the transformation of eighteenth century Protestant Christianity and the transformation of its music in New England: the former was effected by the church leaders, the latter by musicians.... The musicians took over sacred music, originally under the clerical control, not by the usual means of effecting change—defining an issue and debating it and deciding it by action of the clergy or congregation—but by gradual encroachment.... It grew from a tradition rooted in religious ritual, but it has held the interest of later musicians for precisely the reasons that religious leaders objected to it in its own day: it transcended the ritual of public worship and came to flourish as an independent art."

The evolution of sacred music from a part of the church service, integral but subordinate to the preaching, to a form of art that stood on its own is a vital ingredient when looking at the history of sacred music in America, especially the developments in the latter part of the 20th century. This affected audiences as well as musicians and Crawford notes that, "Americans in the 1760s came for the first time to recognize psalmody as an art, as an activity demanding creative inspiration (composing) as well as performance (singing) and requiring technical proficiency of both creator and performer."

The secular influence was felt strongly in sacred music as the church began to be dominated by the culture in much the same way that the Puritan church dominated the secular culture in early New England. Alan Lomax in "White Spirituals from the Sacred Harp" states that, "The editors of the early New England hymnbooks largely included the more formal hymns and psalms from British sources; but from the time of the Revolution forward, more native and more folk-originated material was included ... a large proportion of these tunes were simply religious remakes of secular love songs and dance tunes, exhibiting the traits of traditional folk music in their gapped modal scales and their use of the lowered seventh ... the radical Methodists, like John and Charles Wesley ... brought many British folk and popular tunes into the hymnals by setting religious words to them; and, all-pervasive ... the Baptists, who led the way in the popular religious revivals in Britain and America and thus introduced many folk tunes and much folksy singing into the church."

This influence of folk music, as well as the establishment of singing schools and the Great Revival of the 19th century, established the roots of the *Sacred Harp* and white spiritual traditions and paved the way for 20th century Southern Gospel music.

Chapter 6

ISAAC WATTS

The songs of Isaac Watts may be thought of as rhymed Calvinism. Ironically, though, it was a break from the Calvinist code, which insisted that songs should only come directly from Scripture, that made Isaac Watts such a radical and influential writer of hymns. Still, except for this break with Calvinism in his view of music (although Calvinists and fundamentalists later agreed and joined him), Isaac Watts presented a body of work for the body of believers which embodied the fundamental Christian faith espoused by Martin Luther and John Calvin.

It is difficult to imagine a small, sickly man, standing five feet five, with a hooked nose, small beady eyes, and a head made even larger by the powdered wig topping a frail, emaciated body as a "giant." Yet Watts was (and still is) a giant among hymn writers. He dominated the field in his day and his hymns continue to hold a pre-eminent place in gospel music. Time is a great editor and the fifty or so hymns which congregations still sing may be considered his definitive hymns.

Watts was born in 1674, the son of a religious father whose dissenting views caused him to be jailed several times while Isaac was a youth. Later, his father moved to London and became a wealthy clothier. Isaac's father taught his son at home and the youth learned Latin at four, Greek at eight or nine, French when he was eleven, and Hebrew at thirteen. From his earliest days, Isaac had a penchant for rhyming, a talent that drove his father to frustration and exasperation.

In 1701, at the age of twenty-six, Watts began serving as pastor for the Mark Lane Independent Chapel in London. His parishioners loved him and soon hired an assistant pastor because Watts' ill health would not allow him to preach every Sunday. Still, Watts remained in the Mark Lane pastorate for twenty-two years, holding no other pastorate in his life. The congregation was largely wealthy and prominent, consisting of merchants and politicians. One parishioner, Sir Thomas Abney, was elected Lord Mayor of London in 1700 and once invited Watts to spend a week at his country estate. Watts accepted the invitation and remained there thirty-six years, until Abney died, then moved with the family to another estate until his own death. Except for the earliest hymns, Watts wrote most of his hymns on these luxurious estates.

Isaac Watts was a man of considerable learning. In addition to his hymns—which were really religious poetry set to commonly known melodies—Watts wrote a number of books, including *Logic*; *The Knowledge of the Heavens and Earth Made Easy*; *Divine and Moral Songs*; books on grammar, pedagogy, ethics, psychology; three volumes of sermons; and twenty-nine treatises on theology—fifty-two works in all in addition to his poetry. He received the Doctorate of Divinity from the universities at Aberdeen and Edinburgh and was considered the leading religious poet of his day. A lifelong bachelor, Watts became a member of the Abney family while he shared their home.

Watts began writing hymns at fifteen. Appalled by the horrendous and lamentable singing in churches he attended, he stated that, "The singing of God's praise is the part of worship nighest heaven, and its performance among us is the worst on earth." Returning from a service one Sunday morning, Isaac complained to his father about the singing; his father replied, "Give us something better, young man." Before the evening service, Watts had written his first hymn, "Behold the glories of the Lamb, / Amidst his Father's throne; / Prepare new honors for his name, / And songs before unknown." That evening, the hymn was lined out (a practice where the clerk announced a line, then the congregation sang it) and sung.

Isaac Watts created a revolution in hymn-writing by breaking the strangle-hold of David's Psalms on the liturgy through the substitution of "hymns of composure." He was not the first writer of English hymns, although he is given the title "Father of English Hymnology," but he was the first to thoughtfully develop a theory of congregational praise and provide a well-rounded body of material to be used in the church. Watts' theory held first that religious songs are a human offering of praise to God, and therefore the words should be personal. This contrasted with the Calvinistic theory, which the Church held, that the inspired words of the Bible, particularly the Psalms, were the only fit offerings of praise that man could make. Watts' arguments were sound and finally won out against long and determined opposition. Second, Watts maintained that if the Psalms were to be sung, they should be Christianized and modernized.

Watts took his two theories and two kinds of hymns—the hymns of "human composure," which were his own, and hymns based on the Psalms—and infused his own interpretations and imagination. In these "Imitations of the Psalms," Watts replaced the allegience to Israel and Judah with a patriotism to England and made the Psalms' author speak like the King of England.

Watts' hymns were composed in simple meter and sung to whatever familiar tune was chosen by the clerk. They were sung in the church where Watts preached and composed with the practice of "lining out" in mind. According to Watts, "I have seldom permitted a stop in the middle of a line, and seldom left the end of a line without one, to comport a little with the unhappy *Mixture of Reading and Singing*, which cannot presently be reformed."

The first collection of Watts' songs, *Hymns and Spiritual Songs*, was published in 1707. The composer's intention was "to write down to the Level of Vulgar Capacities, and to furnish Hymns for the meanest of Christians." The poetry should be "simple, sensuous, and passionate." The simplicity is apparent for anyone with a basic intelligence can understand what he means with his verse while his meters are standard—common, long, and short. Watts' sensuousness is obvious as he uses words to conjure pictures in the mind with images from the Bible, nature, and everyday occurrences and experiences. His hymns are passionate because they are charged with the emotion of a true believer. According to Albert Bailey in *The Gospel in Hymns*, "They shed a glow of joy or resound with praise. Even the cold logic of Calvinism catches fire: God is apprehended emotionally, in awe, or dread, or fear; as love, or power, or infinity; Christ is full of human sympathy that evokes from the individual a personal response; a man is filled with hope or fear, with joy or penitence; he is torn by doubts or enraptured by the certainties of heaven. In Watts at his best there is nothing drab or passive; all is vivid and active."

The theology of Watts and Calvin is sung in the hymns. God is an arbitrary and absolute ruler, man is totally depraved, and people fall under considerable conviction of sin. There is no appeal to the lost souls because the concept of predestination precluded a sinner's option to change. Foreordination and election meant that man was powerless to change the status determined for him before the foundation of the world, so it was an exercise in futility for a hymn writer to seek out those souls and attempt to convert them. Not until the Wesleys came along with their missionary zeal and songs of evangelistic outreach did this concept of Christianity change.

Watts' theology derived directly from John Calvin, whose theology was inspired by St. Augustine and the Apostle Paul—the author of basic precepts of earthly Christianity. The followers of these theologians found a dreadful religion with a monster God who outrages our sense of justice and contradicts reason. In the tragedy of human history, Christ is a figure of redemption only for the privileged few chosen for heaven even before their birth. Of course, one can never tell if he is among the elect, but he must put his total trust in Christ then wait to see what happens. If you are not among the elect, you will not be able to put your full trust in Him; however, if you feel a trust it may be a deceit of the Devil to give you that sense of security. In the end, the believer hoped for election with fear and trembling, always sure but never assured.

One of the greatest of Watts' hymns is "When I Survey That Wondrous Cross," written for communion service in 1707. It was inspired by the line in Galatians 6:14, "But far be it for me to glory save in the cross of our Lord Jesus Christ, through which the world hath been crucified to me, and I unto the world." The melody used today is an 18th century English melody.

When I Survey The Wondrous Cross

When I survey the wondrous cross
On which the Prince of Glory died,
My richest gain I count but loss,
And pour contempt on all my pride.

Forbid it, Lord, that I should boast,
Save in the death of Christ, my God:
All the vain things that charm me most,
I sacrifice them to his blood.

See, from his head, his hands, his feet,
Sorrow and love flow mingled down!
Did e'er such love and sorrow meet,
Or thorns compose so rich a crown?

Were the whole realm of nature mine,
That were an off'ring far too small;
Love so amazing, so divine,
Demands my soul, my life, my all.

The song is an example of the complete surrender of the believer to the crucified Christ, whose death atoned for mankind's sins. The term "survey" indicates that Watts (and all who sing the hymn fervently) study the crucifixion, deeply contemplating the meaning of this great sacrifice.

Watts did not write any Christmas songs because the Dissenters believed Christmas to be the celebration of a pagan holiday. However, his "Joy to the World," written from Psalm 98:4, is used almost exclusively as a Christmas carol in the 20th and 21st centuries.

Joy to the World! The Lord is Come

Joy to the world! the Lord is come;
Let earth receive her King;
Let every heart prepare Him room,
And heaven and nature sing,
And heaven and nature sing,
And heaven, and heaven and nature sing.

Joy to the world! the Saviour reigns;
Let men their songs employ;
While fields and flood, rocks, hills and plains

Repeat the sounding joy,
Repeat the sounding joy,
Repeat, repeat the sounding joy.

He rules the world with truth and grace,
And makes the nations prove
The glories of His righteousness,
And wonders of His love,
And wonders of His love,
And wonders, and wonders of His love.

Watts was well aware of the treasure trove of praise songs contained in the Psalms but objected to the indiscriminate use of the Psalms. The Church had failed to discard the obsolete and un-Christian elements in the Psalms. There was a tendency towards anti-Semitism in Watts' time because of the belief that Jews had rejected Jesus as the Savior. Watts sought to eliminate the strong Jewish roots in the Psalms and replace them with Calvinist Christianity.

Watts had tried to "improve" the Psalms for ten years and in 1719 published *The Psalms of David Imitated in the Language of the New Testament, and Apply'd to the Christian State and Worship.* This was a radical work because Watts did not provide a metrical translation or paraphrases but instead produced songs "inspired" by the Psalms which followed the general thought of the original. According to Watts, "Tis not a translation of David that I pretend, but an imitation of him, so nearly in Christian hymns that the Jewish Psalmist may plainly appear, and yet leave Judaism behind." Watts' work eventually dominated the field of Psalmody and superseded the *Old Version* of Sternhold and Hopkins and the *New Version* of Tate and Brady.

A good example of Watts' use of the Psalms as inspiration is his use of Psalm 23 to produce "My Shepherd Will Supply My Need."

My Shepherd Will Supply My Need (Psalm 23)

My shepherd will supply my need;
Jehovah is his name:
In pastures fresh he makes me feed,
Beside the living stream.
He brings my wandering spirit back,
When I forsake his ways;
And leads me, for his mercy's sake,
In paths of truth and grace.

When I walk through the shades of death
Thy presence is my stay;
One word of thy supporting breath
Drives all my fears away.
Thy hand, in sight of all my foes,
Doth still my table spread;
My cup with blessings overflows,
Thine oil anoints my head.

The sure provisions of my God
Attend me all my days;
O may thy house be my abode,
And all my work be praise.
There would I find a settled rest,
While others go and come;
No more a stranger, nor a guest,
But like a child at home.

In "Before Jehovah's Awful Throne," Watts uses Psalm 100 to present Calvinism and the concept of predestination. The concept of the chosen elect, the concept of the all-powerful, arbitrary God, and the replacement of Israel with Europe (in this case Great Britain) as God's chosen land are all found here. Fortunately, the first verse was edited out by the Wesleys before they published it.

Before Jehovah's Awful Throne

Sing to the Lord with joyful voice;
Let every land his name adore;
The British Isles shall send the noise
Across the ocean to the shore.

Before Jehovah's awful throne,
Ye nations, bow with sacred joy;
Know that the Lord is God alone;
He can create, and He destroy.

We are His people, we His care,
Our souls and all our mortal frame;
What lasting honors shall we rear,
Almighty Maker, to Thy name?

We'll crowd Thy gates with thankful songs,
High as the heavens our voices raise;
And earth with her ten thousand tongues,
Shall fill Thy courts with sounding praise.

Wide as the world is Thy command,
Vast as eternity Thy love;
Firm as a rock Thy truth must stand,
When rolling years shall cease to move. Amen.

Isaac Watts wrote from both his head and his heart. He was an intelligent man who mastered the mechanics of writing what he fervently believed. This combination of a skillful writer writing songs from the heart, expressing his deep faith, is what makes the hymns of Watts remain so powerful today. In "Begin, My Tongue, Some Heavenly Theme," Watts could have been expressing his heart, mind, and soul when he wrote the lyrics. It is certainly his personal philosophy as well as that of fundamentalist Calvinism, and an admonition to all who compose hymns.

Begin, My Tongue, Some Heavenly Theme

Begin, my tongue, some heavenly theme,
And speak some boundless thing,
The mighty works, or mightier name,
Of our eternal King.

Tell of His wondrous faithfulness,
And sound His power abroad;
Sing the sweet promise of His grace,
The love and truth of God.

His very word of grace is strong
As that which built the skies;
The voice that rolls the stars along
Speaks all the promises.

O might I hear Thy heavenly tongue
But whisper, "Thou art Mine!"
Those gentle words should raise my song
To notes almost divine.

Chapter 7

THE WESLEYS

The Wesleys, like Isaac Watts, are known for their songs of personal experiences; however, while Watts remained amongst the rich, the Wesleys were involved with the poor as the Great Awakening brought a deep concern for the individual. This contrasted with the apathy inherent in the established church towards the social and economic degradation of the masses of poor who inhabited England at that time. Still, the Wesleys were influenced by Watts (their first hymnal had 70 selections—half composed by Watts) and they encountered some of the same difficulties with the established churches in getting their hymns accepted.

In 1660, the Anglican Church was restored to power in England; naturally, it was a strong defender of the monarchy from which it derived its privileges, class distinctions, wealth, and power. Being political posts of favor, the higher church offices were for sale and ambitious men, regardless of character or ability, filled those offices. However, the ordinary, working rector who performed the day-to-day duties of the church was paid little; the Wesleys' father, Samuel, was a clergyman who spent months in prison because he could not pay debts incurred from the basic expenses of life.

There was a need for a revolution in the social structure: beneath the upper class was a worldly, amoral middle class dedicated to making themselves rich merchants at the expense of the poor. Four out of five children born in England died. But among the poor it was worse; only one in 500 illegitimate children survived to adulthood while gin factories, gambling dens, harlotry and risque theatre performances all contributed to a national degeneracy.

Three great evangelists—John and Charles Wesley and George Whitefield—all confronted these societal problems. Albert Bailey, in his book, *The Gospel in Hymns*, states that, "[They] tackled the problem of reform, not from the economic or social point of view, but from the religious. They believed that the spirit of God could change the hearts of men, could make them desire a better life there, and, trusting in the saving power of God through Christ, could break the chains of sin and cause them to rise to a sobriety and dignity which was theirs by right. Historians can trace the revolutionary effects of their preaching in all fields: personal morality, health, politics, the penal code, class barriers, economic and personal slavery, education, literature, music, and the religious life of all sects."

These evangelists were forbidden by the established church in England to preach in any church and their enthusiasm was "condemned as an excitation of the devil." Despite the condemnation of several prominent clergymen of the time, the Wesleys, both John and Charles, died in full communion with the Church of England; Methodism was not established as a separate dissenting sect until 1808, 17 years after the death of John Wesley.

John Wesley (1703-1791) reportedly traveled over a quarter of a million miles (mostly on horseback) while preaching approximately 40,000 sermons and converting at least 100,000 people. He was known for rising at four in the morning, retiring at ten at night, and never wasting a minute in between, reading hundreds of volumes while travelling on horseback—in spite of being undersized with a frail appearance. He wrote 233 original works, kept a diary for 66 years that accounted for every hour in every day, could read in Hebrew, Greek and Latin, and could preach in English, German, French, and Italian, mastering Spanish enough to pray in that tongue.

On his first voyage to America with younger brother Charles, he learned there were some Moravians on board; immediately he set out to learn German so he could converse with them. The Moravians loved to sing and their services convinced Wesley of the immense value of singing. Wesley would translate a number of German hymns and then sing them in his early morning devotions, in sickrooms, and in larger gatherings on weekday nights and on Sundays.

In 1737, in Savannah, Georgia, John Wesley published these

hymns and psalms in *Collections of Psalms and Hymns*, the first hymnal ever used in an Anglican church. Five hymns came from Wesley's father and another five from his brother, Samuel; Charles had not yet begun to write them. All was not well with Wesley's parishioners, however, as most objected to singing anything but the psalms.

Although John Wesley was a known preacher, his real "conversion" did not come until after his initial American trip when he returned to London and attended some Moravian meetings. Brother Charles had been converted at a Moravian meeting three days earlier and the two would form a team after this with a shared passion for spreading the gospel.

John Wesley's major contribution to gospel music was editing, organizing, and publishing the hymns of Charles. This body of work became one of the most powerful evangelizing tools that England had ever known. Wesley also extensively translated German hymns, bringing a number of them into English, especially those by Paul Gerhardt, Tersteegen, and Zinzendorf.

Charles Wesley (1707-1788) attended university at Christ Church, Oxford, then went to the colony of Georgia as a private secretary to Governor Oglethorpe. He soon fell out of favor with the governor and others because of some escapades with adventuring females, and returned to England. After his conversion at the Moravian rooms at Aldergate, Charles met with his brother, John, and they discussed their mutual experiences; afterward they resolved to become partners in reaching out to the poor and outcast in the United Kingdom. Beginning with the prisoners in London, the brothers preached, encountering hostile mobs and more subtle persecutions while exhibiting tremendous energy, courage, self-sacrifice, as well as a power in their preaching. The converts of the Wesleys fared no better; often they were "outrageously treated—stoned, mauled, ducked, hounded with bulldogs, threatened; homes looted, businesses ruined."

Charles Wesley wrote his first hymn, "Where Shall My Wandering Soul Begin," the day after his conversion. After this, hardly a day or an experience passed without him putting it into a song. He composed in his study, his garden, on horseback—anywhere. In the end, he had composed 6500 hymns of Scripture texts on every conceivable phase of Christian experience and Methodist theology.

John began to select and publish hymn tracts in small collections and, later, in larger ones. In 53 years, there were 56 publications. The culmination of the series was the hymnal of 1780, *A Collection of Hymns for the Use of the People Called Methodists*. Not only was this a complete collection of songs, it was also a complete manual for religious education. This brand of religion was "intense, introspective, and yet so socially concerned; humble yet militant—as if religion, salvation, character, the will to save others, were the most important things in the world."

In discussing the effect of the Wesleys' Methodist movement, Albert Bailey states that, "The Methodist Revival did not concern itself with the reformation of social institutions. It did not tackle evils from the legislative end. It did work a moral transformation in the lives of thousands of people and thus prepared the public conscience and raised up the leaders to enact the legislative reforms of the nineteenth century. John Wesley has expressed the rationale of it: 'The sure hope of a better age is a better man.' Yet the Wesleys were perfectly conscious that institutions needed reformation. They spoke fiercely against human slavery, war, inhuman prisons, barbarous laws, the abuse of privilege, power and wealth, the liquor traffic."

The Wesleys' Methodist theology contrasted sharply with the Calvinistic theology on the issue of "election." Isaac Watts represented the Calvinists, who believed that God had chosen some men to be saved and some to be damned and that man could do nothing to change his pre-ordained state, while Wesley, following the Dutch theologian Arminius (1560-1609), believed man is free and that he himself can decide whether he will be saved. Therefore, Christ's death on the cross atoned for the sins of all men, not a chosen few. This meant that men are subject to persuasion and that the function of Christians is to endeavor to bring men to a decision.

The Wesleys took their songwriting seriously and demanded a high standard from their work. John stated that, "In these hymns there is no doggerel; no botches; nothing put in to patch up the rhyme; no feeble expletives. Here is nothing turgid or bombast, on the one hand, or low and creeping, on the other. Here are no words without meaning. Here are purity, the strength, and the elegance of the English language; and, at the same time, the utmost simplicity and plainness, suited to every capacity."

Richard Dinwiddie, in an article on the Wesleys in *Christianity Today*, quotes Erik Routley, an English hymn authority, who summarized three purposes found in Charles Wesley's hymn writing: (1) to provide a body of Christian teaching as found both in the Bible and in the *Book of Common Prayer*; (2) to provide material for public praise; and (3) to objectify his rich personal faith.

John Wesley's method of choosing hymns for public worship involved first singing them by himself, then trying them out with a few people during early morning devotionals. While visiting the sick he would sing the hymn with them and finally use the hymn during a weeknight service or a Sunday meeting. After using the hymn extensively, he would determine whether it would be printed or not.

Jesus, Lover of My Soul

Jesus, lover of my soul,
Let me to Thy bosom fly,
While the nearer waters roll,
While the tempest still is high;
Hide me, O my Saviour, hide,
Till the storm of life is past;
Safe into the haven guide,
O receive my soul at last.

Other refuge have I none,
Hangs my helpless soul on Thee;
Leave, ah, leave me not alone,
Still support and comfort me!
All my trust on Thee is stayed,
All my help from Thee I bring;
Cover my defenseless head
With the shadow of Thy wing.

Plenteous grace with Thee is found,
Grace to cleanse from all my sin;
Let the healing streams abound,
Make and keep me pure within.
Thou of life the fountain art;

Freely let me take of Thee;
Spring Thou up within my heart,
Rise to all eternity.

This hymn was published in *Hymns and Sacred Poems* in 1740 and was probably connected to John Wesley's conversion in 1738. A number of myths surround this hymn: a bird at sea flew to Wesley during a storm, a dove pursued by a hawk took refuge in his room, or Wesley himself escaped in a time of peril. The melody in contemporary hymnals was written by Simeon B. Marsh (1798-1875), an upstate New York singing teacher.

Christ The Lord Is Risen Today

Christ the Lord is risen today; Alleluia!
Sons of men and angels say; Alleluia!
Raise your joys and triumphs high; Alleluia!
Sing, ye heavens, and earth, reply; Alleluia!

Vain the stone, the watch, the seal; Alleluia!
Christ has burst the gates of hell; Alleluia!
Death in vain forbids His rise; Alleluia!
Christ hath opened Paradise. Alleluia!

Lives again our glorious King; Alleluia!
Where, O death, is now thy sting; Alleluia!
Once He died, our souls to save; Alleluia!
Where thy victory, O grave? Alleluia!

Soar we now where Christ has led; Alleluia!
Following our exalted Head; Alleluia!
Made like Him, like Him we rise; Alleluia!
Ours the cross, the grave, the skies. Alleluia!

Hail, the Lord of earth and heaven! Alleluia!
Praise to Thee by both be given; Alleluia!
Thee we greet triumphant now; Alleluia!
Hail, the Resurrection Thou! Alleluia!

The preceeding song first appeared in *Hymns and Sacred Poems* in 1739. It is considered an Easter hymn and is usually sung at Easter services as the resurrection is celebrated.

Rejoice, The Lord is King

Rejoice, the Lord is King!
Your Lord and King adore!
Mankind, give thanks and sing,
And triumph evermore.
Lift up your heart!
Lift up your voice!
Rejoice! again I say,
Rejoice!

The Lord the Saviour reigns,
The God of truth and love;
When he had purged our stains,
He took his seat above.
Lift up your heart!
Lift up your voice!
Rejoice! again I say,
Rejoice!

His kingdom cannot fail;
He rules o'er earth and heaven;
The keys of death and hell
To Christ the Lord are given.
Lift up your heart!
Lift up your voice!
Rejoice! again I say,
Rejoice!

Rejoice in glorious hope!
Our Lord the Judge shall come,
And take his servants up
To their eternal home.
Lift up your heart!

Lift up your voice!
Rejoice! again I say,
Rejoice!

"Rejoice, the Lord is King" comes from *Hymns for Our Lord's Resurrection*, published in 1746; the melody comes from John Darwall, an English clergyman and amateur musician.

Hark! The Herald Angels Sing

Hark! the herald angels sing
Glory to the newborn King!
Peace on earth and mercy mild,
God and sinners reconciled!
Joyful, all ye nations, rise,
Join the triumph of the skies;
With the angelic host proclaim
Christ is born in Bethlehem!
Hark! the herald angels sing
Glory to the newborn King!

Christ, by highest heaven adored;
Christ, the everlasting Lord;
Long desired, behold Him come,
Finding here His humble home.
Veiled in flesh the God-head see;
Hail the incarnate Deity,
Pleased as man with man to dwell;
Jesus, our Emanuel!

Mild he lays his glory by,
Born that man no more may die,
Born to raise the sons of earth,
Born to give them second birth.
Risen with healing in his wings,
Light and life to all he brings;
Hail, the Son of Righteousness!
Hail, the heavenly Prince of Peace!

The first lines of this hymn were originally "Hark, how all the welkin ring! Glory to the King of Kings," but these were changed by George Whitefield. Its use as a Christmas hymn was established c. 1810 after a number of others had tinkered with the lyrics—a practice that made the Wesleys irate. Charles Wesley once said of his lyrics, "Let them stand just as they are ... or add the true reading in the margin or at the bottom of the page, that we may no longer be accountable either for the nonsense or for the doggerel of other men." Ironically, he had tampered with the lyrics of George Herbert and Isaac Watts to suit his own purposes. The melody came from Felix Mendelssohn-Bartholdy's "Festgesang," although Mendelssohn did not feel that sacred words were appropriate for his melody.

Love Divine, All Loves Excelling

Love divine, all loves excelling,
Joy of heaven, to earth come down,
Fix in us thy humble dwelling,
All thy faithful mercies crown.
Jesus, thou art all compassion,
Pure, unbounded love thou art,
Visit us with thy salvation,
Enter every trembling heart.

Come, almighty to deliver,
Let us all thy life receive,
Graciously return, and never,
Never more thy temples leave.
Thee we would be always blessing,
Serve thee as thy hosts above,
Pray, and praise thee without ceasing,
Glory in thy perfect love.

Finish, then, thy new creation,
Pure and spotless let us be,
Let us see thy great salvation,
Perfectly restored in thee.
Changed from glory into glory,

Till in heaven we take our place,
Till we cast our crowns before thee,
Lost in wonder, love and praise.

The concept of "God as love" was not used much by early hymn writers so Wesley's lyrics in "Love Divine, All Loves Excelling" constituted a fresh take. It first appeared in 1747 in *Hymns for Those That Seek and Those That Have Redemption in the Blood of Christ.* The melody was composed by John Zundel, who was the organist of Plymouth Church, Brooklyn, which was pastored by Henry Ward Beecher.

O For a Thousand Tongues to Sing

O for a thousand tongues to sing,
My great Redeemer's praise;
The glories of my God and King,
The triumphs of His grace.

Jesus, the name that charms our fears,
That bids our sorrows cease;
'Tis music in the sinner's ears,
'Tis life, and health, and peace.

He breaks the power of reigning sin,
He sets the prisoner free;
His blood can make the sinful clean,
His blood availed for me.

My gracious Master and my God,
Assist me to proclaim;
To spread through all the earth abroad,
The honors of Thy name.

Glory to God and praise and love,
Be ever, ever given;
By saints below and saints above,
The church in earth and heaven.

This hymn originally had eighteen stanzas and was written to commemorate the anniversary of Wesley's conversion. The lines "He sets the prisoner free / His blood can make the sinful clean" are indicative of the Wesley's belief that salvation is available to all, not just the "elect." This split in the theology of the "elect" vs. the "free will" of man to choose salvation also caused a split between the Wesleys and George Whitefield; after meeting with Jonathan Edwards in 1740, Whitefield believed in the theology of the "elect."

Chapter 8

THE SECULAR INFLUENCE

During the first hundred years, religious music dominated America; however, in the 18th century, popular music began to grow and blossom and establish itself, although the identity of American music would remain an extension of Europe until the mid-19th century.

There was, of course, secular music from the time of the first settlers, but it was frowned upon by the religious leaders and churches that dominated early society, especially in New England. Still, there is evidence of secular music's popularity in New England. In *American Hymns Old and New*, the authors note that Seaborn Cotton, while a student at Harvard (he graduated in 1651), copied three ballads into his notebook: "The Love-Sick Maid," "The Last Lamentation of the Languishing Squire," and "Two Faithful Lovers." The Puritan leaders were known to have spoken against ballad singing as well as "filthy songs," although some noted that a number of popular tunes were used with religious verses inserted, a practice that drew mixed responses but which seemed to be commonly accepted. Cotton Mather noted the "fondness of people for ballad singing" could be used for religious instruction, observing further that "the minds and manners of many people about the country are much corrupted by the foolish airs and ballads which the Hawkers and Peddlers carry into all parts of the country."

Oscar G.T. Sonneck, in his book *Francis Hopkinson and James Lyon*, states that sacred and secular music developed "simultaneously" throughout the colonies, with sacred music "dominating" in the north (Boston) and secular dominating in the south (Charleston), while in the middle colonies (New York and Philadelphia) both were of "equal weight."

The Great Awakening, which began c. 1734 in New England with Jonathan Edwards and gradually moved south and west, infused a new life into sacred music as it introduced "hymns" into religious music, which had been dominated by psalms taken directly from scripture and usually sung in a slow, drawn-out style. The hymns were more lively and, under the influence of Isaac Watts and the Wesleys, full of personal expressions of faith. In Cotton Mather's time, the words dominated the music and there were only a handful of tunes to fit a large body of texts, which were all marked according to their "meters" or metrical structures.

The rise of the singing schools, which began c. 1717 in Boston, helped re-establish musical literacy and expanded the number of tunes that people knew in addition to correcting the mistakes Americans had injected into the old ones. According to Richard Crawford in his essay, "Make a Joyful Noise," the establishment of singing schools and the publication of tunebooks (which contained melodies as well as texts) were "seminal events in American musical history" because they saw the church commit "for the first time on record" to "supporting the development of musical skill." Crawford notes that some of the results of the success of the singing schools were "the spread of musical literacy, the greater availability of notated music ... many Americans were composing their own music ... [but] congregational singing was once again in the doldrums. The problem was no longer a lack of capable singers but rather that singers in many congregations were forming choirs that dominated the music of public worship. As some improved their skill in singing schools, others lost interest in singing at all."

One of the early singing masters, William Billings, is considered the first major composer in North America and his book, *New England Psalm Singer*, published in 1770, is one of the first books from a singing master. He has been described as "without doubt the most popular composer of the day." A tanner by trade, he loved music, especially choral composition and performance, and had an "enormous vitality," although he was "not a great singer" and had "no gift as an instrumentalist." He did, however, have administrative gifts and a sense for the dramatic and emotionally effective performance. He was somewhat deformed, blind in one eye, one leg shorter than the other, one arm withered, and "given to the habit of continually taking snuff." Musically, he was unsophisticated but he possessed a "vast amount of self-confidence."

Billings established a "Sacred Singing School" in Stoughton, Massachusetts in 1774 with about 48 pupils. He formed the Stoughton Musical Society in 1786 and during 1770-1786 published music books, including *The New England Psalm Singer* (1770), *The Singing Master's Assistant* (1778), *Music in Miniature* (1778), and *The Suffolk Harmony* (1786). He spent his last years in poverty, a victim of his love for music. Credited with composing 263 hymns and psalms, his best-known work is "Chester," a patriotic hymn that was the anthem for the Revolutionary War, and "Columbia," considered one of the "camp songs" of that period. According to Richard Crawford, Billings was the first American to see "psalmody as an art and himself as an artist."

The first major secular composer in the colonies was Francis Hopkinson. Born in Philadelphia, Hopkinson was a member of the first graduating class at the University of Pennsylvania and was known as a painter as well as a musician in the colonies. A signer of the Declaration of Independence, he numbered among his closest friends George Washington, Thomas Jefferson and Benjamin Franklin. His best-known song is "My Days Have Been So Wondrous Free," and though he is sometimes credited with composing "Yankee Doodle," perhaps the most popular song of the Revolutionary War, no conclusive evidence exists that affirms that conclusion.

Hopkinson was an accomplished musician, performing on the harpsichord, and was a leader in the musical life of Philadelphia, organizing subscription concerts as well as public concerts where amateur musicians performed. In addition to concerts, music was also performed in the theater between acts of plays as well as at dances. The subscription concerts, c. 1764, featured choral music by and for young people as well as chamber music, performed by about a dozen of the top amateur musicians in Philadelphia, including Governor John Penn, who played the violin.

A key year for music in the American colonies was 1759 when Hopkinson composed "My Days Have Been So Wondrous Free" and James Lyon composed music for an ode sung at his graduation from Princeton. Lyon is the second major secular composer in the colonies, best known for compiling *Urania*, a landmark volume of

American music. Much larger than any preceding American musical publication, Lyon's book contains 198 pages and 98 compositions. According to Richard Crawford in his essay "The Birth of Liberty," it is significant for a number of reasons. "It represents the earliest American printing of anthems (extended settings of prose text), 'fuging' tunes (psalm tunes with at least one section involving text overlap), and hymn tunes (settings of nonscriptural devotional text). It is also the earliest work to identify compositions as 'new'—that is, composed in the colonies (six pieces in the collection are so identified). Perhaps *Urania's* most significant innovation is that 28 of its pieces are underlaid with text. It is the first American publication to print text with music."

Urania was published in the 1760s, the most fruitful time for music in the colonies, with Hopkinson, Lyon and other composers and musicians bringing music to the public. However, earlier in the century there were some significant developments in secular music too. One of the earliest collections of secular songs in the colonies was the "Mother Goose" rhymes, which established a traditional set of songs that have remained an integral part of childhood since their publication. The book was assembled by Thomas Fleet, who had married Elizabeth Goose in 1715 and to whom a son was born the following year. Fleet's mother-in-law came to live with them and sang to the child constantly. Fleet soon grew weary of her singing; however, he wrote down the words to her songs and published them in a book titled *Songs for the Nursery or Mother Goose Melodies for Children*. Published in Boston in 1719, this book contained songs such as "Little Boy Blue," "Baa Baa Black Sheep," "To Market, To Market," "Little Robin Redbreast," "Sing a Song of Six Pence," "One, Two, Buckle My Shoe," "Snail, Snail," "Bye Baby Bunting," "Peter, Peter Pumpkin Eater," "Jack Spratt," and "Hickory Dickory Dock."

Songs brought from England, Scotland, and Ireland dominated the early 1700s, and George Washington reportedly danced for three hours "with one fair lady" to the music of fiddlers playing "Clock O' the North," "Sellingers' Round," "Strathspeys' Reel," and "Greensleeves" in the Apollo Room at Williamsburg's Raleigh Tavern. In the late 1700s, "The Way-Worn Traveller" is cited as Washington's favorite song, and he reportedly requested it be played a number of times.

Richard Crawford lists two kinds of secular songs that circulated in 18th century England and the colonies. The oldest was the oral-tradition English and Scottish balladry, which was brought over by the earliest settlers and flourished primarily in the south, unaffected by topical currents. The other type was broadside ballads, which developed from Elizabethan times into the 18th century and were the earliest commercial popular music. Crawford states that, "Broadside balladry depended partly on written practice. Texts circulated in broadsides—single sheets printed on one side and sold cheaply—and also in collections, occasionally with melodies but more often only with tune indications." The broadsides brought forth songs of news events, disasters, dying confessions, moralizing poems, and hymns. The Wesleys' "Ah Lovely Appearance of Death," Samuel Sewall's "Once More Our God Vouchsafe to Shine," and the anonymous "Is There No Balm in Christian Lands" were originally published as broadsides.

The ballad opera, which began with John Gay's "The Beggar's Opera" in London in 1728, brought broadside tunes to the theatre. The heyday of the ballad opera was the 1730s and it helped establish the vernacular English musical theatre, which provided another kind of secular music that circulated in the colonies. The 1730s are the time of the first American music concert on record, held in Boston in 1731. The ballad operas were popular in New York beginning in 1732, although its growth was inhibited by the disdain of the religious establishment, which perpetuated the notion that the theatre was a den of iniquity and a haven for sin. However, as more and more people immigrated from Europe, and the population of the new country grew, there was a growing sense of liberalism and a loosening of the stronghold religion held over 17th and early 18th century Americans.

In "The Birth of Liberty," Richard Crawford states that, "Culturally as well as politically, pre-Revolutionary America was a colony of Great Britain; several different kinds of music-making flourished in the colonies, but the most widespread creative response of Revolutionary period America to the war lay in making verses to well-known tunes rather than in composing the tunes themselves." The period just prior to the Revolutionary War, beginning in the 1760s, marked the emergence of a society dominated by secularization and Alan Lomax states in his essay on "The Sacred Harp" that "The Revolution was, for the common man, as much a throwing off of religious as of secular authority." In terms of music, this meant the growing acceptance of musical instruments in homes as well as in churches, which had generally taken a strong stand against the use of instruments with sacred music. The acceptance and use of instruments for composing and performing music provided a striking difference between sacred and secular music. Crawford states that, "The lack of a keyboard instrument can be a decisive determinant of style …[it is] clearer why secular music, rooted in a tradition of melody with keyboard accompaniment, is stylistically distinct from most American psalmody." That difference may be heard in the music of Francis Hopkinson, who composed on the keyboard, and William Billings, who did not, writing instead for four voices which he added successively to the song.

During the Revolutionary War, a number of songs were composed, most of them new texts set to old tunes, primarily concerned with patriotism and the struggle with Great Britain. In "The Birth of Liberty," Crawford states that, "When the colonies went to war with Great Britain, a small amount of new music was composed to commemorate the struggle; a larger amount of propagandist verse was written and sung to well-known British tunes; and an even larger amount of traditional Anglo-American dance music, song, and hymnody having nothing particular to do with the war continued to be played and sung and enjoyed, creating a musical continuity.... The music was functional and hence existed in an unreproducible social context. It relied heavily on oral means for its circulation; its creators' identity was a matter of indifference to its performers. (The songs are likely to be timely parodies rather than original creations.) It addressed a cultural need and was hence accessible. The people whose feelings it expressed were preoccuppied with survival rather than art; anxious to feel morally superior to their enemy; willing to be diverted and entertained.... The music of the Revolution ... was composed not so much to be listened to as to be sung, played, marched to, danced to."

After the Revolutionary War, Americans continued to look to Europe for their music and culture as immigrants came to the new country in large numbers and urban Americans grew wealthier and more desirous of luxury. European musicians took up residence in the major cities and these professionals replaced the native amateur musicians who had dominated the colonial period.

With the establishment of the European professional came the attitude that American musicians and music were not as acceptable. There is some truth to this, as Oscar G.T. Sonneck states in *Francis Hopkins and James Lyon*, that "Our early musicians lacked opportunities accumulated abroad during centuries of musical activity. Their own efforts were restricted to a feeble imitation of European conditions and to the development of our musical life out of a most primitive ... state of affairs."

In *Yesterdays*, Charles Hamm traces American popular music back to English garden music in the 17th century; he also notes that no secular sheet music was printed in America before the 1770s. He attributes the lack of American songs to two reasons: the first national copyright act was not passed until 1790 and there was a ban on theaters and "Play Houses" from 1778 until 1789 because the Continental Congress had decreed that these activities had "a fatal tendency to divert the minds of people from a due attention to the means necessary for the defence of their country and preservation of their liberties."

The English pleasure gardens located in or near cities, were privately owned, and filled with walks, waters, trees, and birds. Those who frequented these gardens paid an admission price and were treated to musical entertainment, food and drink, and the joys of walking through nature tamed and cultivated for civilized man. Musicians who composed for these gardens include J.C. Bach, Handel, and Thomas Arne, who was particularly adept at writing popular songs. Hamm notes that Arne was successful because he wrote music with "immediate accessibility." Knowing it would be "judged on first hearing ... [Arne] did not fill his songs with complex and difficult passages that would interest and challenge other composers and professional musicians.... He wrote strophic songs, so listeners would hear the same music three, four, five, or even more times at a song's first hearing. His songs had simple internal structures, so listeners would hear the chief melodic phrase two or three times within each strophe. They often concluded with a refrain line that was catchy or easily memorable. By the time an audience had heard one of his songs for the first time, they might not be able to sing it from memory, but at the very least they would have some memory of it, could recognize it if they heard it again, and by the end of the song very likely could sing the refrain line at the end of each stanza with the performer."

This garden music never achieved the success in America that it did in England because of the Revolutionary War and because American tastes and lifestyles were different from the English. Still, British musicians and composers came over to America to write and perform popular music and the Americans generally welcomed them. Before the war, the Philadelphia newspapers were full of advertisements by musicians for music lessons as well as dancing lessons. This instruction showed a growing inclination by Americans to learn music; however, after the war, teaching musicians were usually European professionals. Cultured Americans desired to learn music, but they wanted to learn European music. The professionals were classically trained and classical music has never been "popular music" in America as it has in Europe—the cultures can influence each other but they cannot be transplanted. Although the classically oriented music and musicians held a place in America, popular music gravitated towards a folk music that had been brought over a century earlier and nurtured on native soil. These folk melodies would influence secular music as well as sacred music, through the hymns of the Wesleys, Isaac Watts and Bach as well as through the music from native composers.

In sacred music, Alan Lomax identifies four general classes of song—folk tunes, psalm tunes, revivalist hymns and fuguing tunes. The oldest are the folk tunes, originating with the English, Scottish, Irish and Welsh and passed down by oral tradition among ordinary people; the psalm tune is the next oldest, coming from an extensive tradition of church music in northern Europe and passed along by the churches. The revivalist tunes date from the period of the Great Revival (c. 1780-1840) when "many songwriters sought to bring to their music the rousing fervor of the revival meetings." These songs show a clear connection to the older folk and psalm tunes but usually feature the use of "refrain, lively tempos, syncopated choral effects, and a structure that consciously ascends toward a stirring climax." The largest single category was the fuguing tunes, generally older songs from other types put into the new style "by popular demand." The introduction of new tunes, lively, active and vibrant, brought new life to sacred music and threw off the chains of tradition that held religious music in a straightjacket of formalism, sobriety and conservativism. Secular music, too, felt the influence of the Great Revival as it began to develop a distinctive American voice in the 19th century.

After the Revolutionary War, several songs emerged that would influence American music for years. "Hail, Columbia," a song that has been considered one of the most significant written during that era, was composed in 1794 by Judge Joseph Hopkinson of New Jersey, son of Francis Hopkinson. "To Anacreon in Heaven" was written in London by either John Stafford or Samuel Arnold at the end of the Revolutionary War. This was the theme song for the first three American presidents. In 1814, Francis Scott Key, an attorney on board a British ship arranging for the release of a client, wrote the lyrics for "The Star Spangled Banner" to this melody and it later became the National Anthem.

The beginning of the 19th century marked the end of the first two stages of American musical growth—the psalmody of the 17th century and the hymns and secular songs of the 18th century. The next era of American popular music began on July 4, 1826, the day two presidents, Thomas Jefferson and John Adams, died. On that day, while the Star Spangled Banner played (according to legend), Stephen Foster was born; he would live to become the first major American composer with a distinctive American voice and an extensive body of musical work that would change America's music and set it apart from the music of the European heritage.

Stephen Collins Foster was born near Lawrenceville, Pennsylvania, which is now part of Pittsburgh. He had little formal music training but taught himself to play the clarinet at six and soon could play any song by ear. He began composing at fourteen and eventually wrote over 200 songs. He called his minstrel songs "Ethiopian songs" and began composing them in 1845 to take advantage of the minstrel shows becoming popular in the United States at that time. Foster worked with E. P. Christy and the Christy Minstrels, who introduced most of Foster's songs to audiences across the country. The songs proved to be so popular that many of them were adapted for Sunday School use, with the words changed to fit the Christian message but the same melodies retained. His material is an example of Christian churches taking advantage of popular music by incorporating revised tunes in the church.

Foster's downfall was that he was a poor businessman, selling most of his songs that would soon become famous for flat fees or few royalties. Also, the infrastructure was not in place for copyright protection or for a songwriter to earn money from performances. He moved from Cincinnati to New York in 1860 and lived there fighting illness, poverty and alcoholism, until his death in 1864, after the Emancipation Proclamation and just before the end of the fighting in the Civil War.

In his book, *American Popular Song*, author Alec Wilder points out that Foster approached his music from two points of view, the formal and the native. Examples of the "formal" are "Jeannie With The Light Brown Hair" and "Beautiful Dreamer," while examples of the "native" include "Old Black Joe," "De Camptown Races," and "Oh! Susanna." Wilder notes that the latter style was deeply rooted in Negro music and Negro life. Foster was also influenced by early minstrel shows, which were usually white versions of black music.

One of the reasons Foster was so unique was that he was sensitive to and aware of black music and fused this influence into his own music. His death, during the the Civil War, left a musical gap that no one filled until the late 1880s. Wilder states that, "I feel sure that for a long while after the war had ended, the vital, creative energies that had nourished plantation music were subdued." Indeed, the whole country was more concerned about rebuilding itself and re-establishing individual lives than in songs and entertainment. Too, the Negro—who was uneducated—had to learn how to survive in a world that was both hostile and indifferent to him. When the plantations were gone, the social structures that both hemmed in the Negro and allowed him the freedom to play and sing his own music were also gone.

The music from the plantations—jig and cakewalk music, blues and spiritual—would surface later in the 19th century as ragtime, jazz, popular blues, and the original spirituals from the church. However, for the 30 to 40 years following the Civil War there was a musical isolation imposed on both the black and white cultures with whites no longer exposed to music in the slave quarters and blacks excluded from white publishing houses. This period also marks a sharp division in the church life of Americans as blacks established their own churches outside and away from white culture while white churches by and large developed unwritten codes and practices which effectively barred African-Americans from their churches.

Chapter 9

GIVE ME THAT OLD TIME RELIGION

The revival that followed the Revolutionary War was not a highly organized affair and cannot be traced in a logical, sequential manner; rather, it was a number of religious freedom fires which seemed to ignite by spontaneous combustion. As the country pushed westward, these revivals sprang up in various areas of the country over several generations, offending established, organized religion because revival preachers paid no heed to denominational lines, preaching wherever they could gather a crowd.

The Revolutionary War had capped the great concept of "freedom" that had been raging in the colonies. For religion, this meant there was freedom of religion as well as freedom from religion. Many early leaders—George Washington, Thomas Jefferson, and Benjamin Franklin, for example—were quite Deistic and preferred a more distant and rational God than the emotional Puritans. In the urban areas, the rationalism that fueled the French Revolution and provided new breakthroughs in science and philosophy caught hold. However, in the untamed parts of the country, this rationalism had little appeal—the settlers had neither the time nor inclination to ponder intellectual enlightenment. These people needed a faith that was vibrant and alive, full of emotion and comfort, which helped them relate to the lonely, danger-filled wilderness and a life steeped heavily in individualism. Thus, it was a "free" religion that took hold.

Socially, the new free religion was perfect for the common man who was poor. The pursuits of the rich—drinking, gambling and such—were quickly labeled as sinful and railed against. The large urban areas became dens of iniquity while rural America provided the most fertile soil for folk religion. Here, it grew and spread, watered by an emotional spirituality that provided a comfort to the lonely settlers. While this folk religion came under no organizational guidelines, one basic tenet ran through it—all institutional mediacy between a man's soul and his redeemer must be rejected—every individual, no matter what his station in life, had direct access to God.

As the settlers moved westward, they moved beyond the influence of established churches and were served by a new kind of preacher, born on the frontier, or at least familiar with frontier life. Although they generally had little formal education, these preachers did have the ability to move audiences and would preach wherever a group could be assembled. The "camp meeting" was born from the lack of a central church in the vast rural regions and because the settlers lived so far apart. Camp meetings brought people together for several days from a large area, with families bringing food and living in their wagons, the women sleeping inside and the men on the ground underneath or in improvised shelters.

The Baptists were a particularly free group with dissensions breaking out within their sect about predestination, grace, and a number of other theological questions. They were the folky sect of both Britain and America, never accepting a central church authority; in music this meant they were devoted to "free" singing rather than singing songs prescribed to them by a central authority. The spirit of the folk Baptists dominated this time of revivals after the Revolutionary War and the songs they chose to sing differed greatly from the psalms of the Puritans with their long texts. The revival spirituals, born from these mass meetings, emphasized choruses, burdens, refrains, and repeated lines.

In the period 1780-1830, a great body of folk texts appeared in the country-song tradition. Great Britain and the young United States were full of folk tunes, and religious folk often put religious verses to popular secular tunes. The wedding of religious lyrics and folk tunes probably began around 1770 and continued throughout this period. The composed tunes of the pre-Revolutionary War period in America remained unknown to the rural Americans who had moved westward, so they used tunes from the folk tradition for their worship. The source for these American folk tunes was primarily British—from England, Scotland, and Ireland mainly—with only a handful from other sources.

The Kentucky Revival of 1800 established the revival spiritual in America. The Kentucky Revival was not the first and was similar to a number of other revivals that preceeded it; however, the flames there seemed to burn higher and brighter because of a number of favorable conditions. One was the ethnic background of the population—primarily Gaels (Irish, Scots-Irish, Scottish, Welsh) who were known as highly emotional people. Another factor was climatic-geographic. The Kentucky farmers had a period of leisure during the summer from the time their crops were planted until harvesting time (as opposed to their New England counterparts who had a short summer) and the dry roads and trails invited long trips to big gatherings. Too, the dry hot summers lent themselves to meeting outdoors, thereby accommodating large numbers of people. The final factor was the lack of organized, established religion in that area, which meant no religious or civil authorities had to be battled for these revivals to occur.

The revivals were charged with spiritual emotionalism and George Pullen Jackson in *White and Negro Spirituals* describes a gathering in Kentucky, near Lexington, in 1801, where approximately 20,000 gathered. He states that,

> It was a night that the most terrible scenes were witnessed when the campfires blazed in a mighty circle around the vast audience of pioneers...As the darkness deepened, the exhortations of the preachers became more fervent and impassioned, their picturesque prophesies of doom more lurid and alarming...The volume of song burst all bonds of guidance and control, and broke again and again from the throats of the people while over all, at intervals, there rang out the shout of ecstasy, the sob and the groan. Men and women shouted aloud during the sermon, and shook hands all around at the close in what was termed 'the singing ecstasy.' The 'saints' and more especially those who were out to see the show would rush 'from preacher to preacher,' if it were whispered that it was 'more lively' at some other point, swarming enthusiastically around a brother who was laughing, leaping, shouting, swooning...The whole body of persons who actually fell helpless to the earth was computed...to

be three thousand...These were carried to a nearby meeting house and laid out on the floor. At no time was the floor less than half covered. Some lay quiet unable to move or speak. Some talked but could not move...Some, shrieking in agony, bounded about like a fish out of water. Many lay down and rolled over and over for hours at a time. Others rushed wildly over stumps and benches and then plunged, shouting 'Lost! Lost!' into the forest...other 'physical exercises'... included 'jerks' (where) the victims snapped their heads from side to side and front to back with unbelievable rapidity and vim; the 'hops' where frogs were imitated; the 'holy laugh' and the 'barks' whose usually involuntary addicts would 'tree the devil' and then get down on all fours at the foot of the tree and snap and growl.

The crowds at these gatherings had to sing from memory or learn songs that were repetitive and took little effort to learn because there were no song books. Here, the revival songs were in the hands of the people as the real exhortational activity—praying, mourning, and other physical exercises—was by and for the crowd. The singers controlled the songs but the crowds would join in the chorus, on a short-phrase refrain or on a couplet which struck their fancy. This led to the development of revival songs with repetitive passages.

The verse-with-chorus idea spread quickly with some choruses proving so popular they were interjected into other songs with different verses. Two types of revival songs developed—the repetitive chorus and the call-and-response where a line was sung by the singer and the crowd sang the responding line, which always remained the same.

The folk tradition of song—an oral tradition that had begun in Britain and other parts of Europe—took over in religious music. The settlers moving west had little if any music training and possessed neither song books nor established churches. When the revivals caught hold, music was returned to the people who responded with a congregational type of singing reminiscent of the earliest Puritans, albeit much more emotional and active. They had to depend upon tunes they already knew—much as the first Puritans did with their songs. But the nature of the revivals caused a major change—the melodies had to be altered to accommodate choruses that everyone could learn quickly. Thus the song leader would know the verses but everyone could know the chorus and would join on these choruses or on lines that repeated themselves.

This was democracy in action; everyone could feel a part of religion and singing. Too, the choruses spoke the feelings of the settlers. The early religious folk-singing practice took hold in the period 1780-1830, when it enjoyed its greatest vigor. Everyday folk enjoyed the most control over their private and institutional affairs; there was wide participation by the "folk" and there was an interdependence of mass-controlled religion and mass-controlled song.

As the Kentucky Revival followed the Great Awakening, the great Millenial Excitement followed next as religious revival continued to spread across America. This was not the first millenial expectation by American Christians—the Salem witch trials in the 1690s came from a religious fervor heavily doused with the projection of a coming millenium supposed to start in 1700. The millenial movement generally accompanies religious revival in America and centers on the belief that Christ will return and the true believers will either be transported bodily to heaven or an earthly kingdom will be established where peace will reign for a thousand years.

The leader of the Millenial Excitement was William Miller (1782-1849), who declared that the world would end in the spring of 1843. When Judgment Day did not arrive at the appointed time, the faithful reset the date for October 22, 1844. When that date failed to yield the projected result, many committed suicide or entered insane asylums with "Miller Madness" during the early 1840s. Although the earth remained intact after this date, a new sect was born, the Seventh-Day Adventists, founded by Miller, after an evolution that produced a variety of "Adventists" before taking its present form. In addition to the millenialists, there also arose during this time Christian factions against drinking, war, slavery, the Masons, and Catholics.

The old-time religion was a personal, highly emotional relationship between an individual and God; the rise of modern Protestantism brought forth a social-ethical-aesthetic gospel. The religions that were tribes of radicalism soon became cornerstones of the establishment. Methodists and Baptists, Mormons and Seventh-Day Adventists were no longer positioned outside mainstream society; they were now large denominations whose members occupied places of honor and respect and whose denominations spanned the globe.

As the first half of the 19th century ended, the old-time religion faded as the cultural environment gave way to the Industrial Revolution and the Civil War. After the Civil War, the second half of the 19th century witnessed the birth of a new religious trend as the wild, emotion-packed camp meeting style of religion gave way to a more solemn, sober movement, centered in the urban areas and accompanied by the music of the gospel hymns.

The folk hymns and spirituals were the last gospel songs to be perpetuated solely via the oral tradition, although they survive now because they were collected in print and because folklorists collected them on tape. Although some were written by individuals, many of the hymns came from the broadside ballad tradition and the folk songs brought to this country from Europe. The spirituals are often black adaptations of white songs, influenced heavily by the African origins of black Americans but also reflecting the culture of a people united and suppressed in America.

The "all day singing" was unique to the south and families often gathered at the county courthouse to sing from copies of the *Sacred Harp* or *Southern Harmony* and eat picnic lunches together. There was a great deal of harmony singing and most of the songs were written for three or four parts with the tenor generally carrying the melody line. Some of the ballads are reminiscent of the broadside ballads which present the confessions of criminals. One such religious ballad is "Remember, Sinful Youth," which is reminiscent of an earlier song about the fate of the pirate, Captain Kidd.

Remember, Sinful Youth

Remember, sinful youth, you must die, you must die,
Remember, sinful youth, you must die;
Remember, sinful youth, who hate the way of truth
And in your pleasures boast, you must die;
And in your pleasures boast, you must die.

Uncertain are your days here below, here below,
Uncertain are your days here below,
Uncertain are your days, for God hath many ways
To bring you to your graves here below, here below,
To bring you to your graves here below.

The God that built the sky, great I am, great I am,
The God that built the sky, great I am;
The God that built the sky, hath said (and cannot lie),
Impenitents shall die, and be damned, and be damned,
Impenitents shall die, and be damned.

And, O my friends, don't you, I entreat, I entreat,
And, O my friends, don't you, I entreat;
And, O my friends, don't you your carnal mirth pursue,
Your guilty souls undo, I entreat, I entreat,
Your guilty souls undo, I entreat.

Unto the Saviour flee, 'scape for life! 'scape for life!
Unto the Saviour flee, 'scape for life!
Unto the Saviour flee, lest death eternal be
Your final destiny, 'scape for life! 'scape for life!
Your final destiny, 'scape for life!

The traveling preacher Peter Cartwright is credited with writing "Where Are the Hebrew Children." In his autobiography, Cartwright presents one of the rare early accounts of southern folk singing. He wrote that he was in the Allegheny mountains, had not wanted to travel on the Sabbath, and so had been directed to a home where he was invited to preach. At the conclusion of his sermon Cartwright called on the local preacher to conclude. The preacher rose and began singing a mountain song, while patting his foot, clapping his hands, and shouting, "Pray brethren." This led the whole congregation into an emotional release, shouting and singing.

The Hebrew Children

Where are the Hebrew children?
Where are the Hebrew children?
Where are the Hebrew children?
Safe in the promised land.
Though the furnace flamed around them,
God, while in their troubles found them,
He with love and mercy bound them,
Safe in the promised land.
Where are the twelve apostles?
Where are the twelve apostles?
Where are the twelve apostles?
Safe in the promised land.
They went up through pain and sighing,
Scoffing, scourging, crucifying,
Nobly for their master dying,
Safe in the promised land.

Where are the holy Christians?
Where are the holy Christians?
Where are the holy Christians?
Safe in the promised land.
Those who've washed their robes and made them
White and spotless pure and laid them
Where no earthly stain can fade them,
Safe in the promised land.

The form is reminiscent of the 12-bar blues lyric format at the beginning of the verse as the singer sings the same line three times before the phrase, "Safe in the promised land," which also occurs at the end of the verse. The second half of each verse has an a-a-a-rhyme before the repeat of the "safe in the promised land" line, thus making it easy to learn. People could often learn the song as it was being sung and, after a few times through, could sing it fluently.

Cartwright preached to both white and black audiences on southern farms because small congregations were often not segregated. Whites and blacks heard the same songs, although musically the spirituals, born from slavery, became separate from the southern folk songs primarily because of the differences in the black and white cultures and the unique aptitude of the African-Americans for rhythms. The first major collection of spirituals was *Slave Songs of the United States* in 1867, followed by *Jubilee Songs*, issued by the Fisk Jubilee singers. "Hurry On, My Weary Soul" is taken from *Slave Songs*.

Hurry On, My Weary Soul

Hurry on, my weary soul,
And I heard from heaven today,
Hurry on, my weary soul,
And I heard from heaven today.

My sin is forgiven, and my soul set free,
And I heard from heaven today,
My sin is forgiven, and my soul set free,
And I heard from heaven today.

Hurry on, my weary soul,
And I heard from heaven today,
Hurry on, my weary soul,
And I heard from heaven today.

My name is called and I must go,
And I heard from heaven today,
My name is called and I must go,
And I heard from heaven today.

Hurry on, my weary soul,
And I heard from heaven today,
Hurry on, my weary soul,
And I heard from heaven today.

De bell is a-ringin' in de oder bright world,
And I heard from heaven today,
De bell is a-ringin' in de oder bright world,
And I heard from heaven today.

The line "And I heard from heaven today" could have several meanings, a trademark of many spirituals which served as communication between blacks, as did gospel songs. The song can easily be improvised by singers who add "And I heard from heaven today" after a new line. This meant a song could constantly change to fit the mood of the worshippers as well as the individuality of the singer and congregation. It also invited congregations to join in as "And I heard from heaven today" was repeated every other line.

The songs "Didn't My Lord Deliver Daniel" and "When Israel Was In Egypt's Land (Go Down, Moses)" come from *Jubilee Singers and Their Songs*, issued in 1872.

Didn't My Lord Deliver Daniel

Didn't my Lord deliver Daniel,
D'liver Daniel, d'liver Daniel,
Didn't my Lord deliver Daniel,
And why not every man?

He delivered Daniel from the lion's den,
Jonah from the belly of the whale,
And the Hebrew children from the fiery furnace,
And why not every man?

Didn't my Lord deliver Daniel,
D'liver Daniel, d'liver Daniel,
Didn't my Lord deliver Daniel,
And why not every man?

The moon run down in a purple stream,
The sun forbear to shine,
And every star disappear,
King Jesus shall be mine.

The wind blows East, and the wind blows West,
It blows like the judgment day,
And every poor soul that never did pray,
Will be glad to pray that day.

I set my foot on the Gospel ship,
And the ship it begin to sail,
It landed me over on Canaan's shore,
And I'll never come back any more.

When Israel Was In Egypt's Land

When Israel was in Egypt's land,
Let my people go;
Oppressed so hard they could not stand,
Let my people go.

Chorus:
Go down, Moses, way down in Egypt land,
  Tell ole Pharoah, let my people go.

Thus said the Lord, bold Moses said,
Let my people go;
If not I'll smite your first born dead,
Let my people go.

  Chorus

No more shall they in bondage toil,
Let my people go;
Let them come out with Egypt's spoil,
Let my people go.

  Chorus

O let us all from bondage flee,
Let my people go;
And let us all in Christ be free,
Let my people go.

  Chorus

We need not always weep and moan,
Let my people go;
And wear these slavery chains forlorn,
Let my people go.

Chorus

It is easy to see why both of these songs would appeal to slaves with lines such as "and why not every man" and "let my people go." These phrases not only speak of Biblical stories, they tell the slave's story as well, and "When Israel Was In Egypt's Land" equates the plight of the slave with that of the Israelites before Moses led them out. The analogy between America and Israel as God's land, housing God's chosen people, was one employed by the Puritans as well who escaped religious persecution in 17th century England. It is only fitting that African-Americans would also use the parallels between themselves and the Israelites as they sought comfort in their plight through their songs and their religion.

It was not until the 20th century that denominational hymnals included spirituals. "Were You There" was included in *The Hymnal* in 1940 and thus entered the white culture as a church hymn after its long life as a spiritual.

Were You There?

Were you there when they crucified my Lord?
Were you there when they crucified my Lord?
Oh! Sometimes it causes me to tremble, tremble, tremble.
Were you there when they crucified my Lord?

Were you there when they nailed him to the tree?
Were you there when they nailed him to the tree?
Oh! Sometimes it causes me to tremble, tremble, tremble.
Were you there when they nailed him to the tree?

Were you there when they laid him in the tomb?
Were you there when they laid him in the tomb?
Oh! Sometimes it causes me to tremble, tremble, tremble.
Were you there when they laid him in the tomb?

These songs reflect the oral tradition as well as the revival spirit of singing "spontaneously," without books, led by a singer with the congregation joining on key lines, phrases, or the chorus. They are easily learned and easily remembered. They are also easily changed and adapted from singer to singer, and congregation to congregation, with the chorus or key lines remaining and the verse lyrics subject to individual changes. They are timeless songs because of their repetitiveness but also because of their emotional appeal—they can inspire joy or comfort in sorrow, verbalizing people's feelings and thoughts. Within these songs are the roots of blues, country, modern gospel, and rock 'n roll. Musically and lyrically simple, their power rests in their emotional impact and their ability to be learned and sung easily.

Chapter 10

BLACK GOSPEL AND THE FISK JUBILEE SINGERS

The first slaves were brought to Virginia by Dutch traders in 1629. Soon, a whole economy and way of life was based on slavery, particularly in the south where large plantations grew acres of cotton and relied upon slave labor. For thousands of years—even before America was founded—people of most cultures, including Christians, took the practice of slavery for granted and amassed scriptural texts to justify it. Many otherwise humane people saw no inconsistency in the practice of slavery and supported it; it was a very slow and painful awakening that saw slavery cast in the light of injustice and inequality.

Slavery grew quickly in America and soon there was a bustling slave trade spawned by Europeans between Africa and America. From 1720 to the 1760s over 150,000 new African slaves arrived in America. Many Christian whites perpetuated the myth that blacks were descendents of the biblical Ham, wicked son of Noah, and that their bondage was a mark of sin from God. This theory received support from plantation masters as well as scientists from northern universities. Some scholars used research from anthropology, history, sociology, and biology to prove Negroes were inferior, measuring and weighing brains in an attempt to "prove" inferiority because their brains were smaller or lighter.

There was, however, some early concern among white colonial Christians about the salvation of blacks. Cotton Mather, the venerable New England preacher, argued that blacks had souls; however, many whites refused to baptize blacks because this act inferred certain liberties for black individuals that whites were reluctant to bestow. Mather solved the problem somewhat by offering the alternative of huge indentures imposed by masters on Negroes which would insure slavery after baptism. Also, he suggested black children be made to memorize lines like "I must be patient and content with such condition God has ordered for me." The belief that African blacks were slaves because God had ordained it—in spite of evidence to the contrary—was a concept American whites openly embraced and promulgated. These whites also demanded that blacks accept this divine interpretation as well, which many blacks reluctantly did at the time of their Christian conversion.

Even after the Civil War, which officially abolished black slavery, many white Protestants continued in their quest to build a "righteous Empire." However, only certain people belonged in this empire so that blacks, although no longer slaves, were still not equals; thus slavery continued to be a religious doctrine and inequality a way of life to many Christians.

A pivotal figure in the development of the black church is Richard Allen, born a slave in 1760. Allen's family was sold, one by one, by their owner who had fallen on financial hard times. Allen heard the circuit riders—preachers who travelled on horseback from plantation to plantation and community to community—and was influenced by them. He experienced a spiritual rebirth and showed a talent for preaching to his companions. The Methodists, under John Wesley and Francis Asbury, often taught their congregations to set goals for themselves as they sought perfection. Allen's goal was to purchase his freedom, so he and his owner agreed on the terms. Both Allen and his brother became free after meeting the price.

Richard Allen lived in Philadelphia and worked a series of odd jobs to support his preaching. He formed a Free Africa Society and founded a church, named Bethel. In 1816 there were five congregations of this church. This group formed the first Methodist General Conference for free blacks who chose to follow the Methodist Episcopal church doctrine.

Bishop Allen, as he was known, oversaw the 6,748 Methodists in his care around Philadelphia, Baltimore, and Charleston and, though he sought unity amongst freedmen, he saw them oppose each other within black denominations beset with disagreements and riddled with conflicts like those of their white counterparts. Still, he channeled his considerable energies into welfare work, mutual aid, and preaching as he and his colleagues "inspired members with hopes of heaven while they imparted dignity to blacks in their daily struggles."

Even during the early days of the freedom churches, there were militants who inspired slave revolts. These revolutionaries used biblical phrases learned on the plantations to inspire followers and often saw themselves as a Moses, leading the chosen and faithful to an exodus out of Egyptian slavery to the new Canaan, much in the same way that the early American Puritans visualized their flight to the New World. Slaves often combined Christianity with African folk religion to produce a hybrid religion. Two of the more famous—Denmark Vesey and Nat Turner—were killed in 1822 and 1831, respectively, for leading slave uprisings.

Blacks also had to face a movement by whites called the American Colonization Society, formed in 1817, which sought to have them transported back to Africa. However, by then blacks were several generations removed from being Africans and viewed themselves as Americans, with as much right to claim citizenship in the nation as their white counterparts.

Slaves often communicated via a "grapevine" that let others know about their movements. This was particularly needed on southern plantations, which were so far apart that no blacks could effectively congregate. Still, their mixture of African religion and Christianity continued to grow and help them cope with their daily struggles. Their spirituals often had double meanings—the same songs spoke openly of eternal hope beyond the earthly life as well as underground railroads which could lead them to freedom.

The conversion of blacks was guided by the same principles as those for whites—each individual was expected to confront God and make his decision for Jesus, be "born-again" or "get religion." Many white settlers carried their slaves with them during the early camp meetings at the beginning of the 1800s and there blacks heard psalms and camp meeting songs. The slaves made a number of conscious attempts to reproduce the songs they heard but often sang them in a different manner, affecting rhythms which were different from the original and, because of an insufficient vocabulary or inability to recall the words correctly, different lyrics or lyrics which have been published in collections as "Negro dialect," markedly different from white speech.

While the early white settlers placed a heavy emphasis on the words, with the music being incidental—a handful of tunes were used, often interchangable with different sets of lyrics—blacks felt a need to emphasize music over the words. But it was more than just a different melody—it was a whole new rhythm, an entirely new "feel" to the songs which became defined as black gospel. Even though blacks and whites often sang the same words, learned from the same sources, the results were two entirely different songs, with the black gospel songs rhythmical in a way that the white songs never were. These rhythms, often complex, are attributed to the African influence.

Spirituals were created by a people bound in slavery and were an integral part of the culture in the early 19th century. However, it was not until after the Civil War that the spiritual was first recorded. The first major book containing words and music of spirituals was *Slave Songs of the United States* in 1867, but the first real awareness of the spirituals came when the Fisk Jubilee Singers undertook a tour of northern cities in order to raise money for their financially strapped institution. Still, black gospel music was virtually ignored by white Christians and it was not until the 20th century that denominational hymnals included spirituals.

Musicologist and folk music collector George Pullen Jackson noted in the early part of the 20th century that most of the Negro spirituals had white origins and could be traced back to the British folk song tradition and early American camp meetings. Many later called his conclusions racist for denying African origins for these songs. But Jackson was correct in tracing these songs to their source; however, he ignored the musical rhythms that defined black gospel, tracing only words and melodies. Too, he overlooked the development of the "holiness" movement in the latter part of the 19th century, which was a source of the essential difference between black and white gospel music.

Before the Civil War, both the pro-slavery and the anti-slavery forces had one thing in common: they saw blacks as a target for Christian conversion. Southern slave owners justified their practice by saying they were "Christianizing" and "civilizing" the savages from Africa. And many Northern whites in the anti-slavery movement viewed southern blacks as opportunities for mission work. This was an impetus behind the American Missionary Association, formed in 1846, which sent out missionaries who would teach slaves and freed blacks to read and write (so they could read the Bible) and establish churches for them.

In 1863 this organization had 83 ministers and teachers in the field; this number had expanded to 250 by 1864. After the Civil War, the work of this and other, similar organizations, concentrated on establishing schools for former slaves; in 1868 there were 532 missionaries in the South.

In the Fall of 1865, Rev. E.P. Smith, after serving as Field Agent of the United States Christian Commission during the Civil War, became Secretary of the American Missionary Association of Cincinnati. In Nashville, he met Rev. E.M. Cravath, who grew up in a house that served as part of the underground railroad and had served as a chaplain in the Union Army. Cravath was commissioned by the Association to organize schools. Smith and Cravath saw Nashville as an ideal location for a university which would serve blacks. The city had been captured by federal troops early in the war, and remained a federal city throughout the war, escaping the destruction that cities such as Richmond and Atlanta suffered.

Two other men became involved in the establishment of a university for blacks in Nashville. Professor John Ogden, formerly the principal of a school in Minnesota and an officer in the Union Army, lived in Nashville where he was an agent of the Western Freedmen Aid Commission, which merged into the American Missionary Association. General Clinton B. Fisk was in charge of the Freedman's Bureau in the District of Kentucky and Tennessee.

The men searched for land for this institution but were faced with hostility from the city's white population; also, they had virtually no money. However, they managed to purchase some land for $16,000 by not telling the owner what it would be used for. The land contained a one-story frame building erected by the Union Army that had been used as a hospital barracks.

In January 1866, Fisk School opened; Tennessee Governor Brownlow gave a short address for the occasion. During that first year, daily attendance averaged over 1,000 students—many of then barely able to read or write. In 1867, the city of Nashville provided some public schools for "colored children," which allowed Fisk to obtain a university charter. However, the number applying for entrance exceeded the number it could accommodate.

The school suffered from a lack of funds from day one. As the years rolled by, the building fell into decay; meanwhile, money was hard to come by.

The treasurer of the school was George W. White, born in Cadiz, New York in 1838, who had fought in the Union Army at Gettysburg and Chancellorsville. White joined the Freedmen's Bureau in Nashville at the end of the war. He had a talent for teaching music and was especially known for his instruction in vocal music. In the spring of 1867 White's chorus gave a public concert that raised some money; in 1868 they gave another concert and in 1879 presented the cantata "Esther" before a large crowd. White took his choir to Memphis and Chattanooga to perform; they also performed before a convention of the National Teachers' Association of the United States, held in Nashville, even though some members of the organization had strenuously objected to Negroes performing before the organization.

White had the idea that a student group could travel in the North, performing for money, and this idea was discussed for several years. However, many at the school—and in the missionary organization—thought it was too risky. Also, with the treasury almost empty, the association was reluctant to spend money donated for missionary work on such a speculative venture. There was also the objection of students' parents, many of them uneducated people who had not traveled themselves, to let their children travel so far away.

Finally, in 1871 White decided he must take a chance on the idea. He took the last of the school's money and bought provisions for the school, adding his own money and borrowing some against his property. If the venture failed, White would lose virtually everything he had. When the group left Nashville, on October 6, 1871, they had barely enough money to get to Ohio.

Accompanying White on that trip was Miss Wills, principal of the American Missionary Association school at Athens, Alabama, who served as chaperone for the girls in the group. The singers consisted of eleven students: Ella Sheppard, Maggie L. Porter, Jennie Jackson, Minnie Tate, Eliza Walker, Phoebe J. Anderson, Thomas Rutling, Benjamin M. Holmes, Greene Evans, Isaac P. Dickerson and George Wells. Many were quite young; Ella Sheppard was 20, Minnie Tate 14, Jennie Jackson 19, and Eliza Walker 14.

Billed as "a band of negro minstrels" and "Colored Christian singers," the group's first appearance was at a Congregational church in Cincinnati. On the Sunday during their first concert, and the next day, the great Chicago fire was raging. The group took the money they received at this first paid concert—a little less than $50—and donated the entire amount to the Chicago relief fund. On Tuesday evening they performed at Mozart Hall and although Jennie Jackson did a marvelous rendition of "Old Folks at Home," the group's receipts barely covered the expenses of the concert. Furthermore, the main hotels refused to allow them to stay.

Their next stop was at Black's Opera House in Springfield, Ohio, where less than 20 people showed up; however, they sang before a synod of Presbyterian ministers and received $105. From there they went to Yellow Springs, then Xenia—they collected $84 from these two concerts—before singing at Wilberforce University. At Worthington they received $60, then at Oberlin they received over $130, which managed to get them to Cleveland. By this point they hoped that the proceeds of the concert they performed would pay for their hotel rooms and railway tickets to get them to the next appointment. In addition, they had to find money to purchase coats for the cold North.

At Case Hall in Cleveland, one man came forward and gave them $100; three others contributed a total of $40. However, they had to pay $75 to rent the hall and advertising the concert cost $25-50 while hotel bills were usually $20-25 a day.

At Columbus, Ohio, they gave two concerts that didn't make enough money to meet expenses. That night White spent a nearly sleepless night thinking about the group. During that night he made a decision that would have a far-reaching impact: he decided to name the group "The Jubilee Singers" after the year of Jubilee in the Old Testament, which had been a favorite figure of speech of the slaves.

Their fortunes did not improve immediately; at Zanesville the concert didn't meet expenses, but a friend paid their hotel bill; at

Mount Vernon and Mansfield they collected almost no money despite playing before large audiences. In Akron on Thanksgiving Day they received only $20 but feasted on a big dinner. Then it was on to Meadville, Pennsylvania, Jamestown, New York, then Elmira where they performed at the First Presbyterian Church where Rev. T.K. Beecher preached. Beecher's brother was Rev. Henry Ward Beecher, the most famous preacher in the United States, and Beecher sent his brother a letter praising the Jubilee Singers.

Rev. Henry Ward Beecher welcomed the Fisk singers at his Plymouth Church in Brooklyn and the New York Herald wrote an article titled, "Beecher's Negro Minstrels," which publicized their work. This was a turning point for the group; at the Tabernacle Church in Jersey City they received almost $740 and word came they were wanted in Boston.

Concerts were promoted and organized by ministers at various churches. On their way to Boston they performed in Connecticut at Bristol, Winsted, Birmingham, Waterbury, and New Haven and received a total of over $1,200. At Norwich, Bridgeport, and Newark, New Jersey they received over $3,900.

Although they could not obtain lodgings in most hotels, President Ulysses S. Grant received them at the White House, where they sang "Go Down, Moses." At the concerts in Washington the vice president and some members of Congress attended.

From Washington, the Jubilee Singers toured New England, receiving a $1,000 organ for Fisk in Boston as well as $1,235 in that city; they also received books donated to their library. They also had another source of income by this time. Their songs were written out by Professor Theodore F. Seward and published in a book, copies of which were sold at their concerts.

From Boston, the group went to Cambridge, Chelsea, Salem, and Newport, Massachusetts; Portland, Maine; Concord and Hanover, New Hampshire; St. Johnsbury, Vermont; Springfield, Massachusetts; Troy and Poughkeepsie, New York.

This concluded the first tour of the Fisk Jubilee Singers; during the three months they were away, they raised $20,000. For the trip back from New York to Nashville, White purchased first class railway tickets for the group. In Louisville, they went into an unoccupied sitting room where a railway employee gave them notice that "niggers were not allowed" in that room. White objected, pointed out their first class tickets, and asked to see an official with the railroad. An employee got a policeman and the group was ejected while a mob of over a thousand people yelled curses at them.

The Jubilee Singers began their second tour in June 1872 when they were invited to participate in the second World's Peace Jubilee in Boston. On the way they gave concerts in Illinois, Michigan and Ohio before performing before 20,000 in Boston, brought to their feet as the group sang "Glory, glory, hallelujah" in the chorus of "The Battle Hymn of the Republic." This was the greatest triumph of their career.

The group was increased to fourteen for this second tour; part of the reason was so the group could divide in two to perform at smaller venues. However, on New Year's Day, 1873, the troupe was reorganized with eleven members. They were: Ella Sheppard, Maggie L. Porter, Jennie Jackson, Mabel Lewis, Minnie Tate, Georgia Gordon, Julia Jackson, Thomas Rutling, Edmund Watkins, Benjamin M. Holmes, and Isaac P. Dickerson.

During the next three months they performed at the Academy of Music in Philadelphia, the Masonic Hall in Baltimore and in Princeton, New Jersey. Still, despite the large crowds, they suffered humiliations; the hall in Baltimore refused to seat any "colored" in the reserved sections and in Princeton the "colored" could only sit in an out-of-the-way corner of the church.

By 1873 the Jubilee Singers had raised enough money for the school to purchase 25 acres for the permanent location of Fisk University. The property was in North Nashville where Fort Gillem, part of the encircling line of fortifications around the city, had been located. Here, they would build Jubilee Hall, the first building on the campus.

During the winter campaign of 1873-1874 the singers performed in New York City, Brooklyn, Boston, Providence, and Boston, where they received an additional $20,000, bringing the amount they had raised to $40,000.

In 1874 the Jubilee Singers expanded their vision to include England. Carrying letters of introduction from five governors of New England states as well as Governor Brownlow of Tennessee, Rev. Henry Ward Beecher and a number of others, the group attempted to purchase tickets on a steamship to London. All the ship lines refused to carry them until the Cunard Line sold them tickets on the Batavia, which sailed from Boston.

In London, the Fisk Singers were greeted by the Earl of Shaftesbury, who was president of the Freedman's Missions Aid Society, the English auxiliary to the American Missionary Association. Lord Shaftesbury arranged for them to give a private concert on May 6, where they performed before members of the nobility, members of Parliament, and other leading citizens of the city. The major newspapers praised their performances, and overnight they were in demand for more performances than they could fit in.

The Duke and Duchess of Argyll invited them to perform at Argyll Lodge; there they sang "Steal Away to Jesus," chanted the "Lord's Prayer," then sang "Go Down, Moses" before Queen Victoria. At Prime Minister Gladstone's home at Carlton House Terrace, they chanted the "Lord's Prayer" as grace before lunch, then performed "John Brown" and "No More Auction-block for Me" after the meal. After a breakfast with the Gladstones on another date, the Prime Minister presented them with some books for their university library.

The Jubilee Singers spent three months in London, then went to Scotland, where they met Rev. Dwight Moody and Ira Sankey, who were holding revivals. The Fisk group performed with the evangelist during several meetings.

In his book, *The Story of the Jubilee Singers*; with their songs, published in 1881, author J.B.T. Marsh notes that, "From the first the Jubilee music was more or less of a puzzle to the critics; and even among those who sympathized with their mission, there was no little difference of opinion as to the artistic merit of their entertainments. Some could not understand the reason for enjoying so thoroughly, as almost every one did, these simple, unpretending songs."

Colin Brown, a professor at Andersonian University in Glasgow, wrote a series of articles about the Jubilee Singers songs, stating that, "The highest triumph of art is to be natural ... how strange it is that these unpretending singers should come over here to teach us what is the true refinement of music, make us feel its moral and religious power."

The singers were averaging about $1,000 a night for their performances; in January, they received $19,000. They continued their tour throughout Britain and by their closing concert at Exeter Hall had raised almost $60,000 towards the construction of Jubilee Hall.

In 1875 Fisk celebrated its first decade with the opening of Jubilee Hall. Many of its graduates who started illiterate were now teaching in schools. According to Marsh, Fisk students "Conquered the respect of those who began by hating it. It has opened to the vision of vast numbers of colored people new possibilities of Christian attainment and manly achievement. It had demonstrated the capacity of that despised race for a high culture. It had raised up the Jubilee Singers, who had done great things for their people in breaking down, by the magic of their song, the cruel prejudice against color that was everywhere in America, the greatest of all hindrances to their advancement."

That same year, 1875, Fisk got its first president, Rev. E. M. Cravath, and graduated its first college class, some of whom had been there ten years.

Also in 1875, the Jubilee Singers embarked on another tour, but their first without their leader and mentor, Mr. White, whose health was bad. Leading the group was Professor T.F. Seward, who had first written down the Jubilee songs and put them in a book. A series of concerts in the North did not produce good results; the group was reorganized into ten members and sailed for England on May 15, where they joined Moody and Sankey during their London revivals. The tour was undertaken to raise money to build Livingstone Missionary Hall, a companion building to Jubilee Hall.

After a tour of England, the group went to Holland, then Germany where, in October 1877, they performed before the Crown Prince and Crown Princess at their "New Palace" in Potsdam. There they performed "Steal Away," "I've Been Redeemed," "Who Are These in Bright Array" and "Nobody Knows the Trouble I See." Although the Jubilee singers performed in a number of German cities, financially, the tour of Germany was not a success.

Professor T.F. Seward, the leader on this tour, wrote an introduction to their songs, stating that:

> Their origin is unique. They are never 'composed' after
> the manner of ordinary music, but spring into life, ready-
> made, from the white heat of religious fervor during some

protracted meeting in church or camp. They come from no musical cultivation whatever, but are the simple, ecstatic utterances of wholly untutored minds. From so unpromising a source we could reasonably expect only such a mass of crudities as would be unendurable to the cultivated ear. On the contrary, however, the cultivated listener confesses to a new charm, and to a power never before felt, at least in its kind. What can we infer from this but that the child-like, receptive minds of these unfortunates were wrought upon with a true inspiration, and that this gift was bestowed upon them by an ever-watchful Father, to quicken the pulses of life, and to keep them from the state of hopeless apathy into which they were in danger of falling.

Chapter 11

THE GREAT REVIVAL

The 19th century saw America expand geographically and politically and its religion and politics reflected the country as the "land of the free and the home of the brave." Along with the political expansion came moralistic crusades, laissez-faire capitalism, the Industrial Revolution and the Civil War. The two great forces of Christian revivalism and democratic nationalism set the stage for another great revival after the Civil War, which would center on the urban areas.

The Baptists and Methodists had been most active on the frontier and the religious awakening of the settlers put the principle of voluntarism (churches being supported freely by their members) before liturgy, democracy before orthodoxy, and emotionalism before an intellectual, rational approach to religion. Denominational lines were broken and crossed as the church reached the masses. The camp meeting became a social institution which supported the politics of manifest destiny, while revivalism stressed the work of man in salvation as well as the sovereignty of God. There was a democratic character to the idea of a personal encounter with God as well as a linking of politics with religion through the belief that God was actively involved in American life.

America was a growing nation with a population that swelled from 31 million in 1860 to 106 million in 1920. There was an increase in farmers, from six to nine million, but the greatest growth came from the cities as factory workers increased from two million to eighteen million from 1860 to 1880. Even the definition of the city changed from "large village" to "metropolis." In 1850, only six cities contained more than 100,000 people; there were forty-one by 1900.

For religious leaders, the problem of growth was also compounded by the diversity within these cities—there were Catholics, Jews, atheists, and agnostics as well as Protestants.

In addition to the competition from other sects, Christianity also had to deal with science, particularly Darwin's theory of evolution that questioned the Divine origin of man, as well as biblical criticism and the religion of economics, personified in Andrew Carnegie's book, *The Gospel of Wealth*. Americans were worshipping money and their leaders were the self-made entrepreneurs.

The role of the evangelist during the rapidly changing times of the 19th century was to assure believers of the continuity of the ageless faith in a rapidly changing world. It was to convince believers that all good came from God, so the changes that advanced America were proof that God was smiling on the nation. The gap between modern science and old time religion should be seen as a bridge on which scriptural proofs were being revealed and the great truth was again being confirmed.

In London, William Booth, an itinerant minister, found his calling in 1865 and the 19th century witnessed the birth of the Salvation Army. The Army began in London, amongst the poor and outcast who had no notion of religion. While other movements sought to mobilize those asleep in church pews, Booth's movement brought religion to the streets, bringing church to the people instead of drawing people to church. Along the way, he revolutionized the use of instruments in religious music through the Salvation Army band.

Booth loved singing and would "sit up singing until 12 after a hard days work," according to biographer Richard Collier. The General, as he became known, stated that, "I am for the world's salvation; I will quarrel with no means that promises help." It was this intense devotion to the world's salvation that gave Booth the strength to overcome adversity and immense odds to carry the gospel to the streets. Opposed by the churched as well as the unchurched, scorned by the respectable and the derelict, Booth nevertheless made an impact on London—and later the world—through his single-minded devotion to the gospel and his fervor for preaching this message to all listeners.

The Salvation Army band sprang from the same haphazard devotion that spread the Army's cause. In Salisbury, England in 1879, a local builder named Charles William Fry offered Booth the services of himself and his three sons, Fred, Ernest, and Bertram. The Army had been troubled by hooligans roughing up their members and Fry and his sons stepped in as bodyguards, bringing along their instruments as an afterthought. Because Fry and his sons played brass instruments while the Army marched through the streets, the first Salvation Army band was born. It brought attention to the Army's cause and attracted a crowd, which enlisted Booth's support. The instruments accompanied Army members when they sang their songs—Booth banned the word "hymns" because it sounded "too churchy"—using concertinas, tambourines, brass horns, and anything else that made music. The players were mostly spare-time musicians, with the result that the music often sounded "as if a brass band's gone out of its mind."

Booth was a maverick in his approach to evangelism as well as in his use of music. He regularly insisted that well-known secular tunes be used with Christian lyrics, reasoning that if someone knew "Here's to Good Old Whiskey," they could learn "Storm the Forts of Darkness," or if they knew "The Old Folks at Home" they could learn "Joy, Freedom, Peace and Ceaseless Blessing" because the same tunes were utilized. Booth asked, "Why should the Devil have all the best tunes?" and regularly took the secular and made it sacred. Through songs like "There Are No Flies on Jesus," Booth brought Christianity to the street and made it a religion for the poor, the wretched, the socially undesirable and outcast. The Army's music reflected their tactics of spreading the gospel—loud, dramatic, and full of gusto.

Meanwhile, in America there arose two preachers in the 19th century who would dominate evangelism on this continent—Henry Ward Beecher and Dwight Moody.

Beecher was a moderate, mainstream Protestant who attempted to prod Christianity towards modernity. For him, the good in the world was produced by a loving God and Christian thought should be flexible enough to pull in new ideas. From his platform at the Plymouth Church in Brooklyn, Beecher attracted a national following. He injected a healthy dose of humanism into the gospel, urging his members to seek perspiration as well as inspiration, a good day's work to go along with Divine grace. Ward Beecher appealed to the middle class who aspired towards riches, arguing that poverty was a result of sin and that "if a man did not smoke or drink, he could feed his family on a dollar a day." This concept was applauded by Beecher's followers.

The concept of the religious leader as a spiritual salesman was refined by Dwight Moody, a former shoe salesman who used the pulpit to sell Christianity to the masses. Moody was born February 5, 1837, in Northfield, Massachusetts, son of a Unitarian father who died when the boy was four. Moody was converted to Christianity in 1855 at the age of 17 by his Sunday School teacher, Edward Kimble. Ironically, Moody's request to join the Mount Vernon Congregation was turned down for a year because of his ignorance of the Christian faith.

In 1865, Moody moved from Boston to Chicago and became a successful businessman, selling shoes, as well as an active member of the Plymouth Congregational church. Every Sunday Moody reportedly filled four pews he rented with those he had recruited and was so successful at recruiting members for Sunday School that at the age of twenty-three he founded his own Sunday School where he served as administrator and recruiter. Moody was a forceful, though not grammatically elegant speaker, and was cautioned against speaking by members of his church. However, he began preaching one night after the scheduled speaker did not show up. Soon, he devoted himself full time to Christian work and was speaking at Sunday School conventions, to troops, establishing a church of his own, and serving as president of the Chicago YMCA.

Moody could not sing but knew the value of songs and singing in his evangelistic work. He enlisted the support of Ira Sankey in 1871 and together the two travelled to England as well as urban areas in the eastern United States, "reducing the population of hell by a million souls." Moody was clearly the guiding light and visionary for the evangelistic endeavors, but he needed Sankey's songs to attract crowds and set the stage for his message. He would let Sankey begin with songs, then he would preach before having Sankey conclude with a song as the sinners came forth. Moody viewed the Christian conversion as a successful sale—the set up, the hard pitch, and the closing or wrapping up where the convert must make his decision and act on it.

By the end of their careers, the names Moody and Sankey were linked and shared equal billing. A testament to the power of song is that the gospel singer Sankey was as important as the evangelist preacher Moody, their roles supplementing each other and each indispensable to their cause.

The Great Revival brought the evangelistic fervor of conversion to the urban areas and in so doing united Christianity with the Industrial Revolution. Americans began to equate upward mobility with Christian ethics, the blessings of materialism with God's blessings, and the emergence of America as a nation that would dominate the world with the belief that God had chosen the nation for such a role and was guiding her wealth and creating her power. This "Great Revival" closed the 19th century by giving believers an assurance of their salvation and America an assurance of her destiny. The Protestant ethic of hard work, self-discipline and material blessings became an integral part of Christianity as the country moved towards the 20th century as one nation under God, represented by a number of religious denominations. It was a religious fervor that saw them united in their nationalism but divided in their theology, finding in God a source of spiritual as well as material blessings and comforts.

Ira Sankey, as song leader for Dwight Moody's revivals, made the gospel hymn a popular song, presenting the format of verse-chorus-verse-chorus in a way that gave the songs emotional appeal and memorability. In making the hymn a popular song, Sankey evoked the charm of popular music and used the song as an instrument for religion to convict and convert people.

There were revivals in settled communities as well as in churches on the frontier, although the Great Revival came later in the 19th century than the "old time religion" that caught fire in the west. From these urban revivals, the gospel hymn developed to meet the needs of revivals and prayer meetings. The camp meeting hymn was often the work of anonymous singers or the folk tradition but the gospel hymn was created by individual writers and musicians. The camp meeting hymn was characteristic of the frontier and rural areas; the gospel hymn of the great cities.

The gospel hymn is uniquely American. It came from the camp meeting song of the early decades of the 19th century and is evangelical in spirit but focuses on the winning of souls through conversion. Its primary use was in revivals but it was gradually taken over by Sunday schools, Christian associations, and by churches made up of less educated members who preferred the appeals of emotion rather than literary form and quality.

The gospel hymn had certain characteristics that made it appealing to crowds. The mood might be optimistic or pleading, but the music was tuneful and melodic and easy to grasp and learn. A march-like movement was typical and the device of letting the lower parts echo rhythmically a line announced by the sopranos in a fuguing form became a mannerism.

Sankey preferred a small reed organ to accompany his singing. He did not like a professional quartet, or putting the singers behind a screen in back of a minister, preferring a choir of the best singers placed in front of the congregation, near the minister. Part of this desire stemmed from his own view that the singing was as important as the preaching and that he was as important as the evangelist, a view supported by the popularity of the hymns he sang.

Sankey was born in Edinburg, Pennsylvania on August 28, 1840 and throughout his childhood sang hymns with his family. He was a regular church attendee, singing in the choir, and was "converted" at the age of sixteen during a revival at The King's Chapel, a church about three miles from the Sankey home. Sankey's family moved to Newcastle in 1857 where his father was president of a bank. There Sankey finished high school and began working at the bank as well as singing and playing organ at the Methodist Episcopal Church, where he was the leader of the choir.

Sankey joined the Union Army in 1859 and, after his discharge, joined his father again, who was now a collector for the Internal Revenue Service. He married Fanny Edwards in September 1863 and became known for his singing at Sunday school conventions and political gatherings. In 1867, a Young Men's Christian Association was formed in Newcastle and Sankey became involved, first as secretary and later as president of that organization. In 1870, he was appointed a delegate to the YMCA's annual convention, held in Indianapolis that year, where he met Dwight Moody, whom he had heard about because of Moody's work in Chicago.

Moody and Sankey met after a morning prayer meeting where Sankey had led the singing of "There is a Fountain" after Moody had spoken. According to Sankey in his autobiography, *My Life and the Story of the Gospel Hymns*, Moody's first words to him, after an introduction, were, "Where are you from? Are you married? What is your business?" Sankey replied he lived in Pennsylvania, had a wife and two children, and was employed by the government, whereupon Moody replied, "You will have to give that up." Sankey was reluctant to give up his job but Moody pressed him, saying, "You must; I have been looking for you for the last eight years."

Sankey stated that Moody could not sing himself and "therefore had to depend upon all kinds of people to lead his service of song, and that sometimes when he had talked to a crowd of people, and was about to 'pull the net,' someone would strike up a long meter hymn to a short meter tune, and thereby upset the whole meeting."

The day after their meeting, Moody sent a note to Sankey, asking him to meet on a certain street corner. He complied and when he arrived, Moody produced a box and asked Sankey to climb up and sing a hymn. Never one to require much prompting to display his glorious voice in song, Sankey did so and a crowd gathered. After the song, Moody got on the box and delivered a short sermon, then invited everyone present to attend a meeting before asking Sankey to close with another hymn and sing while the crowd was led to the Opera House in Indianapolis where the YMCA was holding its convention.

Moody continued to press Sankey to join him but the singer returned to his home in Pennsylvania. Six months later Moody sent an invitation for Sankey to join him in Chicago and the two met at Moody's home where Sankey once again sang. During the week they were together, the two went around to visit the sick and held meetings with Sankey singing and Moody preaching. The first song Sankey sang at the first house they visited was "Scatter Seeds of Kindness"; this would also be the last song Sankey sang at a public meeting with Moody 28 years later in Brooklyn in September 1899. The song, written by Mrs. Albert Smith with music by S.J. Vail, was popular and was written in the format of verse-chorus-verse-chorus that Sankey would use throughout his singing. It expressed a philosophy of Christianity that made the faith a code of conduct, a religion of gentlemen and ladies. It contained the emotional sentimentality that many of Sankey's hymns did and compared the best of Christianity to the best of nature.

Scatter Seeds of Kindness

Let us gather up the sunbeams,
Lying all around our path;
Let us keep the wheat and roses,
Casting out the thorns and chaff,
Let us find our sweetest comfort
In the blessings of today,
With a patient hand removing
All the briars from the way.

Chorus:
Then scatter seeds of kindness,
Then scatter seeds of kindness,
Then scatter seeds of kindness,
For our reaping by and by.

Strange we never prize the music
Till the sweet-voiced bird is flown!
Strange that we should slight the violets
Till the lovely flowers are gone!
Strange that summer skies and sunshine
Never seem one half so fair,
As when winter's snowy pinions
Shake the white down in the air.

Chorus

If we knew the baby fingers,
Pressed against the window pane,
Would be cold and stiff tomorrow
Never trouble us again
Would the bright eyes of our darling
Catch the frown upon our brow?
Would the prints of rosy fingers
Vex us then as they do now?

Chorus

Ah! those little ice cold fingers,
How they point our mem'ries back
To the hasty words and actions
Strewn along our backward track!
How those little hands remind us,
As in snowy grace they lie,
Not to scatter thorns but roses
For our reaping by and by.

Chorus

Again Moody pressed Sankey to join him but again the singer declined, returning to the security of his job and life in Pennsylvania. However, upon discussing the offer with his minister and some friends, Sankey was urged to join the evangelist, and he moved to Chicago in 1871. Based at Moody's Illinois Street Church, the two made the rounds in Chicago, singing and preaching at daily noon prayer meetings as well as at regular services.

During the great Chicago fire, Moody's church and home burned. In his autobiography, Sankey goes into great detail about how he labored all through the night to save his material belongings, finally procuring a boat so he could sit safely in Lake Michigan with his possessions. Moody was involved in waking up the neighbors and helping them flee, saying later, "All I saved was my Bible, my family and my reputation." After the fire, Sankey left Chicago for Pennsylvania and did not see Moody for two months. The evangelist finally called him back though and began to rebuild the church, using his skill at raising money to provide the funds.

Dwight Moody and Ira Sankey visited England for the first time together in June 1873 and, beginning with some small gatherings in York, soon achieved fame that saw them preaching and singing before 20,000 in London. Sankey had begun compiling a musical "scrapbook" with words and music to use during his singing. People often wanted to borrow it, sometimes not returning it in time for Sankey to lead the next service, so he had some words of hymns printed on small cards. Soon he compiled a book containing some of the hymns and began selling them for sixpence each; there was a quick demand and he soon sold all he had printed. This was the start of his songbook, which popularized numerous songs including "Rock of Ages," "Onward, Christian Soldiers," "Whiter Than Snow," "It is Well With My Soul," "Jesus Loves Me," "Blessed Assurance" and others and caused the hymns he sang to be popularized in the print tradition as well as the oral tradition. It was Sankey's songbooks which perpetuated his songs—and furnished a healthy income—and the popularity of these songs is directly attributed to the fact he not only performed them during revivals but made them available in print as well.

Sankey was a large man, pompous and impressed with his own singing talent. He had a full, rich voice and was quite proud of the recognition he received for it. He seemed to be vain about his singing as well as full of the assurance of salvation and his own election as one of God's chosen. He was born in the privileged upper middle class and remained there all his life. The Christianity he sang about was a social gospel but a social gospel for the middle and upper classes, drawn from the urban areas. For Moody and Sankey, Christianity was almost like a club, with members entitled to the privilege of Heaven as well as earthly benefits of peace and prosperity. Everyone who was not a member was an infidel, hopelessly lost and living in error.

One of Sankey's most popular songs was "The Ninety and Nine" and reflected the concept of conversion as joining the elect. Sankey sang it often and his rendition of Elizabeth C. Clephane's words is reported to have convinced many who had strayed from the fold of righteousness.

The Ninety and Nine

There were ninety and nine that safely lay
In the shelter of the fold,
But one was out on the hills away,
Far off from the gates of gold—
Away on the mountains wild and bare,
Away from the tender Shepherd's care,
Away from the tender Shepherd's care.

"Lord, Thou hast here Thy ninety and nine;
Are they not enough for Thee?"
But the Shepherd made answer:

"This of mine has wandered away from me,
And, although the road be rough and steep,
I go to the desert to find my sheep,
I go to the desert to find my sheep."

But none of the ransomed ever knew
How deep were the waters cross'd
Nor how dark was the night that the Lord pass'd thru'
Ere He found His sheep that was lost;
Out in the desert He heard its cry—
Sick and helpless and ready to die,
Sick and helpless and ready to die.

"Lord, whence are those blood-drops all the way
That mark out the mountain's track?"
"They were shed for one who had gone astray
Ere the Shepherd could bring him back,"
"Lord, whence are Thy hands so rent and torn?"
"They are pierced to-night by many a thorn."
"They are pierced to-night by many a thorn."

But all thro' the mountains, thunder-riven,
And up from the rocky steep,
There arose a glad cry to the gate of heaven,
"Rejoice! I have found my sheep!"
And the Angels echoed around the throne,
"Rejoice! for the Lord brings back His own!"
"Rejoice! for the Lord brings back His own!"

Since Moody and Sankey conducted "revivals" where the stated purpose was to convert souls, it is obvious there would be many songs intended to convict and convince the wayward sinner to return to the fold of Christianity. The story of the prodigal son is an ideal topic for such a sermon and Moody delivered it a number of times while Sankey sang this song, based on the prodigal son story, at meetings.

There are three characters in the story—the father and two sons. One son left and the other remained faithful to the father; when the lost son returned the father was overjoyed while the son who remained was jealous of the attention received by the "other" son who was, in a sense, rewarded for squandering his father's wealth. It can be read as a parable where the father is God, the faithful son the church which has remained with God and the errant son the lost sinner who abandons Christianity. Moody and Sankey put themselves in the role of the father—God—inviting the wayward son to return, ignoring the angry faithful son of the story. Since Sankey adapted the songs he sang for himself, expressing his point of view, it seems obvious he viewed himself and Moody as father figures in Christianity and the sinners as lost children. The jealous son, in the form of the church, caused the evangelist and singer some problems throughout their career though, disliking some of their tactics and accusing them of "sheep stealing" on occasion.

The Prodigal Child

Come home! come home!
You are weary at heart,
For the way has been dark,
And so lonely and wild;
O prodigal child!
Come home! oh, come home!
Come home! Come, oh, come home!

Come home! come home!
For we watch and we wait,
And we stand at the gate,
While the shadows are piled;
O prodigal child!
Come home! oh, come home!
Come home! Come, oh, come home!

Come home! come home!
From the sorrow and blame,
From the sin and the shame,
And the tempter that smiled,

O prodigal child!
Come home, oh, come home!

Come home! come home!
There is bread and to spare,
And a warm welcome there,
Then, to friends reconciled,
O prodigal child!
Come home, oh, come home!

Although Moody and Sankey often seem Calvinistic in their rigid approach to religion and their belief in the self-imposed discipline of the believer, the Lutheran concept of justification by faith was also deeply imbedded in them. Yet, somehow, they managed to be among Calvin's chosen elect, divinely ordained from the beginning of time, and saved by the merciful grace of God, too. It almost seems as if they adapted Calvinism's concept of preordination to include a moment of self-revelation where grace allowed them to see their salvation and become aware of their predestined fate.

The song "Saved by Grace" was written by Fanny J. Crosby with music by George C. Stebbins. Crosby and P.P. Bliss were particular favorites of Sankey, and he sang and printed a number of their songs in his songbooks, setting a number of Crosby's lyrics to music as well.

Saved By Grace

Some day the silver cord will break,
And I no more as now shall sing,
But, O, the joy when I shall wake
Within the palace of the King!

Chorus:
And I shall see Him face to face,
And tell the story—Saved by grace;
And I shall see Him face to face,
And tell the story—Saved by grace.

Some day my earthly house will fall,
I cannot tell how soon 'twill be,
But this I know—my All in All
Has now a place in heav'n for me.

   Chorus

Some day, when fades the golden sun,
Beneath the rosy-tinted west,
My blessed Lord shall say, "Well done!"
And I shall enter into rest.

   Chorus

Some day, till then I'll watch and wait,
My lamp all trimm'd and burning bright,
That when my Saviour ope's the gate
My soul to Him may take its flight.

Sankey provided the music for many poems and hymns he found from various sources that included periodicals as well as his hearing the song in another version or his receiving poems from people. He did, however, write several songs, including "Out of the Shadow-Land."

Out of the Shadow-Land

Out of the shadow-land, into the sunshine,
Cloudless, eternal, that fades not away;
Softly and tenderly Jesus will call us;
Home, where the ransom'd are gath'ring to-day.

Chorus:
Silently, peacefully, angels will bear us
Into the beautiful mansions above;
There shall we rest from earth's toiling forever,
Safe in the arms of God's infinite love.

Out of the shadow-land, weary and changeful,
Out of the valley of sorrow and night,
Into the rest of the life everlasting,
Into the summer of endless delight.

Chorus

Out of the shadow-land, over life's ocean,
Into the rapture and joy of the Lord,
Safe in the Father's house, welcomed by angels,
Ours the bright crown and eternal reward.

This song—words and music—was written by Sankey alone. It was the last song he wrote and he did so for the occasion of Dwight Moody's funeral in 1899. The self-assurance of salvation by Christians is obviously present and Sankey has no doubt of his or Moody's reward, with phrases like "Safe in the arms of God's infinite love" and "Into the summer of endless delight" giving proof that he knew the fate of the believer. There is also the philosophy of the monarchy of believers—that God is a King and those who enter heaven are welcomed as royal subjects which is present in lines like "Ours the bright crown and eternal reward" and "Into the beautiful mansions above." Like many of Sankey's hymns, there is an abundance of emotional sentimentality in the lyrics and a romantic view of religion that contrasts with the harsh darkness of life on earth. Perhaps it was Sankey's intense devotion to the sentimental view of salvation and heaven that made it so appealing and struck an emotional chord in listeners' hearts.

Chapter 12

THE PENTECOSTAL AND HOLINESS MOVEMENTS

A major religious movement began during the turn of the century which would play an active role in guiding American Christianity throughout the 20th century. Pentecostalism would have a major effect on religion in the United States as well as on music—particularly in the South—because a number of musicians came from this movement. This period also marked the beginnings of "Fundamentalism." Although it may be argued that most of the major Christian revivals in this country since the Great Awakening have been fundamental in nature, it was not until the 20th century that this became a doctrine and a widely used term.

The roots of Pentecostalism have been traced to two sources in the United States. Charles Fox Parnham began Bethel Bible School in Topeka, Kansas in October 1900. In late December 1900, before he made a trip to Kansas City, Parnham instructed his students to study the Bible individually and learn about the baptism of the Holy Spirit. When he returned, the students told Parnham that in Apostolic times, whenever believers were baptized with the Holy Spirit there was speaking in tongues.

The source for this is Acts, Chapter Two, and after this meeting members of the college began to pray and seek for this baptism and gift of tongues. On New Year's Eve, as about forty students and seventy others outside the student body gathered for the traditional "Watch Night" service, Miss Agnes Ozman requested that members lay hands on her so she might receive the Holy Spirit. Parnham demurred but, after repeated urgings, consented to do this.

After only a few moments of prayer, Miss Ozman began to speak in Chinese and could not speak English for the next three days. The other believers accepted speaking in tongues, or glossolaia, as the outward sign that someone had received the gift of the Holy Spirit. The rest of the student body began to pray earnestly and soon most were speaking in tongues. This led to a major evangelistic effort by Parnham and his students, which resulted in Pentecostalism spreading through the midwest, south, and southwest.

Parnham opened another school in Houston, Texas in 1905. Like the one in Topeka, there was no tuition charged (just "faith" offerings), the only textbook was the Bible and the only lecturer was Parnham. One of his students there was William J. Seymour, an African-American preacher. Seymour was invited to preach at the Nazarene mission in Los Angeles after another student, Neely Terry, also an African-American, had received the Holy Spirit baptism in Houston and began speaking in tongues. She had recommended Seymour to her home church after returning from Houston.

Seymour's first sermon offended a church member and he found the doors barred to him after the first service. Invited to the home of Richard and Ruth Asberry (relatives of Neeley Terry), he conducted services there. On April 9, 1906, seven of the worshippers received this baptism of the Holy Spirit and began speaking in tongues, shouting and praising God for three days and nights, according to records. Soon, the small congregation moved into an old frame building, which once served as a Methodist Church, on Azusa Street and here The Apostolic Faith Gospel Mission, under the leadership of the one-eyed preacher, William J. Seymour, heralded in a revival whose effects would be felt all over the world.

The Azusa street meetings were integrated so the Black Holiness movement and the white Pentecostal movement came from the same seeds; however, within a short while, the congregations segregated.

The Holiness movement's roots actually go back to the 1890s and the "Latter Rain Movement," which sought to "irrigate the dry bones" in churches. Pentecostal congregations, characterized by this intense emotionalism in the worship service, developed all over the country, especially among the poor and depressed. The term "holy rollers" came from this movement because people were liable to scream, shout, dance, jump, or roll on the floor for Jesus. These churches placed a heavy emphasis on "saved, sanctified, and filled with the Holy Spirit," which means a possession by the spirit so the person is not chained to this world but free to act or say whatever God wants done or said, using the individual's voice and body. Speaking in tongues, or "glossolalia" (a fluent gibberish with a number of Hebrew-like sounds), is often practiced. Although the Pentecostal and Holiness movments began as an integrated movement, within a few years they became segregated, with whites becoming "Pentecostal" while African-Americans used the term "Holiness" for their churches.

Both the Pentecostal and Holiness churches feature a great amount of singing and dancing in their services, with half of the service usually comprised of music. These churches were the first to use musical instruments in the service, instruments that churches had long considered "of the Devil." Conservatism has long been a staple of American Christianity, and the mainstream black churches, while usually more emotional than white churches, generally rejected the intense emotional involvement and extreme physical activities the holiness churches introduced as a regular part of their service.

There are foot-stomping and hand-clapping up-tempo songs in Pentecostal and Holiness churches, but the Holiness songs tend to have more complex rhythms. The archetypal Holiness song is a slow chant, often begun as church starts or later, during a prolonged series of shouts and outbursts. The ministers, with their strong personal charisma and elaborate showmanship, are required to lead the church to a spiritual high during the service that will enable the congregation to face six hard, troublesome weekdays.

For those attending, religion is a way of life and almost every night is filled with some church-related activity. The congregants come well-prepared for the Sunday service, ready and willing to begin the shouting and praise when they enter the door. There is a strong current of anti-intellectualism and, with all the physical and emotional activity at a fever pitch, the air is often heavy with repressed sexuality. The faith is composed of mystery, divinely inspired intuition and visions that cannot be explained in this world. Holiness church is the antithesis of rationalism.

By definition and nature the holiness churches are usually small and generally "store-front" churches, without elaborate trappings or extensive networks of denominations. Each church, like each individual, is intensely individualistic in its faith and expression of that faith.

The significance of the Holiness church in black gospel as well as pop music is that its individualism has led to many innovations. It has served as a leader and catalyst in bringing new forms of music into the black church, including the addition of musical instruments, once considered "of the Devil" because they made the music sound "worldly" or like contemporary secular music.

Too, the Holiness church has encouraged and inspired African-Americans to express their own culture, rather than be black versions of white churches. This has meant that the evolution to a mainstream church has been much different from that of their white counterparts. With churches so segregated, this has served to divide Christianity and gospel music into two distinctive camps—black and white. While each may borrow songs and musical influences from the other, and the performers watch the opposite race to incorporate ideas into their own performances, the congregations remain separate, often unaware of the music of their racial counterparts.

American fundamentalism began as an ideology among urban intellectuals and sought to keep modernism at bay through conservative and traditional values during a time when America was undergoing radical social changes. The term came from a series of booklets issued from 1910-1915 which defined the proper Christian doctrines and dogma as belief in the deity of Christ, the Virgin birth, bodily Resurrection of Christ, imminent Second Coming, substitutionary atonement, and the verbal inspiration and inerrancy of the entire Bible. These doctrines would not only come to define and dominate American Christianity, they would also be the central themes of gospel songs throughout the century.

Fundamentalism is not unique to any one denomination but cuts across all denominational borders and represents an effort to establish doctrines and propositions which are universal and unchanging within the Christian faith. Fundamentalists generally see any deviation from essential doctrines as a compromise of the truth, a weakness of the faith, and a betrayal of the gospel. They often have difficulty accepting someone as a Christian if this person does not affirm the truth of a wide variety of necessary articles of faith or accept a common dogma of biblical authority. These dogma include an insistence on the Genesis account of creation, the acceptance of Adam and Eve as parents of the race of man, Christ's virgin birth, sacrificial atonement, bodily resurrection, the reality of his miracles, and a literal Second Coming. Fundamentalists are often rigidly secure in their faith, speaking unwaveringly on matters of faith and morals with a tendency to distinguish between those whom are "true" Christians from those who they believe do not measure up because of ungenuine faith.

Chapter 13

BILLY SUNDAY AND HOMER RODEHEAVER

One of the most famous people in America during the early 1900s was Billy Sunday. Born on November 19, 1862 in Ames, Iowa, William Ashley Sunday was the son of German immigrants whose name had originally been Sonntag. His father, a private in the Union Army at the time of his son's birth, died about a month after the birth and never saw his son. At home were three older brothers. About six years afterward, his mother married someone named Heizer, who fathered two more children and then disappeared in 1874. Young Willie lived with his grandfather and at the Soldiers' Orphan Home in what is now Davenport, Iowa.

Willie left the orphanage when he was fourteen and moved back in with his grandfather. After a hot-tempered dispute, he left for Nevada, Iowa, where he landed a job as a hotel errand boy and never returned home again. Fired from his first job, Sunday landed a job as stableboy for Colonel John Scott, who had been lieutenant-governor of Iowa, and the Scotts helped send him to high school, where he attracted attention as a fleet track star. He came to the attention of the Chicago Whitestockings baseball team in 1883 after the Marshalltown team he played on won the state championship. In the major leagues for eight years—1883 to 1891—Sunday was known as a daring base stealer (he reportedly held the record for most stolen bases until Ty Cobb broke it in 1915) and a poor hitter, carrying a .259 lifetime average.

Billy Sunday's conversion occurred in 1886 when he went to the Pacific Garden Mission in Chicago after first hearing a group from that organization singing hymns outside the saloon where he and his teammates had been drinking. Married in 1888, Sunday continued to play baseball, moving to Pittsburgh and then Philadelphia but giving up drinking, swearing, going to theaters, and playing baseball on Sundays. In the towns where he played, he often spoke to groups of young men at the YMCA, telling of his conversion and lecturing on "Earnestness in Christian Life."

Sunday began working full-time for the YMCA in the winter of 1890-1891 when he was made assistant secretary of the religious department. In 1893, he took a job with a well-known evangelist, J. Wilbur Chapman, and assisted with setting up revivals in the Midwest through the last part of the 19th century. Sunday was the "advance man" for Chapman—who was considered a leading evangelist of his day—and worked for Chapman from 1893 to 1895. In December 1895, Sunday received a telegram from Chapman, who said that he was quitting revivalism in order to pastor a church in Philadelphia leaving Sunday with a wife, two children, and no job. This was remedied when an offer came from the town of Garner, Iowa, for Sunday to conduct a revival campaign.

Chapman had taken Sunday under his wing and attempted to train him as an evangelist, but the young man was a poor speaker and suffered from stage fright whenever he had to speak before a large crowd. He could not sing either, and did not have a singer to travel with him (Chapman worked with P.P. Bilhorn). Still, the revival was a small success and Sunday was asked to speak in other small towns in Iowa. Along the way, he hired Joseph E. Van Winkle to lead the singing.

Sunday quickly became a successful evangelist and a number of people were converted during his revivals. By 1900, Sunday was successful enough to hold revivals in large tents and hire a gospel singer—Fred Fischer—full-time. Fischer sang familiar hymns like "When The Roll Is Called Up Yonder," "In the Sweet By and By," and "We'll Gather by the River" with Sunday for ten years before he left.

Sunday's revivals were criticized because of their entertainment aspect. Like Dwight Moody, Sunday advertised his revivals in the entertainment section of the newspaper and, also like Moody, he hired a handsome singer. He also sometimes employed a female singer, Miss Mamie Lorimer. But Moody was a man of proven devotion and his singer, Ira Sankey, always prefaced his songs with a prayer—which Fischer did not do—and accompanied himself on the reed organ. Fischer used a piano accompanist and encouraged local cornet and trombone players to join him on stage during the hymns. Encouraging audience members to compete with one another in singing (the men vs. the women) and turning the music portion of the revival into a community songfest were techniques also used by Charles Alexander, the choirster for Reuben A. Torrey (and later Chapman), who was considered the leading gospel singer of the day. But Alexander performed mostly in cities while Sunday held most of his revivals in rural areas.

Billy Sunday continued to attract larger and larger crowds. Musically, his revivals took a major turn when he hired Homer Alvin Rodeheaver to replace Fred Fischer in 1910. It was Rodeheaver who revolutionized the musical portion of the revivals and began, in essence, the gospel music industry of the 20th century with his mixture of ministry and entertainment and his creation of an independent record company as well as publishing interests.

Rodeheaver was born in Cinco Hollow, Ohio in 1880 and grew up in Jellico, Tennessee. He learned to play the cornet as a boy and, when he went to Ohio Wesleyan in 1896, switched over to the trombone while playing in the college band, serving as a cheerleader and taking a number of music courses. His education was interrupted by the Spanish-American War, so Rodeheaver never obtained a degree, although he stayed at Ohio Wesleyan until 1904. He left school to work for evangelist William E. Beiderwolf, where he served for the next five years as choirster.

Rodeheaver was the perfect man for the job with Sunday. He was genial and created an atmosphere of enthusiasm and friendliness, which gave the revivals a tremendous popular appeal and made them entertaining. He had a rich baritone voice and incredible stage presence with his dark, wavy hair, moderately handsome face, and what has been described as an "ingratiating" personality. Always smiling, he was affable and mixed well socially with a wide range of people, perfecting the chorister role that Charles Alexander had first established. But Rodeheaver had more than just flair and style—he soon proved to have skill as a singer, a trombonist, a talent for evangelistic speaking, and the ability to coordinate and direct both children's and adult choirs. Musically, he was a bit more daring than his predecessor as he sought out new gospel songs instead of relying solely on old hymns, and experimented extensively with group singing.

A premier showman, Rodeheaver had the ability to win over a large crowd with a funny story, a magic trick, producing various "noises" from his trombone, and pulling a practical joke on another team member on the stage. He encouraged his choirs to be enthusiastic and advised them to "go at it like selling goods." A bachelor, Rodeheaver was the first chorister to have an overt appeal as a "lady's man" or sex symbol. That, combined with a lively sense of humor, his musical ability, a thick southern accent, and his ability to catch the feeling of a crowd made him an invaluable asset to Sunday. It is not fair to say that Billy Sunday would not have succeeded without Homer Rodeheaver, but it must be acknowledged that the chorister was a major drawing card and source of appeal for Sunday's revivals. His polish and grace stood in a marked contrast to Sunday's physical acrobatics and hoarse shouting, serving to lend a tone of dignity to the meetings. Although a number of newspaper reporters privately felt him to be a little too smooth, suave, and unctous to be sincere, the public crowds loved him and affectionately called him "Rody."

The songs Rodeheaver used were not very different from those of Ira Sankey in terms of doctinal content, but differed greatly in terms of tone, tempo, and style. Rody tended to favor the lively, optimistic songs rather than the sentimental songs that Sankey preferred. For example, one of Sankey's favorite numbers was "The Ninety and Nine," while joyous numbers like "Brighten the Corner" tended to dominate Sunday's revivals. There were a few songs popular in both eras—"Ring the Bells of Heaven," "Bringing in the Sheaves," and "Pull From the Shore" are examples, but songs such as "Safe From the Law," "Christ Is My Redeemer," and "There is a Fountain Filled with Blood" were less popular with Sunday than in Moody's time. Dwight Moody had tended to favor songs of humility such as "Oh, to Be Nothing," while Sunday preferred the self-confidence of "Onward Christian Soldiers," "I Walk with the King, Hallelujah!," "The Battle Hymn of the Republic," and "The Fight is On." The atmosphere in the revivals of these two great evangelists was markedly different as well: for Moody, salvation was a lonely wailing while Sunday struck up a militant pose that encompassed the brashness of a righteous soldier. In fact, the songbook Homer Rodeheaver compiled and published contained an entire section entitled "Warfare" that featured a number of militaristic songs, equating the Christian walk with an open warfare against sin, the secular world, and the ways of the Devil.

Rodeheaver went into the publishing business in 1910. Inspired by the example of Ira Sankey, it was perfectly natural for a chorister to compile songs, old and new, and sell them at revivals. Rodeheaver wrote a number of hymns and employed the services of such quality songwriters as B.D. Ackley and Charles Gabriel. In the thirty-minute musical program before the sermon, designed to warm up the crowd and get them in the proper mood for Sunday, Rodeheaver would generally begin with some old hymns which the crowd already knew and gradually introduce newer compositions. As a result, these newer gospel songs became popular and demand for the songbooks was created and sustained. One of those songs, "Brighten the Corner," written by Gabriel, with words by Ina Duley Ogdon, was initially criticized because of its entertainment appeal. Rodeheaver answered the critics by stating that, "(This song) was never intended for a Sunday morning service, nor for a devotional meeting—its purpose was to bridge that gap between the popular song of the day and the great hymns and gospel songs, and to give to men a simple, easy, lilting melody which they could learn the first time they heard it, and which they could whistle and sing wherever they might be."

Brighten the Corner

Do not wait until some deed of greatness
  you may do,
Do not wait to shed your light afar,
To many duties ever near you now be true,
Brighten the corner where you are.

Brighten the corner where you are
Brighten the corner where you are
Someone far from harbor
You may guide across the bar,
Brighten the corner where you are.
Just above are clouded skies

That you may help to clear,
Let not narrow self your way debar
Tho' into one heart alone
May fall your song of cheer,
Brighten the corner where you are.

There was an obvious secular appeal to this song as well as others, such as "If Your Heart Keeps Right," and Rodeheaver knew he was appealing to the audience's need for entertainment with these tunes. Too, he was firmly and confidently establishing an area for gospel songs outside the church, independent of a religious service, and congruent with the American spirit of optimism, democracy, and success through hard work.

If Your Heart Keeps Right

If the dark shadows gather as you go along,
Do not grieve for their coming, sing a cheery song,
There is joy for the taking, it will soon be light—
Ev'ry cloud wears a rainbow, if your heart keeps right.

If your heart keeps right,
If your heart keeps right,
There's a song of gladness in the darkest night;
If your heart keeps right,
If your heart keeps right,
Ev'ry cloud will wear a rainbow,
If your heart keeps right.

Is your life just a tangle full of toil and care;
Smile a bit as you journey, others' burdens share;
You'll forget all your troubles making lives bright,
Skies will be blue and sunny if your heart keeps right.

A major reason for the increasing popular appeal of gospel songs was phonograph records, and Homer Rodeheaver probably began the first gospel label, although there is other evidence that suggests James Vaughan in Lawrenceburg, Tennessee may have been responsible for the first gospel recordings. At any rate, the time was ripe for gospel music to be marketed with the new technology and Rodeheaver's company, Rainbow Records, was instrumental in presenting many of the new gospel songs, actively competing with the secular labels for the consumer's dollar. When Rodeheaver began with Sunday, the major source of revenue for music came from the copyrights in the songbooks; however, shortly after 1916, when he began his record company, the sales of records accounted for more income than sheet music sales. It was a sign of the times and the times to come that the new technology would dominate the music industry and that records would replace songbooks and sheet music as the financial backbone of this industry. It was also a harbinger for the emergence of gospel music on independent labels later in the century, which assured the development of the music towards a Christian consumer rather than any attempt to appeal commercially to the culture-at-large. Rainbow Records was only the first of a number of small labels which recorded only gospel music and which nurtured this music.

During the time just before World War I, a number of patriotic songs were sung at revivals and found their way into the songbooks. Patriotism has long been a civil religion in America and Christians have often equated the love of God with the love of country and the flag as nearly equal in importance to the Bible, so it is not surprising that songs such as "America" and "Song to the Flag" were often a part of the services. Temperance was a major issue and Billy Sunday (as well as a number of evangelists) ushered in the era of Prohibition with a steady stream of sermons against liquor. Rodeheaver had songs about "Temperance" listed in the topical index of his songbooks. One of these was "De Brewer's Big Horses," written in Negro dialect, apparently from the influence of popular vaudeville shows.

De Brewer's Big Hosses

> Oh, de brewer's big hosses comin' down de road,
> Totin' all around ole Lucifer's load;
> Dey step so high, an' dey step so free,
> But dem big hosses can't run over me.
> Oh, no, boys, oh, no!

De turnpike's free wherebber I go,
I'm a temperance ingine, don't you see,
And de brewer's big hosses can't run over me.

Oh, de licker men's actin' like dey own dis place,
Livin' on de sweat ob de po' man's face,
Dey's fat and sassy as dey can be.
But dem big hosses can't run over me.

Oh, I'll harness dem hosses to de temp'rance cart,
Hit 'em wid a gad to gib 'em a start,
I'll teach 'em how for to haw and gee,
For dem big hosses can't run over me.

This song was written in 1887 but was first introduced into revivalism by Rodeheaver in 1911 and soon proved immensely popular with its rousing melody and fighting lyrics.

Songs like this were aimed at entertaining audiences. Since Sunday's services were not held in churches—they were generally held outdoors in a specially-built "tabernacle"—Rodeheaver actively used all the tools of secular entertainment without any fear of disrupting the decorum of the sanctuary. He also employed various show biz tactics, such as encouraging audiences to sing and making them an active part of the musical program, encouraging competition among choirs, and of course, exercising his own considerable talents in showcasing his show biz tendencies.

The choirs between 1912-18 were generally large and this allowed Rodeheaver to popularize numerous new songs with them. With a large number of voices, the chorister could create jazzy arrangements, do "call and answer" type numbers (often by placing some members of the choir in the back of an auditorium), and manipulate a song so that it contained many melodramatic flourishes and effects. Since a large number of people learned the new songs and often sang them after the revivals left town, the popularity of new songs was assured.

Although local talent was encouraged to participate on the revival stage, and although Rodeheaver made use of large choirs during the services, it was Rody himself who provided the key thread which tied it all together. He served as host and master of ceremonies for the revivals in addition to his role as soloist and chorister. He also welcomed the special delegations who held special seats each evening and required special attention from the revival team. And, of course, when Billy Sunday made his plea for converts, Rodeheaver was responsible for selecting the right song and leading it as the people came forth as an act of faith.

In many ways, Homer Rodeheaver set the standard for the gospel music industry in the 20th century. Through the creation of his publishing company he promoted and popularized a number of new songs (including "The Old Rugged Cross") and through the formation of his record company he reached large numbers of people with new gospel songs, establishing the independent label as the primary outlet for gospel music.

During the early days of recording, many recording companies went into the field, recording singers in rural areas of the south, and collected a number of hymns. These were mostly old songs carried from the oral tradition or learned from songbooks. But it was the records produced by independent companies like Rodeheaver's which began to create the Christian culture in 20th century America, as the gospel consumer became part of a segmented market. As radio and secular records created a national market for music, gospel music evolved from being a separately identifiable form of music—such as the hymns of Sankey or the spirituals—into songs which sounded much like their pop counterparts, the only difference being in the lyrics. Homer Rodeheaver was the first to bridge this musical gap and establish the trend of religious music mimicking pop music in an attempt to draw large audiences and appeal to those both in and outside of religion.

Chapter 14
THE RISE OF RADIO AND RECORDS

The 20th century began with the development of two technologies which transformed music by taking it from the oral tradition to a new electronic tradition. These two developments, the phonograph and the radio, would spread music and preserve it in a fixed, definitive form—the recording—instead of letting it be subjected to the nuances of each performer and performance. These developments also let music reach the masses in a way it had never done before, creating national trends in music as well as national acceptance and popularity. Thus, music went from a local event to a national entity.

Thomas Edison invented the phonograph in 1877 and by the 1890s there were a number of firms competing in the phonograph market. Edison originally envisioned his invention as a business machine but it was soon apparent its real potential lay in the entertainment field. Edison's company, The Edison Phonograph Company, soon began making its own recordings for sale with the phonographs. These original recordings were on cylinders and caused problems with storage as well as with bootlegging. With recordings so easy to make—it could be done on the same machine that played the cylinders—the market soon became flooded with recordings made by nearly anyone who had a machine. The recording quality was not particularly good but neither was the playback quality, and since this was such a new phenomenon, consumers tended to overlook this problem in the first recordings. It wasn't until 1902 that the obvious superiority of studio recordings became apparent and that the control of recordings came to rest with the record manufacturing companies. These companies, which manufactured discs for 120 or 160 rpm, included The National Phonograph Company (an extension of Edison's original company), Columbia, and Victor (later RCA).

Emile Berliner first introduced commercial discs in 1895. By 1898, the quality of the discs had improved with the substitution of wax for zinc in the recording and shellac for rubber in the records and an important advantage began to emerge—storage space. Fifty of the discs could be stored in the same space alloted to four standard cylinders or one concert cylinder.

In 1903, Victor began manufacturing a twelve-inch disc which increased the playing time of recordings to three and a half minutes. The cylinders had previously recorded about two minutes. The significance of this development was that it defined the length of a popular song, which remained around three minutes throughout the 20th century.

The development of the coin-in-the-slot phonograph, or jukebox, allowed recorded music to be made public because these machines were placed in public places, particularly saloons. Comic songs, monologs, whistling and band records tended to attract the most popularity initially, although hymns were also popular in some saloons. The coin-in-the-slot phonographs also became popular in movie houses during the early 1900s as that industry began to develop. The chief rival to these early jukeboxes were coin-operated player pianos, first introduced in 1908. The initial heyday for jukeboxes was from 1890 to 1908 but their major boost to the record industry came during the Depression years of the 1930s when record sales dropped and the coin-operated machines created a market which virtually saved the recording industry and provided a key outlet for minority music not played on the radio. These machines were instrumental in the development of the market for country or "hillbilly" music for rural whites and "race" records for blacks.

The "Blues" was first recorded in 1920 by Okeh Records, a small label financed by the German company, Carl Lindstrom. The country was in a major depression after World War I and labels, having saturated the major urban markets in the East, were looking for new markets; black Americans represented an untapped source for record sales.

"Crazy Blues" was written by Perry Bradford, who insisted that black Americans would buy recordings if blacks were allowed to make the recordings. Mamie Smith had been singing the song, titled

"Harlem Blues" in a New York musical revue, *Made in Harlem*. After he had been turned down by Columbia and Victor, Bradford approached Otto Heineman, head of Okeh, who agreed that Bradford's songs could be recorded if Sophie Tucker did them. When Tucker could not do the sessions, Mamie Smith, Bradford's original choice, was allowed to record "Harlem Blues," renamed "Crazy Blues" to avoid copyright litigation from the Revue backers. That recording reportedly sold over 75,000 copies during the first month of its release and over one million copies during the first year.

This marked the beginning of "blues" recordings, although some African-Americans had recorded the blues earlier and songwriter W.C. Handy had written and published "Memphis Blues," "St. Louis Blues," and several other "blues" songs before World War I. The first black gospel group recorded was "The Dinwiddie Colored Quartet" by Victor in 1902, but there was no follow-up to this group, who performed spirituals a capella.

The first "blues" singers were generally women in New York vaudeville like Mamie Smith, Sippie Wallace, Sara Martin, Victoria Spivey, Ma Rainey, Ida Cox and Alberta Hunter and these "vaudeville blues" singers provided the initial "hits." But with the introduction of "field recordings" after microphones and the electrical recording process had been introduced, the labels did extensive recordings in cities like Dallas, Memphis, Atlanta and Chicago. This ushered in the era of "Delta blues" (generally a man with a guitar) as artists such as Blind Lemon Jefferson, Charlie Patton, Robert Johnson and others emerged before World War II.

The first commercially successful "country" or "hillbilly" recording was done by Fiddlin' John Carson in Atlanta in 1923 by Okeh Records. The recording was made because Polk Brockman, manager of a store that sold phonographs and Okeh Records, insisted the company record the fiddler for the local market. Since this was a major account, the label sent a talent scout and engineer to Atlanta to record Fiddlin' John doing "Little Old Log Cabin Down the Lane" and "The Old Hen Cackled and the Rooster's Gonna Crow." The record executives in New York thought the record was "pluperfect awful" and didn't even give it a number; however, Brockman quickly ordered more copies and the sales success inspired the recording executives to rethink their ideas for the white southern market.

In 1925 a New York singer from Texas, Vernon Dalhart, recorded "The Prisoner's Song" and "Wreck of the Old '97" and that record sold over a million units; after this, recording executives regularly looked for "country" songs and performers, recording extensively in the South during the 1926-1929 period.

The commercial success of "blues" or "race" and "country" or "hillbilly" music led the recording companies to record widely for the southern white and black markets. White performers regularly sang both gospel and secular songs, so both were recorded and released. Blacks generally sang either blues or gospel—but recording executives saw it all as one market. And so southern gospel quartets and black gospel singers were recorded in the 1920s and 1930s.

The development of the technology for radio occurred about the same time as Edison was developing the technology for the phonograph and the first radio communication signals were sent by Guglielmo Marconi of Italy in 1895. At first, the technology was used for ship-to-shore communication but experimental broadcasts in the United States began around 1910. That was the year Lee De Forest produced a program from the Metropolitan Opera House in New York featuring Enrico Caruso. Other stations began to broadcast as well and the United States issued the first broadcast license for radio in 1920. Soon network broadcasting, begun by RCA-owned NBC, began to link the country.

The Golden Age of Radio broadcasting is generally considered to be from 1925 to 1950 when radio was the primary source of family entertainment. During the 1930s, in particular, radio came into its own with live musical shows, soap operas, comedy shows and dramatic series and news, especially Roosevelt's "Fireside Chats" from 1933 to 1945 which linked the Presidency to the people in a way that had never been done before. The Golden Age of Radio ended in the early 1950s with the advent of television, which replaced radio as the chief source of family entertainment in the home. However, radio emerged as the primary carrier of music to teenagers in the mid-1950s with the rise of rock 'n roll. This gave radio a new youth-oriented direction and a new, important function—the spread of new kinds of music which had mostly been kept off the airwaves when the networks controlled radio.

Two other events in the early part of the 20th century also had a profound effect on music: the Copyright Act of 1909 and the formation of the American Society of Composers, Authors and Publishers (ASCAP) in 1916. The Copyright Act provided protection for songwriters and legitimized the song as both a commercial and literary form. But it also demanded that compositions be "original," and thus the long tradition of "borrowing" from other sources began to come to an end. No longer could songwriters take old songs, or other people's songs, change and adapt them, and use them as their own (although this folk tradition still continued through World War II); now they must create totally new material.

The formation of ASCAP provided a means for songwriters and publishers to make money from music performances. Later, other performing rights organizations, Broadcast Music, Inc. (BMI) and SESAC, would form and have a major impact on music as well. These performance rights organizations lifted songwriting from a mostly amateur status to that of a full-fledged occupation. Both of these events affected popular music immediately and directly but gospel, folk, blues, and country really did not feel the full effect until after World War II.

Science and technology played a key role in America's development into a world power in the 20th century, although these scientific advances often played a divisive role in the Christian community. The roots again date back to the 16th century and the Copernican Revolution, which took man out of the center of the universe and made him just one speck in the cosmos. This change in the position of man in the universe also changed man's view of God, and the scientific revolutions during the next 500 years produced a chameleon God whose image and role changed with each new scientific discovery.

But science and religion did not always clash when science was used for practical applications. Christianity quickly embraced radio and preachers began to broadcast their sermons and influence over the airwaves too, taking sacred music outside churches and revivals and putting it into the American home.

Religion discovered radio very early. The first commercially licensed radio station, KDKA in Pittsburgh, Pennsylvania, began broadcasting on November 2, 1920; on January 2, 1921, it broadcast a church service. The service was from the Calvary Episcopal Church and was a Sunday evening service conducted by Rev. Lewis B. Whittemore. The broadcast came about because one of the

Westinghouse engineers at KDKA was a member of the church choir; the broadcast proved successful and soon the services were a weekly Sunday feature. Other evening services were aired in Chicago by Paul Radar in 1922 and in Omaha, Nebraska by R.R. Brown in 1923, whose "Radio Chapel Service" was the first nondenominational service.

Religious broadcasting generally occurred on Sundays and most of the programs were worship or church services. The Federal license requirements were minimal and stations could operate at whatever level of power they wished over whatever frequency they chose. That ended in 1927 when the Federal Radio Commission (FRC) was formed. The FRC established regulations that required regular broadcast schedules, an assigned frequency and channel, and the use of modulation equipment. This ended the era of radio mavericks, including religious broadcasters, who could not keep up financially because of the cost of equipment and dropped out. However, some pioneers hung on, including KFUO in St. Louis, which began in 1925; KFGQ in Boone, Iowa, which began in 1927; KPOF in Denver, which began in 1928; WWBL in Richmond, which began in 1924; KPPC in Pasadena, California and WCAL in Northfield, Minnesota, which both began in 1922.

The first program of gospel music on radio was the work of two students from the Moody Bible Institute in Chicago who produced a Sunday evening program in 1925 over the school's radio station, WMBI. Wendell Loveless, a gospel composer, was the station's first program manager and served as announcer, pianist, vocalist and preacher on a number of programs. However, there was always music on gospel radio when the services were broadcast because singing was part of the service, traditionally preceding the sermon. The music on WMBI was confined to standard hymns and classical numbers.

As the FRC regulations essentially ended the chance for any individual to begin a radio station, religious programming moved over to secular radio where it purchased time on established stations. This was the era of network radio and Donald Grey Barnhouse was the first to purchase network radio time for a religious program. During the 1930s, a number of others also did this as shows such as "Radio Bible Class," "Radio Revival," "Heaven and Home Hour," "Haven of Rest," "Back to God Hour," and "Back to the Bible" were heard.

THE RISE OF RADIO AND RECORDS

Walter A. Maier is a key figure in early religious radio programming because he started "The Lutheran Hour," which was broadcast over the CBS network. The price for broadcasting a season of half-hour weekly shows in 1930 was $200,000 and Maier provided $100,000 in seed money from his own church. The other half came from listeners after the show went on the air in October 1930, on WHK in Cleveland. Barnhouse received a lot of money from listeners and so did Charles Fuller, who began the Gospel Broadcasting Association. Fuller was so successful that in 1943 he spent $1,556,130 for time buys and was the Mutual Broadcasting Network's best customer. That year—1943—was the peak year for religion on radio, as contributions reached an all-time high.

However, the networks banned paid religious broadcasts, basically because Father Charles E. Coughlin and Rev. Robert "Fighting Bob" Schuler were proving to be too popular and too controversial with their vitriolic attacks on President Roosevelt during their broadcasts. This forced the religious programmers to purchase time on independent stations and this trend continued from 1944 until 1949 when the drop in radio advertising revenue, caused by the introduction of television, saw radio look again to the religious broadcasters for time buys.

The beginning of the television era in 1950 spelled the decline of network radio but not the decline of radio, which became even more influential and pervasive as it became more independent. It was here that radio had to begin playing records because it did not have the income to support live bands. Too, it had to program music because it could not compete with television's shows—thus radio became the dominant medium for records and the dominant medium to reach those with differing tastes in entertainment.

Musically, the turn of the century is marked by the emergence of the first truly "American" voice in songs. These songs are often linked directly to the theater, which has always been a leader in introducing new styles and trends to American music. The year 1890 serves as a good starting point, although there were breakthroughs in American music before that. This period is when popular music came of age in America, although this date fails to acknowledge the tremendous influence Stephen Foster had earlier in the 19th century as he became the first composer to be uniquely "American" in the field of song writing.

A major difference between Americans and Europeans at the turn of the century was that Americans were less formal, less inhibited, and more inclined to create wild dances outside the European tradition of waltzes, polkas, and gallops. These "informal" dances needed a music that was less structured that that of European music and Americans found it in the music originated by African-Americans. Popular music and popular dance evolved together as a new dance would often create demand for a song or vice versa.

In 1912 W.C. Handy published the first blues song. Handy, called "the father of the blues," was actually the promoter and publisher of the blues, a music which had been around since before the Civil War and dates back to early work songs. Handy had the first successful black-owned publishing company which put down on paper the music of blacks, allowing white musicians to play the music. Musicians such as Eubie Blake and James P. Johnson—whose piano playing style was later made famous by Fats Waller—influenced white musicians, songwriters and audiences. Irving Berlin published "Alexander's Ragtime Band" in 1912 (which was really not a "ragtime" song) and the floodgates were opened as songs from white songwriters influenced by black music poured through.

The early part of the 20th century was particularly rich with musical developments as cowboy music in the west, folk music from immigrants, black spirituals (first popularized by the Fisk Jubliee Singers), hillbilly music from whites in the south, blues from blacks in the south, and the musical theater on Broadway all began to grow and influence one another. The technology of phonographs and electricity, which led to the practice of doing field recordings of musicians playing different forms of music in their own genre and culture, allowed Americans all over the country to hear the music that had previously been limited to a particular race, sub-culture, or region. Thus, music and technology grew hand in hand throughout the first half of the 20th century.

Chapter 15
THE ROOTS OF BLACK GOSPEL

After the end of the Civil War, African-Americans were in conflict with their past. Living as slaves before the war, considered less than human, many wanted to prove they were cultured, educated, sophisticated people, to "move up" in this world. The traditional Negro music from the slavery period was considered base, backwards, and a remnant of the past they were trying to escape; many turned their backs on their heritage and sought to improve themselves by adapting formal church services, ignoring the music and culture of their past, and seeking education in newly formed black universities.

During the 19th century, the Fisk Jubilee Singers performed old Spirituals, but in a European style, very formal, standing erect, singing with trained voices. The mainline Baptist and Methodist churches were emblems of social respectability, giving their congregants the dignity of a formal worship service. But the Holiness movement challenged this formality and threatened the mainline churches with a service heavy on emotion and physical release. The music provided a release from troubles, rather than the quiet, inner strength to tame the spirit that mainline churches sought to impart.

The old spirituals became more respected within the African-American community through the efforts of John Wesley Work, Sr. and his brother, Frederick J. Work. John Work taught Latin and history at Fisk until 1900, when he re-organized the defunct Fisk Jubilee Singers. For the next sixteen years, Work led the group around the United States, performing concerts. He also collected and arranged black folk music. The Work brothers published *New Jubilee Songs* in 1901 and *Folk Songs of the American Negro* in 1907. By putting these songs in books, and using musical notation, Work sought to make the spirituals the music of "educated Negroes" and encouraged the study of these songs at black colleges.

Although Work's efforts did not end blacks' resistance to their folk heritage—especially among the young, the educated, or the choir directors in large urban churches—he was a major force in urging blacks not to forget their past. He was only moderately successful during his time, but Work's books have been a treasure trove for scholars of black folk music and spirituals ever since.

The conflict between the Holiness and mainline churches was played out over a number of years, with the Azusa Street Revival as the major catalyst for changes in African-American worship services and, ultimately, in the development of a distinctive sound for black gospel music. A major conflict that would have far-reaching consequences came to a head in Mississippi in the early 1900s.

Charles Price Jones was born near Rome, Georgia in 1865; when he was 17 his mother died, and he left home and moved around throughout the South. He began preaching in 1885 and was licensed to preach in the Baptist church in 1887 while he was living in Arkansas; he then entered the Arkansas Baptist College at Little Rock, graduating in 1891. Jones was the pastor of the Tabernacle Baptist Church in Selma, Alabama in 1894 when he came under the influence of the Holiness movement. On June 6, 1897 a Holiness Convention for a small group of Baptist preachers was called by Jones; it was held in Jackson, Mississippi. During the next convention, in 1898, the Holiness faction decided to change their name from the Mt. Helm Baptist Church to the Church of Christ. The Baptist Association sued and dismissed them; in 1899 in Lexington, Mississippi the new church held its first independent convention.

In 1906 several church representatives from this Holiness group attended the Azusa Street Revival. Charles Harrison Mason, J.A. Jeter, and W.S. Pleasant all attended the Revival, although Jones himself did not. When Mason returned to Mississippi, he and Jones had a disagreement over doctrine, which caused them to split and form two separate churches. The Church of Christ (Holiness) was formed by Jones while Mason organized the Church of God in Christ.

Charles Price Jones was a self-taught musician and songwriter who began publishing his work in 1899; his most famous song is

"I'm Happy with Jesus Alone." Although Jones was an influential songwriter, he wrote for a congregation that sang without any instrumental accompaniment because he could not find any mention of instruments used in worshipping Jesus in the New Testament. Consequently, his church did not have a major influence on the gospel music that developed in the 20th century. The other church that developed from this split would have a profound effect on 20th century gospel music.

Charles Harrison Mason was born near Memphis, Tennessee in 1866 and moved with his family to Plumbersville, Arkansas in 1878. He converted and was baptized in the Mt. Olive Baptist Church in 1880 after a miraculous recovery from a long fever. Mason's brother was pastor of the Mt. Olive church and in 1893 Charles preached his first sermon there before entering Arkansas Baptist College. Mason stayed at college for only a few months, then left and became a traveling evangelist. He met Jones in 1895 at the first Holiness convention.

Mason spent five weeks at the Azusa Street Revival where, in March 1907, he began speaking in tongues. After splitting from Jones, he settled in Memphis in late 1907 and started his church, the Church of God in Christ, called COGIC, which soon attracted a large following. Although Mason wrote songs, he never published them (not until 1982 was the hymnal *Yes, Lord!* first published). His most important compositions were "I'm a Soldier in the Army of the Lord" and "Yes, Lord," also known as the "COGIC chant." By 1934 COGIC had a membership of 25,000 and would eventually go on to become the largest black Pentecostal church in the world. It would also spawn a number of influential gospel performers in the coming years, including Sister Rosetta Tharpe, Andrae Crouch, Walter and Edwin Hawkins, the O'Neal Twins, the Banks Brothers, the Boyer Brothers, and Vanessa Bell Armstrong.

Another major influence on black gospel at the turn of the 20th century was Charles Albert Tindley, who was born in 1851 in Berlin, Maryland and moved to Philadelphia in 1875 after he married. While working at the John Wesley Methodist Episcopal Church, Tindley studied for the ministry and, beginning in 1885, pastored congregations in New Jersey and Delaware. In 1902 he moved back to Philadelphia to pastor the Bainbridge Street Methodist Church—the same church that had formerly been the John Wesley Methodist

Episcopal Church. From an initial congregation of about 200 members, the church grew to over 10,000 and Tindley became an influential preacher, civil rights worker and gospel hymn writer. His most influential songs are "What Are They Doing in Heaven?," "Nothing Between," "Some Day" (also called "Beams of Heaven"), "Stand By Me," "Let Jesus Fix It For You," "Leave It There," "We'll Understand It Better By and By," and "I'll Overcome" (later altered to "We Shall Overcome").

The black gospel quartet has its roots in Fisk University in Nashville. In 1905 Fisk made a decision to feature a male quartet instead of a mixed choir of Jubilee Singers. The school led the way for mixed choirs with the Fisk Jubilee Singers; they were followed by "Jubilee singers" from Hampton, Tuskegee, Utica, Mississippi and Wilberforce Universities, which also developed singing groups.

The first quartets were formed at black universities and generally operated as clubs, electing officers, paying dues, wearing uniforms and singing formal arrangements at concerts that were pre-arranged. These quartets were primarily Baptists, who generally ridiculed the Holiness singers and their improvisation, emotionalism and untrained singing; the Baptists preferred trained voices, singing the melody in a "concert demeanor"—standing erect, with proper enunciation, in a formal, reserved style. This, they felt, elevated the music and themselves. The Holiness singers, on the other hand, would sing spontaneously during a church service, as audience participants rather than special guests.

The "Jubilee quartets" often found themselves in front of audiences who responded with shouts of "Amen," "Hallelujah," and "Praise the Lord" during their songs. Gradually, the quartets began "borrowing" some of the emotional style of singing from the Holiness singers. The quartets became so popular that members of a community or church, not a university, began forming four-man groups.

R.C. Foster, born in 1899, was a student of Vernon W. Barnett, a graduate of Tuskegee Institute who taught quartet-style singing. In 1915 Foster moved to Bessemer, Alabama and started a group called the Foster Singers. This would be the pioneer group that moved from the formal, university-based group to a traveling, black gospel quartet. Members of this original group were Foster (tenor), Norman McQueen (lead), Fletcher Fisher (baritone), and Golius Grant (bass).

A major difference between the university quartets and the quartets formed in communities and churches was the untrained voice. Rhythmically more free, the quartets moved on stage and used gestures with their hands, such as patting their thighs and swaying back and forth.

Soon, other quartets were formed—the Famous Blue Jay Singers and Birmingham Jubilee Singers (both begun in 1926); the Ensely Jubilee Singers and the Ravizee Singers (both in 1929) in Alabama. The Ravizee Singers were a family group with mixed voices. In 1935 they moved to Bessemer in Jefferson County, Alabama, which became known as the center for black gospel quartets.

Quartets were formed in other parts of the South as well. In Norfolk, Virginia, the Silver Leaf Quartet was known for the falsetto of William Thatch instead of the usual tenor as the top voice. This would have a major influence on later doo-wop groups. The Fairfield Four, based at the Fairfield Missionary Baptist Church in Nashville, was formed in 1921; the Dixie Hummingbirds were organized in Greenville, South Carolina in 1928.

Although these quartets were influenced by the Holiness movement, they did not use instruments. They sang a cappella. And although the Baptists and Methodists grew, particularly as large numbers of blacks left the South and moved North during the World War I era and joined these established churches, the Holiness movement expanded by "planting" churches—finding a community and setting up a "store-front" church. Music was an important part of the Holiness churches, which appealed to the less-educated and those who wanted to feel a connection to their Southern roots.

The Holiness singers wanted to have a piano accompany their singing. The first-known gospel pianist was Arizona Dranes, a blind woman, from Dallas, Texas. Dranes played for Emmett Morey Page as he went about setting up churches. Back in Dallas, Dranes became pianist for another preacher, Samuel M. Crouch, Jr. During the early 1930s, Crouch moved to the Los Angeles area where he founded the Emmanuel Church of God in Christ.

Dranes introduced the "gospel beat" to the piano—adding a syncopated rhythm akin to ragtime, with a heavy left hand driving the rhythm. She sang in a high, nasal voice and was an effective song leader. Richard M. Jones, a talent scout for Okeh Records, heard

Dranes play at one of Crouch's services and Jones arranged for her to record in Chicago where she cut "My Soul is a Witness for My Lord." Between 1926 and 1928 she recorded over thirty songs for Okeh, including "I Shall Wear a Crown."

In 1921 the National Baptist Convention published *Gospel Pearls*, edited by Willa A. Townsend, who worked at Roger Williams University in Nashville. Although the 163 songs in the book contained many standard Protestant hymns, such as "Battle Hymn of the Republic," the book also included "Stand By Me," "We'll Understand It Better By and By," "Leave It There," and "I'm Happy With Jesus Alone," by Charles Price Jones, "Shine for Jesus," by E.C. Deas, and "If I Don't Get There," the first gospel song published by Thomas Andrew Dorsey. When The National Baptist Convention put its stamp of approval on these songs, they became widely accepted in black congregations across the country. In fact, they transcended Baptist congregations and were found in Methodist and Pentecostal churches as well.

Gospel Pearls broadened the style of music available to Baptists and led to the formation of several important groups. The Tindley Gospel Singers, organized in 1927 at the Tindley Temple Methodist Episcopal Church in Philadelphia, was the first male group to be accompanied by the piano. The Golden Gate Quartet was organized in Norfolk, Virginia, in the late 1920s by students attending Booker T. Washington High School. The original members were Henry Owens (lead), Clyde Reddick (tenor), Willie "Bill" Johnson (baritone), and Orlando Wilson (bass). Willie Langford later replaced Reddick. In 1925 the Golden Gate Quartet was heard live on radio over WBT in Charlotte, North Carolina.

The worlds of blues and gospel were, literally, worlds apart. Gospel music was for the church while blues was for the honky tonks and dives; blues appealed to man's carnal nature while gospel sought to purify and elevate the soul. Blues was aligned with the "the Devil" while those who sang gospel did "God's work." Still, the popularity and commercial success of blues recordings during the 1920s helped black gospel because the recording companies saw both as music for the black market.

The success of Mamie Smith's recording of "Crazy Blues" in 1921 ushered in an era when blues singers were sought out by the recording companies. With the introduction of microphones and the electrical process in recording, recording companies began to travel throughout the South in search of black performers; some of these performers sang blues while others sang gospel. As long as the recordings sold, both genres were recorded—often on the same days.

The major companies recording blues during the 1920s were Victor, Paramount, Columbia and Okeh. They regularly sent talent scouts with recording equipment into cities such as Atlanta, Memphis, Dallas, San Antonio, and Chicago to record local singers. In April 1926, the Birmingham Jubilee Singers, organized by Charles Bridges, recorded "Southbound Train," "He Took My Sins Away," and "Birmingham Boys" for Columbia in Atlanta. That same year Arizona Dranes recorded "My Soul is a Witness for My Lord" in Chicago.

Labels also recorded sermons by black preachers. The first preaching record was done by Reverend Calvin P. Dixon for Columbia in 1925, and by 1927 six preachers had been recorded; that year 30 were recorded and eventually 750 sermons on record were released. The market for these sermons was the 5.2 million black church members in the United States, who were increasingly found in urban areas such as Detroit, Chicago, Indianapolis and Philadelphia. In 1927 there were approximately 100 million records sold; blues accounted for about five percent of that total and one artist, Bessie Smith, probably accounted for about a million—or about 20 percent of the total number of blues records sold. There were also over 70 recordings of quartets issued in 1927.

The key figure in black gospel songwriting and publishing is Thomas Dorsey, who became known as a great personality, composer, publisher, performer, teacher, choir director, and organizer as well as minister of music for the Pilgrim Baptist Church in Chicago. More than any other individual, Dorsey defined contemporary black gospel music, even though he was not the first African American to have his songs published. But it was Dorsey himself as well as his songs that unified the movement which became black gospel, giving a definition to the music that survived throughout the 20th century.

Thomas Dorsey was a great songwriter, able to capture the spirit and essence of "soul-singing" and compose in the unique black idiom. But his influence and popularity is also attributed to his practice of reproducing his words and music on single sheets for sale, selling them directly to churches and singers, whose alternative was to purchase large collections of songs in books. W. C. Handy, the "Father of the Blues," also did this in the field of secular music.

Dorsey, of course, was a gigantic figure in gospel music outside of his publishing. He trained and accompanied countless singers and fought for recognition with ministries and church musicians who were opposed to adding his songs to church services. Finally, the National Baptist Convention (Negro), which convened in Chicago in 1930, allowed the performance of two Dorsey songs, "How About You" and "Did You See My Savior." The positive reaction from delegates charted the direction for black gospel.

Thomas Andrew Dorsey was born in Villa Rica, Georgia, in 1891, son of a Baptist minister, Reverend T.M. Dorsey and his wife, Etta. He moved with his family to Atlanta in 1906, where he was influenced by early blues and jazz as well as Isaac Watts hymns. Although his parents disapproved of show business, Dorsey was clearly attracted to it and mastered several instruments in his youth. In his teens he began playing blues and ragtime in Atlanta. In 1916 his family moved to Chicago, but Dorsey often went back to Atlanta to play piano in clubs. During the latter half of 1919, Dorsey moved permanently to Chicago.

In Chicago, Dorsey was frustrated by his inability to read music, so he enrolled in the Chicago School of Composition and Arranging and learned musical notation; with this knowledge he was able to obtain work with publishing companies as a composer/arranger. This led to him copyrighting his first composition, "If You Don't Believe I'm Leaving, You Can Count the Days I'm Gone," in October 1920.

Dorsey worked for the Chicago Music Publishing Company, which was aligned with Paramount Records. This led to Dorsey organizing a band and playing for Paramount recording artist Ma Rainey from 1924 to 1926.

Throughout the 1920s Dorsey was a prolific composer of blues songs. He was initially "saved" through a song, "I Do, Don't You," at a Baptist convention in 1921. During the following years, he kept a foot in both worlds—gospel and blues—and performed all kinds of music. He always returned to the church after recovering from a grave illness, but the demands to support his wife led to his continued involvement in the blues field.

Dorsey had first made a name for himself in blues music, under the name "Georgia Tom," writing "Tight Like That" with Hudson Whitaker, known as Tampa Red. The success of "Tight Like That" led to Georgia Tom and Tampa Red writing more of these double entendre blues, including "Pat That Bread," "You Got That Stuff," "Where Did You Stay Last Night," "It's All Worn Out," and "Somebody's Been Using That Thing." During the late 20s and early 30s, Georgia Tom and Tampa Red made over 60 recordings.

In gospel, Thomas Dorsey found his calling, and his true genius took root and flourished. As director of the gospel choir at Pilgrim Baptist Church in Chicago, Dorsey helped a number of singers and had a forum for writing and experimenting with new songs he composed. He was heavily influenced by preachers, and he composed for those who would use his songs as a mini-sermon, singing a line, then expounding while the audience shouted. The choir would join in on the chorus while Dorsey played the accompaniment on the piano.

Dorsey's new songs ushered in a new era for black gospel at the same time some great gospel singers emerged, most of whom came out of choirs (often Dorsey's) as soloists. As black gospel was recorded and released, these singers would go on to establish national reputations and influence others who would never have seen or heard them otherwise. This served to unify black gospel and increasingly brought it to the attention of white churches and singers, who were influenced by the style and rhythms and often copied some of the songs and bought the records.

Dorsey's first gospel song was "If You See My Savior, Tell Him That You Saw Me." Initially, Dorsey mailed copies of the sheet music to churches around the country, but the first order did not come until two years later. The breakthrough for Dorsey and his gospel songs, as noted earlier, occurred in 1930 at the National Baptist Convention for blacks in Chicago. The musical directors there, Lucie Campbell and E.W. Isaac, invited him to sell his music and this launched Thomas Dorsey as a gospel songwriter.

As his music became more accepted in the churches, Dorsey's stature as a songwriter grew until he was, in the words of Mahalia Jackson, "our Irving Berlin."

Chapter 16

THE BEGINNINGS OF SOUTHERN GOSPEL

The roots of Southern Gospel can be traced back to the singing schools and shaped note song books, as well as to revivals in rural areas in America. The singing school movement actually began in New England in the 1720s with the intent to increase musical literacy in churches so that congregations could sing from songbooks. In 1721 John Tufts developed a musical notation of F, S, L, and M to correspond to the syllables, fa, sol, la, and me and published *Introduction to the Singing of Psalm-Tunes* in Boston. In 1798 William Little and William Smith used Tufts' basic ideas but created "character notes" or "shaped notes" and published *The Easy Instructor*. This new method caught on fairly quickly.

During the 1790s a series of revivals began in New England and with settlers who had moved west of the Appalachian Mountains. The revivals solved the problem of musical illiteracy by using songs with an easily learned chorus that would re-occur throughout the song and with which the congregation could join in singing.

In 1816 *Kentucky Harmony*, a collection of songs using the four shaped notes, was published by Ananias Davisson, and during the period from the 1830s until the Civil War, Joseph Funk sold *Genuine Church Music*, a songbook he published originally in 1832, at the singing schools he taught at in Virginia. William "Singin' Billy" Walker published The *Southern Harmony* in 1835, and in 1844 Benjamin Franklin White published *The Sacred Harp*. Two years later Jesse Aikin published *The Christian Minstrel*, but Aikin's book added three more shaped notes to make a total of seven shaped notes.

Although the shaped note books were popular, particularly in southern rural areas, there was a backlash against them on the part of trained musicians who insisted the traditional "round notes" were the only way to learn music. Part of this involved a class conflict—with shaped notes, the educated elite no longer had control of musical literacy. Further, the rural "unlettered" Southerners were more likely to embrace folk tunes instead of music from the European classical tradition. And so the urban areas shunned shape notes while the rural areas embraced them; this would set the pattern for the future of what eventually became known as Southern Gospel music.

The fourth edition of Joseph Funk's *Genuine Church Music* was published in 1851 as *Harmonia Sacra*. Two years later Ephraim Ruebush became an apprentice bookbinder with Funk's publishing company. To promote his songbooks, Funk established a monthly magazine, *The Southern Musical Advocate and Singer's Friend*, in 1859. The next year Joseph Funk's grandson, Aldine Silliman Kieffer became an active part of the company. Kieffer, born in 1840, lived with his parents in Saline County, Missouri, until his father died in 1847, when the family moved back to Mountain Valley, later renamed Singer's Glen. He learned the shaped note songbook business from his grandfather and uncles and was soon conducting singing schools. Ruebush and Kieffer grew close personally, and then became brothers-in-law when Ruebush married Virginia Kieffer, Aldine's sister.

The Civil War began in the spring of 1861 and caused a split between the two men; Ruebush joined the Union Army while Kieffer served in the Army of Northern Virginia for the Confederacy. In 1862 Joseph Funk died. After the Civil War, Kieffer, his brother and two uncles formed The Patent Note Publishing Company and established a periodical, *The Musical Million and Singer's Advocate*.

Ruebush returned to Virginia and joined the firm, which continued to publish songbooks with four shaped notes. But William "Singin' Billy" Walker published *Christian Harmony*, which used seven shaped notes. Both *The Christian Minstrel* by Jesse Aikin and *The New Harp* published by Marcus Lafayette Swan used the seven-note system in their books.

In January 1872 Ephraim Ruebush gained control of the day-to-day business while Kieffer, the driving creative force, continued to edit the magazine. In August 1874 the company opened the Virginia

Normal Music School and hired Benjamin C. Unseld as principal. Unself, who had previously taught at the New England Conservatory of Music in Boston, favored the "round notes" and convinced the company to teach both systems at the singing school. This school, which was really an annual gathering of students held in New Market, Virginia, became a major training ground for singing school teachers. These teachers would teach from the Ruebush-Kieffer songbooks, which increased sales for the company.

A relative of the Funk family, Anthony Johnson (A.J.) Showalter came to the Virginia Normal School in 1876 when he was 18. Showalter, born in 1858, had been teaching at singing schools since he was 14. Showalter would publish his first songbook in 1880 and eventually establish his own company, modeled on the Ruebush-Kieffer organization, becoming a major force in shaped-note publishing. James David Vaughan, who would also establish a major shaped note publishing company, attended a singing school conducted by James Berry from the Ruebush-Kieffer Company. Vaughan also attended the Shenandoah Seminary, which had branched off from the Virginia Normal Singing School in October 1879.

Meanwhile, the problem of two competing systems—the four-note vs. the seven-note—was resolved when Ruebush-Kieffer changed over to the seven note system after Jesse Aikin came down to Virginia and convinced them to do so.

In 1880 A.J. Showalter taught during the summer at the Shenandoah Seminary, where 101 students met for the four-week course. The following year Showalter conducted singing schools and sold songbooks for Ruebush-Kieffer in Mississippi, Alabama, Texas, South Carolina, Georgia, Arkansas, North Carolina, and Missouri. In 1884 he moved to Dalton, Georgia and established a branch office there for Ruebush-Kieffer. He also established his own business, publishing the songbook *Good Tidings* and a periodical, *The Music Teacher* (originally named *Our Musical Visitor*). He established branch offices in Dallas, Texarkana, and Chattanooga for his company and in 1885 began a singing school, the Southern Normal Institute, which later became the Southern Normal Conservatory of Music. One of his students at this school was Jesse Randall (J.R.) Baxter, who would later become a major publisher of shaped-note songbooks. In 1890 Showalter married and moved to Cisco, Texas.

James D. Vaughan taught his first singing school in 1882 and, to publicize the school, created a family quartet that would become the forerunner of all Southern Gospel quartets. Vaughan sang lead, his 15-year-old brother John sang bass, while 12-year-old Will and 7-year-old Charles sang tenor and alto, respectively. This quartet demonstrated the songs and showed how a trained quartet could promote the selling of songbooks.

Around 1896 Vaughan and Ephraim Timothy Hildebrand, another protege of Reubush-Kieffer and a graduate of the Shenandoah Seminary, published two songbooks, *Onward and Upward* and *Onward and Upward No. 1*. Vaughan had moved his family to Cisco, Texas, but in 1899 a cyclone hit the town, destroying Vaughan's home while the family huddled, unhurt, inside. This led Vaughan to pack up and move back to his native Giles County, Tennessee, where he became a school principal in Elkmont Springs. Vaughan continued his involvement with singing schools—conducting several—and published some songs. In 1900 he published Gospel Chimes and in 1902 left his job as school principal, moved to Lawrenceburg, Tennessee and took a job as an office clerk in the County Register of Deeds while he built his James D. Vaughan Music Company.

In May 1910 Vaughan sponsored the first Vaughan Quartet, consisting of his brother Charles singing lead and accompanied by Joseph Allen, George Sebren, and Ira Foust in order to advertise and sell his songbooks; by this time he was publishing a new songbook every year. During the first appearance by the Vaughan Quartet, at the annual Cumberland Presbyterian Assembly in Dickson, Tennessee, the group sold 5,000 songbooks; this convinced James D. Vaughan that the best way to sell songbooks was to hire quartets to sing the songs. This began the shift in gospel publishing away from congregation singing to that of an audience watching a trained quartet performing the songs.

In January the following year, Vaughan established the Vaughan Normal School of Music and began publishing a periodical, *The Musical Visitor*.

Most singing schools, called "Normals," held classes over a ten-day period with classes often conducted at night. The students were drilled in sight-reading shaped notes, harmony, and pitch. At the end of the ten days, the graduating class generally put on a "concert" in which they demonstrated their ability to sing from shaped-note song-books. For a rural youngster raised on a farm who had a talent for singing, this was a mark of prestige and honor. Watching the singing school teacher, many saw a way out of southern farm life and a chance to make a living doing what they loved—singing.

Singing conventions, usually held annually, were social as well as musical events and it didn't take song publishers long to realize this was fertile ground for songbook sales. But there was also resistance to these singing conventions from the traditional churches, who felt the theology was shallow and the "acrobatics" of the singers distasteful and "ungodly." But the Holiness and Pentecostals were a group of individualists who loved spirited, emotional singing, were not biased against non-traditional church music, and generally ignored—even disdained—the views of so-called "experts" in church music. And so shaped-note songbooks, singing conventions, and trained quartets performing new songs became widely accepted in the rural South. These Southern Pentecostals were usually open to instrumental accompaniment, particularly from "folk" instruments like the guitar.

Young Southern farm boys saw singing school teachers and traveling quartets as people they admired, respected, and wanted to emulate. The major evangelists of the day, Billy Sunday and Sam Jones, had songleaders who also led the congregation in spirited singing. Homer Rodeheaver, who performed with Billy Sunday, and E.O. Excell and Professor Marcellus J. Maxwell, who performed with Jones, were "heroes" and figures of renown to numerous young men who also wanted to stand in front of a crowd and lead them in singing.

By 1912 several gospel publishers were doing extremely well; A.J. Showalter had sold millions of songbooks by this time and had written, with Elisah Hoffman, "Leaning on the Everlasting Arms." Vaughan had proven that a traveling quartet was an excellent way to demonstrate new songs and sell songbooks, selling about 60,000 books annually by this time.

Still, there was a constant need for trained singing school teachers who could travel throughout the South. In order to increase enrollment at his school, and train more students to become singing school teachers, Vaughan hired 70-year old Benjamin Unseld, formerly with Ruebush-Kieffer, to become dean of his school in Lawrenceburg. As he did in Virginia, Unseld insisted the "round-note" system be taught along with the shaped-note system; he also edited Vaughan's periodical, *The Musical Visitor*.

In 1914 V.O. Stamps attended the Vaughan Music School in Lawrenceburg and the following year returned to his home in Texas as a traveling representative of the Vaughan Music School. Stamps, born near Gilmer, Texas in 1892, attended his first singing school in that area in 1907. After he joined Vaughan, he worked selling song-books and recruiting students for Vaughan's school in Lawrenceburg, which sponsored a four-week session each winter. In 1916 the term was extended to six weeks, with day and night sessions running parallel.

V.O. Stamps was the best salesman James D. Vaughan had. He joined the Vaughan Quartet in 1917; that same year Vaughan established branch offices in Greenville, South Carolina, Midlothian, Texas and Fitzgerald, Georgia. Vaughan also established a saxophone quartet that played instrumental music.

In 1918 A.J. Showalter organized a quartet which promoted the *Big Quartet Book*. That same year the Hartford Music Company was formed by Eugene M. Bartlett, John A. McClung and David Moore in Hartford, Arkansas. The company's roots can be traced to Moore, who opened the David Moore Music Store in 1904, then teamed with Will M. Ramsey to form Central Music Company. When Ramsey moved to Little Rock, one of the employees of the firm, Eugene Bartlett, convinced Moore and McClung to establish the Hartford Music Company. Also in 1918 Vaughan transferred Stamps to Timpson, in east Texas; the following year Stamps moved to Jacksonville in that state and remained there for five years, building the most successful branch of the Vaughan Music Company.

In 1919 V.O.'s brother, Frank, joined the Vaughan company and sang bass in one of the quartets. That year Vaughan changed the name of *The Musical Visitor* to *Vaughan's Family Visitor* and also purchased the *Lawrenceburg News*; he would publish that newspaper for the next twenty years.

The technologies of radio and recordings had an effect on Southern Gospel, beginning in the 1920s. In 1921 Vaughan Phonograph Records started up in Lawrenceburg; the initial recordings, by a quartet, included "Couldn't Hear Nobody Pray," "Steal Away," "Magnify Jesus," "Look for Me," "Someday," and "Waiting at the Gate." The phonograph company led to the formation of a new group, the Vaughan Recording Quartet. Comprised of Glenn Kieffer Vaughan (lead), Hilman Barnard (tenor), Walter B. Seale (baritone) and Roy L. Collins (bass), the quartet did not record exclusively for Vaughan, recording for Homer Rodeheaver's Rainbow Records as well as the Gennett label, owned by the Starr Piano Company, in Richmond, Indiana, in 1921. This was two years before the first "country" recordings, which led to a number of gospel songs being recorded by individuals, family groups, and quartets.

In November 1922 James D. Vaughan received a license for a non-commercial radio station in Lawrenceburg; the involvement in radio came about through Vaughan's friendship with Fred Green, a local resident who'd served in the Signal Corps during World War II. In early 1923 WOAN went on the air with 150 watts, playing Vaughan music and selling Vaughan songbooks. This development led to the formation of the Vaughan Radio Quartet, comprised of William B. Walbert, Hilman Barnard, Otis McCoy and Adger M. Pace; this group remained together until the early 1930s.

That same year James D. Vaughan began a four-year term as Mayor of Lawrenceburg. He was also president of one of the local banks and, politically, was a prohibitionist.

The biggest event in the world of shaped-note publishing occurred early in 1924 when V.O. Stamps broke away from the Vaughan Company and formed his own firm, the Virgil O. Stamps Music Company; his first publication was *Harbor Bells* (V.O.'s brother, Frank, formed a traveling quartet to promote the songbook). The quartet was comprised of Frank Stamps, J.E. Hamilton, Lee Myers and Johnny E. Wheeler, although personnel changed frequently over the next several years. Also in 1924, the V.O. Stamps School of Music began, offering instruction to singers and teachers.

By 1926 Stamps's company was struggling, which led to him acquiring a partner, Jesse Randall (J.R.) Baxter, Jr. Baxter was a singing school teacher who had worked for the A.J. Showalter Company, operating a branch office in Texarkana, Texas. Baxter decided to merge with Stamps in March 1926 and moved to Chattanooga while Stamps remained in Texas. Frank Stamps moved to Chattanooga with his quartet and recorded for the Dixie Phonograph Company. In November of that year the V.O. Stamps School of Music expanded, holding a six-week session in Chattanooga that month and another session in January in Dallas.

Another major event in Southern Gospel occurred in 1926 when a young songwriter, Albert E. Brumley, born in 1905 in Spiro, Oklahoma (it was Indian Territory at the time) joined the Hartford Music Company. Brumley came to the school without enough money for tuition but was willing to work; soon, he was staying at Eugene Bartlett's home and helping out. In 1927 Brumley published his first song, "I Can Hear Them Singing Over There"; during the coming years he would become the most popular Southern Gospel writer of all time, penning such classics as "I'll Fly Away," "I'll Meet You in the Morning," and "Turn Your Radio On."

In 1927 V.O. Stamps' company was renamed The Stamps-Baxter Music Company, with Stamps continuing to operate out of the home office in Jacksonville, Texas while J.R. Baxter operated the branch office in Chattanooga. That same year the periodical *Stamps-Baxter News* began operations and the Frank Stamps Quartet made some recordings for Victor Records; Frank also hired pianist Dwight Brock as an accompanist. Prior to this, a quartet usually sang a cappella, although sometimes a member played piano. But the addition of the "fifth man" was a revolution in the quartet line-up. Another revolution was Brock's piano playing; he introduced the idea of what became known as the "turnaround," playing a short improvised solo between verses that added a "lift" to a song and gave the singers time to catch their breath for the next verse while keeping the audience entertained.

The Vaughan Recording Quartet also hired a piano player, Luther Heatwole, brother to bass singer F. Pierce Heatwole, in 1927; this group, comprised of Glenn Kieffer Vaughan (lead), Walter B. Seale (baritone), Claude Sharpe (tenor), and F. Pierce Heatwole (bass) performed on the Grand Ole Opry that year.

In 1927 Ralph Peer began doing field recording sessions for Victor Records; in August, he recorded the Carter Family and Jimmie Rodgers in Bristol, Tennessee. The Bristol sessions would mark the first recordings of these two acts and usher in a new era in country music, giving the field its first superstar, Jimmie Rodgers, and intro-

ducing a collection of songs that included "T for Texas," "Waiting
For a Train," "Peach Pickin' Time in Georgia," "Miss the Mississippi
and You," "Mother, the Queen of My Heart," and the "Blue Yodels"
all recorded by Rodgers, and "Wildwood Flower," "Jimmie Brown the
Newsboy," "Keep on the Sunny Side," "I'm Thinking Tonight of My
Blue Eyes," "Wabash Cannonball," "Worried Man Blues," and
numerous others recorded by the Carter Family.

In October 1927, two months after these historic recordings,
Peer recorded the Frank Stamps Quartet in Atlanta. The quartet,
comprised of Stamps, Odis Echols, Roy Wheeler, Palmer Wheeler
and Dwight Brock recorded "Bringing in the Sheaves," "Rescue the
Perishing," and "Give the World a Smile." The following year, the
Vaughan Recording Quartet made recordings for Victor.

The development of the microphone and the electrical recording
process led recording companies to leave New York and travel widely, doing "field recordings" of talent, particularly throughout the
South. During the early years of field recordings, from 1926 to 1930,
a number of gospel songs and performers were recorded. The dominant labels involved in field recording during the 1920s were Okeh,
Paramount, Brunswick, Vocalion, Victor, Gennett, and Columbia.
These recordings, which provided the beginnings of the country
music industry, were made primarily in Atlanta but also in Johnson
City, Tennessee, New Orleans, Dallas, and Memphis; the resulting
sales of these records were primarily in the South. Historian and
author Charles Wolfe has stated that Columbia's recordings from
1925 to 1931 were electrically recorded and released on the 15000-D
series. These recordings resulted in eleven million records containing
twenty-two million songs (one on each side of the record) released in
the South at a time when its population stood at just under 30 million. During these field sessions, over 300 different groups were
recorded but only six accounted for half the releases. One of those
six, the Smith Sacred Singers from north Georgia, was the top gospel
group.

The most successful quartet in the recording industry, the Smith
Sacred Singers, was not aligned to any publishing firm; in fact, it
could almost be considered an "accidental" quartet. Frank Smith was
a barber from Braselton, Georgia, who formed a quartet on WSB in
Atlanta on Sunday afternoons. In April 1926, Smith's Sacred Singers

had their first recording sessions for Columbia; during the next four years they would record 66 songs for the label. However, Smith did not want to become part of a publishing company enterprise, preferring to remain independent and sing old standards.

Gospel accounted for about 20 percent of the releases during this time, with the material consisting of "sacred harp material, quartet material, convention songs, and solos or duets of sacred material," according to Wolfe. The material included both pre-war and post-war material, some traditional songs as well as songs from the widely circulated paperback convention books.

Overall, the sales of gospel releases accounted for about 15 percent of the total sales from the Columbia 15000-D series. An "average" sale was 15,600 per record, with 15 records selling over 100,000 units each. However, the "smallest average sales" occurred with the gospel releases. An exception was the Smith Sacred Singer's record of "A Picture of Life's Other Side," which sold over 100,000 copies.

By the end of the 1920s two major firms, the James D. Vaughan Music Company and Stamps-Baxter, stood at the forefront of shaped-note publishing, though there were numerous other companies vying for business. Albert Brumley was in a quartet sponsored by the Hartford Music Company, which recorded "Victory in Jesus" and "Everybody Will Be Happy Over There," both written by Eugene Bartlett. The company had opened the Hartford Musical Institute, which held sessions in January and June, and published a monthly periodical, *The Herald of Song*.

V.O. Stamps formed a quartet called "The Old Original Quartet" that sang in the Dallas area, where he had relocated his headquarters in 1929. James D. Vaughan sponsored about 15 quartets, but sold his radio station, WOAN, to WREC in Memphis for $9,000. The radio station could never make money because of its non-commercial license. The following year Vaughan issued the final releases of the Vaughan Recording Quartet. Vaughan was growing older (he turned 66 in 1930) and had decided to stick to his shaped-note publishing business rather than expend energy in the fields of radio and recording. Also, Vaughan was more interested in the religious aspects of his company; he had expanded his school to five-month terms, added Bible instruction, and renamed it "The Vaughan Conservatory of Music and Bible Institute."

Chapter 17

BLACK GOSPEL DURING THE 1930s

During the 1930s there was a widening gap between mainline churches and the Holiness/Pentecostal denominations that were creating a new style, music, language, and behavior in their services. Further, the Holiness/Pentecostals were more interested in personal salvation—"heaven or hell" was their rallying cry—than in assimilation. Their services were filled with emotional ecstasy, with members giving dramatic testimonies, clapping their hands, stomping their feet, singing forcefully, and making music with drums, tambourines, guitars, pianos, or any other instruments they could find. The music was loud, rhythmic, and jubilant, and a song, accompanied by a "shouting session," could last half an hour or more. Women fainted and men jumped during these services; it was not uncommon for someone to be "slain in the spirit"—or "knocked out cold" for God—or for someone to be seen dancing in the aisle, oblivious to anything else.

A reserved sense of decorum, a withholding of emotion so as to present a dignified appearance, that was part of the mainline services was ejected from the Pentecostal service. The stoic demeanor was replaced with an emotional release that proclaimed joy, strength, and jubilation. The music of these services reflected this.

In 1927 Sallie Martin moved to Chicago from Pittfield, Georgia; she worked as a domestic and joined Thomas Dorsey's church where Dorsey taught her music by ear. Also in 1927 Theodore Frye moved from Fayette, Mississippi to Chicago and joined Dorsey's church. Frye was known as a singer who could "move a house"—get an audience emotionally involved in his song—and he influenced Dorsey, who played piano for him.

Mahalia Jackson was born in 1911 and moved to Chicago in 1927 after quitting school. Soon she was singing with the Greater Salem Baptist Church choir, often doing the lead vocal. She supported herself as a domestic, doing laundry and serving as a maid. She joined the Johnson Gospel Singers, organized by Robert Johnson, son of the pastor of the church that she attended. Along with Robert's brothers, Prince and Wilbur, and Louise Barry Lemon, the five-member group became professional—one of the first in black gospel—earning their living with gospel music. According to black gospel historian Tony Heilbut, their style was "advanced and free" and Johnson played a "distinctive boogie-woogie piano geared to the Dorsey bounce." They also performed a series of plays Robert wrote, with Mahalia and Robert usually singing lead in these church dramas. During the early 1930s the group played a number of local churches, but by the end of the decade the group had split and each member was singing solo.

Thomas Dorsey first heard Mahalia sing around 1928, during the time she was with Johnson's group. The group was thrown out of one church by a pastor who told them, "Get that twisting and jazz out of the church." Mahalia was a "shouter" and, according to Dorsey, she originally approached him wanting him to be her vocal coach. She also wanted to sing some of Dorsey's songs. Dorsey spent about two months teaching her his songs and training her to sing them; he also worked on her timing and performance.

One of the keys to Dorsey's success was finding key collaborators, and he found his best in Sallie Martin, Roberta Martin (no relation), and Mahalia Jackson. In 1932 Dorsey organized a gospel choir at the Pilgrim Baptist Church in Chicago; Roberta Martin was his first choir director and Sallie Martin was a principal soloist who also became a business partner. In 1932 Sallie Martin organized Dorsey's publishing business and made it profitable; until that time, Dorsey was a disorganized businessman who kept few records. Mahalia Jackson sang at Dorsey's church when she wasn't on the road performing concerts.

Thomas Dorsey toured throughout America between 1932 and 1944, performing concerts of the new gospel music he called "Evenings with Dorsey." The singers included Sallie Martin, Mahalia Jackson, Roberta Martin, Theodore Frye, and others he had trained.

Admission was nominal and sheet music was sold at the concerts for a nickel a song. It proved to be an effective way of building a publishing company as well as of promoting the songs, for he also left copies at churches for others to perform wherever he went. In many ways, this sense and knack for self-promotion was as great a gift as the songs themselves.

Dorsey was helped by finding Sallie Martin, who, in addition to being a great singer, helped him organize his publishing business. Dorsey was a teacher as well as a choir director; he studied each singer and worked to improve her strengths. These personal appearances were the key factor in Dorsey's songs becoming known in the church world.

Also key in the development of Thomas Dorsey into the "Father of Black Gospel" was his formation, in 1933, of the National Convention of Gospel Choirs and Choruses. Along with several associates, Dorsey held these conventions in various cities, attracting choirs and soloists he instructed. They also learned his songs. The National Baptist Convention was another key for Dorsey; this annual convention drew thousands of black Baptists from all over the country. In 1935 his song "Take My Hand, Precious Lord" was sung four times; it was the first step toward this song becoming a gospel standard.

"Take My Hand, Precious Lord" came after a particularly traumatic time in Dorsey's life. He stated that: "This song is very dear to me. I left my home one morning with another fellow driving to St. Louis to sing in a revival at a Baptist church. My wife was going to become a mother in a few days. We got 24 miles outside of Chicago, and I discovered I had left my briefcase with all my music in it. I turned around, drove back to Chicago and went home. My wife was sleeping, and I didn't disturb her. When I got back in the car, the other fellow said he had changed his mind and decided not to go. As it was, Providence was trying to tell me not to go away. But I went on to St. Louis anyway. Next night, I was working in a revival, and I received a telegram: 'Your wife just died. Come home.' Some fellows volunteered to drive me to Chicago, and when I got home the next day, I had the body moved. I had a bouncing boy baby. But that night, the baby died. That was double trouble. I felt like going back on God. He had mistreated me, I felt. About a week later, after we had put the baby and the wife away in the same casket, I was sitting with Theodore Frye, just drowsing. Just like water dropping from the crevice of a rock, the words dropped into the music, 'Take My Hand, Precious Lord.'"

Actually, Dorsey was playing an old hymn, "Must Jesus Bear the Cross Alone"—noodling on the piano, really—when the "feel" of "Precious Lord" came to him. He originally began with "Take my hand, blessed Lord" but after playing it for Frye, the preacher insisted Dorsey change the lyric to "precious Lord."

Dorsey said of "Peace in the Valley," "It was just before Hitler sent his war chariots into Western Europe in the late thirties. I was on a train going through southern Indiana on the way to Cincinnati, and the country seemed to be upset about this coming that he was about to bring on. I passed through a valley on the train. Horses, cows, sheep, they were all grazing and together in this little valley. Kind of a little brook was running through the valley, and up the hill there I could see where the water was falling from. Everything seemed so peaceful with all the animals down there grazing together. It made me wonder what's the matter with humanity? What's the matter with mankind? Why couldn't man live in peace like the animals down there? So out of that came 'Peace in the Valley.'"

Other songs Dorsey wrote include "I Surely Know There's Been a Change in Me," "It's My Desire" (popularized by Guy Lombardo), "When I've Done the Best I Can," "How Many Times," "I'm Gonna Live the Life I Sing About in My Song," "Singing in My Soul," "Life Can Be Beautiful," and "The Lord Will Make a Way."

Throughout the 1930s Mahalia Jackson sang at Dorsey's church; Dorsey accepted her as a gospel singer and gave her a "gospel home" whenever she was in Chicago. Throughout her career, a number of people wanted Mahalia to use her rich and powerful vocal talents to sing music other than gospel. The first of these was her first husband, Isaac Hackenhull, whom she married in 1936. Hackenhull wanted her to sing classic pop songs and jazz and Mahalia made some attempts; however, the church was embedded in her too deeply. Wracked by guilt, she abandoned this music after only a few attempts and returned to gospel, where she was clearly most comfortable musically, spiritually, and emotionally.

Always a good businesswoman, Mahalia opened a beauty salon

and then a florist shop, and both succeeded for a short time. Like a number of other gospel pioneers who survived in the field, it was her business acumen which was as much a key to her success as her talent. She was not the only one—Thomas Dorsey, Sallie Martin, and Sam Cooke also made smart business moves which assured them successful musical careers throughout their lifetimes.

Mahalia's first recording was "God's Gonna Separate the Wheat from the Tares" in 1937 b/w "Keep Me Every Day." The first song was one Mahalia had adapted from the wakes she had attended as a child in New Orleans, and the second an old Baptist hymn. This first record brought her national recognition and made her name equal to that of the other great soloists in Chicago during that time: Willie Mae Ford Smith, Sallie Martin, Madame Lula Mae Hurst, Mary Johnson Davies, Roberta Martin, and Louise Lemon. It was a rich time for female soloists and Mahalia was just one of a number, but her strong southern influence, which manifested itself in the moaning, growling, strutting, and skipping during stage performances, soon caused her talent to be in front of all the rest.

Black gospel was also heard on the radio during the 1930s. In 1930 the Southernaires, a group formed the year before in New York City, began singing over WMCA and WRNY; in 1933 they were on an NBC network program, "The Little Weather-Beaten Whitewashed Church," which lasted a decade. The group also recorded for Decca Records.

A number of black gospel quartets were formed during the 1930s. The Dixie Hummingbirds was formed in Greenville, South Carolina by James Davis. The group, comprised of Davis (tenor), Barney Gipson (lead), Barney Parks (baritone), and Fred Owens (bass), traveled throughout the South performing at churches.

The Soul Stirrers was formed in Trinity, Texas in 1934; bass singer Jesse Farley joined in 1935. Almost from the very beginning, the Soul Stirrers stood apart from most other quartets, who sang spirituals and jubilee songs, by singing newer "gospel" or original compositions. They also were innovative in their use of lead singers, employing two and bringing the lead vocalist out front. Through Rebert Harris, their first lead singer, they virtually created the gospel quartet tradition. Among Harris's innovations were the technique of ad-libbing within a song and singing delayed time—off the regular meter from the rest of the lyrics. The group was among the first traveling quartets who were full-time performers and their early success with concerts caused many other quartets to adapt the newer "gospel" songs instead of the more traditional spiritual and jubilee songs.

According to Harold Boyer in his book *How Sweet the Sound*, four different types of songs emerged for quartets. The "sentimentals" or "gospel ballads" had a moderate to slow tempo; the "minors" or "Baptist lining hymns" had a slow tempo and used minor, diminished and augmented chords, known as "off chords." The "Jubilees" had a moderate to fast tempo and the "Chop Jubilees" or "shout songs" had a rapid tempo with a "short vocal phrasing, chopped, staccato-like attack" on the song's lyrics.

Another important, influential performer was Sister Rosetta Tharpe, born Rosetta Nubin in Cotton Plant, Arkansas. Daughter of a mother who traveled from church to church as a "missionary" (women could not be evangelists or preachers), "Little Rosetta Nubin, the singing and guitar-playing miracle" was a child prodigy. She was unique because she played the guitar instead of the piano; she and her mother joined evangelist P.W. McGhee and settled in Chicago during the 1920s, then moved to New York and settled in Harlem in 1934. Rosetta married Wilbur Tharpe and, though the marriage did not last, kept his name throughout her life.

In 1937 the Golden Gate Quartet began recording for Victor. Inspired by the Mills Brothers, with their smooth vocal sound, the group did "Jonah" in that first session. On December 23, 1938 John Hammond presented his first "From Spirituals to Swing" concert at Carnegie Hall. Included in that concert were the Golden Gate Quartet, the Mitchell Christian Singers, and Sister Rosetta Tharpe. Although numerous jazz historians have cited this event as pivotal to demonstrating the importance of African-Americans in jazz, it was equally important for black gospel, showcasing this music to an audience who had never heard it, or heard very little.

Tharpe began recording for Decca in October 1938 but the label would not allow her to sing with just her guitar. Instead, they put her with the full Lucky Millinder jazz orchestra and she did "Rock Me," "That's All," "My Man and I," and "Lonesome Road."

Although black gospel singers traveled during the 1930s and 1940s, most disliked doing so. In the South there were segregated restaurants, hotels and businesses—most black-owned restaurants did not open before 6 p.m. or so because the owner generally had a day job. The groups could always find a meal and a place to stay in someone's home, and the church groups could count on a collection from the congregation to help them out. But the quartets were stranded if the promoter would not pay—they generally survived from concert to concert.

Although African-Americans had written and performed in hit musicals on Broadway from the 1920s, with *Shuffle Along, Blackbirds, Hot Chocolates,* and *Runnin' Wild*, which introduced the "Charleston" to America, there wasn't much black gospel on Broadway. In 1933 *Run, Little Chillun* used old spirituals and folk songs but it wasn't until 1937 when *Heaven Bound* was produced that original black gospel songs were used. In 1941 *From Auction Block to Glory*, written by Memphis minister W. Herbert Brewster, came to Broadway. Also during the 1930s Paul Robeson did operatic versions of Negro spirituals for white audiences in New York.

The 1930s were a difficult time in the United States especially for blacks, whose unemployment rates for men reached 75 percent in many areas. Because there was less money to buy recordings, fewer recordings were produced. And there was very little music from blacks on radio, which was dominated by the Big Bands. When Prohibition ended in 1933, "blues" could be heard on jukeboxes in dives; but that was no place for black gospel. The saving grace was the church, and here black gospel grew and developed, aided by the Pentecostal/Holiness movement. Here is where black gospel found the "voice" which would define the music throughout the rest of the 20th century.

Unlike many other forms of gospel music, black gospel has a distinctive, identifiable sound. Thomas Dorsey was a leader in introducing jazz rhythms and blues singing in the church, adding gospel lyrics to the blues tradition. According to Mahalia Jackson, "The basic thing is soul feeling ... gospel music ... is soul music. When they talk about jazz, the Holiness people had it before it came in. They would take a song like 'What a Friend We Have in Jesus' and give it personal expression. They gave it a joyful expression ... expressed by things they couldn't speak. Some called it gospel music for years but it did not come into its own until way late ... when the Holiness people helped to emphasize the beat."

The emotional impact of black gospel came from the Holiness Church and from Southern singers, who moved North. There, they found the opportunity to connect with a large African-American community. Although the mainstream churches in this community originally rejected the Holiness sound, in time they would embrace it as "black gospel" developed its own unique sound, rooted in the black experience in the United States, which came from a deep-felt emotionalism anchored in a certain hopelessness about their earthly life balanced by a shining hopefulness about the Heavenly life to come.

Chapter 18

SOUTHERN GOSPEL MUSIC DURING THE DEPRESSION

During the 1930s the Stamps-Baxter Company in Dallas emerged as the top shaped-note publisher, eclipsing the James D. Vaughan Company. These were not the only companies publishing shaped-note books; others included the Teachers' Music Publishing Company in Hudson, North Carolina; the Morris-Henson Company in Atlanta; Athens Music Company in Athens, Alabama; the Benson Company in Nashville; the Trio Music Company in Waco, Texas; the Central Music Company of Little Rock, Arkansas; and the Tennessee Music and Printing Company in Cleveland, Tennessee. These companies sponsored singing schools; the personal relationships that developed between teachers, students and company representatives led to loyalties to a particular company. Quartets aligned with these companies were not allowed to sing songs published by their competitors; they were required to sing only songs published by their sponsor.

But there were changes on the horizon, primarily because of radio. As the quartets, which had depended on an affiliation with a shaped-note publisher, obtained radio shows, they reached larger audiences, which increased the demand for personal appearances. Also, as they played on the radio, they obtained recording contracts and the records carried their music even further. The advent of radio also meant that people could be entertained in their homes by professionals—they did not have to depend on going to a singing convention, church, or concert to hear music. They didn't need to learn to play or sing to have music around, and this led to a decline in the demand for songbooks.

The Southern Gospel quartets had a major advantage over their counterparts in black gospel because radio welcomed white performers but not black ones. Hence, a good white country or gospel singing group could obtain a regular broadcast while a black gospel quartet could not. Black gospel quartets had to depend on recordings—which declined during the Depression—and personal appearances. For rural audiences as well as music performers in country or southern gospel music, radio was the dominant medium during the 1930s.

At the same time, the recordings of black gospel quartets were heard by Southern white gospel groups, who began to learn and use their songs. The influence worked both ways—black gospel quartets heard southern quartets on the radio and learned some of their songs.

There was a conflict between rural and urban audiences that developed during the 1930s. The music that came from urban areas—particularly jazz and rhythm and blues—was deemed "dirty" by the rural audiences, who extolled the virtues of rural living and insisted on "good, clean family entertainment." This split between the sacred and the secular did not affect country and gospel music at this time; most country performers did gospel songs and most gospel groups included some country or "folk" songs in their repertoire.

There was resistance within the church world toward gospel music. Many ministers saw the traveling quartets as a threat and criticized the lack of spiritual depth in the songs and performances. Those who take religion seriously tend to demand a serious religion; increasingly the gospel quartets put on a good show, which angered religious conservatives. New musical forms such as jazz were also threatening to those who liked "traditional" sounds. Finally, radio was deemed an enemy because, the argument went, entertainment led the serious-minded Christian astray.

Those in gospel music countered that singing gospel music was just as pleasing to God as preaching and prayer. Further, they argued they were promoting the gospel—not disparaging it. And, the argument continued, radio and records were another way to reach "the lost," who would not otherwise go into a church.

The performers in both country and southern gospel shared a rural heritage and a common motive for wanting to sing: it was a way off the farm and away from the southern agricultural life that was difficult, demanding, and unpredictable. Performers were widely respected, and many young farm boys and girls dreamed of the day when they could sing for a living, rather than walk rows with a hoe, chopping weeds.

The difference between country and gospel was that country performers could charge admission for their concerts while gospel groups could not. The church frowned on "entertainment," and "paid concerts" were part of that world. Gospel acts had to depend on "free will" offerings wherever they sang, taking up a collection, hoping there was enough money in the hat at the end of the evening to pay their way to the next church. This was difficult during the hard times of the Depression when audiences didn't have much money in their pockets. These hard times also affected the gospel music publishers, whose audience often could not afford songbooks.

A number of important gospel groups formed during the 1930s. The Speer Family joined the Vaughan organization, while the Blackwood Brothers were affiliated with Stamps-Baxter. The LeFevre brothers, Urias and Alphus, from Smithville, Tennessee, sang as a trio with their sister, Maude; later another sister, Peggy, replaced Maude. After singing with the Homeland Harmony Singers, Urias married Eva Mae Whittington and she joined the trio. This trio sang on WGST in Atlanta and in evangelistic meetings.

In 1931 Otis Leon McCoy, a former employee of James D. Vaughan, began the Tennessee Music and Printing Company in Cleveland, Tennessee, an affiliate of the Church of God in Cleveland. McCoy formed the Homeland Harmony Quartet from the church's Bible Training School. Those who performed in the quartet included the LeFevre brothers, Urias and Alphus, Aycel Soward, Fred C. Maples, Connor B. Hall and songwriter Vep Ellis.

The Chuck Wagon Gang got their start on a 15-minute daily radio program on KFYO in Lubbock, Texas in 1935. Dave Carter, born in Milltown, Kentucky in 1889, had moved with his family to north-central Texas; he married in 1909 after meeting his future wife at a singing school in Clay County, Texas. Carter got a job on the railroad and worked in Missouri and Oklahoma where, in 1927, he was hurt in a railroad accident and could no longer work. The railroad would not pay him for the disability, so the family moved back to

Texas where the couple sang wherever and whenever they could—some gospel but mostly country music. When one of his children got sick, Carter, out of desperation for money, walked into radio station KYFO and asked for a job singing on the air; surprisingly, he got it as well as an advance of some money for medicine for his sick child.

In 1936 Carter landed a job on Fort Worth's WBAP on a show sponsored by Morton Salt. The family group sang mostly western tunes on a morning program, "The Roundup." But Bewley Flour Mills sponsored a group, The Chuck Wagon Gang, on a program. The Chuck Wagon Gang traveled to local towns and sang, demonstrating the flour by cooking biscuits during their appearances. Since this group wanted to continue to travel, and couldn't make it back to the radio station each day for their on-air program, another group was needed. Dave Carter agreed to do the radio program, and changed the name of his family group to "The Chuck Wagon Gang." For the next 15 years, they would play on this program, heard over the Texas Quality Radio Network all over the state, and become one of the most popular groups on southern radio stations. Although they began singing western and folk songs, with one gospel number per program, they eventually switched over to all-gospel.

In November 1936 the Chuck Wagon Gang made their first recordings for Columbia in San Antonio; the following year they recorded in Dallas. Although they originally recorded a mixture of secular and sacred songs, by April 1940 they were recording only gospel.

The Texas Centennial Celebration was held in 1936 and out of this event came a gospel group, the Texas Rangers Quartet. Comprised of Vernon Hyles (guitar & lead), his brother Arnold Hyles (bass), Walter Leverett (baritone), and George Hughes (tenor), the group moved to Louisville, Kentucky in late 1936 where they landed a job on WHAS. In 1939 the group moved to WBT in Charlotte, North Carolina, where they also performed on CBS's Dixie Network.

The Swanee River Boys were formed in Chattanooga in 1939. Affiliated with the Vaughan company, they sang on WNOX in Knoxville in the late 30s. In 1941 they moved to Atlanta, where they appeared on the WSB Barn Dance. The John Daniel quartet was formed in 1940, consisting of Wally Fowler (baritone), "Big Jim"

Waits (bass), and the brothers John and Troy Daniel. The Sunshine Boys began in 1939 as a country group on WMAZ in Macon, Georgia; in 1941 they moved to Atlanta where they performed on WAGA.

The V.O. Stamps Quartet performed on KRLD in Dallas, opening each program with their theme song, "Give the World a Smile Each Day." They also sent transcriptions to XERL in Del Rio, Texas. This station, which operated just across the border in Mexico, had no restrictions on their power—the Federal Communications Commission had no jurisdiction over Mexican radio stations. And so the station blasted 500,000 watts across the United States. The result was that Stamps-Baxter's 15-minute programs were heard several times a day and night, increasing their popularity.

In 1938 V.O. Stamps promoted his first "All-Night Singing" in Dallas at the State Fair Grounds; it was broadcast live over KRLD. These "All-Night Sings" would become increasingly popular after World War II.

By the mid-1930s, the groups affiliated with Vaughan were the Vaughan Office Quartet, the Speer Family, the Vaughan-Daniel Quartet, the Oliver Jennings Family, Vaughan's Sand Mountain Quartet (with Erman Slater), the Vaughan Melody Girls, the Vaughan Victory Four, and the LeFevre Trio. In 1935 Vaughan closed down his recording label, and the groups who'd recorded with him moved on to other labels. Also, these groups increasingly found outlets on radio stations throughout the South, often on 15-minute programs in the morning.

Groups associated with Stamps-Baxter at the end of the 1930s included Virgil Stamps Original Quartet, Frank Stamps' All-Stars, W.T. "Deacon" Utley's Smile-A-While Quartet, the Daniel Stamps-Baxter Quartet, the Deep South Quartet, the Blackwood Brothers, and the Herschel Foshee and Stamps-Baxter Melody Boys. Each of these groups sang regularly on a radio station.

In the summer of 1941, just before the United States became involved in World War II, over 500 students attended the Stamps-Baxter school in Dallas. Clearly, young men still saw these singing schools, and the music publishers, as an important step towards entering the field of gospel music. But World War II would change a great many things in America. The changes in Southern Gospel music were already in the wind as the first generation of southern quartets, who needed an affiliation with a publishing firm during the 1920s and 1930s, became celebrities on radio and recordings. This marked a transition in southern gospel music from being part of the publishing industry to standing as an industry of its own.

On August 19, 1940, Virgil Stamps died in Dallas; less than six months later, on February 9, 1941, James D. Vaughan died in Lawrenceburg, Tennessee. The deaths of these two publishing giants marked the end of the first era of southern gospel music. The American involvement in World War II would also halt the development of this industry, which would emerge after the war into its Golden Era.

Chapter 19

GOSPEL IN THE MAINSTREAM AFTER WORLD WAR II

George Beverly Shea and Billy Graham

At the beginning of World War II, the Great Depression was still with America. The unemployment rate in 1939 was 17 percent—down from 25 percent in 1933, but still considerable. The jobless rate in 1943 was 1.7 percent. Those employed included the 12 million men—or about 75 percent of those born between 1918 and 1927—in the military. By the end of the War, 16.3 million Americans had served in the military.

War-time employment peaked at about 60 million, with about a third of the work force comprised of women. In 1940 the average worker earned less than $1,000 a year and only 7.8 million Americans made enough money to pay taxes; by 1945 the population had risen to 140 million and 50 million of those made enough to pay taxes.

Prior to the war Americans were united in entertainment, especially the movies and radio. Musically, the radio was dominated by the networks (CBS, NBC—which had two networks—and Mutual). The most popular music was Big Band groups led by Benny Goodman, the Dorsey Brothers, Duke Ellington, Harry James, Glenn Miller, and others. Popular soloists included Bing Crosby, Frank Sinatra, Perry Como, Patti Page, and Jo Stafford.

Although country music had become a national music through the Singing Cowboys movies, with Roy Rogers, Gene Autry, Tex Ritter, the Sons of the Pioneers, and others developing a national following, the country music from the South was known as "hillbilly" music and was mostly confined to the South. "Blues" music was not recorded a great deal from the beginning of the Great Depression until World War II (blacks were hit hardest by the Depression and couldn't afford to buy records). During the war a new sound, known as rhythm and blues, was increasingly heard.

The government began to build 37,000 new miles of highways in 1947; in 1956, with the passage of the Interstate Highway Act, there was an additional 42,500 miles built—90 percent financed by the government. Although the original intention of the interstate system was national defense—allowing the Armed Forces to move men and equipment across the country quickly—the interstates soon became commuter roads serving the suburbs.

William J. Levitt created the idea of mass production in housing with his planned suburb, Levittown, in Long Island. In 1944 there had been only 114,000 new single houses started; by 1946 that number was 937,000, then 1,118,000 in 1948 and 1.7 million in 1950. In 1947, five million Americans shared housing, usually with parents, in-laws, siblings, uncles and aunts. This obviously created tension, which the growth of the suburbs strove to alleviate by providing many with the "American Dream"—a single-family home and a car in the suburbs.

The growth in housing led to a boom in consumer spending for household goods; food spending rose by 33 percent in the five years following World War II, clothing expenditures rose by 20 percent, and purchases of household furnishings and appliances combined soared by 240 percent.

Between 1950 and 1980, 18 of the top 25 cities in the United States lost population while the suburbs gained 60 million; about 83 percent of the nation's growth took place in the suburbs. By 1955, the Levitt-type subdivision accounted for three-fourths of all new housing starts.

Federal GI benefits were available to 40 percent of the male population between the ages of 20-24 which permitted a whole generation of men to expand their education and improve their job prospects without foregoing marriage and children.

The government underwrote the real estate industry by insuring private, home ownership lenders, lending directly to long-term buyers, subsidizing the extension of electricity to new residential areas, and building highways to the suburbs.

Before World War II, banks required a 50 percent down payment on homes, and limited mortgages to 5-10 years. After World War II, through the Federal Housing Administration and the Veterans Housing Administration, policies required only 5-10 percent down for a home purchase and guaranteed mortgages of up to 30 years, with interest rates of 2-3 percent that guaranteed protection against inflation. The Veterans Administration asked for only $1 down from veterans. Almost half of all housing in suburbia depended on federal financing.

But there was a catch to most of these loans: you had to buy a new house; entire sections in cities were declared ineligible for loans. Thus the government's programs encouraged housing construction and ownership in the suburbs, which caused the country to become a nation of suburbs over the next 50 years. The cities were left to those who could not afford to move or who were denied access to loans; increasingly this meant poor blacks were left in the inner cities while whites moved to the suburbs. Blacks, in fact, did not have much choice—the new suburban developments specifically denied any blacks the right to buy homes and become part of the community. This was done in order to encourage white buyers.

The post-war generation was united by their experiences in World War II, a war that was popular at home and which united the country in a single cause like it had never been united before. For this generation, patriotism and manhood were defined by a willingness to join the armed services. The support they received at home while they were away and again when they returned would define their view of the world for years to come. It also taught them how to manage large undertakings, and the value of teamwork.

In addition to a popular war that united the country, this group of young American men had other advantages past and future generations would not have. During the 1920s there was an anti-immigration movement that culminated in a series of acts that severely restricted immigration into the United States. From 1924 until after the war, this limit on immigration caused the work force to be mostly restricted to those born in the country. Further, the birth rate during the 1930s during the Great Depression was the lowest of any time in the history of the nation; thus this generation of men came of age when the competition for jobs was extremely limited. Accepted discriminatory practices against women and blacks further enhanced the position of the white male, who was living in a booming economy that demanded skilled workers in which to grow and thrive.

The GI Bill made a college education available to any veteran who wanted one. This led to a highly educated work force at the management level after the war, a decided advantage in an economy that would shift from being a blue collar industrial and manufacturing economy to a white-collar information-based economy during the following 50 years.

During World War II about eight million women entered the work force in large numbers because male workers were overseas fighting and "Rosie the Riveter" was born. But after the war the majority of these women were replaced by men as soon as the servicemen came back home; about 800,000 women were fired from jobs in the aircraft industry within two months after the end of World War II and within two years, two million women had lost their jobs.

During the 1930s, 26 of the 48 states prohibited hiring married women and in all the states, 43 percent of public utilities, 13 percent of department stores, and over half of the public schools had rules against hiring married women. World War II changed that—but old habits died hard. Although many women yearned for a home and family after World War II, they did not want to be denied the opportunity to work. Also, the move to the suburbs tended to separate women from the workplace.

The media, especially magazines such as *Ladies' Home Journal*, *Redbook*, *McCall's*, and *Mademoiselle*, defined the feminine woman as one who did not work; instead, she was devoted to her family, supported her husband, kept her house spotless, got dinner ready on time, and remained attractive and optimistic. The husband was the leader and hero, out there braving the treacherous corporate world each day to win a better life for his family. The wife was his domestic mainstay.

Post-World War II women provided a commitment and stability that was important to the growing society and economy of this period. For the organization men this meant free child care and a home life that was taken care of so they could pursue a career full force, which they did with dedication and zeal. This was augmented by a business culture that virtually guaranteed lifetime employment for loyal employees with the promise that things would get better every year. This generation grew up with pessimism, nurtured by the Great Depression, so they were cautious and learned optimism slowly. The following generations were born with an optimism that things would always get better and learned a pessimism as they grew older. This became an essential difference in the World War II generation and those born later.

As some have noted, the "self-made" men whose "rugged individualism" shaped the country after World War II needed the federal government and a "true" woman to accomplish all they did.

The business climate could not have been better after World War II. The sensitivity to the environment or concern about energy was not there; there was no thought (and generally no knowledge) about the harmful effects of pollution. Auto and gas manufacturers thought of new ways to sell big cars with no concern for the price of gas because it was so cheap.

The mainline churches were at their peak in membership and influence in society after World War II. But the membership in mainline churches began to decline during the 1960s while membership began to increase in evangelical denominations and individual religious groups. Actually, membership in all churches increased up until the 1960s, but the cultural shift during that period led many people away from traditional social institutions.

The conservative theology espoused after World War II tended to affirm traditional American culture, especially the values of patriotism, free enterprise and the validity of financial rewards. Although mainline churches have usually been identified as a culture-affirming religious tradition, during the period immediately after World War II, the evangelistic and fundamentalist movements also embraced American culture while at the same time preaching a radical transformation for the individuals in this culture.

For Christianity and gospel music, George Beverly Shea and Billy Graham are the prime examples of an evangelical Christianity with mainstream appeal after World War II. Previously, the evangelicals and fundamentalists were on the fringes of American religion; Shea and Graham put it in the mainstream.

Singers who have appeared on evangelistic crusades with famous evangelists—like Rodeheaver and Sankey—had been major "stars" in their own right. They brought the church to the public arena and, with their singing, put the crowd in the right spirit because they were great soloists, great song leaders who delivered songs of faith to audiences comprised of both believers and non-believers. But George Beverly Shea became the first international singing "star" of the gospel world. He achieved this position from his solos on the Billy Graham Crusades and his exposure on television, radio, and records. His songs, delivered with reserved emotion, a controlled passion, have been assimilated into hymnals and choir books. Musically, he was not a trailblazer, but he achieved his fame and position of respect by providing audiences with messages carefully encased in the tradition of Protestant Christianity in America.

The son of a minister, George Beverly Shea was born February 1, 1909, the fourth of eight children. He spent his teenage years in Ottawa, Canada and sang with a quartet at Houghton College, which he attended briefly before having to drop out because of lack of money during the Depression. He moved to New York with his family in 1936 when his father was offered the pastorate at the First Wesleyan Methodist Church in Jersey City, across the Hudson River from Manhattan.

Shea obtained a job as a medical secretary with the Mutual Life Insurance Company, where he worked for nine years. But he also had his foot in the door of a singing career at this time, doing 30-minute programs from 7-7:30 a.m. on WKBO in Jersey City, singing on Erling C. Olsen's program "Meditations in the Psalms" on WMCA, and taking voice lessons after work.

During his years with the life insurance company, Shea sang at weddings, in church, during tent meetings, on radio, and wherever else he could. He also wrote the music to "I'd Rather Have Jesus" from the poem by Mrs. Rhea Miller and began singing this in services. His first recording was for Decca after talking with A & R man Jack Kapp, who offered him the proposition that "If you do better than the singer we have in mind, we will give you a contract. If not, you'll have to take the records on yourself." He recorded "Jesus Whispers Peace," "Lead Me Gently Home, Father," "I'd Rather Have Jesus," and "God Understands," accompanied by Mrs. Percy (Ruth) Crawford on organ. Initially 500 records were pressed and eventually 7,000 were sold.

Shea's major break came when Dr. Will Houghton, president of

Moody Bible Institute of Chicago, offered him a job with the radio station at the school. Shea sang each week on Houghton's program, "Let's Go Back To the Bible" on WMBI, and in 1939 became a staff announcer with duties that included emceeing, interviewing, newscasting, continuity writing, programming, administration, auditioning, and singing.

Billy Graham was a student at nearby Wheaton College, and one day he stopped by the station and told Shea how much he enjoyed hearing him sing on the program "Hymns From the Chapel" each morning at 8:15. This relationship would prove valuable in the future as Graham would become the major figure in American religion in the 1950s, but for now Shea continued doing weekend concerts around the Chicago area.

In 1942 Shea took a leave of absence to join Jack Wyrtzen for a summer of crusades in the New York area. He spent this summer traveling throughout New Jersey, New York, and Connecticut, singing at youth rallies while also singing on WHN on Sunday mornings. When Shea returned to Chicago in September, he talked with Torrey Johnson about conducting youth meetings in that area and soon "Chicagoland Youth For Christ" was held in Orchestra Hall on Michigan Avenue with Shea singing and young Billy Graham speaking. From that initial concert came the "Youth For Christ International" organization which Torrey Johnson was to head.

Shea resigned from WMBI in 1944 to accept a position with "Club Time," a 15-minute radio program broadcast weekdays sponsored by Club Aluminum over WCFL. "Club Time," which initially had only a 13-week contract, continued to be renewed and was eventually put on the ABC network, where it began in September 1945 and lasted seven years. Shea's job was to host the program and sing several songs, including the favorite hymn of various famous people. It was on "Club Time" that Beverly Shea became George Beverly Shea at the insistence of the advertising agency; it seems they felt most listeners were confused by a man named "Beverly."

When Billy Graham, then a young pastor at The Village Church in Western Springs, Illinois, took over the WCFL program, "Songs in the Night," from Torrey Johnson in 1944, he persuaded Shea to sing on the program. This led to a lifelong friendship and working relationship that was interrupted temporarily by World War II. Graham joined the Army for a year before being released (he contracted a severe case of mumps), while Shea continued to sing on "Songs in the Night" and "Club Time." After Graham was discharged from the Army, the young preacher began preaching for "Youth for Christ" and traveled to Great Britain, where he held meetings for six months.

When Graham returned to the States, he contacted Shea about singing for some gospel meetings in Charlotte, North Carolina, which became the unofficial launching of his Crusades. The year was 1948 and Billy Graham had to overcome a number of obstacles, mostly owing to the bad reputations of itinerant evangelists who had attempted to replicate the success of Billy Sunday in the 1920s and 1930s. His big break came in September 1949, when the troupe brought their "city-wide" campaign to Los Angeles and received international coverage from the Hearst newspapers. The conversion of some celebrities, chief among whom was Stuart Hamblen, a popular radio entertainer who later wrote "It Is No Secret" and a number of other gospel classics, as well as 1936 Olympic star Louis Zamperini and underworld figure Jim Vaus, also helped propel Graham's career.

In 1951 Shea signed with RCA, where he would enjoy major recording success in the 1950s. The first session was produced by Stephen H. Sholes and featured Shea backed by the Hugo Winterhalter Orchestra on an album titled *Inspirational Songs*. Among the songs included on this first RCA album were "Ivory Palaces," "Known Only to Him," "Tenderly He Watches," "If You Know The Lord," and "It Is No Secret."

During Shea's first four years with RCA, his records did not sell enough copies to pay for the costs of recording and pressing. Still, the label believed in him and continued to release recordings, produced first by Sholes and later by Brad McCuen and Darol Rice.

Shea was the beneficiary of a big break received by Billy Graham when Henry Luce featured the evangelist in *Life*, which led to a White House visit with Harry Truman. The "Hour of Decision" radio broadcasts began on December 5, 1950 from Atlanta with the first program broadcast over 150 stations. By the fifth week, it had the largest audience of any religious program in history. By 1952 Shea was singing regularly on "The Hour of Decision" broadcasts (many of his performances were taped) and "Club Time," both national weekly broadcasts, as well as on "Songs in the Night," also a weekly show broadcast over WCFL in Chicago. But in that year "Club Time" ended and Shea turned over his duties on "Songs in the Night" to Glen Jordan, after eight years on the program, to devote all his energies to the Billy Graham Evangelistic Association (BGEA).

During his first Crusade abroad in 1954, Shea found a song which would be linked with him throughout his career—and the success of both men would owe a great deal to this connection. The song was "How Great Thou Art."

The sheet music was given to Shea by George Gray, who worked with the publishing firm of Pikering and Inglis, Ltd. after a chance encounter between the two men on Oxford Street in London. Several months after his return to the United States, Shea was going through his notes and found the leaflet and sang it to himself. He liked the song, as did Cliff Barrows, music director for Graham, who had also received a copy. Shea performed it first on the Toronto Crusade in 1955 at the Maple Leaf Garden and the song had an immediate impact.

The song was originally written in 1885 or 1886 in Sweden by Reverend Carl Robert and titled "O Store Gud" (O Great God). Robert was a preacher and religious editor who died never knowing the impact the song would have on the world. The first translation from Swedish to German had been done in 1907 by Manfred von Glehn and it had been translated into Russian in 1912 by Reverend Ivan S. Prokhanoff. It was included in a book of Prokhanoff's hymns published in 1922 (in Russian) by the American Bible Society as well as in a second book of hymns, published five years later. This second book came into the possession of Mr. and Mrs. Stuart K. Hine, a missionary couple who used the song in their work in the Ukraine. Hine translated the first three verses into English and added a fourth stanza in 1948; this was printed in a Russian gospel magazine published by Hine in 1949. Other missionaries saw the song and requested copies, so Hine had some leaflets printed; it was one of these leaflets which Shea received from Gray in 1954.

"How Great Thou Art" became a standard during the 1957 Crusade in Madison Square Garden, where Shea performed it with the choir 99 times during the 16-week Crusade. The average attendance for this Crusade was 19,000 per night and it resulted in 14

Saturday night television programs. In the ensuing years, Shea won a Grammy and was given an award by RCA for selling over a million albums. He recorded the song three times with RCA and several times with other labels in addition to performing it countless times live.

The tall, genial man became a major "star" in the gospel world through singing this and other songs in his rich bass voice. The songs he sang fit perfectly in church—a key to their success—and Shea's voice is the epitome of the great choir soloist. His exposure on the Billy Graham Crusades and in the electronic media made him a household name in gospel circles as he became the first major gospel singing "star" to emerge in the second half of the 20th century, preceding (and laying much of the groundwork for) the boom in gospel music during the latter half of the 20th century. It was Shea who first proved that a religious artist could reach a sizeable market recording only gospel music directed at the Christian audience whose focal point is the church.

Chapter 20

SOUTHERN GOSPEL AFTER WORLD WAR II

For rural Southerners, life in the military during World War II was often better than the life they had known at home. Many had, for the first time, a steady job, a regular paycheck, regular meals, new clothes, and good housing. For some farm boys, it was the first time they'd ever worn shoes. When the draft was first instituted in 1941, over three-fourths of the new recruits had been declared physically unfit for service because of the effects of malnutrition; as the war progressed, however, the newer recruits drafted were healthier, a sign of better times.

The United States had seen a decline in its rural population in the 20 years before World War II. In 1920, slightly less than half of all Americans lived on farms; in 1940 it was a little over 20 percent. But only ten percent of those farms had flush toilets. During the war, approximately 27 million Americans—or about 20 percent of the population—moved, and farm workers dropped by 16 percent between 1940 and 1944.

Before the war, the South had been an isolated region. But most of the Army's training camps were in the South because large tracts of available lands could be used to establish bases and the climate allowed for year-round training. About half of all those who served in the military during World War II spent some time in the South, which meant about six million non-Southerners were exposed to the region for the first time.

In the long run, World War II would help Southern gospel music because so many Southerners who grew up with this music were sent all over the country—and to foreign countries—and carried their love of quartet singing with them. These young men introduced others to this kind of singing and, when the war was over, there was an awareness of Southern gospel music outside the South which resulted in demands for appearances by Southern gospel groups all over the country. This led to a national awareness instead of just a regional appeal, although the South certainly remained the stronghold for the quartet sound.

However, the war itself disrupted the gospel world; gas and tire rationing meant that groups could not travel and many young men in quartets were drafted, so groups disbanded or had to constantly look for new members.

For some quartets, the war provided opportunities. The John Daniel Quartet got a morning program on WSM in Nashville and appeared regularly on the Grand Ole Opry. Songwriter Albert Brumley organized his own music publishing firm in 1943 and later purchased the Hartford Company, which had published his earlier songs.

After the death of Virgil Stamps, a number of groups left the Stamps-Baxter company. In 1945 Frank Stamps left the company and formed a rival firm, the Stamps Quartet Music Company. This left J.R. Baxter to struggle with the Stamps-Baxter legacy formed in 1926. Frank Stamps and J.R. Baxter held competing singing schools and published competing songbooks. Frank Stamps began a periodical, *Stamps Quartet News*, and convinced some groups to go with his new company. Among the established groups who joined Frank Stamps' organization were the Stamps Quartet, Frank's old Stamps All-Stars, the Blackwood Brothers, the Deep South Quartet, and Harley Lester's Stamps Quartet. New recruits included the Blue Ridge Quartet, at WBBB in Burlington, North Carolina; the Dixie Four from WIBC in Indianapolis; and the Weatherford Quartet from KGER in Long Beach, California.

The split weakened the old Stamps-Baxter Company and, when combined with the growing independence of individual quartets, the power in the Southern gospel industry shifted dramatically during the 20 years after World War II. As the quartets depended more on radio and recordings, they depended less on a single publisher to supply material. Some begin writing their own songs but all quickly learned a lesson: in order to survive, they had to find the best material available, no matter who published it. The old days of only doing the songs of a single publisher were rapidly coming to an end.

The success of both black and Southern gospel music after World War II was aided by the success of Pentecostalism in the second half of the century. Pentecostals accepted new musical styles much more quickly than mainline churches and were more open to new ways to spread the Christian message. Because Pentecostals were evangelistic, they embraced the idea that popular music with Christian lyrics could reach people that traditional music and church services could not. Promoting "worldly pleasures within a sanctified form," most of the black and Southern gospel performers after World War II were Holiness/Pentecostals who increasingly saw their shows as a ministry every bit as viable as that of a traditional pastor in a mainline church.

The development of "new" music like rhythm and blues and gospel was helped by the booming economy; by the end of the 1940s there were over 400 companies listed in Billboard. Many of these companies specialized in country, rhythm and blues, or gospel; Bibletone and White Church were independent gospel labels.

Some of the gospel groups still sang secular tunes as well as gospel. In 1945 the Sunshine Boys went to California where they appeared in about 24 western films over the next seven years with Eddie Dean, Lash Larue, and Charles Starrett. The group sang western tunes as well as spirituals. However, as the 1940s progressed, gospel groups had to face the decision of whether to be all-gospel or get out of the field altogether. Increasingly, audiences demanded that groups make this choice. Gospel lyrics with popular melodies and sounds were fine—but "pop" songs reeked of the wicked, sinful, fallen world they railed against.

After World War II the rural singing conventions began to die out. The inexpensive entertainment they provided was replaced by radio—and soon, by television—as well as by the touring gospel groups that were now appearing in their area. And, as the singing conventions died, the shaped-note publishing business began to die as well because these singing conventions were a major source of their income.

But as one source of entertainment was dying, another was coming into its own. Electricity was increasingly available to rural residents and so were radios—by 1948 about 95 percent of the house-holds in the United States had a radio. Sound systems, electric gui-tars, and microphones all improved; the tape machine developed by the Germans was discovered at the end of World War II and taping technology would revolutionize recording. Television had its first full season in 1948; gospel groups intent on increasing their fame and spreading their message would look to TV as they looked at radio in the 1930s—a prime outlet for their music and message.

A number of new gospel groups were formed after World War II. In Macon, Georgia, The Segos, consisting of brothers James, W.R. and Lamar, were joined by bass singer Charlie Norris. Elmo Fagg formed the Blue Ridge Quartet; the group moved to Spartanburg, South Carolina where their line-up consisted of Fagg (lead), Ed Sprouse (tenor), Burl Strevel (bass), and Kenny Gates (baritone).

After World War II the Homeland Harmony Quartet, now head-ed by tenor Connor Brandon Hall, moved to Atlanta, where they per-formed on WAGA. Their membership included many who would become prominent in the history of this music; singers James McCoy, Paul Stringfellow, Wayne Groce, Jim Cole, Bob Shaw, Jim Waits, Aycel Soward, George Younce, Rex Nelon and pianists Hovie Lister, Lee Roy Abernathy, Reece "Rocket" Crockett, Wally Varner, Jack Clark and Livvy "Lightnin'" Freeman were all alumni.

When Lee Roy Abernathy, born in Canton, Georgia in 1913, joined the Homeland Harmony Quartet in 1947, he brought along a song he had written, "Everybody Gonna Have a Wonderful Time Up There (Gospel Boogie)" and convinced the group to record it for White Church Records. It was released in 1948. The sound, with a heavy "boogie" rhythm, caused an uproar in gospel circles. This was not sedate music—this was music akin to the rhythm and blues heard on independent labels. Critics lambasted the song. Charles Wolfe quotes Rupert Cravens, who wrote an editorial in a magazine of one of the singing convention publishers, that states:

> The cause of gospel singing is too sacred and universal for anyone conscientiously to take up some phase of it for personal economic, political or social purposes ... it is a flim-sy excuse when a godless, Sabbath-desecrating quartet or singing group will say, after one of their typical Saturday

night or Sunday shows, 'We are doing this for a living'....
Why should people who love the Lord and clean Christian
society have to listen to the music of the 'juke box' to find a
medium of expression toward God? ... Why should men who
are supposed to love the Lord make for their most popular
phonograph records and 'song-hits' a type of song that is too
cheap in the light of God's holy purpose to deserve mention?
Why should a so-called Christian audience go crazy over an
all-night jamboree which is so often opened with a prayer but
is thereafter carried on as if there were no God.

Although Cravens was reacting to the death of the singing conventions as well as out of genuine religious conviction, there was a
strong vein of truth in his editorial. Many Southern gospel singers,
whose roots ran back to those days, recalled that those times were
marked by an emphasis on entertainment rather than "ministry" and
that oftentimes many of the singers were not true believers but rather
boys who had been raised in the church and in Christian homes and
loved to sing. They looked upon the quartets as a way to make a living doing something they enjoyed, feeling the lure of the spotlights
much more intensely than any lure from the eternal light.

A factor that often entered into an acceptance by both audiences
and performers of the entertainment aspects was that Southern-style
religion preached that a person must serve either God or the Devil.
Since the Devil was represented by secular music and the honky
tonks, this was a road to be avoided; however, God was represented
by gospel music and churches so if someone performed in church
singing gospel music, it was "safe" for their souls as well as good
entertainment. In the rural South, these gospel singings and gatherings served many needs—cultural, social, political, and personal—so
they were deemed vital. Too, the congregation heard preaching and
received a heavy dose of the gospel on Sundays and weekday nights,
so there was an aversion to a heavy dose of religion in these concerts
felt by the audiences—they wanted some safe, wholesome family
entertainment and the gospel concerts provided it.

The year 1948 also proved to be key in other areas as well. In
June, Wilmer B. (W.B.) Nowlin promoted the DeLeon Peach and
Melon Festival with Eddy Arnold as the star attraction. But, con-

cerned that the country star alone could not draw a crowd, Nowlin booked Frank Stamps and His All-Star Quartet to open the show and the Stamps-Ozark quartet to close it. The event was a huge success and convinced Nowlin there was a big audience for gospel music.

On November 5 of that year, Wally Fowler held the first "All-Night Sing" from the Ryman Auditorium, home of the Grand Ole Opry in Nashville. During the spring of 1949 Fowler began holding a gospel sing at the Ryman on the first Friday of each month.

Fowler had originally been a country performer, playing on the Grand Ole Opry with a group called the Georgia Clodhoppers. The group regularly did gospel shows as well as country shows. In August 1945 Fowler re-named the group the "Oak Ridge Quartet" when they performed gospel. That was the same month the atom bombs had been dropped on Japan, ending World War II, and Oak Ridge, Tennessee was home to secret projects that helped develop the bombs. When it was revealed that Oak Ridge had played an important part in this Tennesseans were proud of their achievement; Fowler capitalized on this in re-naming his gospel group after the town. Members of the Clodhoppers/Oak Ridge Quartet were Fowler (lead) Johnny New (tenor), Lon "Deacon" Freeman (baritone), and Curley Kinsey (Bass).

With the success of the All-Night Sings at the Ryman, all-night shows soon spread to cities and towns throughout the South, often promoted by Fowler. Fowler at this point decided to go "all gospel" and the Georgia Clodhoppers simply ceased to exist. The Oak Ridge Quartet added Neal Matthews, Jr. and pianist Boyce Hawkins to join Joe Allred (tenor), Bob Weber (bass), Pat Patterson (baritone), and Billy Joe Campbell (guitar and lead vocal when Fowler did not appear with them). Fowler, who joined forces with W. B. Nowlin in promoting concerts, was so busy as a gospel promoter that he only sang with the group on weekends.

Also in 1948 one of gospel's most influential groups, the Statesmen Quartet, was formed in Atlanta by 21-year-old pianist Hovie Lister. Lister, born in 1926 in Greenville, South Carolina, grew up in a Baptist church, sang with his father and uncles, then played piano for evangelist Mordecai Ham. He attended the Stamps-Baxter School of Music during World War II, then played piano for the Rangers, LeFevres, and the Homeland Harmony Quartet. In 1947 he was a disc jockey on WEAS in Decatur, just outside Atlanta. He got a show on WCON, a new station in Atlanta owned by the *Atlanta Constitution*, through his friendship with Barry Howell, the son of the newspaper's owner, Major Howell. Lister played on shows at 6 in the morning and 12 noon.

Because he was given a hefty "budget" ($50 a week) to pay each member in his group, Lister could entice members of other groups to join him. His first group consisted of Mosie Lister (lead), who had previously sung with the Sunny South Quartet and Melody Masters Quartet; Bobby Strickland (tenor), who had sung with the Sand Mountain Quartet and Harmoneers; Bervin Kendrick (baritone), and Gordon Hill (bass). The group went on the air in October 1948 and took their name from Georgia Governor Herman Talmadge's newsletter, "The Statesman." Since Lister did not want to travel outside Atlanta, he was soon replaced by W. Jake Hess, who had been a member of the John Daniel Quartet.

In 1949 the Statesmen began recording for Capitol Records. That summer their line-up consisted of Jake Hess (lead), Bobby Strickland (tenor), Bervin Kendrick (baritone), and James "Big Chief" Wetherington (bass), with Lister on piano. During the next two years Claris G. "Cat" Freeman replaced Strickland and Doy Ott replaced Kendrick. Because Ott could also play the piano, Lister could play host and emcee and sometimes joined as a fifth voice.

The driving force behind the Statesman was Lister, a bright, energetic, ambitious and forceful young man who drove the group towards a "vision" of what he thought a quartet should look and sound like. They perfected the art of taking spirituals such as "Get Away Jordan" and adopting them as their own.

Several other influential groups emerged after World War II and were instrumental in increasing the popularity of Southern gospel music in the 20 years after the war. Southern gospel had long called itself a "family," presenting a "family" type of music, so it is not surprising that two of the most influential groups in Southern gospel would be families—the Speers and the Blackwoods.

"Mom and Dad" Speer were Tom Speer and Lena Brock; he was born 1891 in Fayette County, Georgia, the fourth of 18 children to J.J. and Emma Speer, and she was born in 1900 in Shady Grove Hill, Alabama (in Cullman County). Soon after Lena's birth, the Brock family moved to Lawrence County, Tennessee, then again to Center Point, Tennessee.

The Speers were cotton farmers who knew the rigors of a hard, rural life. In 1902, young Tom's mother passed away and his father married Mary Estes Seymour, with whom he completed his family. Unable to attend school in his youth, Tom Speer entered the third grade when he was 23 and finished the seventh grade at 25; this would be the end of his formal schooling. Captured by his love for gospel music, Tom felt God had called him to be a gospel singer at an early age. His mother often sang gospel songs at home and young Tom often gave music lessons to his younger brothers and sisters. In World War I, he served in the Army in France and, after his return, met Lena Brock at a country church singing in Leoma, Tennessee. Lena's father taught singing schools and went to singing conventions all over Alabama and Tennessee; Tom Speer quickly became a pupil of Mr. Brock and courted Lena until February 27, 1920, when they were married in Athens, Alabama.

In December 1920 their first child, Brock, was born, followed by Rosa Nell and Mary Tom and, in 1930, by Ben. They quickly became a singing family group with Lena playing the organ and Tom, or "Dad," leading. During these early years, Tom farmed to support his family in addition to his work as a singing school teacher. As a teacher, Tom traveled all over Alabama, Georgia, Mississippi, and Tennessee and on weekends sang at conventions and in concerts. There were a number of "all-day singings" which served as a social gathering, church picnic, and entertainment for poor rural Southerners and this is where the Speer family cut their teeth in gospel music. It was all centered on the church and these rural churches would usually sponsor a "homecoming" once a year as well as monthly gatherings in the summer where members would gather, play, socialize, eat, and sing. Later, these events would become larger and more organized and soon the county meetings grew into state conventions which attracted thousands of people in some of the larger cities in the South, such as Birmingham and Nashville. As these conventions attracted larger crowds who demanded "special attractions," the quartets became better known.

In 1929—just after the Wall Street stock market crash—the Speer family moved to Lawrenceburg, Tennessee, home of the James D. Vaughan Music Company. Tom Speer was selling insurance but the Depression soon took that business away and the singing schools also declined as he began collecting a bushel of beans or some other barter for his fees. But things began looking up in spring 1934 when Tom got a job with the Vaughan Music Company for $50 a month. Among his duties were editing music for the songbooks, writing lyrics, teaching harmony and sight singing, and conducting the Vaughan Singing Schools.

Tom Speer was a determined, ambitious man and in his desire to further himself as well as gospel music, he had identified radio as the chief medium. The family was used to hearing gospel music on their car radio as they came from Sunday night singings when they would tune in a Stamps-sponsored quartet. Since Lena Brock's brother, Dwight, worked as an executive for Stamps-Baxter, based in Dallas, they had connections there. So, after the death of James D. Vaughan in 1941, they joined the Stamps organization.

The family moved to Montgomery, Alabama, where they began a gospel radio program. The group advertised Stamps-Baxter song-books over the air and people sent in money. Stamps-Baxter received most of the money (the groups received a commission). Too, the group developed a following and performed in concerts within the listening area where they also sold songbooks for Stamps-Baxter. The major income for the groups came from ticket sales at these concerts, usually held in small churches or school houses. At WSFA in Montgomery, the Speers performed a 15-minute program at 6 a.m. each weekday morning.

World War II saw the oldest son, Brock, join the Army for four years. The war was the cause of the demise of a number of these small groups but the Speers managed to find replacements and continued singing gospel music, adding a patriotic segment in honor of Brock during each of their shows. After the war, when Brock returned, the group moved to Nashville so he could attend college. Brock, who wanted to be a preacher, eventually received his divinity degree from Vanderbilt and married Faye Ihrig in 1948. When "Dad" had his teeth pulled, Brock took over the emcee duties and thus found a way to combine his call for preaching with his love for gospel music.

The first recordings by the Speers came in the late 1940s on Bullet Records; later they recorded for the Skylite Company, a gospel label formed by the Statesmen and Blackwood quartets.

The Speers had a radio show on WSIX in Nashville and in the 1950s appeared on television station WLAC. In 1964 they were regular performers on "Singing Time in Dixie," a popular syndicated TV show taped in Atlanta. They often appeared with the LeFevres on another television show, "Gospel Caravan."

As gospel publishers began forming record companies, a number of new gospel labels emerged from companies whose source of revenue was shifting from the songbooks to album sales. The John T. Benson Company, formed in Nashville during the early part of the 20th century as a publisher, formed Heartwarming Records in the early 1960s; the Speers signed with the company in 1965.

The career of the Blackwood Brothers parallels that of the Speer family, but the roots were planted about 20 years earlier, on Christmas Eve, 1900, when Roy Blackwood was born to William Emmett and Carrie Blackwood near Fentress, Mississippi. In 1905, daughter Lena was born while two other sons, Doyle and James, were born in 1911 and 1919, respectively.

The Blackwoods, like the Speers, were farmers but two of the sons, Doyle and James, had a tremendous drive to become gospel singers, probably inspired by watching visiting groups perform in their local churches. Doyle learned to play a Russian balalaika and soon he and James formed a duet. In their biography, *Above All* (written with Kree Jack Racine), Doyle states that, "My first and most lasting ambition was to learn everything possible about singing, and then to become a professional Gospel Singer." He tells of early practices and states that: "[There were] many tree stumps in the fields my Dad worked, and these became my 'stages'.... I would go out in the fields, pick a stump to stand on, and pretending I was on the stage of a big hall, I would sing through every song I knew. Then I would run back to the house to get Mama's opinion of my voice projection and to see if my diction was remaining full and clear. As time passed I used stumps farther and farther away from the house, and the power of my stomach muscles, diaphragm, and vocal cords really did develop. I tried continually to widen my technical scope by listening to, and copying as closely as I could, the styles and techniques of well known performers of the day ... like the Delmore Brothers and Jimmie Rodgers.... I was quite familiar with the guitar and soon had learned—

by ear—almost every song he had recorded complete with yodels."

James was soon bitten by the gospel bug too, and he and Doyle would often discuss their future. In their autobiography, James states that, "In discussions as to what we would do when we got out of school, our ambitions centered, more and more, on Gospel Singing. I had attended several 'All Day Singing Conventions,' and R.W. in his travels with Roy and Susan, had attended even more. We enjoyed immensely the Christian fellowship and the programs at these Conventions. We greatly admired the professional singers who we knew were making their living this way.... As the years progressed, R.W. and I became firmly set in our conviction that Gospel Singing should become our life's work. We promised each other to learn everything possible about Gospel Music and Gospel Singing until such time as we could set out on our own, and do our very best to establish our name of Blackwood as a household word in Gospel Singing circles."

R.W. Blackwood was the son of Roy Blackwood, James' older brother. This made R.W. the nephew of James, but the age difference—only two years—made them more like brothers. Since Roy Blackwood was a minister, the family moved around quite a bit, from church to church as pastoring jobs ended or opened up. But he always tried to make it back home for Christmas and that holiday in 1933 was particularly eventful for the Blackwood Brothers gospel act because Roy brought back a Victrola—the first any of them had ever seen—and a number of records by gospel groups. Doyle, James, and R.W. were soon avidly studying these records.

James stated that, "We had learned a great deal from listening to these records and the various arrangement of the songs. We found it was even better for us, technically, than listening to live presentations, because we could play a record over and over, until we understood thoroughly what was being done to achieve certain effects."

It was during this holiday that the brothers and R.W. began a serious discussion about a full-time family quartet which would go under the name of "The Blackwood Brothers." The first step towards that goal was realized when they enrolled in a ten-night singing school at the Clear Springs Baptist Church under the tutelage of a Mr. Ray. From that school came their first quartet, with Doyle singing baritone, James alto harmony, Gene Catledge, a distant relative, singing bass, and Mr. Ray singing lead. Mr. Ray was apparently a demanding taskmaster and required much practice and dedication from the Blackwoods. They immersed themselves in it totally. They state that: "He (Mr. Ray) would require us to analyze the words until he was sure we understood the song message thoroughly. Then, the melody would be analyzed, phrase by phrase. Next, we would run through the parts until the intonation was exactly right. At this point, we were ready to consider phrasing (the breathing points in the song), and the word 'cutoffs.' When this was perfected we would select what we considered the best tempo for presentation of our arrangement of the song. Lastly, came the dynamics (the 'softs' and 'louds') and where and what extent they should be applied."

After a number of practice sessions such as this one, the group made their first appearance at the "All Day Singing" at the Concord Baptist Church, near Ackerman, Mississippi. Just before they sang they named themselves the "Chocktaw County Jubilee Singers." After this appearance, the group sang at a number of other engagements—including some that paid—for about a year and then broke up.

In September 1934 Roy and his family moved back to Mississippi and a family quartet was soon formed with Roy singing lead, R.W. alto, James baritone, and Doyle bass. They sang together, pursuing their dream of making themselves a household name with a "Blackwood sound" until late 1935 when Roy was offered the pastorate of a church in Ft. Worth, Texas, and Doyle was offered a position with the Homeland Harmony Quartet in Birmingham, Alabama. James, who was then 16, continued to sing with groups in the area. Two years later, the Blackwoods re-formed with James, now 18, singing lead (his voice had finally passed the "changing" period), R.W. (who was now 16) on baritone, Roy singing first tenor, and Doyle singing bass and providing musical accompaniment on guitar. The group decided to try to land a radio program and auditioned at WHEF in Kosciusko, Mississippi.

James notes that, at this time on small, rural radio stations, "The broadcasting field was wide open to any one who could carry a tune, make a speech, scrape a fiddle, pick a banjo ... or, for that matter ... whistle! Most anybody who was willing and able to get the body to the station ... was welcomed with open arms." Their audition came just 15 minutes after they walked through the station's front door and was broadcast live. The owner had taken them straight to the mike and told them they had a 15-minute program in which to prove their stuff. According to James Blackwood, "Before we had finished our first number, the phones began to ring. Listeners were calling and congratulating the station on the program, and making requests for songs ... instead of 15 minutes ... our air time stretched out to an hour and 15 minutes." The owner scheduled them to appear every Sunday morning for a 30-minute show. This led to personal appearances, and the Blackwoods would announce their availability during the program as well as advertise where they would be appearing the coming week. The average income for the group was four to six dollars a night with admission priced at ten cents for children and 15 cents for adults. Their first big pot of gold came when they collected $27 one night at the high school in Noxapater, Mississippi and $55 another night in Houlka, Miss.

In 1938 the Blackwoods moved to WJDX in Jackson, Mississippi, where they had a daily broadcast. Tirelessly promoting themselves, they soon invested in a public address system that ran off the car battery with speakers attached to the top of their car. When they reached the area where they were to give a concert that evening, they always drove around—in town as well as on the rural backroads—announcing where they would be that night and the time of the concert. Those speakers covered a mile radius and showed the Blackwoods to be both determined and innovative in their approach to promoting gospel singing. In fact, the key to the success of the Blackwoods seems to be that they "out-promoted" most other gospel quartets. This pursuit of publicity and promotion—which most others left to chance—as well as their ability to stay together over a long period of time, set them apart from other gospel groups and eventually made them a household name in gospel singing circles.

The Blackwoods' first big success came when they moved to KWKH in Shreveport. They had two daily broadcasts—at 6:15 a.m. and at noon—and by mid-afternoon would be traveling to an evening engagement. Since KWKH had 10,000 watts, the Blackwoods' engagements carried them all over Louisiana, east Texas, and southern Arkansas. It was also while they were in Shreveport that they became associated with the Stamps organization.

Roy Blackwood had first met V.O. Stamps in 1929 in Boaz, Alabama. The Stamps organization had contacted the Blackwoods because of their success on the Shreveport station, which meant they were traveling enough to sell songbooks. The business arrangement was that Stamps would assist with the booking arrangements, securing bookings the Blackwoods would normally not get (such as large conventions), would provide a pianist and furnish a late model automobile. In return, the Stamps organization would receive a percentage of the gross income after a stipulated amount had been earned. The Blackwoods would take the Stamps name as part of their calling card; they changed their name to "The Blackwood Brothers Stamps Quartet" to advertise their association with this organization.

Since V.O. Stamps was adamant that the piano was the proper form of accompaniment for gospel singing, he insisted all groups carrying his name have a piano player and, to that end, provided piano players from the main office for each group. The first piano player for the Blackwoods was Joe Roper, who was replaced a few months later by Wallace Milligan, who remained with them until 1940.

Another perogative of Mr. Stamps was that he would assign the quartets territories. The Blackwoods had been successful in Shreveport, but V.O. wanted his younger brother, Frank, who was based in Shenandoah, Iowa, to be closer to the home office so he assigned Frank to Shreveport and sent the Blackwoods to Iowa. The Blackwoods took up their new chores on station KMA in mid-summer, 1940. They had three daily broadcasts—5:30 a.m., 7:30 a.m., and 12:30 p.m. The first was a transcription recorded the day before while the following two were live broadcasts. From their location in Iowa, the Blackwoods reached 27 states and Canada and their concert bookings took them to Iowa, Nebraska, Missouri, Kansas, Minnesota, and North and South Dakota. Their pianist was Hilton Griswold.

The first major setback for the Blackwoods occurred when World War II began. Since most of their income depended upon personal appearances, and since gas and tire rationing made this kind of travel impossible, the Blackwoods had to give up their career. Too, some of the members were of draft age and knew that life in the Army was only a letter away.

During the war the Blackwoods moved to San Diego, California, and took jobs working in defense plants. In the evenings, they continued to sing at nearby churches and schools and were even active in the War Bond Drives. R.W. Blackwood was the first to be drafted and he left in June 1944. Doyle's health had begun to fail and so pianist Hilton Griswold took over the baritone part until he was drafted. Griswold was replaced by A.T. Humphries, was in the Navy and stationed at San Diego, and his wife, LaVera, who served as pianist. James Blackwood was turned down by the draftboard while Roy Blackwood and his family returned home to Mississippi. Although this was a setback of sorts for the Blackwoods, it would prove to be a blessing in disguise in the long run as the Blackwoods made a small name for themselves on the West Coast and were responsible for introducing their gospel quartet sound to that part of the country.

World War II ended in August 1945 and on October 1 of that year, the Blackwoods were back at KMA in Shenandoah, Iowa to resume their career. Their line-up was Roy on first tenor, James on lead, Don Smith on bass, Hilton Griswold on baritone and piano. Doyle, an announcer on WAPO in Chattanooga, could not join them but retained his full interest and share in the group. R.W. Blackwood joined them again in mid-December 1945 after his discharge from the service.

Ever alert to business and professional opportunities, James Blackwood had calculated that the group could sell albums from their personal appearances and generate more income as well as promotion for the Blackwood sound and name. Terry Moss, program director for KMA, had the equipment necessary for the recording as well as some contacts to get the pressings done. The Blackwoods began selling records at their concerts and through mail order, which led them into the publishing business as they began finding songs to record whose copyrights would generate additional income.

Don Smith returned to California and was replaced by Bill Lyles and, in 1948, Doyle re-joined the group. The demand for concerts was so great that it was impossible to fill them all, so the Blackwoods decided to form two groups, with the second group containing Roy and Doyle, along with Johnny Dixon on baritone, Warren Holmes on bass and Billy Grewin on piano. The first group was comprised of James and R.W. Blackwood, Bill Lyles, "Cat" Freeman on high tenor, and Hilton Griswold handling the piano chores. The Blackwoods doubled their income from personal appearances and added opportunities to sell records and songbooks with this arrangement.

By 1950 the mail order business had grown to the point that quartet number two was disbanded and Roy and Doyle devoted all their energies to record promotion and filling mail orders. During this year the Blackwoods left Shenandoah, Iowa, after ten years, and moved to Memphis, Tennessee, where they would establish their permanent headquarters.

In Memphis they appeared on WMPS. The line-up was James on lead, R.W. on baritone, Aldon Toney first tenor, Bill Lyles bass, and Jack Marshall on piano. Marshall had replaced Hilton Griswold, who had decided to remain in Iowa. In 1951 they were signed to RCA Victor by Steve Sholes, the legendary A & R man, who contracted them to record singles. There was some conflict as the Blackwoods kept their own record label and insisted on putting out albums of their own (for the increased profits) while recording for RCA, which offered them national distribution.

In 1952 the Blackwoods and Statesmen formed a partnership in which they toured together; for the next 15 years Southern gospel fans could see two of the top acts in Southern gospel on the same evening.

Perhaps the biggest break for the Blackwoods came in 1954 when they appeared on the "Arthur Godfrey Talent Show" on CBS (TV and radio). Singing "Have You Talked to the Man Upstairs" on June 12, 1954, they won the contest (from audience applause) and appeared throughout that week on the network on the "Godfrey Show."

For the Blackwoods, the "Godfrey Show" was their biggest exposure to date and was followed by their greatest tragedy a couple of weeks later.

On June 30, 1954 the Blackwoods were appearing in Clanton, Alabama. R.W. Blackwood and Bill Lyles, who had been flying the plane the Blackwoods were then traveling in, took the plane up during the afternoon. Something went wrong during the landing and the plane crashed, killing R.W. and Lyles. A huge memorial service and funeral was held on July 2 at Ellis Auditorium in Memphis, and news of the tragedy was broadcast nationally, made pertinent by the Blackwood's recent network appearances.

The ever-opportunistic Blackwoods resumed their concert schedule two days after the funeral with an engagement in Fort Worth, Texas, and on July 10 they began a series of "Memorial Sings" in Tupelo, Mississippi with Cecil Blackwood, R.W.'s brother, joining the quartet on baritone, and J.D. Sumner taking on the bass chores (he had formerly been with the Sunshine Boys Quartet). One month after the tragedy, on August 4, 1954, the Blackwoods appeared at a Memorial Sing in Clanton, Alabama, where the crash had occurred. RCA had released "Have You Talked to the Man Upstairs?" and it became a best seller.

That same August the Statesmen appeared on Godfrey's show and sang "This Ole House," a song written by Stuart Hamblen, who was one of the pioneers of country music in Los Angeles. This song would also become a huge hit.

Another innovation came out of the Blackwood tragedy: the Blackwoods gave up travel by airplane and went back to cars. In 1955, they bought a bus and refurbished the interior for travel and sleeping, becoming the first Southern gospel quartet to utilize this mode of travel, which soon became the major means of transportation for long tours not only in gospel but country and rock music as well. Traveling by bus had previously been a necessity for black performers, who often could not stay in hotels while touring and needed a place to sleep as they traveled.

Chapter 21

BLACK GOSPEL AFTER WORLD WAR II

The "Golden Age" for black gospel was during the 20 years following World War II. Mahalia Jackson joined forces with Thomas Dorsey in the early 1940s, creating more national attention as Dorsey toured the nation. She sang such songs of his as "Precious Lord" and "If You See My Savior" in a way that was distinctively hers, changing the melody and meter, stretching out the song, slurring her words, and projecting an image that was both spirit-filled and sexy at the same time. This caused Dorsey much consternation as he tried to coach Mahalia to sing his songs in the manner in which they had been written, but Mahalia's fiery spirit soon made Dorsey's attempts futile until he finally resigned himself to her individuality. By 1945 she was famous in the black churches. Dorsey would become firmly established as the "Father of Black Gospel" while Mahalia became the most famous gospel singer of her time.

Mrs. Bess Berman signed Mahalia to Apollo Records, a small firm based in New York, in 1946. Although the relationship with Berman was at times volatile and argumentative, Mahalia produced a string of recordings over the next eight years which were both brilliant and definitive. Her third release, "Move On Up A Little Higher," reportedly sold over a million copies. Her concerts were equally memorable and sometimes she would spend almost half an hour on "Move On Up" or some hymn.

In 1950 another career breakthrough occurred when Chicago journalist Studs Terkel began featuring Mahalia Jackson on his television show. The show was centered on jazz and the resemblance to

Bessie Smith and natural jazz vocalizing was inherent in Mahalia's style. On October 1, 1950 she gave her first concert at Carnegie Hall. International acclaim came in 1952 with her recording of "I Can Put My Trust In Jesus" as a duet with James Lee, which won a prize from the French Academy. Her first European tour followed and the international attention increased when her recording of "Silent Night" became a top seller in Norway.

Back in America, Mahalia continued to play churches, booked by her nephew Alan Clark and accompanied by young singers and musicians. She became famous to white American audiences and began to embody the quintessential gospel singer—a black Kate Smith who was saintly, stately, and who sang with incredible power. She had her own radio and television programs beginning in 1954, the same year Columbia Records signed her and instigated a tremendous national publicity campaign on her behalf. A special feature in *Life* followed as commercial success on Columbia catapulted her fame even higher.

Black gospel quartets also experienced a "golden age" from 1945 to 1965. They were aided by the fact that a number of independent labels were formed to market music to the black audience. Most of these labels were interested in rhythm and blues; the United States was a segregated nation with "black" and "white" sections of town. Entrepreneurs saw that jukeboxes in black sections could not get recordings of the music they wanted and so they began labels that recorded black singers and groups. This, in a nutshell, is the story of how rhythm and blues got on record. The labels formed after World War II included Apollo, Gotham, Excello, Atlantic, Imperial, Vee-Jay, Savoy, Specialty, Peacock, Chess, Aladdin, and King.

Because these rhythm and blues records sold well, the major labels became interested, signing the acts, buying the labels, and hiring A&R representatives to scout black talent. The success of rhythm and blues on small labels led directly to the rock 'n' roll revolution of the 1950s when the sound of R & B became the backbone of rock 'n' roll.

A number of African-American acts got on white radio stations because of this revolution. This occurred because television replaced radio as the dominant mass media in the United States, so the networks shifted their programming to TV. This left radio in a dilemma:

they could not compete with TV, so how could they survive? The answer lay in playing records instead of live talent, and appealing to the young audience of teenagers and young baby boomers born after the war who wanted a "new" music.

Black gospel was more influential than white gospel in providing a "sound" and performers for rock 'n' roll, although most of the mainstream churches found the new music disturbing, to say the least. Their world was divided between the sacred and the secular, like the white world, but, in a segregated United States, blacks remained more united than whites. In the areas where blacks lived, and where black businesses were located, churches and bars were in close proximity. African-American youth were likely to hear both R & B and gospel as they walked down the main thoroughfare in a black community.

The "Great Migration" brought African-Americans to the cities in large numbers in the post-World War II era, which made Chicago a center for black music. There were 44,000 African-Americans living in Chicago in 1910; that figure grew to 109,000 by 1920, then 234,000 by 1930. During the Depression this migration slowed, but during the 1940s the black population in Chicago rose from 278,000 to 492,000. During the 1950s the population increased to 813,000 or, to put it another way, an average of 2,200 African-Americans moved to Chicago every week during the 1950s. During the two decades after World War II, Chicago saw its black population increase by over half a million. These figures were mirrored in other major cities as African-Americans increasingly fled the rural South to move North to cities.

The 1930s was the age of white Southern gospel on radio, but the period after World War II brought black gospel to the airwaves. This came about because a large number of new radio stations were licensed after World War II, combined with the advent of television, when radio had to find new programming to replace the network programs that previously dominated radio. While there were few black-owned stations, and few that programmed black music, the stations featuring a program of black music increased in number throughout the late 1940s and 1950s.

The biggest station was WLAC in Nashville, where late-night programming was a mixture of rhythm and blues and gospel. Disc jockeys John R. Richbourg ("John R."), Gene Nobles, and "Hoss" Allen played records on a 50,000 watt station that could be heard over most of the United States. With shows sponsored by Ernie's Record Mart and Randy's Record Shop, the station alternated 45 minutes of R & B with 15 minutes of black gospel from 9 p.m. until the early morning hours. These two sponsors also developed record labels for black music; Ernie's founded Excello while Randy Wood began Dot.

The disc jockeys at WLAC sold everything from baby chicks, hair pomade, and recordings to garden seeds, choir robes, and skin-lightening cream. Covering 38 states, the station reached 8-12 million listeners.

Other important stations that played black gospel programs included WDBJ in Roanoke, Virginia; WDIA in Memphis; WIS in Columbia, South Carolina; WOKJ in Jackson, Mississippi; WLIB in New York; WLOF in Orlando, Florida; WMMB in Miami; WNOX in Knoxville, Tennessee; and WXLW in St. Louis.

Perhaps the most important disc jockey was Joe Bostic in New York, who hosted "Tales From Harlem" from 1937 to 1939 on WMCA, then worked for WCMW and WLIB. Beginning in 1950 Bostic also promoted shows; he organized the first "Negro Gospel and Religious Festival" at Carnegie Hall with the Selah Jubilee Singers, the Herman Stevens Singers, and Mahalia Jackson.

The "sound" of the black gospel quartet was four men and a piano. The groups were sharp dressers, choreographed their moves on stage, and developed the "swinging lead" where two men would trade the lead vocal, as well as a soaring tenor—which often reached into falsetto—with smooth harmonies on the chorus. Increasingly, the music had a driving beat and, because the Holiness/Pentecostals demanded an emotional service, the music often brought crowds to their feet.

During World War II several important groups, first formed before the war, developed into full-time, professional groups. Archie Brownlee and the Original Five Blind Boys of Mississippi were first formed in 1932; all its members had attended the Piney Wood School for the Blind in Piney Wood, Mississippi. Their group was first called the Cotton Blossom Singers and founding members were Brownlee, Sam Lewis, Lloyd Woodard, Lawrence Abrams, and Joseph Ford. In

1944 they changed their name to the Jackson Harmoneers; later they changed their name again, to the Original Five Blind Boys of Mississippi and moved to Chicago, where their members were Brownlee, Abrams, Woodard, J.T. Clinkscale and Reverend Percell Perkins. Among the "hits" they recorded were "I'm Willing to Run," "Will Jesus Be Waiting," and "I'm Going to Tell God."

Clarence Fountain and the Five Blind Boys of Alabama were formed in 1937 at the Talledega Institute for the Deaf and Blind. The group came from the Glee Club and was originally comprised of Johnny Fields, George Scott, Olice Thomas, and Velma Bozman Traylor; they called themselves the Happy Land Jubilee Singers. In 1944 they changed their name to the Five Blind Boys of Alabama; in 1948 they became professional and began recording for Coleman Records. They were known for the "mother" songs, beginning with their first hit in 1949, "I Can See Everybody's Mother, But I Can't See Mine."

In 1936 Joe Johnson formed the Pilgrim Travelers at the Pleasant Grove Baptist Church in Houston; in 1944 they toured with the Soul Stirrers. By 1944 the Soul Stirrers had sung in all 48 states and were the first group to have a regular weekly radio show, on WIND in Chicago, on Sunday mornings.

The Four Harmony Kings began in 1938 in Kentucky with Claude Jeter, his brother, and two others. The group moved to Knoxville and changed membership with Jeter singing first lead and tenor, Bobby Womack second lead, John Myles baritone, and Henry Bossard, bass. The a cappella group did barbershop harmony and landed a Sunday morning spot on WDIR. However, there was another group called the "Four Kings of Harmony" and, to avoid confusion, Jeter's group changed its name to the Silvertone Singers. Because their show was sponsored by Swans Bakery, the group added the sponsor's name to become the Swan Silvertone Singers. In 1948 the Silvertones moved to Pittsburgh, where their new lineup consisted of Jeter, Louis Johnson (second lead), Paul Owens (alternate lead and second tenor), Myles, and William "Pete" Connor (bass).

In 1945 the Highway QCs, a "farm team" for the Soul Stirrers, was organized; the original members were Sam Cooke, Spencer Taylor, Lee Richardson, Creadell Copeland, and Charles Richardson. The Fairfield Four had a program on WLAC in Nashville and recorded for the Bullet, Delta, Dot, Champion, and Old Town labels.

Other groups and singers popular during the decade after World War II include The Dixie Hummingbirds, the Nightingales, the Famous Davis Sisters from Philadelphia, the Royal Sons Quintet (which recorded secular music as the Five Royales), the Golden Gate Quartet, Swan Silvertones, the Soul Stirrers, Wings Over Jordan Choir, Southernaires, Sonny Til and the Orioles, Delloreese Patricia Early (later known as Della Reese) in the group Meditation Singers, Gospel Harmonettes, Dorothy Love Coates, the Clara Ward Singers, the Angelic Gospel Singers, Aretha Franklin, and the Drinkard Singers, whose members included Cissy Houston, mother of Whitney, and Marcel Warwick, father of Dionne.

Perhaps the best-known preacher in black gospel was Clarence LaVaughn (C.L.) Franklin, who preached his first sermon at the Bethlehem Baptist Church in Detroit in January 1946. Franklin was born in Indianaola, Mississippi; his father served in World War I and, after the war, abandoned his family. Franklin's mother remarried; the second husband's name, "Franklin," was adopted by C.L. The new marriage produced one child, a daughter Aretha. C.L. became a preacher when he was 17 and pastored churches in Clarksdale and Greenville, Mississippi; Memphis; and Buffalo, New York before moving to Detroit. While in Memphis, in 1942, the Franklins had a daughter he named "Aretha" after his sister; she, too, would become a legend in black gospel. But during the war, Franklin's wife, Barbara, died, leaving him with four children to raise. When he moved to Detroit, the female members of his congregation helped raise those daughters while he concentrated on preaching.

In Detroit, Mattie Moss Clark became the most powerful woman in black gospel through her position as choir director at the COGIC conventions. These gatherings provided a showcase for new gospel talent while her daughters, Elbernita (Twinkie), Jackie, Denise, Dorinda, and Karen formed a popular group, the Clark Sisters, who wrote "Save Hallelujah" and "Salvation is Free."

In Memphis, W. Herbert Brewster, pastor of the East Trigg Baptist Church, wrote the musical drama, *From Auction to Glory*, which was first staged in 1941. Brewster also wrote "I'm Leaning and Depending on the Lord," "Move On Up a Little Higher," "I Never Heard of a City Like the New Jerusalem," "Just Over the Hill," "Faith Can Move Mountains," and "Let Us All Go Back to the Old Landmark."

In 1947 Rebert Harris organized the first National Quartet Association of America, which hosted an annual convention for quartet singers. Also in 1947, Robert Anderson organized the first Gospel Caravan; Albertina Walker was in this group, which would later become identified with her.

During the 1950s Albertina Walker and The Caravans produced more gospel stars than any other group or choir; they were, in essence, an ensemble of soloists. Singers who came out of the Caravans include Bessie Griffin, Shirley Caesar, Inez Andrews, Cassietta George, Dorothy Norwood, and Albertina Walker. Walker, born in Chicago in 1930, began her career in 1952 at the West Point Baptist Church with a group that included Ora Lee Hopkins, Elyse Yancey, and Nellie Grace Daniels. Among their "hits" were "Think of His Goodness to You," "Blessed Assurance," and "All Night, All Day."

The Mighty Clouds of Joy were formed in 1959 by Willie Joe Ligon (lead), Elmore Franklin, Johnny Martin, and Richard Wallace at a high school in Los Angeles; by 1962 they were one of the leading quartets in gospel music.

During the early 1950s rhythm and blues was increasingly popular with white audiences while "hard gospel" dominated the Pentecostal churches. This "hard gospel" featured a voice strained to the limit, singing to the end of the vocalist's range, in an emotional and spiritual ecstasy, dramatically delivering the lyrics while ad-libbing commentary. It involved "acting out" songs and taking the audience for an emotional ride during the evening. Dorothy Love Coates and Shirley Caesar were particularly good at this.

Numerous R & B groups were influenced by the Soul Stirrers, Pilgrim Travelers, and Dixie Hummingbirds, whose charismatic singers were combined with tight harmony background singing; many of these individuals and groups began in gospel, then shifted to R & B. Pianists used large, "heavy" chords in the middle of the keyboard with accents provided in the upper registers and a rolling bass underneath. Some of the most influential pianists were Curtis Dublin (with the Davis Sisters), "Pee Wee" Pickard (and the Original Gospel Harmoneers), Mildred Falls, Mildred Gay, Jessy Dixon, James Herndon, Clara Ward, Roberta Martin, Alex Bradford, James Cleveland, Edgar O'Neal, Raymond Raspberry, Charles Taylor, and Lucy Smith.

On the R & B side, artists like Ray Charles, James Brown, and Little Richard all emerged. Although each was influenced by gospel music, borrowing songs and styles, none of them was ever a "gospel" singer. The first singer who proved that gospel could be the training ground for a pop star was Sam Cooke.

Born in Mississippi in 1931, Sam Cook (no "e") grew up in Chicago, where his father was a Church of Christ Holiness minister. He joined his two sisters and brother in a group called "The Singing Children" when he was nine and became a member of the Highway QC's a few years later. This latter group was an offshoot of the Soul Stirrers, perhaps the most popular black gospel quartet of the day, who wanted to form a group of young singers as a sort of "farm club" for the parent organization. Here, Cooke was coached by Soul Stirrer member R.B. Robinson, who brought him into the Soul Stirrers when lead singer R.H. Harris left in late 1950.

When Sam Cooke joined the Soul Stirrers they were already the biggest name in black gospel quartet circles. Their sex appeal was also known—it was the reason Harris, a devout man, quit—and their reputation as musical innovators was established. But it was Sam Cooke who brought the young people in droves to gospel concerts and who became the first "sex symbol" in the music, which he used as a launching pad into pop stardom. Along the way he created a distinguishable style characterized by his semi-yodel, developed into a first-rate songwriter in both the gospel and pop fields, and created the pattern of success which so many others—from David Ruffin to Jerry Butler, Lou Rawls, and Johnny Taylor—sought to emulate. In other words, it wasn't just his vocal style that made Cooke so influential, it was his lifestyle as well.

Cooke had just passed his 20th birthday when he sang on his first recordings with the Soul Stirrers in 1951; this first session yielded the Cooke-penned hit, "Jesus Gave Me Water." His singing style, which touched on imitations of Harris and some attempts at "shouting" like other popular lead singers of the day, was quickly settling into his trademark of sophisticated sanctification, effortless emotions which somehow still touched the depths of passion. He became the rage of the gospel world as young girls lined up outside venues to wait for him. Cooke, with his movie-star good looks, was the perfect male sex symbol—young and pretty, with a voice that could send chills up any spine. His charisma during performances brought the youth down front to the stage where they would stand all performance long—and the result was that the covert sexuality of gospel suddenly became quite overt with Mr. Cooke.

Cooke had flirted with the idea of crossing over to pop for a number of years before he actually did so. He wanted to appeal to the white audience—there was more money, prestige, and fame there—and he knew he could do it best through pop music. Still, he was reluctant to take the step because of the usual inhibitions gospel singers feel when singing for "the world." It was 1957 when he took that step, and even then he tried to step back into the gospel world and plant his feet in both places. But it could not work that way.

Cooke was certainly not the first singer to leave gospel for pop music. Dinah Washington had done it years before, and Ray Charles, only a year older than Cooke but already a veteran in the recording studio (he had begun recording in 1948 when he was 18), had shown the powerful appeal inherent in gospel music when he took a traditional gospel song, put some secular lyrics to it, and delivered it with the gusto and delivery of a sanctified holiness preacher resulting in the hit "I Got A Woman" in 1953. This heralded the rhythm and blues explosion of 1953 and 1954 when a number of white teenagers discovered black music and modified it into the rock 'n' roll revolution that began in 1955 when Bill Haley and the Comets's "Rock Around the Clock" hit number one on the charts.

Other precedents for black success in the white market were quartets like the Mills Brothers, the Ink Spots, and the Orioles, who presented a supper-club type harmony on songs like "Crying in the Chapel." The key year is 1954. This is when Elvis Presley made his first recordings in Memphis for Sun Records, Roy Hamilton had a pop hit with the gospel song, "You'll Never Walk Alone," and Ray Charles had a pop hit with a gospel-influenced performance of the bawdy "I Got A Woman." Then in 1955 and 1956, a succession of black acts, beginning with Little Richard, Chuck Berry, Fats Domino, the Coasters, and the Platters opened up the way in the musical world for black artists to appeal to white audiences. It was a world ripe for Sam Cooke, but he was hesitant and did not make his move until 1957.

Perhaps it is because he had more to lose than the others—he was the major superstar in gospel and would lose that following if he "went pop"—that caused him to defer his decision, but more likely it was his own inner religious convictions and the sermons he must have heard from black preachers who were admonishing their people to refuse the temptation of the sinful world and be assured of their salvation by staying with the church.

The Soul Stirrers had been recording for the Specialty label, an independent Los Angeles-based firm, since 1949. The label had begun recording another top black gospel quartet, the Pilgrim Travelers, a year before. The Soul Stirrers were brought to label owner Art Rupe by the head A & R man, J.W. Alexander. Producer Bumps Blackwell was producing the group and decided to cut Cooke on some pop songs, although Rupe was against the move since he had been having success with gospel and did not want that jeopardized. The first pop single from Cooke, titled "Loveable" and released under the name Dale Cook in 1957, sold about 25,000 copies but raised Rupe's ire to the point that it ended Cooke's and Blackwell's career with the label. Since Rupe owed Blackwell money, they made a deal whereby the producer would get the unreleased tapes from the pop session he had cut with Cooke. He took these over to another small label, Keen Records, which put out the record.

That record was "You Send Me," and it was released in the fall of 1957 and quickly went to the number one position on both the R & B and pop charts. That began Sam Cooke's pop career and songs like "Wonderful World," "Only Sixteen," and "Everybody Loves a Cha Cha Cha," which he either wrote or co-wrote, followed before he went with RCA. His career continued to thrive with the release of his third single, "Chain Gang," and culminated with perhaps his finest song, "A Change Is Gonna Come," written after he had heard Bob Dylan's "Blowin' in the Wind" for the first time. This became a hit after his death in 1964.

Cooke's death, both tragic and grisly—he was shot to death by a prostitute after allegedly threatening her and roughing her up—though the true details of that night have never been fully known—was gist for sermons. Those in the gospel world saw it as a just reward for someone who had turned his back on his gospel roots while others saw it as perhaps the logical conclusion of a phenomena that had been thinly disguised in the past—church folk dabbling with loose women.

Still, this does not diminish Sam Cooke's considerable achievements in the gospel field in the early 1950s: he was the first gospel sex symbol and brought young people in the droves to gospel concerts, proving that the music could have an appeal for the young as well as the old. Too, he showed that a performer with gospel roots could have a major effect on the pop world, that the talent of gospel performers was first-rate and that the church—via musicians and singers who received their early training and experience there—would be a major influence on pop music in the rock 'n' roll revolution from the mid-'50s through the '60s. Since the rise of soul music paralleled the rise of the Civil Rights Movement (as noted by Peter Guralnick), this places the career of Sam Cooke in the strategic center where gospel, soul, and social activism all fused to bring about a major social revolution.

During the 1950s Mahalia Jackson had her own CBS radio program (it premiered on Sunday, September 26, 1954), appeared as a guest on Dinah Shore's television show, appeared on the Ed Sullivan Show on CBS, performed at the Newport Jazz Festival and Carnegie Hall, toured Europe—playing the Royal Albert Hall in London—and at the end of 1954 began recording for Columbia Records, which promoted her as the "World's Greatest Gospel Singer."

In 1956 Mahalia became involved in the Civil Rights movement when she went to Alabama and sang for free in support of the Montgomery bus boycott. From this point on, she became a regularly featured performer at civil rights seminars and rallies.

During her career Mahalia Jackson played a major role in moving black gospel from the relatively small, limited base of African-American churches into the larger world of American music. She also played a major role in bringing the world of black gospel into the Civil Rights movement. This movement would redefine life for African-Americans in the United States during the 1960s.

Chapter 22
THE 1950s AND ELVIS PRESLEY

The 1950s were a "pro-family" decade, but rather than the "norm" in American history, as has been portrayed, especially by Christian fundamentalists, they were really an aberration. First, the previous decades were horrible for families; the Great Depression during the 1930s saw men withdraw from family life, humiliated by their inability to find work. They turned to domestic violence while children quit school to work at dead-end jobs just to keep the family afloat.

As late as 1940, ten percent of American children did not live with either parent; during the 1940s, less than half of those entering high school finished. After World War II, a third of all marriages ended in divorce, a result of "war brides" and quick marriages where a couple married soon after they met and just before the man departed for foreign shores.

But at the end of the 1940s, the divorce rate—which had been rising steadily since the 1890s—dropped sharply. The age at which people got married dropped to a 100-year low and the birthrate soared as young people "caught up" with their lost years and the "baby boom" began.

During the 1950s, 90 percent of all households in the country were made up of families; 86 percent of children lived in a two-parent homes and 70 percent of these were biological parents. Almost 60 percent of children were born into a male breadwinner-female homemaker family, with a sharp division of labor between husband and wife. The 1950s were a time of the old-fashioned "mom" instead of the modern "mother."

On television were such family-oriented shows as "I Love Lucy," "The Adventures of Ozzie and Harriet," "Leave It To Beaver," and

"Father Knows Best." These shows served an important function: they showed how families were supposed to live. They were more than entertainment; they also served as advertisements, manuals for marriage and child raising, and lessons in basic social etiquette. There were no communist witch-hunts on these programs, no conflicts with race or class; the father knew best and the mother always stayed cool in a crisis and did housework in a dress and high heels; teenagers were glad to have dinner with the family and soak up parental wisdom.

It is interesting to note than when people who grew up during the 1950s remembered that decade years later, they often confused their real lives with the lives of those they saw on television. TV had brought a new reality into American homes, and Americans sometimes felt closer to the families on television than to their own kin or neighbors. However, despite the glow that encircles memories of that era, these television shows were not documentaries.

During the 1950s real wages grew so that a 30-year-old man could buy a medium-priced home with 15-18 percent of his salary. Most women specialized in child raising as family life and gender roles became much more predictable, orderly, and settled than in the previous two decades (or the next two decades).

There was, of course, another side to the 1950s. The homogeneous neighborhoods allowed people to ignore and avoid racial and political repressions outside the suburbs. The poverty rates were higher, but were not concentrated in identifiable pockets and were declining. There was a high rate of teenage pregnancies—the highest rate occurred in 1957—but pregnancies were generally followed by a wedding. High school graduation rates were lower in the 1950s than during the following decades, but there were good jobs with a future available for high school drop-outs. This would be the last generation who would be able to reach middle-class status without post-secondary schooling.

The '50s began with the promulgation of fear; on February 9, 1950 Senator Joseph McCarthy made a speech claiming there were communists in the State Department; he never produced the list of names he claimed he had, but nonetheless conducted a "witch-hunt" for the next several years. In June 1950 the Korean War began.

Americans had a great deal of confidence in government, business, education and other institutions during the 1950s. The government was activist, but federal assistance programs were more widespread and generous than later years. Before the 1950s, the elderly had been the poorest segment of the population, but Social Security began to build a large safety net for them.

Government spent a good deal of money on public works; it was almost 20 percent of total expenditures in 1950 (it would drop to less than 7 percent in 1984). During the decade of the 1950s, funding of sewers and waterworks rose by 46 percent, construction expenditures for new schools rose by 72 percent, and non-military, non-residential public construction rose by 58 percent.

Between 1945 and 1960 the gross national product grew by almost 250 percent and per capita income by 35 percent. By 1960, 62 percent of American families owned their homes; it had been 43 percent in 1940. By the mid-1950s, 60 percent of the population had what was labeled a middle-class income ($3,000 to $10,000 a year). It was a period when business profits soared and America became a nation dominated by the middle-class. The tax burden was carried by corporations, who had a tax rate of 52 percent and provided 32.1 percent of tax revenues in 1952; it would decline to 12.5 percent of revenues in 1980 and 6.2 percent in 1983. For individuals, the top tax bracket took almost 90 percent of a person's income until President Kennedy lowered it to 50 percent.

The middle-class of the 1950s was square and proud of it, and the corporate world was comprised of a group defined by the title of a book published in 1956, *The Organization Man*. In his book, *The Fifties*, author David Halberstam writes about the corporations that produced these organization men, "The culture was first and foremost hierarchical: An enterprising young executive tended to take all signals, share all attitudes and prejudices of the men above him, as his wife tended to play the sports and card games favored by the boss's wife, to emulate how she dressed and even to serve the same foods for dinner. The job of a junior executive was to know at all times what the senior executive desired at any given moment, what kind of snack or alcohol he wanted in his hotel room on the road, what his favorite meal at a favorite restaurant was in a given city and to have an underling there several hours early, standing guard to make sure that nothing went wrong—that the right table was available, that the restaurant did not run out of the favorite food or wine."

The essential goodness of the corporation was never questioned, and General Motors was the largest, richest corporation in the world, the first corporation to gross a billion dollars. It was headed by Charlie "Engine" Wilson, who told Congress that what was good for General Motors was good for the country. In 1953 General Motors had 45 percent of the automobile market; in 1956 GM sold 51 percent of the cars in America. The growth in actual numbers is impressive: in 1950 General Motors sold 49.3 million vehicles; in 1959 it sold 73.8 million.

The car wasn't just a means of transportation—it was a reflection of class and status. The Chevrolet was for blue-collar workers or young couples just starting out; the Pontiac was for those a bit more successful who wanted a sportier car; the Oldsmobile was for the bureaucrat or manager; the Buick was for the doctor or lawyer in town; and the Cadillac was the ultimate status symbol, reserved for the top executive or owner of a large, successful business.

General Motors did not depend entirely on Americans developing a love affair with cars on their own; beginning in 1932 they had formed a consortium with Firestone, Standard Oil, and Mack Truck which would buy or shut down the electric trolleys and streetcar systems in cities and replace them with buses. By 1940, public transportation ridership had shrunk by two billion riders; still, in 1953, 1.5 million people traveled by rail each day. But by 1956 this cabal had bought out the last of the electric rail lines and finished converting the public transportation to buses. Public transportation by rail effectively ended in the United States in 1956, replaced by big buses, which most riders found unappealing. Between 1946 and 1980, government aid to highways totaled $103 billion while railroads received $6 billion in assistance.

During the 1950s, Eugene Ferkauf created the first big discount store, E.J. Korvettes; by the end of that decade, it had annual total sales of $157.7 million. Out in California, the McDonald brothers, Dick and Maurice ("Mac") had a hamburger stand in San Bernardino; in 1954 Ray Kroc visited and offered the brothers a deal to begin franchising. In 1955 the franchising began, and Kroc bought the company for $2.7 million. By the beginning of the 1960s, the company was opening a hundred new restaurants a year. Similarly, in Memphis, Tennessee, Kemmons Wilson developed the idea of "Holiday Inn" in

1951—he took the name from the popular Bing Crosby movie that had introduced "White Christmas" to the public—and began franchising this motel chain in August 1952; in 1957 he took the firm public.

The counterculture in the 1950s was centered in Greenwich Village in New York, where folk singers and Beat writers congregated. During the 1930s, the Left criticized America and capitalism for its failure; during the 1950s America and capitalism was criticized for its success. The Left argued that success had a darker side—affluence, bigness, corporate indifference, the homogenization of mainstream culture, and bland jobs corrupted the human spirit. Religion was criticized for being a social club rather than a radical force for change. With these criticisms, the Left planted the seeds for the counterculture of the 1960s.

In 1954 French forces were defeated in Vietnam; this led to the division of Vietnam into North and South and began the American involvement in that country's civil war. That same year the Supreme Court ruled in the Brown vs. Board of Education decision that segregation was illegal and ordered all schools to be integrated, an act that brought the Federal government into the Civil Rights struggle. During the 1960s the Left would embrace these two issues—Vietnam and Civil Rights—and these issues would propel the liberal agenda.

In 1950 there were 108 series that had been on radio for ten years or more; 12 had been on for 20 years or more. But things would change with the advent of television. In 1949 there were a little over a million TV sets in American homes; 450,000 of these were in New York City with the remaining sets mainly in Philadelphia, Washington, Boston, Chicago, Detroit and Los Angeles. In 1952 there were 19 million television sets in the country and there were a thousand new stores opening each month to sell TVs. But the growth of TV stations during the early years was slow because President Truman froze the licensing of new stations for four years at the beginning of the Korean War; consequently, there were 108 TV stations in 1953 but only 24 cities had two or more stations.

Even in the earliest days of television its effect was felt; in 1951 cities with one TV station reported drops in movie attendance of 20 to 40 percent, in New York 55 movie theaters closed while the number was 134 in California, and minor league baseball began a serious decline because people could see major league games (and other things) on television.

The biggest cultural force in music of the 1950s—indeed, of the entire 20th century—was Elvis Presley and rock 'n' roll. The rock 'n' roll revolution, led by Elvis, changed everything: music, language, clothes, and created a new social revolution.

Elvis came along at a time when the nation was obsessed with the issue of "juvenile delinquency." There was concern that the mass media had usurped parental control and thus caused an outburst of "delinquency" and youthful viciousness; in 1955 there were over 200 bills related to delinquency discussed in Congress.

Before Elvis, "pop" music was aimed at the upper middle class; it was really an extension of the big band music that produced soloists such as Frank Sinatra, Bing Crosby, Rosemary Clooney, Perry Como, and Patti Page. Country music and rhythm and blues were music of the lower classes; blue collar music limited to those outside the mainstream. Respectable people did not listen to such music.

In 1951 Alan Freed, a disk jockey in Cleveland, started "The Moondog Show," on which he played rhythm and blues for white kids. This was the first radio show which gave teenagers their own music, totally and completely different from their parents. Rock 'n' roll came at a time when young people had money of their own; during the 1930s teenagers put the money they earned into the family pot to help make ends meet. In the 1950s parents could afford to give their teenagers money while the money teenagers earned was spent on themselves. In 1956 there were 13 million teenagers in the United States with a total income of $7 billion a year; the average teenager had a weekly income of $10.55. During that year, Elvis sold $75,000 worth of records a day; by the late 1950s, 10 million portable record players were sold each year.

Elvis had recorded his first single, "That's All Right, Mama" b/w "Blue Moon of Kentucky," on July 5, 1954 in Memphis for a small independent label, Sun Records, owned by Sam Phillips. The record was a regional hit and Elvis began touring, exciting audiences with his uninhibited stage movements. His next recordings increased his popularity in the South and, to a smaller extent, the national level.

On January 5, 1956, Elvis did his first session for RCA. The session was held at 1525 McGavock Street in the studio owned by the

Methodist TV, Radio, and Film Commission. The producer of the session was Steve Sholes, who had negotiated the purchase of Elvis's contract and all masters previously recorded by Sun in Memphis from Sam Phillips for $35,000 plus a $5,000 bonus to Elvis. Also at this session were Colonel Tom Parker, who was not Presley's full-time manager yet (Bob Neal had been managing Elvis in Memphis and was still performing that duty part-time), guitarist Chet Atkins, Elvis' road musicians Scotty Moore (guitar), D. J. Fontana (drums), Bill Black (bass), and the Jordanaires.

During the three-hour session, Elvis recorded three songs: "Heartbreak Hotel" was the first he completed, then "I Want You, I Need You, I Love You," which would be his second single from RCA, and "I Was The One," which was issued on the "B" side of "Heartbreak Hotel."

In 1956 Elvis exploded, selling ten million records and making appearances on television shows with Jackie Gleason, Milton Berle, Steve Allen, and Ed Sullivan, all of which combined to launch him as a teen idol and cultural icon. The remaining songs on Elvis' first album were recorded in New York at RCA's studio with three songs from the Sun tapes added to round out the release.

Although religious leaders and parents railed against him, the roots of Elvis were firmly planted in gospel music. This was proven in later years when Elvis consistently recorded gospel albums and sang gospel songs in his performances throughout his career. All of Presley's gospel albums sold well—even the one recorded in 1957 when he was at the height of his notoriety as a rock 'n' roller, dangerous to youth's morals and the perceived enemy of preachers who openly accused rock 'n' roll as being the Devil's music and Elvis as being the Devil himself.

Presley looked at gospel music as his heritage as well as a source of spiritual strength. Gospel was his boyhood, his cherished memories of childhood, his mother's favorite music, and a tradition too deeply ingrained to ever let go of. It became a faith taken to the point of superstition, but in the beginning it was a child-like faith in the confusing and complex world that rock 'n' roll was creating in the 1950s. When he sang gospel Elvis was not only fulfilling a spiritual obligation (self-imposed) but also bringing back pleasant memories of his childhood. He was showing his mama he loved her, showing himself that he had not forsaken his roots or his God, and perhaps showing God—in the best way he could—that he was still a good boy, still God-fearing, and that he wanted salvation.

Presley's first gospel recording came soon after he joined RCA, at the height of his rock 'n' roll popularity—after he had sold ten million records in one year (1956) and presented himself to the nation on the major network television shows of the day. It came at a time when the younger generation was increasingly turning their backs on the religious heritage of their parents, shaking off all the inhibitions that religion had instilled, in order to pursue rock 'n' roll, a music that released rather than restrained them, a music that fueled their mood for rebellion.

The first gospel album from Elvis was *His Hand in Mine* and the cover shows a carefully groomed young man, albeit with hair a little long for the era, dressed in a tuxedo and seated at a piano. Except for the fact that it is Elvis, it is not untypical of gospel record covers of the day. Inside, the songs were primarily old gospel standards but done with a beat. Elvis, though respectful of gospel music, still made it exciting.

Calling Elvis Presley the most important figure in the history of rock 'n' roll is not an original thought. Ditto the notion that he is the most important figure in shaping American popular culture and music in the latter half of the 20th century. These ideas may not be totally accurate—musical movements and social changes hinge on more than just one person, even a performer as dominant as Elvis Presley—but it is interesting to note that many of the things which attracted so much initial attention to Elvis—like his long hair, flashy clothes, and flair for showmanship—came from the Southern gospel world. J.D. Sumner, a former member of the Blackwood Brothers in Memphis and later with the Stamps Quartet when they performed with Elvis during his final years, remembers that "Southern gospel singers always wore flashy clothes, even back in the early '50s. And we had real long hair combed back before long hair ever came in style." Sumner also notes that during the early days of Elvis, the singer "lost jobs because he was trying to wear his clothes and hair like gospel singers."

Elvis admitted to copying the singing style of Jake Hess, telling Johnny Rivers once as one of the Statesmen's records was playing

(Hess was lead singer for this group), "Now you know where I got my style from." It is perhaps ironic that the source for so much of Elvis Presley's music and personal style came from the Southern gospel world. The attitudes, tastes, and style in his dress and performances were then passed on to a whole generation of teenagers who had never heard of Southern gospel or, if they had, probably despised it. Meanwhile, the man who stood alone at the top of the rock world, inspiring countless others to pick up a guitar, gyrate, and sing, always had a yearning in his heart to be a member of a gospel group.

Elvis came from a Pentecostal background and this Bible belt religion was infused in him from earliest childhood by his mother. His attraction to gospel music came naturally—he loved singing and was deeply religious so the notion of being a gospel singer seemed to be the best way of reconciling these two drives. He heard a number of gospel groups in Memphis and tried out for at least one of them.

Jim Hamill and Cecil Blackwood had a quartet, The Songfellows, which they began while in high school in Memphis in 1952. When Elvis was a teenager driving a truck for an electrical company, he auditioned for the group. According to some versions of this story, Hamill put his arm around Elvis' shoulder and said, "Son, you better stick to driving that truck. You can't sing a lick!"

But, according to Hamill, the story is a bit different. "I did not tell Elvis he couldn't sing," said Hamill. "I told him he couldn't hear harmony—and he couldn't. As long as he was singing lead, he was fine, but when the baritone or the tenor took the lead, then someone had to sing harmony, and he could not harmonize. He'd sing baritone a line or two, then switch off to tenor for a couple of lines, and wind up singing the lead part. That was the reason we didn't take him into the quartet with us."

A few months after being turned down by the Songfellows, Elvis signed with Sam Phillips and Sun Records. However, also around this same time, Elvis was hearing harmony better and so Hamill and Cecil Blackwood asked if he'd like to join the quartet. This offer came because Cecil was leaving to join the Blackwood Brothers after two members of the original group (including his brother, R.W.) had been killed in a plane crash. According to Hamill, Elvis even discussed getting out of his Sun contract to sing gospel with Sam Phillips. This was certainly not the end of Elvis' involvement with gospel music. Until his death in 1977, Elvis continued to sing gospel, follow the careers of gospel quartets, and feature some of those quartets on his records and shows.

Gospel songs were no strangers to the pop world during the 1950s. The Recording Industry Association of America (RIAA), the organization which monitors record sales and awards "Gold" and "Platinum" records, began awarding gold records in 1958 and that year "He's Got the Whole World In His Hands" by Laurie London achieved gold status. It also reached the number one position on the charts in April of that year. This was Laurie London's only success in the charts; ironically, Mahalia Jackson also recorded this old gospel song and released it at the same time but Mahalia's version only reached number 60 on the charts.

In 1959 Tennessee Ernie Ford's album, *Hymns*, was awarded gold status and in 1961 his *Spirituals* album achieved that summit. He had two other gold albums in 1962, *Nearer the Cross* and a Christmas album, *Star Carol*. Ford, who hosted a popular weekly television show during this time, saw none of his gospel singles on the pop charts and was more known for his hit "Sixteen Tons."

There were gospel hits on the radio, beginning in 1955 with "Angels in the Sky" by the Crew Cuts, "The Bible Tells Me So" by Don Cornell, and two recordings of "He," one by Al Hibbler and the other by the McGuire Sisters, which all reached the top 15 in *Billboard*'s pop charts that year. In 1956 "Every Time (I Feel His Spirit)" by Patti Page, "Give Us This Day" by Joni James, "The Good Book" by Kay Starr, and "Sinner Man" by Les Baxter all reached the charts. In 1957 "Peace in the Valley" by Elvis Presley and "There's a Gold Mine in the Sky" by Pat Boone charted. In 1958 "A Wonderful Time Up There" by Pat Boone as well as the two versions of "He's Got The Whole World in His Hands" were on the charts; "Battle Hymn of the Republic" by the Mormon Tabernacle Choir, "Deck of Cards" by Wink Martindale, and "When The Saints Go Marching In" by Fats Domino all charted in 1959.

As radio gave up live entertainment in favor of records in the 1950s because of economics (the advertisers shifted their ad buys to television), recordings achieved a new significance. Two single records, which each reached number one on the music trade charts, reflected large social movements which began in the 1950s. In 1955 Bill Haley and the Comets had a number one hit with "Rock Around the Clock," marking the official beginning of the rock 'n' roll era; in 1958 the Kingston Trio had a number one song with "Tom Dooley," ushering in the folk music movement.

Rock 'n' roll separated the kids from their parents; folk music gave them a social conscience. Rock 'n' roll divided the generations because of its music, while folk divided them because of its lyrics. As the Jesus Movement developed and spread in the late 1960s, it was heavily influenced by both of these musical forms—rock 'n' roll moved the body, folk moved the mind.

Chapter 23

BLACK GOSPEL AND CIVIL RIGHTS: FANNY LOU HAMER

On May 17, 1954, Chief Justice Earl Warren of the Supreme Court issued the unanimous opinion in the Brown v. Board of Education suit that had been brought against school segregation. The Court said the doctrine of "separate but equal" had no place in education, that separate meant inherently unequal. This ended the legal and moral legitimacy of segregation, but it did not end segregation right away. It did begin a decade of violence connected to the struggle for Civil Rights.

The Southern states had been spending twice as much to educate white children, and four times as much for school facilities, as they had for black children. There was basically no transportation for black children to and from school and the salaries of black teachers were approximately 30 percent lower than those of their white counterparts. At the college level, the Southern states spent $5 million on black colleges while they spent $86 million on white colleges. And the Southern political establishment kept blacks from voting through the poll tax; in the presidential election of 1940, only 2.5 percent of the black population in the deep South voted.

In August 1955 Emmett Till, a 14-year-old African-American from Chicago visiting relatives in Tallahatchie County, Mississippi, was killed for talking "fresh" to Carolyn White, a 21-year-old white woman. Her husband, Roy Bryant, with his friend, J.W. Milam, took Till into the woods, stripped him, shot him, and threw him in the river. This murder made national news and brought the "code" of Southern segregation into American living rooms via the television screen.

Later that year, on December 1, 1955, a 42-year-old seamstress, Rosa Parks, was riding home on a city bus in Montgomery, Alabama. It was the practice of buses to require blacks to sit in the back and whites to sit up front; further, if a white person got on and there was no seat, black was required to give up his/her seat to the white. But on this particular day, when the driver ordered Rosa Parks to get up from her seat and move further back, she'd reached the limits of her endurance and simply refused. This incident sparked the Montgomery Bus Boycott, which lasted through most of 1956 and brought the first national fame to Reverend Martin Luther King, the 26-year-old pastor of the Dexter Avenue Baptist Church who had been in Montgomery for 15 months.

King was arrested and his home was bombed in 1956 but, as he stated, "There comes a time when time itself is ready for a change." That time had come.

Also in 1956, Central High School in Little Rock, Arkansas was scheduled to become integrated for the first time. But Governor Orval Faubus called out the Arkansas National Guard to stop the integration; this forced President Eisenhower to federalize the Guard and call in the army's 101st Airborne to protect the African-American students. This, too, became another turning point in the struggle for Civil Rights.

These events were the major catalysts for the Civil Rights Movement of the 1960s. But they did not happen in isolation—there was a huge foundation built for the movement by the time it arrived.

The "Great Migration" had brought a number of African Americans from the South into northern cities such as Chicago, Detroit, Toledo, Cleveland, Philadelphia and New York. African-Americans had been urged to move by the *Chicago Defender*, the leading newspaper for African-Americans. Founded by Robert S. Abbot in 1905, it was circulated in the South by Pullman porters. The North offered jobs and opportunities for African-Americans from the South, and many went North before and during World War II for that reason. But the invention of the mechanical cotton picker, and the widespread use of farm machinery after World War II, dried up most of the remaining agricultural jobs held by Southern blacks, so this became an added incentive.

Network television also helped the Civil Rights movement, and changed the politics in American homes, because it brought the Civil Rights struggles into the American living room.

The black church and politics have often been linked with preachers serving as a lightning rod for political issues. A number of African-American political leaders have come from churches and the Civil Rights Movement itself owes the major portion of its victory to the grassroots support of church members. Since music is a key focal point for the black church, it is logical that black gospel music would play a pivotal role in the Civil Rights Movement. Although there are a number of television clips of people singing "We Shall Overcome," "Blowin' in the Wind," and other songs while their arms are locked together, it was the old black gospel standards which provided the foundation for that movement. That, and people like Fanny Lou Hamer, who had the courage to become leaders of the movement.

Rural Mississippi in 1964 was not the most comfortable place to live if you were black. The public bathrooms were marked "Men," "Women," and "Colored." There were "White" water fountains and there were "Colored" water fountains. All public places, including restaurants, movie theaters, and bus stations, were either segregated with special places for blacks or reserved for whites only.

In the summer of 1962, the Student Non-Violent Coordinating Committee (SNCC) came to Ruleville, Mississippi to work on a voter registration drive. Blacks were required to pass a literacy test in order to vote—a requirement not applied to white voters. This literacy test had them copy and interpret an arcane section of the Mississippi state constitution to the satisfaction of the county examiner. The SNCC volunteers knocked on doors to get African-Americans to go to the courthouse in Indianola, about 26 miles away. After a week, they held a mass rally to stimulate some community interest; finally, the registration day arrived and 18 people boarded a bus for the trip to the courthouse.

According to Charles McLaurin, who was in this group of volunteers, a "short, stocky lady" was the first to step off the bus and go in to register. The others followed—all taking the literacy test and all failing.

That lady was 43-year-old Fanny Lou Hamer and she had lived on the Marlowe plantation in Sunflower County with her husband

and two adopted daughters for 18 years. After the group had taken the test, they boarded the bus to return home. However, a police car stopped them on their way out of town and informed the driver he was under arrest for driving a bus the color of a school bus. They took him to jail and everyone else was "shaking with fear," according to McLaurin. No one knew if they would all be put in jail or whether they would just be left there on the road.

Then a voice was heard singing some old hymns and spirituals. It was Fanny Lou Hamer. Somebody on the bus said, "That's Fanny Lou, she know how to sing." And she did know how to sing as she sang with a power in her voice that calmed and comforted the others on the bus. It was a voice that carried the power of Jesus, and she sang the gospel songs that expressed a faith that was like a rock in her life.

When the police came back to the bus, they informed everyone that the driver needed $52 to pay his fine; a collection was taken, the money was raised and all went home except the driver, Robert Moses, who was jailed. But there were problems waiting for Fanny Lou. The plantation owner where the Hamers lived as sharecroppers had been told that she tried to register and informed her husband, Pap Hamer, that Fanny Lou had to go back to the courthouse and withdraw her name or she would have to move. With that, Fanny Lou packed her belongings and moved into Ruleville, where she stayed with some friends. That night, nightriders shot up the home where she was staying. They also fired into the homes where other SNCC members were staying. Fanny Lou Hamer would never again go back to that sharecropper's shack that had been her home.

Several weeks later Fanny Lou went to Nashville for an SNCC conference. There she was asked to sing and began singing "This Little Light of Mine," "Ain't Gonna Let Nobody Turn Me Around," and other songs that became part of motivating people in the Civil Rights movement. The "Freedom Singers" were born that night and this group from the SNCC toured college campuses in the North to raise money for the SNCC. They also cut several albums.

Living the Christian life is risky business and carrying the message of the gospel is dangerous; Fanny Lou Hamer and many others proved that during the Civil Rights movement in the 1960s. Although she performed some of her gospel music while she was in her 40s in a concert setting before warm, appreciative audiences, most of Hamer's life was spent singing gospel music because that was where she found her strength.

Fanny Lou Hamer demonstrated to people the power of gospel music. She also showed them the power of love. She and other SNCC workers faced constant threats and beatings by Southern police; once in Charleston, South Carolina, Hamer and a group of workers were held for three days in a jail and brutally beaten. She suffered kidney damage and developed a blood clot in her left eye that permanently impaired her vision. Still, she refused to consider turning to hate or revenge. "It wouldn't solve any problem for me to hate whites just because they hate me," she once said. "There's so much hate. Only God has kept the Negro sane."

Fanny Lou Hamer chose to stand up for her Civil Rights and believe that God had created blacks equal to whites. When her husband and two daughters left the plantation to join her in town, the plantation owner confiscated all their belongings, claiming they owed him money. The day after Hamer attended a Mississippi Freedom Democratic Party meeting, her husband was fired from his job.

The sharecropper's life was tough—they were provided with a house and food, seed, fertilizer, and farm equipment on credit from a company store owned by the plantation owner. After the crops were harvested, the owner would receive half the income and the share-cropper the other half. However, the bill at the company store always managed to exceed what sharecroppers got for their crops.

After the Hamers left the plantation, they were so destitute that Fanny Lou applied at the welfare office for emergency surplus food. But the clerks would not accept her application until someone appealed to the Federal government in Washington. Because of her stand she was destitute, homeless, and her life and the lives of her family, were in constant danger.

Fanny Lou Hamer was the youngest of twenty children. She was semi-literate, except in the area of biblical wisdom. As she became active in Civil Rights, she sought to help others; she attended seminars and workshops until she received a certificate stating she was qualified to teach literacy and citizenship.

On Thanksgiving Day, 1963, less than a week after President John Kennedy had been assassinated, Fanny Lou Hamer was at

Howard University in Washington for a SNCC Conference. The day before, Lyndon Johnson had given a speech to a Joint Session of Congress, stating he would push forward on Civil Rights. At the conference, Fanny Lou Hamer sang "Go Tell It On the Mountain." In Hattiesburg, Mississippi, during "Freedom Day" marches, Fanny Lou led the crowd singing, "Which Side Are You On?" At countless other gatherings, she song gospel songs in her strong, powerful voice, giving herself—as well as others—the courage to face the challenges of changing the South.

Fanny Lou Hamer knew more than her share of troubles during her time. When she distributed food and clothing to destitute African-American families while encouraging them to register to vote, the Mayor of Ruleville complained to the Mississippi State Sovereignty Commission—a state agency funded by the legislature to defend white supremacy after the Brown decision—and wanted bribery charges brought against her.

When Hamer decided to run for Congress, her campaign manager was Charles McLaurin. While McLaurin was driving in Mississippi, he was stopped by a Highway Patrol officer in Starkville, who found campaign leaflets for Fanny Lou in his trunk. The officer took McLaurin and another man riding in the car into the Lowndes County jail where they were beaten until McLaurin admitted he "was a nigger rather than a Negro."

At a hearing in Washington, Fanny Lou said, "Not only have I been harassed by the police. I had a call from the telephone operator after I qualified to run as congresswoman. She told me, 'Fanny Lou, honey, you are having a lot of different callers on your telephone. I want to know do you have any outsiders in your house? You called somebody today in Texas. Who was you calling, and where are you going? You had a mighty big bill.'"

Hamer's politics were linked directly to the gospel. She wrote in 1968, "I think the sixth chapter of Ephesians, the eleventh and twelfth verses helps us to know … what it is we are up against. It says, 'Put on the whole armor of God, that ye may be able to stand against the wiles of the devil. For we wrestle not against flesh and blood but against principalities, against powers, against the rulers of darkness of this world, against spiritual wickedness in high places.' This is what I think about when I think of my own work in the fight for freedom."

Fanny Lou once stood up in a meeting and said, "I've been sick and tired for so long that I'm sick and tired of being sick and tired." That phrase—"sick and tired of being sick and tired"—stuck with her during the Civil Rights movement and is now etched on her tombstone in Ruleville, Mississippi. She died in 1977 and is buried on land purchased by the Freedom Farm Cooperative.

Chapter 24

THE 1960s:
PEACE, LOVE, AND MUSIC

The 1960s were characterized by intense social turmoil in the midst of the search for love, peace, and brotherhood. In many ways—and for many people—the social revolution of the '60s began as a spiritual quest. Youth rebelled against an increasingly technocratic and bureaucratic society, as well as the perceived hypocrisy and materialism of their parent's generation. They sought "truth" and a higher calling in life, a calling that would bring meaning and purpose and would be deeper than the selfish pursuit of materialism and blind acceptance of the status quo.

When people discuss "the '60s," they generally refer to the period from the end of 1963 to 1974, or from the assassination of President Kennedy to the resignation of President Nixon. During this roughly ten-year period, the United States underwent a social and cultural upheaval sparked by Civil Rights, the Vietnam War, and Watergate. It was a time when the country split between old and young, conservative and liberal; it was the World War II generation vs. the Baby Boomers, born from 1946 through 1964. It was a time when revolution was in the air: there was a feminist revolution, a sexual revolution, a drug revolution, a musical revolution, and a political revolution. The Beatles provided the soundtrack and their music—and their attitude—would affect the United States for the rest of the 20th century.

Spiritual searches in the 1960s led some to experiment extensively with drugs, others to seek out the Eastern religions and still others to turn to Jesus. Through it all, the common denominator was music. The irony of the anti-materialism in the '60s generation was that a good stereo system and a large collection of the "right" albums were essential and as much a part of their lives as breathing. On these records were the voices of their generation, singing messages to this whole counter-culture. It was a form of expression, a natural outlet for expressing whatever they were thinking and doing. It was only natural that those who became "Jesus people" would still look to music as a very vital and important part of their lives.

In *The Greening of America*, a book which captured the shift in consciousness perhaps better than any book of that era, author Charles Reich discusses the importance of music to this generation. He states that: "Music has become the deepest means of communication and expression for an entire culture.... For the new consciousness, this music is not a pastime, but a necessity, on a par with food and water ...(it) is a daily companion to share, interpret, and transfigure every experience and emotion."

The success of gospel songs on the pop charts in the late '50s and early '60s is an early indication of the spiritual revival that was to take place in the mid-to-late-'60s. This spiritual revival preceded the Christian revival which took place at the end of that decade. In some ways, this spiritual movement paralleled the career of Peter, Paul and Mary, who came to national attention in 1962 with "Lemon Tree" and "If I Had a Hammer." In August 1963 they reached the number two spot on the charts with "Blowin' in the Wind," a song which defined this spiritual movement for many. The folk movement was filled with old, traditional gospel songs and Peter, Paul and Mary were on the charts with some of these numbers, providing a political activism filled with spiritual overtones (or undercurrents) during this period.

The 1960s began with Ferlin Huskey's "Wings of a Dove" reaching the number 12 position; in 1961 there was chart activity for "Child of God" by Bobby Darin and the number one song "Michael" by The Highwayman; in 1963 The Singing Nun had a number one song with "Dominique" and Steve Alaimo reached the charts with his version of "Michael"; in 1964 "All My Trials" by Dick & Deedee, "Amen" by the Impressions, "I Believe" by the Bachelors, "Oh Rock My Soul" by Peter, Paul and Mary, "Michael" by Trini Lopez, "Tell It on the Mountain" by Peter, Paul and Mary, and "You'll Never Walk Alone" by Patti LaBelle & the Blue Belles all reached the charts. In

1963 *The Lord's Prayer* by the Mormon Tabernacle Choir was awarded a gold album.

In 1965 "Turn, Turn, Turn," which was a rewriting of the biblical Ecclesiastes, was a number one song for The Byrds and "Eve of Destruction" by Barry McGuire also reached that spot. "People Get Ready" by the Impressions was a hit that year. "I'm a Believer" was not a song about Christianity but that title reflected the religious undercurrent in 1966 when it became number one. "Crying in the Chapel" by Elvis reached number three in 1965 and "Blowin' in the Wind" became a top ten song for Stevie Wonder in 1966.

In June, 1967 the Beatles released the album *Sgt. Pepper's Lonely Hearts Club Band*, which ushered in the Summer of Love; at the end of 1967, the Beatles reached number one with "All You Need is Love," which also achieved gold status and personified that period. In 1968 Elvis Presley was awarded a gold record for his gospel album, *How Great Thou Art* while Simon and Garfunkel broke the invisible barrier pop radio had put up against the word "Jesus." That was the year of *The Graduate* soundtrack and the number one single, "Mrs. Robinson" featured the line, "Jesus loves you more than you will know" in the chorus.

In addition to *The Graduate* at movie theaters, there was *Hair* on the Broadway stage, and Woodstock, the ultimate concert. And all of these were somehow "spiritual" experiences as well as entertainment for this generation. Perhaps this "spiritualness" was best expressed in the song "Abraham, Martin, and John" by Dion DiMucci.

In May 1969 "Oh Happy Day" reached the number four position on Billboard's chart. The song was an old spiritual recorded by The Edwin Hawkins Singers, a black youth choir with a leader from Oakland. Outside of Mahalia Jackson, who reached the charts several times but never had a top ten single, The Edwin Hawkins Singers were the only genuine gospel artists to have a hit single on secular radio. All through this period of the late '60s, a number of spiritual and gospel-flavored songs would be hits, but they would have to be done by secular artists. Also in 1969 came the anthem "Get Together" by The Youngbloods, which was a rock song ready-made for campfire gatherings, as well as "Jesus is a Soul Man" by Lawrence Reynolds, which put Jesus in the middle of the Black Movement.

The year 1969 is crucial in tracing the roots for contemporary

Christian music because "Crystal Blue Persuasion" and "Sweet Cherry Wine," both by Tommy James and the Shondells, "Dammit Isn't God's Last Name" by Frankie Lane, "Kum Ba Ya" by Tommy Leonetti, "That's the Way God Planned It" by Billy Preston, "Turn! Turn! Turn!" by Judy Collins, and "You'll Never Walk Alone" by the Brooklyn Bridge all reached the charts with a Christian message in the lyrics.

Writers Andrew Lloyd Webber and Tim Rice had written a 15-minute operetta titled *Joseph and the Amazing Technicolor Dreamcoat* in 1968 about the Joseph in Genesis. It was written for the schoolboy choir at Celet Court School in London and was well-received. Since they had done so well on their first project, the two decided to do another more elaborate rock operetta; the result was *Jesus Christ Superstar*. Financed by MCA Records, the Broadway play and subsequent movie had a profound effect on America, producing several hit singles for pop radio as well as giving the public a new version of Jesus—one of a "superstar" who was a questioning man. The church (by and large) attacked it because they did not like this new version of Jesus. Too, the writers left Jesus in the grave at the end—there was no resurrection—so the result was Jesus portrayed as a man, not as Divine. Theologically, it was on shaky ground with traditional Christianity but it brought a widespread awareness of Jesus and rock music to the American public that could not be ignored when it premiered on October 27, 1970.

Two songs from the rock opera *Jesus Christ Superstar* became hit singles—"I Don't Know How To Love Him," recorded originally by Yvonne Elliman and then by Helen Reddy, and "Superstar," with its chorus of "Jesus Christ, Jesus Christ/Do You think You're what they say You are," which provided this generation with some more questions that had begun with the question "How many roads must a man walk down?"

In addition to the songs previously mentioned, there was "Amazing Grace" by Judy Collins, "Are You Ready" by the Pacific Gas & Electric, "Church Street Soul Revival" by Tommy James, "Holy Man" by Diane Kolby, "I Heard the Voice of Jesus" by Turley Richards, "Oh Happy Day" by Glen Campbell, "Spirit in the Sky" by Dorothy Morrison, "Stealing in the Name of the Lord" by Paul Kelly, "Stoned Love" by the Supremes, and versions of "Fire and Rain" by

James Taylor, R.B. Greaves and Johnny Rivers which all reached the charts in 1970.

In 1971 there were two more gospel songs that were hits—"Put Your Hand in the Hand" by Ocean and "Amazing Grace" by Aretha Franklin. Both achieved gold status. Also on the charts in 1971 were "All My Trials" by Ray Stevens, "Come Back Home" by Bobby Goldsboro, "Deep Enough For Me" by Ocean, "Mighty Clouds of Joy" by B.J. Thomas, "My Sweet Lord" by Billy Preston, "Take My Hand" by Kenny Rogers and the First Edition, "Life" by Elvis Presley, "Grandma's Hands" by Bill Withers, "Think His Name" by Johnny Rivers, "Top 40 of the Lordy" by Sha Na Na, "Turn Your Radio On" by Ray Stevens, and "Wedding Song (There is Love)" by Noel Paul Stookey.

Godspell, another rock opera based on the life of Jesus, appeared in 1972 and was also awarded gold status. The play, which pictured Jesus as a gentle clown, again offended the religious establishment but caused youth to take another look at Christianity. The movie was not as big a hit as the play but one of the songs, "Day by Day," did become a hit single. In 1972 "I'd Like To Teach The World To Sing," which began as a commercial for Coca Cola, became another spiritual anthem for brotherhood. A country hit also reached the pop charts: "Me and Jesus" by Tom T. Hall provided a chorus which articulated the stand of defiance many were taking regarding Christianity: "Me and Jesus got our own thing going/... got it all worked out/... And we don't need anybody to tell us what it's all about."

Concert for Bangla Desh by George Harrison and Friends came out in 1972 and provided one of the first attempts by rock artists to put their social conscience into action. Featuring appearances by Harrison, Eric Clapton, Bob Dylan and others, it served as a model of how not to raise money for a worthy cause because much of the money somehow disappeared or was eaten up by extravagant overheads.

Other gospel-related songs which reached the charts in 1972 were "Amazing Grace" by the Royal Scots Dragoon Guards, "I'll Take You There" by the Staple Singers, "Joy" by Apollo 100, "Jesus is Just Alright" by the Doobie Brothers, "Jubilation" by Paul Anka, "Morning Has Broken" by Cat Stevens, "Speak to the Sky" by Rick Springfield, "That's The Way God Planned It" by Billy Preston,

"Wedding Song (There Is Love)" by Petula Clark, and "Wholly Holy" by Aretha Franklin.

The year 1973 brought a platinum album for the movie soundtrack of *Jesus Christ Superstar* as well as an answer from Glen Campbell: "I Knew Jesus Before He Was a Superstar." 1973 also saw an album by Kris Kristofferson, *Jesus Was a Capricorn*, that featured "Why Me, Lord," one of the most overt Christian songs ever to be a major hit. "Jesus is Just Alright," which was a top ten single for the Doobie Brothers, furthered the cause.

There was less gospel activity on the pop charts from 1974 through 1976, although gold records were awarded to "The Lord's Prayer" by Jim Nabors as well as another version of that song by Sister Janet Meade; "I Don't Know How to Love Him" by Helen Reddy and "Did You Think to Pray" by Charley Pride also went gold. But 1977 was a different story as Debby Boone had a number one single and platinum album with *You Light Up My Life*. Daughter of former pop star Pat Boone, who had left the pop world to become a Christian celebrity, she soon followed her father's footsteps after a few more attempts in the secular market.

Perhaps the most significant musical event in 1977 was the gold record given to *Alleluia—Praise Gathering for Believers*. This was a Christian musical released on Benson, a gospel label, and marked the first time a gospel label had ever achieved this sales success. Also in 1977 the first president to publicly declare himself "born again" took office. After Jimmy Carter, the Jesus Movement ceased being an underground phenomenon and took its place in the mainstream of American life. At least it ceased being viewed as a radical element and became comfortable for middle America.

Musically, the Jesus Revolution paralleled the career of Bob Dylan, who began in the '60s singing and writing folk songs, including "Blowin' in the Wind," then went into rock. He released *John Wesley Harding*, a haunting album full of biblical allusions in 1968, before returning to rock. By the end of the 1970s, Dylan was releasing gospel albums as "The Voice of a Generation" continued to stay a little ahead of musical trends and produce culturally definitive works.

Chapter 25

GOSPEL MUSIC IN THE 1960s

In the 1940s and 1950s in America, Christ was an awesome figure; during the 1960s he became accessible. The youth, who had moved away from the stern God of their parent's church, readily embraced the warm, loving God of the '60s who was concerned about peace, love, social justice, and most importantly, each individual's life. As young people rejected the values and culture of their parents, they discarded the old Christianity as well. But somewhere they found a new Jesus, one they could relate to and one their parents were often repelled by. In the 1940s and 1950s, Jesus was a safe, middle-class figure, comfortable in country clubs; in the '60s He had gone to the streets and become a radical. Those were the images of the two competing versions of Jesus at the beginning of the Jesus Revolution.

Just as there was a spiritual revolution going on outside the church in the 1960s, there was also another one taking place inside the churches. This was first reflected in the career of Bill Gaither, whose songs became anthems for church-goers and whose career paralleled the rise of renewal within the Christian world. Gaither, his wife Gloria, and brother Danny were all from Anderson, Indiana and, like so many others, had a gospel group that sang whenever they could. They recorded their first commercial album in 1964 and its success soon surpassed everyone's expectations. Nearly 300,000 copies of that first album were sold—an unheard of number in the Christian market—and their following albums did just as well. The key was the songs Bill and Gloria Gaither composed, which were quickly adapted by church congregations.

Bill Gaither is the Godfather of Contemporary Christian music. He dominated the field of gospel music beginning in the mid-'60s.

Along the way, he captured the first gold album by a gospel artist on a gospel label for his musical *Alleluia* and became a performer who could regularly fill 10,000-seat auditoriums with his group, the Bill Gaither Trio. He did all this before the explosion of contemporary Christian music brought gospel music to the attention of the secular world. For Gaither and his group, however, there was little secular recognition because he was firmly entrenched in the Christian world, playing for Christians. To them, he was a major star; to those not of this world, he was an unknown.

Bill Gaither began as a songwriter and his contributions include "He Touched Me," "Because He Lives," "The King is Coming," "There's Something About That Name," "I Am a Promise," "I Am Loved," and countless others that have made their way into churches where congregations sing them regularly. His early songs brought him to the attention of Bob Benson and the Benson Company, a Christian record and publishing company. Bob Benson was in Anderson, Indiana, the Gaithers' hometown, to watch the Imperials perform in the early '60s. Gaither, who had booked the show, opened as a warm-up act with his trio.

The Trio had pressed a custom album; Benson asked if they could sell a couple thousand on their own and Gaither said he'd give it a shot. The agreement was that Gaither would be responsible for the sale of several thousand—guaranteeing that many sold—and the Benson Company would distribute it to Christian bookstores, trying to garner additional sales.

Bill Gaither had grown up in Anderson, Indiana and attended Anderson College, where he graduated in 1959. While in college, he met Gloria Sickle, whom he married after her graduation in 1963. The couple then began teaching at Alexandria High School; he taught English while she taught French.

As a child, Bill had learned to play piano and organ and performed whenever he could, in recitals and as an accompanist. After his college graduation, Bill taught high school for seven years, acquiring a Masters degree in Music at Ball State in Muncie along the way. He formed his original Trio in the mid-1950s, playing for civic clubs, Farm Bureau meetings, and in churches. In 1967 Gaither quit teaching school so as to devote all his time to gospel music.

Gaither's songs were recorded by the Imperials, Doug Oldham, George Beverly Shea, and others. These songs have been described by

Gaither as "like a brush fire that kept getting out of control." At this early stage, the Bill Gaither Trio was a family affair consisting of Bill, his brother Danny, and his sister Evelyn. His sister left to get married and there was the problem of replacing her; the solution would determine the future of the Trio as a recording act. That problem was solved when his wife, Gloria, joined the trio.

In 1968 the group recorded an album that contained "The King is Coming" and "Jesus, There's Something About That Name." The album was a landmark for the Gaithers and for gospel music. "Back then, 25-30,000 was a great number to sell and for us 5,000 was a big number," said Gaither. "And I'll never forget when we made that record, it went 10,000, then 20, then 30, then 50,000 and we couldn't believe those kinds of figures. Then it went 100,000, then 150, then 200, then it went 250,000 and in our field that was totally unheard of." The album had spread through word of mouth, through the Benson company learning how to market to the Christian bookstores, and through the Gaithers' own personal appearances and the extensive mailing list they had compiled. But the reason it sold was because of songs like "The King is Coming," "Jesus, There's Something About That Name," "The Family of God," and others which would become standards and establish the Gaither songwriting talent in gospel music.

That album was not particularly well produced, but the following albums saw more money allotted for production and more time spent on vocals. Several live albums reached a quarter million in sales and two children's albums sold 300,000 each. The Gaithers had found their audience of young Christian adults who were the key church audience and this audience found writers and performers they could trust to say something meaningful to them and their lives. Soon the group was filling 10,000-seat auditoriums.

The key to understanding Bill Gaither lies in understanding his motive. "All I have ever wanted to do with my life, ever since I was a kid, was make meaningful moments for people who are serious about life. Now that's a limiting thing right there," he said, "because most people are not serious about life. I get up every morning and I'm still excited about running our publishing company, writing material, getting our stuff in the hands of churches, who, for the most part, are serious and motivated about dealing with the serious issues of life.

What's life all about? What are you going to do with it? Are we going to use our resources to bring Christ to the world? I can still get excited about that. If I were just in music—well, the music has changed so much I wouldn't be doing the kind of music I really love now. So, if I continued doing music that less and less people gravitated to, I would have to find some kind of outside stimulation to keep me excited about that because music itself is not fulfilling enough. I understand why some of the secular guys are on drugs or have stimulants and that kind of stuff. Music by itself is not enough."

Although many have asked why he's never tried his hand at writing pop songs or country tunes through the years, Gaither freely admits he has never felt the urge to do that. "I just don't have any interest," he said. "That's not the way I was wound up."

Many gospel artists come from Christian families, attending church all their lives and feeling drawn to stay within the Christian culture to deliver their message. It is a world they are comfortable with. It is Bill Gaither's story.

During the 1970s and 1980s, Bill Gaither's audiences were comprised mostly of Christians, church-goers who came for an evening of spiritual entertainment. He did not have to convince them of the Christian way of life or defend his faith. They believed together. "I don't think my big motive has ever been to save the world," said Gaither. "I think our motive has been to minister to the body of Christ. I don't think there's a lot of non-Christian people coming to our concerts. There are probably very, very few. I've never tried to kid myself from the beginning so, because of that, we have never given many 'invitations' for people to accept Christ. Not that I'm against that. God has used mass evangelism in a very powerful way. I just don't feel called to be an evangelist."

Bill Gaither was not just a successful songwriter and artist, he was a successful businessman as well, owning the publishing to his songs and operating Spring House, which booked concerts for artists and marketed material to the churches. Except for the publishing company, which is based in Nashville, all his other ventures are based in the small town of Anderson, Indiana. It is where Bill and Gloria Gaither grew up and lived as they raised their three children. It is from this town in Indiana that the music of Bill Gaither originated and took shape. Gaither has said, "you can't keep a good song down"

Evie Tornquist was the first contemporary Christian music "star" in the mid-1970s.

Petra emerged as a Christian rock band during the 1970s and had to overcome a prejudice against rock music in the Christian world.

Michael W. Smith emerged as a one-man boy band during the 1980s. One of the most talented musicians and songwriters in Christian music, Smith influenced a whole generation of artists.

Jimmy Swaggart combined his talents as a musician, singer and evangelist to become a superstar on television and with his recordings during the 1970s and 1980s.

Jarrell McCracken founded Word Records, the label that dominated Christian music during the 1970s and 1980s.

Tennessee Ernie Ford had a Gold album with his "Hymns" LP during the 1950s.

Albertina Walker led the "Gospel Caravans," which became a training ground for a number of top singers and musicians in gospel music.

Billy Ray Hearn founded Sparrow Records in 1976.

Larry Norman was the first "Jesus Rock" star. His "One Way" sign (a single finger pointed heavenward) was the gesture that ignited Jesus Rock audiences.

Amy Grant became the contemporary Christian artist who crossed over to the secular field, achieving success in both fields.

Debby Boone, daughter of 1950s pop idol Pat Boone, had a number one pop hit with "You Light Up My Life" in 1977 and seemed destined to become the artist who would bridge the gap between pop and gospel. But she elected to marry and devote herself to her family instead of pursuing stardom.

Sandi Patti became the dominant singer of "praise and worship" songs during the 1980s and, with Amy Grant, dominated contemporary Christian music during that period.

The Speer Family was a cornerstone of southern gospel music. With their roots going back to the James D. Vaughn singing school, The Speer Family later emerged as radio and recording artists who career has spanned over 60 years.

The Clark Sisters came out of Detroit and became one of the leading female groups in black gospel music.

Shirley Caesar emerged from The Caravans to become a leading soloist. She also was ordained a preacher and led a ministry based in her home state of North Carolina.

The Cathedrals were a premier southern gospel group whose early fame is traced back to appearances with TV evangelist Rex Humbard on his "Cathedral of Tomorrow" show.

The Masters V; bottom row, l to r: Jake Hess, J.D. Sumner and Hovie Lister. This group was formed by several gospel "legends." Hovie Lister founded The Statesmen Quartet, Jake Hess founded The Imperials, and J.D. Sumner sang with The Blackwoods, The Stamps, and Elvis. Watching this group during the 1980s, fans got a glimpse at history on stage.

Tramaine Hawkins, a member of The Walter Hawkins Family during the 1970s and 1980s, stepped out on her own to become a major star in black gospel during the 1990s.

Mylon LeFevre was the original "bad boy" of gospel music during the 1970s. After an early Jesus Rock album, LeFevre, from the famous Singing LeFevre family, backslid for several years before recommitting himself to his faith and becoming a major contemporary Christian music artist.

The Imperials bridged the world between southern gospel and contemporary Christian music. They were pioneers in moving southern gospel towards a more contemporary look and sound, and were the first southern gospel group to find a home in contemporary Christian music. They also starred with Jimmy Dean and Elvis in Las Vegas, but decided to follow gospel rather than secular success.

The Bill Gaither Trio; l to r: Bill Gaither, Gloria Gaither, and Gary McSpadden. Bill Gaither became the single most important figure in gospel music during the latter half of the twentieth century. He is the "Godfather" of Contemporary Christian music, and then rejuvenated Southern Gospel during the 1990s.

The Blackwood Brothers; top right is J.D. Sumner, bottom left is James Blackwood. The Blackwoods began as a family group during the 1930s; their long career has made them legends in the field of gospel music.

Clarence Fountain & The Original 5 Blind Boys emerged after World War II during the "golden age" for gospel groups. They were known for their "mother" songs.

Edwin Hawkins had the first genuine gospel "hit" in the secular field with his recording of "Oh, Happy Day."

no matter where it comes from. You can't keep a good man down either, no matter if he lives in Anderson, Indiana, or one of the music capitals of the world.

In his book *Why Should the Devil Have all the Good Music*, author Paul Baker traces the beginning of the Jesus Movement in America to 1967 when the Christian World Liberation Front opened the first Christian coffeehouse in the Haight-Ashbury district of San Francisco. It was headed by "Holy Hubert" Lindsey, who had preached in Berkeley at the University of California in 1965 when that school came to national fame with its anti-war riots. There were other seeds as well—a number of other small coffee houses and small underground newspapers. These paralleled the rise of "head" shops in the secular culture, small gathering places where drug paraphernalia and underground rock albums were sold. In the Christian world, there was the same funky decor, the same ambiance, but no drugs.

The folk movement of the early '60s spawned hootenannys, which influenced countless youths to sit around campfires at Bible camps and youth meetings and sing songs such as "Kumbaya," "Amen," "I've Got the Joy, Joy, Joy," "Give Me Oil in My Lamp," "When the Saints Go Marching In," "Do Lord," and a other sing-along type songs. Although many of the youths attending church knew these songs, the music never made it inside the sanctuary; the religious leaders preferred 200-year-old hymns. However, there were several traveling groups from evangelistic organizations like Youth For Christ which began appearing at churches and schools. These groups were well-scrubbed, wholesome and had All-American looks and smiles—models of youth—so the adults could easily accept them.

Billy Graham's organization had produced a number of Christian films before *The Restless Ones* in 1965 but this was different because of the music, which was contemporary and aimed at the '60s protest audience. The music, scored by Ralph Carmichael, was tame by later standards, but contained the song "He's Everything to Me," which immediately proved popular. The fact that it came from a Billy Graham film made it acceptable to church audiences who viewed the film.

The year 1965 was also the time for Good News, the first Christian folk musical. *Good News* was composed by Bob Oldenburg,

Billy Ray Hearn, Cecil McGee and a few others. The idea was sparked by large road shows like Up With People which were touring the country. The second major Christian musical, *Tell It Like It Is* by Ralph Carmichael and Kurt Kaiser, proved to be even more popular with church youth as the Jesus Movement caught fire within the Christian world.

The first commercially released Jesus rock album was *Upon This Rock* by Larry Norman, released on Capitol in 1969. Norman had been a member of the group "People," whose recording of "I Love You (But the Words Won't Come)" reached number 14 on the pop charts in 1968. Norman wanted to title the follow-up album *We Need a Whole Lot More of Jesus and a Lot Less Rock 'n' Roll* and put a picture of Jesus on the cover. The label balked and the day the album was released Norman broke with the band. A year later he was invited by Capitol to record a solo album and the result was *Upon This Rock*, which included the song "I Wish We'd All Been Ready." This song was recorded by secular acts as well and quickly became an underground classic in Christian circles. Norman also provided another anthem for the Jesus Revolution, "Why Should the Devil Have All the Good Music," that answered the question of why rock and religion should mix.

Norman had a profound influence on the Jesus movement with his "one way" sign (one finger pointed heavenward). With his incisive lyrics, long blond hair, sharp wit and controversial stage appearances, Norman shook the foundations of many traditional church goers but ignited a number of young people, Christians and non-Christians alike, who realized Jesus could be hip and contemporary and the Bible could be applied to the current world.

Another early Jesus music album was *Mylon* by Mylon LeFevre on Cotillion Records in 1970. Mylon had grown up in southern gospel, serving as a member of the famed LeFevre Singers and performing gospel with his family since he was five. He had also written a number of gospel songs before this first album, including "Without Him," which was recorded by Elvis Presley. The album was an underground classic but LeFevre's own life led him away from his Christian roots and into rock 'n' roll where he "backslid" into drugs before recommitting himself to the straight and narrow in the late '70s and recording albums for gospel labels.

The Everlastin' Living Jesus Concert was the first album released by Maranatha! Music. It appeared in 1971 at a time when Calvary Chapel in Costa Mesa, California was drawing thousands of youths to their services. Calvary Chapel was headed by Chuck Smith and featured a "hippie" preacher named Lonnie Frisbee. Because so many talented musicians attended the church and because so much music originated there, Maranatha! Music was formed. The label would become a leader in "praise and worship" music but its first release (later titled simply "*Maranatha! 1*") was a live recording of a contemporary Christian concert.

Although this first album was important and influential, it was not as influential as Calvary Chapel itself, which continued to be the spiritual home of a number of early contemporary Christian musicians. Some of those who attended were Debby Kerner, Ernie Rettino, Children of the Day, The Way, Country Faith, Karen Lafferty, Good News, Mustard Seed Faith, Blessed Hope, Gentle Faith, Selah, and Kenn Gulliksen. The first group to emerge from Calvary Chapel was Love Song, comprised of Chuck Girard, Jay Truax, Tom Coomes, and Fred Field.

Love Song's first album was released on Good News Records in 1972 and proved to be an immediate success in both the gospel and secular worlds, where it was distributed by Liberty Records. It was the first "hit" album to emerge from the Jesus Movement. Other early albums of Jesus music included *Truth of Truths*, a rock opera; *The Armageddon Experience* from Campus Crusades contemporary group; *Born Twice* by Randy Stonehill; *Songs From the Savior* by Paul Clark; and *Agape* from the first hard rock Christian group by the same name.

Another early group in contemporary Christian music was Andrae Crouch and the Disciples, first formed in Los Angeles in 1965. Crouch, whose father was a preacher, worked with Teen Challenge helping alcoholics and drug addicts and played only part-time until 1970, when he began performing full-time. His first single, "Christian People," was on Liberty Records and he appeared in the early '70s on Johnny Carson's "Tonight Show." On the show he was backed by "Sonlight," a group consisting of Fletch Wiley, Bill Maxwell, Harlan Rogers and Hadley Hockensmith, all of whom would become top studio musicians for contemporary Christian acts.

Most of early contemporary Christian music came out on secular labels—Norman's album on Capitol, LeFevre's on Cotillion—or brand new labels formed for contemporary music—Maranatha! for the Calvary Chapel artists and Good News for Love Song's initial recordings. The established gospel labels, primarily Word and Benson, were apprehensive. The church also questioned whether the Jesus Movement was indeed really Christian. However, as the movement spread and the major Christian labels saw more and more young people attracted to the music, they began signing acts like Randy Matthews, who was the first successful Jesus rock artist for Word Records.

Chapter 26

SOUTHERN GOSPEL IN THE 1960s AND 1970s

During the 1960s and 1970s, the Southern gospel world seemed to be caught in a time warp, left behind by the flower children whose spiritual quest could not stomach such an outdated, outmoded and outlandish form of rural religion. Even the Jesus music revolution could not relate to those in the Southern gospel world—this was a music and culture of the past and the Jesus people wanted a current, hip Jesus, not an old-fashioned icon from history.

But the 1960s was a period of contradictions; there was the "liberal" movement of the cultural revolution and a "conservative" movement that was defined by a hawkish attitude towards Vietnam, opposition to Civil Rights, and social conservatism. The world of Southern gospel represented this anti-liberal trend in the 1960s. Still, it was a vibrant time for this music and several groups define the era.

The Florida Boys began in 1947 when J.G. Whitfield and Roy Howard formed the Gospel Melody Quartet in Pensacola, Florida. Whitfield had always wanted to sing and before World War II had sung with a group called the Happy Hitters. After the war, Whitfield and Howard put together the group that included Guy Dodd on tenor, Edward Singletary on baritone, and Tiny Merrell at the piano with Howard singing lead and Whitfield singing bass. Generally, they sang at conventions, churches, schools, and wherever else they could around Pensacola.

Tragedy struck the quartet in 1951 when, after singing at a Pensacola radio station, Roy Howard died suddenly of a heart attack. But the group kept going and in September 1952 Glen Allred joined, playing guitar and singing baritone, while Les Beasley, singing lead, was added in the spring of 1953.

The name of the group changed to The Florida Boys around 1954. The change came because the group—still calling itself the Gospel Melody Quartet—was being promoted by Wally Fowler, who had earlier popularized the all-night sings in Southern gospel. Fowler insisted the group's name was not distinctive enough, so on posters that advertised their concerts he would put "The Boys From Florida." According to Les Beasley, "Wally is really the one who made us change our name. He was the biggest guy in our life as far as promotion was concerned so we went on with the change."

According to one story, the "official" name change took place one morning when Whitfield walked into a rehearsal. "Fellows," he reportedly said. "As of today, we're the Florida Boys." Les Beasley asked, "Just like that?" Whitfield replied, "Just like that. That's the only way we can do it." Nobody argued with his reasoning and from that time on the group was The Florida Boys. Group members included Beasley, Allred, Whitfield, Buddy Mears on tenor, and Emory Parker on piano.

J.G. Whitfield quit the group in 1958; he had already gotten involved in promoting concerts and saw his interest heading more in the direction of the business of gospel concert promotion. After his marriage in 1957, Whitfield turned the group over to Beasley, Allred, and Derrell Stewart, who joined as the piano player, while Whitfield settled in Pensacola and ran a local business.

Although Whitfield continued to sing through the years, as well as promote concerts, his biggest contribution to Southern gospel came with the introduction of *The Singing News*, the paper for Southern gospel which he began in 1969 after getting a list of 100,000 possible subscribers from his own mailing lists (for promoting concerts) and the lists of two other gospel promoters, W.B. Nowlin and Lloyd Orrell. The idea came from *Good News*, a newsletter published by the Gospel Music Association, which was then headed by J.D. Sumner.

After Whitfield left the Florida Boys, there were several slow years. But in 1959 the group received a break with the advent of their 30-minute television show, "The Gospel Songshop." The Chattanooga Medicine Company had been sponsoring gospel music on radio with the LeFevres in the 1930s and 1940s and wanted to get involved in television. The company could not get the LeFevres because they already had a show, "Gospel Music Caravan," sponsored by Martha White. Since the account representative for the company knew Whitfield, he was approached about doing a television show which first played in a test market in Greenville, South Carolina on a Saturday in the late afternoon and was a huge success.

The Chattanooga Medicine Company purchased 31 weeks of air time a year for the show and the rest of the year local sponsors purchased ads. This ran for several years before the Chattanooga Medicine Company discontinued this arrangement. Noble Dury and Associates, an advertising agency, then stepped in. Jane Doughten, a vice-president with the company, and Les Beasley came up with the concept of the "Gospel Singing Jubilee," which would feature several groups in an hour-long program. They sold 15 minutes to the Chattanooga Medicine Company, and allotted 30 minutes to each local station to sell time.

Later the agency confronted an anti-trust ruling that said they could not be both a producer and an agent so they formed a separate company, Show Biz, headed by Bill Graham, which produced the show.

"The Gospel Singing Jubilee" was one of the first gospel singing programs to be on Sunday mornings and opened up Sunday morning television for Southern gospel music. The show began in 1964 and at one time was on in virtually every major television market in the United States. The show ran for twenty-five years and closed after winning a number of Gospel Dove Awards (for "Best Television Program").

During the late 1970s and early 1980s "The Gospel Singing Jubilee" had a better rating and larger audience than any of the high-profile televangelists.

The first recordings by the Florida Boys were on their own label, which was a subsidiary of King Records in Cincinnati. The recordings, on 78s, were sold over their radio show and at personal appearances. There were also a number of transcriptions made from their local radio programs—there would be three or four 15-minute shows each day in Pensacola which were aired on other stations.

The first big "break" in recordings came through Bill Beasley (no relation to Les Beasley) from Cincinnati, who had a label that recorded a number of sound-a-likes (recordings of popular hits that sounded as close to the original as possible), which he sold for 33 cents apiece. The Florida Boys made some of these sound-a-likes. Then Bill Beasley formed a gospel label called Faith in 1959 and offered the Florida Boys a $1,000 advance per album to record. Since the group had never really gotten any money from their records, this seemed like the big time.

In 1963 Jarrell McCracken, president of the fledgling Word Records in Waco, called Les Beasley to ask him if the group would consider recording for Word. McCracken had seen the group on television and wanted to start a Southern Gospel division. The Florida Boys became the first artists signed to Canaan Records, headed by Marvin Norcross, which began Word's involvement in Southern gospel.

The first big hit for the group was "There's a Leak in This Old Building," which received additional fame when Elvis Presley sang it in the movie *Love Me Tender*. That first hit happened around 1954 and their next big hit was "Surely I Will." The first real album came out in 1958 and was called *The Eleventh Anniversary*. It was the first time the group had ever recorded an album's worth of material on a 33 rpm vinyl record; previously they had recorded single songs on 33s after recording single songs on 78s.

The gospel heritage runs deep for the Florida Boys—deeper than all the years they have been together. For Les Beasley, these roots go back to the 1930s and 1940s in the Texas and Louisiana area where he first heard the Stamps-Baxter gospel singers on radio. He soon developed a love of gospel music growing up in his father's church and always felt drawn to the male quartet sound. In 1946 he began singing with the McManus Trio in New Orleans. This husband-wife team, along with Les, did a number of Youth For Christ rallies and one-nighters all over Louisiana. After a stint with the Marines in Korea, Beasley returned to this group.

The Cathedrals began as a trio with Rex Humbard in 1963. The group was comprised of Glen Payne, Bobby Clark, and Danny Koker. George Younce had been in the Blue Ridge Quartet with Jim Hamill (later with the Kingsmen) when Rex Humbard called and asked him to come back to the Cathedral of Tomorrow—the church Humbard had established in Akron, Ohio, with his national television ministry—and sing. He did and the Cathedral Trio became the Cathedral Quartet in November 1964.

Glen Payne and George Younce, the two cornerstones for The Cathedrals, met for the first time in Stow, Ohio, when George came to join Glen's group. The first time George met Glen was not the first time George met Rex Humbard. Their relationship went back 13 years to when the Weatherfords were part of the Humbard team. That was in 1956 but later that year George, along with Jim Hamill, Danny Koker, and Tallmadge Martin, moved to Milwaukee to re-form the Watchmen Quartet.

The beginning of the Cathedral Quartet was not the beginning of singing gospel music for either Glen Payne or George Younce. Glen had first wanted to be a gospel singer "around six or seven when I sang with my Granddad," he said. "I was raised in a Christian home and our type of music had always been gospel. I had heard quartets since I was knee high and that's what I wanted to do."

The big turning point came when he was 17 and Frank Stamps called to give him a job with the Stamps Quartet. Later, Glen would be drafted into the service. When he came back, he returned to gospel singing, joining the Lester Stamps Quartet and then the Stamps-Ozark Quartet until he joined the Weatherfords in 1957. Glen moved from his native state of Texas to Ohio and stayed with the Weatherfords until 1963, when he started the Cathedral Trio.

George Younce was bitten by the gospel singing bug in Lenoir, North Carolina. "I went to hear a group called the Harmoneers," he said. "And I was just a teenager. They were playing in Gainesville, North Carolina, at a high school there and when I heard them that night, I'll never forget it, I knew that's what I wanted to do."

George, too, had come from a Christian home where gospel singing was part of everyday life. His father was a bass singer and sang in the choir and in Sunday afternoon singing conventions. The first group George was in was called the Spiritualaires; he switched from lead to bass when his voice changed.

George became a full-time gospel singer through an odd set of circumstances. "I was in the service with a boy from West Virginia and he got killed," said George. "I went to visit his parents—I didn't know them but I knew Bill—and when I was there I met a quartet who was there that day and their bass singer had just moved to California. So we rehearsed a little bit and they said, 'Move on up here.' I wanted to sing so bad that I moved on up there and lived with one of the boys and we sang on weekends. Whatever they made they took out for the gas and the car—they all had jobs—and they'd give me what money was left over because I didn't have a job at the time. Of course, living with them it didn't take anything."

That was 1954 in Beckley, West Virginia, and the group was the Watchmen Quartet, who teamed with Rex Humbard in 1956. From there, George re-formed the Watchman Quartet before joining the Blue Ridge Quartet in 1957 with whom he stayed until he joined the Cathedrals in November 1964.

There were a number of Cathedral members through the years, including Bobby Clark, Danny Koker, Mack Taunton, George Amon Webster, Lorne Matthews, Roger Horne, Roy Tremble, Bill Dykes, Jim Garstain, and Haskell Cooley. In 1979 a big change occurred for the Cathedrals. Three members—Roy Tremble, George Amon Webster and Lorne Matthews—all decided to leave the group. That left the two cornerstones, Glen and George, standing alone.

"Glen and I were talking one day over at my home," said George, "and I said, 'Maybe this is the Lord's way of saying He wants us to retire or something.' So we prayed, 'Lord, if this is it, then make it impossible for us to get anybody we can sing with and want to be with.' And the Lord proved to us from the first member that he wasn't through with us yet. That was when Kirk Talley called."

Gospel music takes its toll on the singers and their families through the incessant traveling it entails. It is not easy to constantly have to leave home, a wife, and growing children, and climb aboard a bus to go to distant places and sing. Those who leave this gospel world generally do so because they tire of this life week after week, year in and year out. For that reason, those who continue to travel and sing must feel a special call, a special mission to do what they do. Glen reflected on this when he stated that, "After years of traveling I think you realize your days are numbered when you travel as much as we do on the road. I think you realize it's more a ministry. When you first start out, the glamour of it all is important to you. As you get a little older you realize to sing the gospel means seeing somebody saved. Blessing people's hearts becomes more important to you."

A third major group in the history of Southern gospel is The Kingsmen. In an era when Southern gospel, like other forms of gospel, sought to upgrade itself and cut the ties from its rural

Southern heritage, the Kingsmen are unique because they clung to that heritage. Lead singer Jim Hamill referred to their music as "three chords and a cloud of dust" and it was this decision to shun pretenses and stay close to their roots that ensured the Kingsmen of a continuing appeal.

The leader of the Kingsmen was Eldridge Fox, who decided he wanted to be in Southern gospel when he was a youngster in the first grade. That was when he went to his first concert and, according to Fox, "From that moment on, my dream and my goal was to be a gospel singer and have a gospel quartet."

While in high school in Asheville, North Carolina, Fox formed a quartet called The Silvertones with Frank Cutshall, Charles Stoll, Jim Kirby, and Lena Elliot. In their junior and senior years they sang on weekends. After graduation in 1954 most of the members entered the armed forces. Fox joined The Ambassadors, playing piano and singing lead in 1955 and 1956 before spending time in the Army in 1956 and 1957. He still managed to sing with the quartet on weekends in Atlanta where they backed Wally Fowler. He also worked for Hovie Lister and the Statesmen, running their Faith, Henson, and Vep Ellis music companies.

After the Silvertones disbanded, another group formed in Asheville. Comprised of Charles Collier, Louise McKinney, Raymond McKinney, Reese McKinney, and pianist Charles Mathews, the group was named The Kingsmen. Mathews, who named the group, died and was replaced by Martin Cook—later with the Inspirations—on piano.

In 1957 Charles Cutshall returned to Asheville from the Air Force and joined the Kingsmen, replacing Louis McKinney, who had been killed in an automobile accident. In 1958 Fox moved back to Asheville from Atlanta and replaced Martin Cook as pianist. The Kingsmen were weekend singers, holding down regular jobs during the week, and the group soon disbanded because of the conflicts between their jobs and the singing. Fox, who still dreamed of owning a quartet, bought out the other members of the group and retained the name "Kingsmen."

In July 1970 Eldridge Fox hired Jim Hamill to sing lead, Jerry Redd to sing tenor, Ray Dean Reese to sing bass, and Charles Abee to play piano, with himself singing baritone. Fox proved adept at managing until he reached the point where managing the group took most of his time and he became a part-time singer, only singing with the group occasionally while handling their business the rest of the time. The group thrived but as Fox moved out of the spotlight, another figure became known as the personification of the Kingsmen on stage. That man was Jim Hamill.

Hamill was born in Big Stone Gap, Virginia and began singing lead in church when he was seven. At 12 he sang with his grandfather, aunt, and grandmother at the Tri-State Singing Convention. His family moved to Memphis where his father pastored the First Assembly of God Church which the Blackwoods attended. Hamill got to know the Blackwoods and formed a quartet in high school with Cecil Blackwood in 1952. This group, The Songfellows, is the group Elvis Presley auditioned for and was turned down.

When Cecil left the Songfellows to join the Blackwoods in 1954, after the deaths of R.W. and Bill Lyle, Hamill attended Bible college but soon grew dissatisfied because he was not singing. He was offered a job with a group—also called The Songfellows—in Shenandoah, Iowa and went to work for them, broadcasting over KMA.

After the Songfellows, Hamill joined the Melodymen, then the Weatherford Quartet, before landing with The Foggy River Boys on Red Foley's "Ozark Jubilee." Hamill then sang with the Blue Ridge Quartet, the Rebels, the Oak Ridge Boys and then the Rebels again until 1971, when he joined the Kingsmen. When Fox decided to concentrate on the business side of the industry and Hamill took over the songs and stage shows, he elected to mold the quartet into an emotional, rough-edged group with a strong backbone of fundamentalism. Hamill told the group when he was making the change that "as long as there were fundamental, Bible-believing churches we'd always have a place to sing the old-time Gospel."

In the mid-'60s there was no contemporary Christian music as it later became known; the Imperials and the Oak Ridge Boys, although part of the world of Southern gospel music, were contemporary Christian music. The moves they made to contemporize were more than just changes in the music—they were changes in attitudes and appearances. The problems, pitfalls, dilemmas, and decisions they faced would be faced by others in Christian music over and over again. The first to act on this were the Oak Ridge Boys.

The Oak Ridge Quartet was originally the Georgia Clodhoppers, led by Wally Fowler. The Clodhoppers were a country group and played on the Grand Ole Opry; they also performed gospel songs and sometimes did gospel shows. After World War II, Fowler renamed the group "The Oak Ridge Quartet" and eventually the Clodhoppers ceased to be. In 1949 this first group of singers quit and Fowler formed a new group. In 1956 the second group disbanded and Wally Fowler, who had sold the Oak Ridge Quartet's group and name, was forming a group called the Country Boys. Fowler hired E. Smith "Smitty" Gatlin as lead and then Ronnie Page. The Country Boys became the "Oak Ridge Quartet," filling the gap that opened up when the Oaks disbanded. They added tenor Hobart Evans, pianist Powell Hassell, and bass singer Bill Smith.

After a week of rehearsals, the group debuted at a New Year's Eve all-night singing in Birmingham. Bass Bill Smith soon dropped out and was replaced by Herman Harper. The group was young—the oldest member, Powell Hassell, was only 22—and they sang songs made famous by the previous Oak Ridge Quartet.

In 1957 Marty Robbins hired the group for a series of fair dates; in late 1957 Hassell quit and was replaced by Tommy Fairchild; then Hobart Evans left and was replaced by tenor Willie Wynn. Fowler owned the Quartet, but owed them about $3,000; he offered to "give" the group to Smitty Gatlin in return for forgiving the debt. Gatlin agreed.

The Oaks recorded first for Cadence Records out of Chicago, then in 1959 recorded an album for Monument and two for Skylite, the company owned by the Blackwood Brothers and Statesmen. In the early 1960s they recorded two albums for Starday and one for United Artists. In 1962, after Gary McSpadden joined on baritone, they recorded two albums for Warner Brothers and changed their name from the Oak Ridge Quartet to the Oak Ridge Boys.

When McSpadden left the group, Jim Hamill joined, but he never quite fit in and was replaced by Bill Golden in 1965. The group was a pioneer in gospel fashion; they were the first to go on stage in sports coats and turtlenecks—not neckties—and were criticized for this. Some churches even forbade them to play in their sanctuaries. In 1965 they signed a booking agreement with Don Light, who had just formed the first exclusively gospel booking agency, at a time when most other acts booked themselves.

In Spring 1966 Smitty Gatlin left the group and was replaced by Duane Allen. Golden and Allen would be the nucleus of the group;

both were ambitious and wanted the Oaks to push further than other gospel groups. In fall 1968 Herman Harper resigned and joined Don Light's talent agency; he was replaced by Noel Fox.

The group put an emphasis on "clean entertainment," not ministry. They performed some dates with Andrae Crouch and saw themselves as gospel entertainers, not gospel evangelists. They were criticized by other groups for their long hair, mod clothes and contemporary sound. They were also the most successful gospel group on the road, attracting young and old to their shows.

In 1968 they began a TV show, "It's Happening with the Oak Ridge Boys," from Shreveport on KTAL-TV; in 1970 they toured Sweden and in 1971 appeared on Johnny Cash's network TV show. In 1972 bass singer Noel Fox left the group and was replaced by Richard Sterban; less than a year later, Willie Wynn left and the group added Joe Bonsall. This was their 40th change in singers since 1956—but it would be the line-up that lasted.

In 1973 the Oaks left HeartWarming, a gospel label, and signed with secular giant Columbia Records. Columbia thought they could sell gospel to country audiences and had found themselves some "gospel rebels" to attract young people. But Columbia did not service gospel stations and so the Oaks lost on two fronts—country radio would not and gospel stations could not play their recordings.

In August 1974 the played the Las Vegas Hilton with Johnny Cash and had a minor hit on Columbia with "The Baptism of Jesse Taylor." The next year they sang back-up on a Jimmy Buffett song, "My Head Hurts, My Feet Stink, and I Don't Love Jesus," which caused a further split with the gospel world.

Five promoters controlled the bookings of Southern gospel groups; the Oaks had been used to doing 150 dates a year for them but in 1975 they were booked on only three dates. Their last gospel date, in Roanoke, Virginia, ended their career in gospel. The Kingsmen made disparaging remarks about them from the stage, and about 200 members of the audience stood up and walked out when the Oaks took the stage.

The idea that a top gospel group could sell to the secular market doing gospel songs was proving to be a bust; so was the idea that the most popular act in gospel music could have a secular appeal. The Oaks had fallen between the cracks; finally, they signed management and booking agreements with Jim Halsey, who also managed Roy Clark, then signed with a new record label, ABC/Dot. In 1977 they recorded a country song, "Ya'll Come Back Saloon," that was a major country hit. From this point, they would be country stars with a gospel heritage. Their days in gospel music were over.

The Imperials are a different story. They were formed in 1964 by the hottest gospel singer of the day. Jake Hess wanted a super group and had his own theory of how a gospel group should look and perform. He handpicked what he felt were the best talents from other groups for the Imperials—Armand Morales (from the Weatherford Quartet), Shirl Neilson, Gary McSpadden, and pianist Henry Slaughter.

Hess required all group members to sign moral contracts, stating that they would not dally with members of the opposite sex they were not married to or otherwise conduct themselves in a manner fast, loose, libertine, or unbecoming to a personal representative of God. Because the other groups dressed alike in shiny matching suits, the Imperials dressed more casually, wearing sports coats of different colors while their vocal harmonies were smooth and tight instead of the more ragged sound prevalent at the time. Because of the tremendous popularity of Hess, the group immediately had a full schedule of bookings and because of the new look and sound, they took the Southern gospel world by storm, ushering in a new era in this music.

After about a year, Shirl Neilson left the group and was replaced by Jim Murray. A short while later Henry Slaughter resigned and Joe Moscheo was hired to play piano. To give an idea of the relative wealth of gospel performers during this time, pianist Joe Moscheo was hired for $150 a week while each of the singers was making $200-250 per week. This was c. 1966-1976. Then, as now, with a number of Southern gospel groups, someone owned the group and was responsible for management, maintaining an office, buying clothes, paying the hotel bills, and generally running the group like a small private business. That someone was Jake Hess. The Imperials were doing well in the Southern gospel world, making anywhere from $600-1000 a night for their performances.

The next step was to sign a recording contract with a major Christian label—in this case, The Benson Company. The Benson Company helped the group buy a bus for touring and released a record, making the Imperials one of the first professional groups on what had previously been basically a custom record company.

A custom record is one where the artist or group pays for the recording out of his own pocket instead of the label paying the initial costs. Then, the artist is responsible for selling the albums himself, without distribution to stores. This is usually done by selling the records at live appearances and wherever the artist can find willing buyers. The custom record business serves somewhat like a farm club system for gospel acts and labels keep their eyes on these performers—when they sell a large number on their own, a major company is then willing to sign them up.

Hess had health problems—a bad heart—and in 1965 he decided to quit the road, so Moscheo, Jim Murray, and Armand Morales purchased the group from him. When Hess left there was an immediate reaction in the gospel world and 93 scheduled dates were cancelled by gospel promoters who had booked the Imperials because Hess was the lead singer. This left the group broke, with hardly any dates for the coming year. They played some churches for love offerings (collections where the audience puts in what they wish at the end of a performance), getting $50-100 a night sometimes, trying to keep the group together and themselves fed.

The Imperials' office was in the RCA building on Music Row in Nashville. Through their friendship with Mary Lynch, Chet Atkins's secretary, they were booked for an Elvis Presley session—the one that yielded the gospel album *How Great Thou Art*. For these sessions, RCA wanted a choir sound so the Jordanaires—Elvis's long-time back-up group—-and some female background singers were hired as well as the Imperials. This was the Imperials' first contact with Elvis and it allowed them to make some money singing background on studio sessions.

Mary Lynch also connected the Imperials with Jimmy Dean, hot off his ABC-TV show, who had a recording date scheduled but did not know any of the songs. The Imperials worked with him, teaching him the songs, and for this were given the job of singing back-up for Dean. Dean and the Imperials' got along so well that he invited the group to travel with him to California where he was performing. There, they were to sing on his show as part of The Cimarron Singers, a group of background singers from New York dressed in cowboy garb. For the Dean trip, the Imperials were given $1000 for a week's work; since they were making much less than that in Nashville, they gladly took it. Soon, Dean dropped the rest of the Cimarron Singers (there were about 12) and hired the Imperials alone to sing behind him as well as perform some opening numbers in his show. Jimmy Dean was a very hot country act, having had "Big Bad John" and a number of other hits, and soon the Imperials found themselves playing Las Vegas, Lake Tahoe, Reno, state fairs, rodeos, and the top theaters in the country.

In 1969 Elvis called the Imperials to ask them to perform on his show and soon the group was performing with Elvis as well as Dean—which meant even more Vegas appearances. Working with Elvis was very prestigious, but the Imperials made a lot of sacrifices. Colonel Tom Parker, Presley's manager, would call two weeks before a tour and tell the group where they would play. The problem was that the group often had other bookings in the gospel world. They would scramble to cancel these bookings, making a lot of people in the gospel industry irate.

After several years of doing this, the conflict of performing with Dean and Elvis became so great that the Imperials had to reevaluate their position. Elvis offered only a background slot and lots of glamour while Jimmy Dean offered the same amount of money, a back-up slot, and a solo part of his show as well as participation in his new syndicated TV show. The Imperials decided it was a better move for their career to stick with Jimmy Dean.

Their resignation as back-ups to Elvis raised more than a few eyebrows because of the glamour and prestige involved, but the group felt strongly they should do it. After they left, Elvis hired J.D. Sumner and the Stamps Quartet to be part of his show; they remained with him until his death.

In 1975 the Imperials reached a crossroads. There were two groups in gospel music who were at the top of the field—the Imperials and the Oak Ridge Boys. The talk was strong that gospel music could hit the secular world in a big way with one of these groups. Because of the exposure each group had received, both within and outside the gospel community, it was thought secular success was just around the corner.

The Oaks decided to make that move—taking their music to the secular marketplace—and, after starving for a couple years, hit it big in country music. But because they had to abandon gospel music to achieve success, they proved that the secular industry would not buy a gospel artist as they had originally thought. The Oaks had definitely given it a good, strong shot but had come up short. Meanwhile, the Christian audience, who have been known to bury their wounded, abandoned the Oaks and cut them off from that world.

The Imperials watched what happened to the Oaks and decided they wanted to immerse themselves more deeply in the gospel industry, continuing to record for gospel labels. Imperials member Jim Murray admits the group had an identity crisis during this time. "Sometimes we didn't know who we were or who we wanted to be," he said. The Vegas circuit was very lucrative and some of the lounges where they had performed were wanting them to return. TV shows such as Merv Griffin, Mike Douglas, and Dinah had them on and welcomed them back. But the Imperials decided not to go that route.

Gospel audiences frown heavily on an act performing in Las Vegas and with secular artists. It's all or nothing, they say, and the Imperials decided to stake their all in the Christian world—a move they did not regret but one they nonetheless had to make. They believed God was calling them to sing about Him and not perform the Vegas circuit. Too, they desired to be more heavily involved in the ministry, less in show biz entertainment.

Another insight into the gospel audience regarding the Imperials: the group proved their progressive thinking by hiring Sherman Andrus, an African-American, to sing with the group in 1972. Andrus was the first black to enter the Southern gospel world and, like Jackie Robinson and James Meredith, he paid a price. The Imperials were rewarded for this move by having a number of dates cancelled and by finding themselves forbidden to play in a number of places where they had once performed. But that was just part of the Christian way of life in the South during the early 1970s.

The Imperials became accepted not only in the Southern gospel world, but also in the contemporary Christian world—two worlds which had not always been compatible in the past. For a long time the Southern gospel world looked on the Jesus Movement of the late 60s and early 70s as a bunch of hippies polluting gospel music. The Jesus People responded by accusing the Southern gospel world of carrying on a religion riddled with hypocrisy and following a conservative redneck Jesus who, they felt, did not capture the true spirit of the original.

It was the bridge that the Imperials built between the contemporary and Southern gospel worlds and even the secular world that was their greatest contribution. They showed there were no boundary lines—these worlds which were once so far apart had far more in common than either one had originally thought. The Imperials proved their talent as well as their faith and priorities, arriving at a point where they were possibly the group who reached more people with more diverse tastes with the Christian message than any other musical ministry in Christian music.

This desire to promote the ministry was shared by a number of groups and individuals who saw contemporary Christian music as a way of reaching kids in the pop culture with the gospel message. Many of these groups came from strong Christian backgrounds, growing up with the radio on a rock 'n' roll station. For them, playing gospel rock 'n' roll was somewhat like missionary work, but instead of going to a foreign country, they went to the church world. Unfortunately, they often found some ugly Americans in the Christian world.

Americans have always shown an affinity for gospel songs done by non-religious artists. This is best exemplified by Tennessee Ernie Ford's success recording gospel music in the late 1950's, and with Elvis Presley.

The first gospel quartet Elvis was closely associated with professionally was the Jordanaires, who recorded with him on his earliest RCA recordings. Elvis had first met the Jordanaires at the Grand Ole Opry when he performed there in 1955. They had been formed in 1948 in Missouri but Gordon Stoker, first tenor, was the only original member left. Hoyt Hawkins, baritone, had joined in 1950 and in 1953 Neal Matthews, second tenor, joined and Hugh Jarrett was added on bass. All had studied music in college and sung spirituals as well as barbershop quartet songs. Their performance of spirituals was the reason they were performing on the Opry and the reason Elvis asked them to record with him.

Elvis had gone from being a teen heartthrob to a member of Uncle Sam's Army and, when he got out in 1960, he spent the next decade in Hollywood making movies. As a result, Elvis had not performed before live audiences—except on movie sets—for nine years when he decided to return to the stage in 1969. He hired the Imperials to perform with him after the Jordanaires turned down his invitation to play Vegas and tour because, as studio singers, they felt they could not afford to be away from Nashville so much.

After the Imperials left, Elvis instructed Charlie Hodge, one of his "Memphis mafia," to call Sumar Talent for another gospel group. Heading the agency at the time was J.D. Sumner, and he suggested the Stamps Quartet, who had been re-formed and were coming along well as a group. Sumner was wanting to get off the road and go into management and booking and had hired another bass singer, Richard Sterban (later with the Oak Ridge Boys), to sing with the Stamps. The rest of the line-up included Bill Baize, Ed Enoch, and Donnie Sumner, J.D.'s son.

J.D. saw this booking as a short-term replacement for the Imperials, which Sumar also booked. In short, he felt he was protecting his client, the Imperials, who were facing a double booking problem and he expected the Imperials to re-join Elvis at some future time.

J.D. Sumner first met Elvis around 1949 when Elvis was 14 and J.D. was a member of the Sunshine Quartet. Elvis had always been a fan of gospel music and Memphis was a hotbed for this activity, the home and headquarters for the Blackwood Brothers. When J.D. joined the Blackwoods, he continued to see Elvis at concerts, letting him in the back door at the Memphis Coliseum occasionally so he would not have to pay. For the young Elvis, people like J.D., the Blackwoods, and other gospel quartets were idols and he set his sights on someday singing gospel with them. Thus, when Elvis saw Sumner sitting down while the Stamps assembled on stage to rehearse, he promptly asked, "Why aren't you up here?"

J.D. replied that he had just come as a manager and booker looking out for his group. Elvis told him in no uncertain terms to get himself on stage and pointed out that J.D. had his own microphone set apart to sing into and Elvis wanted some of those deep bass drops during his show that Sumner was so noted for. And so it was done.

Later, Elvis told the Stamps he wanted them to open his show with about a 20-minute performance. The Stamps gathered and began naming songs they could do—secular tunes—but Sumner made the decision to stick with gospel. Their first solo performance was in

Greenville, South Carolina, and the group received two standing ovations. Later that night, Elvis called J.D. to his room and thanked him for the gospel performance, then gave him a check for $10,000 and asked if the Stamps would continue to sing gospel to open the show. J.D. looked at the check and replied, "Why certainly, boss."

J.D. Sumner has often recounted touring with Elvis, how after almost every show Elvis would gather the singers together to sing gospel songs.

Sumner spent a good deal of time at Elvis' home and was always amazed at how many gospel albums Presley owned. "All he listened to was gospel," said J.D. "He didn't even listen to his own records." Sumner relates a story that occurred when a whole group was at Elvis' home in Memphis to record. Elvis would only record when he felt like it and on this particular Saturday evening he apparently did not feel like it, although RCA had set up a studio in his home. Finally, just before eight on Sunday morning Elvis came down and told the group he did not want to record and that he was going to watch the Florida Boys, whose show was coming on television in a few minutes.

Sumner was surprised and rushed back to his hotel room to watch the show too. He told the Florida Boys about the incident, and they were pleased and surprised, but they would never have known that Elvis was a fan unless Sumner had told them. This underscores a unique situation: although Elvis was a big fan of Southern gospel, and many in Southern gospel were fans of his, there was no communication between the two. Part of this was because of the isolation of Elvis, but part of it was also because rock and Southern gospel are literally worlds apart. They only came together because of Elvis Presley using Southern gospel groups on his show.

Much more can be said about Elvis' affection for gospel music but it can all be summed up by noting that at his funeral in Memphis in August 1977, Kathy Westmoreland—who sang with Elvis in his shows and on his records—sang "My Heavenly Father Watches Over Me," Jake Hess and two members of the Statesmen sang "Known Only To Him," James Blackwood with the Stamps sang "How Great Thou Art," and, finally, the Stamps sang "Sweet Sweet Spirit."

It is difficult to gauge Presley's effect on gospel except to note that by influencing popular music in general, he certainly had an effect on gospel, which often incorporates popular musical trends in songs and reflects those trends in recordings. The effect gospel music had on Presley is also difficult to ascertain but at the end of his life, it is obvious that Presley kept in touch with his religious roots through gospel music. Indeed, it may be argued that after 1956, gospel music was Christianity for Elvis. He seemed to find spiritual nourishment there and used the music as a way to keep in touch with his earlier days before he became the rich and famous rock 'n' roll star.

In many ways Elvis was a phony because he could only sing the message, he could not live it. He remained haunted by gospel music and the gospel itself all his life but somehow could not reconcile his later life to his boyhood beliefs. Still, it is through Elvis that so many rockers and rock writers know about the gospel roots of early rock 'n' roll. The music has moved far away from those roots through the years, especially with the British influence and their lack of religious roots in rock, but the emotional fervor and dramatic intensity so prevalent in southern religion is still encased in the best of rock 'n' roll.

In the end, the biggest contribution made by Elvis to gospel is that he made the rock 'n' roll world aware of the music and gave it a platform on his shows and a sense of respectability in the rock world. He showed his audiences that at the heart of his own music was gospel, and he shared the songs and influences which formed the core of his being.

Chapter 27

THE CATHOLICS

The Catholics have long been a "breed apart" from mainline American Protestantism and have generally had little if any effect on the Christian revivals in early America. Their rigid structure and control by the Vatican left their faith basically unchanged while the American Protestant religions were changing dramatically. However, the major changes brought about by Vatican II in the 1960s were felt by American Catholicism and musically led the way towards introducing contemporary music into their religion through the "folk masses" of the mid-60s. This introduction of folk music into the church service preceeded the introduction of contemporary music into Protestant churches. With this move—and their overtures to Protestants to unite under the banner of Christianity—the American Catholic church for the first time affected a major Christian revival: the Jesus Revolution of the late 60s and early 70s. Too, John Kennedy became the first Catholic president in 1961, challenging many of the traditional fears and superstitions held by American Protestants about Catholics.

The history of music in the Catholic church begins with the establishment of the priestly liturgic chant, which had replaced the songs in public worship as early as the 4th century. This chant was exclusively vocal and evolved from the selection and integration of certain prayers, Scripture lessons, hymns, and responses woven together until a "religious poem" emerged which expressed the relation of Christ to the church. This great prayer was primarily composed of contributions from the Eastern church during the first four centuries, which were adopted and transferred to Latin by the Church of Rome. Its form was basically completed by the end of the 6th century.

This "religious poem" or "great prayer" is the Mass and several kinds of Masses have been developed: High Mass, Solemn High Mass, Low Mass, Requiem Mass or Mass for the Dead, Mass of Presanctified, Nuptial Mass, Votive Mass, etc. However, there is little difference in the essential elements of these Masses and virtually no difference in the words of the High Mass, Solemn High Mass, and Low Mass, only in the performance and degree of embellishment.

The Christian church began as an extension of Judaism and the early church had no formal break with the Judaic tradition. The disciples assembled regularly in small gatherings modeled on that of the synagogue. With the passing of the Apostolic Age (c. 33 to 100) the young church entered a period of expansion as well as controversy and persecution. The center had shifted from Jerusalem to Antioch to Ephesus and then, by the end of the 2nd century, to Rome and Alexandria. Rome offered the world great wealth and prestige while Alexandria had the early thinkers, philosophers, and apologists.

For music, the early Christians used Hebrew melodies and cultivated the habit of antiphonal or responsive chanting of the psalms. But as the church grew, it became more organized and the shift from the homogeneous, democratic system of the apostolic age to a hierarchical organization occurred under the Western popes and Eastern patriarchs who developed an elaborate system of rites and ceremonies which were "partly an evolution from within, partly an inheritance of ancient habits and dispositions, which at last became formulated into unvarying types of devotional expression." Music was part of this ritualistic movement and it rapidly became liturgical and clerical as the laity stopped sharing in the worship through song. A chorus, drawn from minor clergy, took over the highly organized body of chants which were almost the entire substance of worship music and remained that way for a thousand years.

The independent songs of the people were replaced by the sacerdotal and liturgical movement and the people's part of the service became limited to responses at the end of the verses of the psalms. Originally, the singing of psalms and hymns by a group of worshippers was the custom of the early churches at informal assemblies but the progress of ritualism and growth of sacerdotal ideas put all the initiative of public devotion—including songs—on the clergy. This shift from a people-centered service to a clergy-centered and controlled one was complete by the middle of the 4th century, if not earlier. The reason appears fairly simple: doctrinal vageries and mystical extravagances as well as unified teaching could serve as a control for the religion through these ritualistic, clergy-centered services. Too, Christianity was becoming a political as well as religious power.

The idea that songs should be used to instruct converts in the faith goes back to the first days of Christianity, to the time of the apostle Paul and his allusion to "psalms, hymns, and spiritual songs." Here, he divides songs into three categories, probably meaning ancient Hebrew psalms for "psalms," hymns taken from the Old Testament for "hymns," and songs composed by the early Christians themselves for "spiritual songs." In 112, it was recorded that Christians were "coming together before daylight and singing hymns alternatively to Christ."

This early music was a combination of Greek and Hebrew. Paul wrote his Epistles in Greek and the earliest liturgies are in Greek while the Hebraic influence was felt in the sentiment of prayer and praise. The use of songs for worship worked because it was impressive and easily remembered; Edward Dickinson, in his *Music in the History of the Western Church*, notes that, "The injunction to teach and admonish by means of songs also agrees with other evidences that a prime motive for hymn singing in many of the churches was instruction in the doctrines of the faith."

As the church grew, so did the opposition to musical instruments. The prejudice against instruments came about primarily because of the association of these instruments with superstitious pagan rites and their connection with the theater and circus, two degenerate forms of entertainment. Thus the purely vocal chants emerged as the dominant form of music in the church. This was a split from the Hebraic tradition where instruments were used in the temples and from the Greek and Roman song tradition.

The Greeks and Romans sang songs that were metrical but the Christian psalms, antiphons, prayers, responses, etc. were unmetrical as church music moved away from rhythm to a mystical chant. As the music moved away from rhythm, it also moved away from the people to the sole authority of the clergy. At the Council of Laodicea— held between 343 and 381—it was decreed in The 13th Canon: "Besides appointed singers, who mount the ambo and sing from the book, others shall not sing in the church." The musical roles of clergy and laity had been set by law.

A large body of liturgic chants had been classified and systemized by the middle or latter part of the 6th century. The teaching of the form and tradition of their rendering was the role of the clergy. The liturgy, which was basically completed during or shortly before the reign of Gregory the Great (590-604), was placed in a musical setting. This liturgical chant was made the law of the Church, on equal footing with the liturgy itself, and the initial steps to impose one uniform ritual and chant upon all congregations of the West was completed.

The first six centuries of the Catholic Church were essential in the organization and structure of Christianity and the Church controlled the direction of her music, as well as all art. Christian music separated itself from the secular, pagan world by embracing a vocal music without the support of instruments, unencumbered by the antique metre which kept Greek and Roman music in strict prosodic measure. The result was a mystical music that was uniquely the Church's, centered on vocal melody, not on rhythm, which differed dramatically from any other style of music. The music of the Church, like the Church itself, separated itself from secular culture and developed a music and culture all its own. This Church music defined a universal mood for prayer and reinforced the concept that the expression of the individual was to be subjugated to the whole body.

The first major split in the Christian church occurred in 1054 when the church separated into east and west with the west becoming the Roman Catholic Church and the east evolving to the Greek Orthodox Church. This split came after a long series of disagreements that involved differences in politics, geography, the expressions of faith, the way to worship, details of administration, and language. An unofficial boundary line was established, running the length of the Adriatic and extending south to the Gulf of Libya in Africa, with all those living to the east primarily Greek-speaking, while those living to the west were generally Latin-speaking. Although there are a number of differences between the two branches of Catholicism, the primary difference is that the Roman church is headed by a pope while the Greek Orthodox prefer to be governed by a board.

THE CATHOLICS

This split led to Europe coming under the Roman Catholic Church as Christianity spread westward. The next major split in the Roman Catholic Church occurred in the 16th century with Martin Luther's Protestant Reformation, which began in Germany and soon encompassed most of Europe. England's split with Catholicism in Great Britain created a schism between Anglicans, Protestant puritans and reformers, and Catholics, which led to the first Catholic settlement in America by Lord Baltimore (George Calvert) in Maryland in 1634.

The Calverts were a genteel family who had converted back to Catholicism in Protestant England—not a popular move—but remained in favor with King James I and later Charles I. George Calvert's son, Cecil, received a charter for the colony in 1632 and the settlers first landed in spring 1634. The colony soon found itself in the midst of strong anti-Catholic sentiment in the new country as most of America was settled by Protestants. This led the Marylanders to pass a religious tolerance act which forbade religious dissension and eventually served as a model for the rest of the colonies in religious tolerance.

The major problem Catholicism faced during the Protestant Movement was that Catholics continued to hold an allegiance to Rome and the Pope while the Protestants felt they alone could be aligned with a particular nation and its leaders without compromising their faith. Catholicism was often considered a threat to religion in the Protestant era and many saw Catholicism as denying God's ability to speak to each and every individual. The highly structured, ritualistic service did not seem to fit the new country whose religions were increasingly individualistic and whose new beginnings sought to cut old ties and leave the past behind. In a land where religion came from the people, the Catholic style of clergy-oriented religion was a bit impractical as well as undesirable—the laity wanted to be active, not passive, and Catholicism tended to snuff out sparks of the individualistic and pioneering spirit inherent in the young country.

Catholicism did not spread quickly in America because the Catholic missionaries did not do well against the zealous missionaries from such Protestant sects as the Baptists, Methodists, Lutherans, etc. Still, Catholicism did grow and become a dominant religion in the United States, centered primarily in the large metropolitan cities where immigrants from Catholic countries in Europe settled.

Since Catholicism is a universal church, the same mass with the same music is used all over the world. This meant the masses in Rome or Rio de Janiero were no different from those of Detroit or Cleveland, and those Masses are basically the same in the 20th century as they were in the 16th century, which was basically the same mass that had been performed for centuries before that. The music did not change either and so the chant-song still predominated until the mid-20th century.

To a large extent the Catholic Church became a universal church by adopting a universal language—Latin—for its services. This meant a believer could go into a Catholic church anywhere in the world and hear the same Mass. Also, the church could be assured that believers everywhere were of one mind and one allegiance—subjucating differences and denying individuality—through the hierarchy of Pope, Cardinals, Bishops, and Priests, who spoke for and controlled the silent laity. This changed significantly with Vatican II.

Vatican II was convened in 1962 by Pope John XXIII and completed under his successor, Pope Paul VI, in 1965. The most significant results of this church council, held in three different sessions, were that the old Latin in the Mass was discarded and replaced by the vernacular or local language and that the laity was encouraged to participate more fully in the Mass and take initiative in both religious and temporal affairs. These sessions also sought to end the isolationism of Catholicism by embracing all of Christianity and, indeed, all the peoples of the earth as God's creatures.

The major growth in American Catholicism occurred in the mid-19th century when a flood of immigrants descended on America. A number of these immigrants were European Catholics and they tended to settle in major cities in the North and East. Catholicism met with resistance in the South where many southern religions considered the Pope to be the anti-Christ and felt suspicious about the lack of emotionalism—a trademark of Southern Christianity—in Catholicism. Catholicism differs from Protestantism in its concept of sacraments (baptism, confirmation, communion, marriage, holy orders or the ordination of priests, penance, and extreme unction or last rites), and the concept of salvation, which is not tied to one dramatic experience that brings immediate salvation but rather a lifelong experience incorporating the faith of the individual and resulting good works.

Musically, Vatican II meant the introduction of a whole new set of songs in the Mass and the encouragement of individuals writing songs for the services. The "folk mass" was born as the antiquated faith renewed itself through modernization. This modernization led to a musical movement in the Catholic Church which embraced the popular music of the day, using it for church, and in turn paved the way for the Jesus Movement in the late 1960s, which also took popular music and used it to celebrate faith, making it relevant to contemporary youth. This first folk mass, "Mass for Young Americans," was produced by Ray Repp in 1964.

The result of these movements within the Catholic organization was a charismatic renewal in which many individual Catholics felt they could develop a direct personal relationship with Christ and the Mass became more "people-oriented." This, in turn, resulted in a great demand for liturgical music as almost overnight every Catholic church in America had to have songbooks, songs, and books of readings to accompany the new Mass. This led to the formation of Catholic groups and songwriters who could write this material for the Mass. Perhaps the most influential group was the St. Louis Jesuits.

The St. Louis Jesuits were all Jesuit priests who first united at St. Louis University, where they met while pursuing their studies. Individually, they are known as Bob Dufford, Dan Schutte, John Foley, Roc O'Connor, and Tim Manion and they began composing and developing their music in the early 1970s.

The first among the group to begin composing music for liturgical use was John Foley. Foley and John Davanaugh met at the Jesuit novitiate in Florissant, Missouri, in the '60s and inspired each other with their folk-guitar compositions for the liturgy. Both arrived in St. Louis in the mid-'60s to study philosophy and during this time they wrote numerous compositions. Foley's music and reputation soon spread and by the time he left St. Louis for a teaching position in Denver in 1967, his music had already become popular within Jesuit circles.

Bob Dufford was familiar with Foley and his music because he, too, had studied in St. Louis and been involved with the choir there. When Dufford left for Omaha, Nebraska to teach high school, he too began to compose songs.

Dufford met Dan Schutte when he visited the Jesuit Novitiate in St. Bonifacius, Minnesota in the spring of 1968. Schutte had written several songs for the congregation there on guitar and John Foley's songs had begun to filter into the novitiate. Roc O'Connor was in the same novitiate in Minnesota with Schutte and offered his skills as an accomplished guitarist to the choral groups that Schutte and others organized for their community liturgies.

Dufford and Schutte arrived in St. Louis in 1970 and began working with Roc O'Connor and John Foley on providing music for the group who worshipped on Sundays at Fusz Memorial, the Jesuit house of studies. Word of their music soon spread and they were besieged with requests to perform. Meanwhile, Tim Manion arrived in St. Louis in 1971 from the novitiate in Florissant, Missouri. Tim had been a part of the liturgy music in Missouri and was familiar with the music of Dufford, Schutte, and Foley.

During the next two years, this group began to investigate ways to publish their music. Discouraged and disheartened after their contact with religious music publishers, they decided to produce and publish a collection of 57 songs on their own and record a set of albums which would aid the performance of their songs. In the midst of this project, the young priests were approached by a relative newcomer in the field of Catholic publishing, North American Liturgy Resources, that made them an offer to record and publish their music. Impressed that NALR could do far more than the Jesuits could on their own, and flattered by NALR's interest and desire to work with them, the group agreed to the offer. Their first project, *Neither Silver Nor Gold*, was issued in June 1974.

In 1975 the Jesuits (except for Tim Manion) all left St. Louis to be scattered in Omaha; Berkeley, California; and Toronto. They continued to collaborate, though, and spent a summer together in Berkeley composing new music for their second collection. The result was *Earthen Vessels*, released in December 1975, which sold over half a million units.

The success of the St. Louis Jesuits parallels the success of Catholic music. The fact that it has grown since the mid-'60s is well-documented; however, for those not in Catholic circles, this growth, music and influence has gone largely unknown. In fact, most of those involved in the contemporary Christian music world are not even aware of Catholic music, although an occasional act appears on the charts. Perhaps the best-known act producing music for Catholics was John Michael Talbot, a contemporary Christian musician who became a third order Franciscan monk and whose albums reached both the Catholic and contemporary Christian markets, giving the gospel mainstream a taste of liturgy music.

There are almost 19,000 Catholic parishes in the United States administered by nearly 200 dioceses. All of these parishes, or churches, have needed hymn books, song sheets, and chorus scores since the Mass was changed into English. This fact, along with the spiritual renewal in the Catholic charismatic movement—paralleling the charismatic and evangelical Christian movement in American since the Jesus Revolution of the late '60s—have been responsible for the tremendous growth of the Catholic music market.

Chapter 28

CONTEMPORARY CHRISTIAN MUSIC: THE EARLY YEARS

The counterculture in post-World War II America began with "the Beats" and rock 'n' roll in the 1950s; it entered the mainstream through Civil Rights, anti-Vietnam War sentiment, and the Beatles during the 1960s. By the end of 1974, with the end of Watergate and the resignation of President Richard Nixon, the country was returning to a sense of "normalcy." By the mid-1970s, young radicals of the 1960s era were beginning to mature. Too, the issues they had fought for most passionately—Vietnam and Civil Rights—had been somewhat resolved, or at least a peace permeated this group, who were now older, getting jobs, and starting families.

Although the counterculture was criticized at the time for being "un-American," and even "communist," in truth it was an attempt to purge the darker side of capitalism, to rein in the excesses of America abroad, and right the wrongs present in America at home. Underlying the counterculture was an idealism, an attempt to make life—and the United States—the way they thought it should be.

The Jesus Revolution was a product of the 1960s counterculture; it was also the counterculture of mainstream Christianity. This, too, was an idealistic attempt to return religion to a "purer" Christianity. The early participants in the Jesus Revolution were young and innocent and the music they produced was filled with hope and idealism. But, as in the American countercultural movement, there was also a strong anti-establishment and anti-business bias, especially in the music industry, where large corporations were seen as the enemy of "pure" music. Terms like "honest," "real," and "true" were self-proclaimed for their music while the corporations that produced and marketed it were often considered phony, corrupt, and out of touch with the music and the audience. The prevailing view was that corporations were filled with grey-suited men in grey-carpeted offices whose little grey cells could not comprehend the colorful world outside their grey walls.

(The irony of the music industry is that consumers love the product—musical recordings—but tend to hate the industry that makes these recordings available to them.)

By 1975—when the last Americans left Vietnam—mainstream music was filled with introspective self-absorption, articulated by intensely sensitive acoustic singer-songwriters. The corporations found ways to capture the youth market—usually by hiring the hippest and brightest people they could find—and the counterculture soon became the mainstream again, although it would never again look like the mainstream of the 1950s.

Within Christianity, the fundamentalist counterculture entered the mainstream in 1976 when Jimmy Carter, a "born-again" evangelical, was elected President. This brought an immense amount of media coverage to the evangelical movement in the United States. In a 1976 survey, the Gallup Poll found that one out of every three Americans considered themselves a "born-again" Christian; that same year, for the first time since World War II, church attendance increased rather than decreased.

These revelations caught the basically agnostic mainstream press off guard. Scrambling quickly to recover, they discovered a huge Christian culture that included books, records, television, radio, bookstores, and churches all doing a booming business. They discovered a culture in America that had size as well as strength—led by no less than the President of the United States and accounting for hundreds of millions of dollars in revenue.

In the mid-1960s the church had been on the decline, with attendance decreasing and interest from the youth waning. The Jesus Revolution of the late 60s and early 70s took the gospel back to the street, largely via music. Christian musicians had a hard time making ends meet—but their commitment to spreading the message of the gospel kept them going in spite of a rejection from both the church and society towards their gospel in the pop/rock music format. The church, accustomed to 200-year-old hymns, often considered the music to be of the Devil and those involved with street-level Christianity to be cultish and suspect, while the secular culture simply did not want to hear about Jesus through their loudspeakers. Because the major gospel record companies and Christian radio stations generally sided with the conservative churches and Christian bookstores, the result was a stifling of Christian music by the Christian culture itself.

By the mid-1970s this had begun to change as churches realized that contemporary music was a way to reach the youth while the record companies and radio realized there was a demand for this music. Too, the musicians and others involved in the Jesus Movement proved themselves to be sincere, dedicated Christians who involved themselves in local churches, so the fears of conservative church members were generally quieted as they realized this movement was not composed of wild hippies on the loose. As a matter of fact, churches realized that the audience for contemporary Christian music was sitting in their pews.

America underwent a spiritual awakening, and Christianity that was fundamental in its beliefs, active in its faith, and in touch with the contemporary culture became acceptable. The term "born-again" became known, accepted, and practiced, with many Americans undergoing a rebirth in their spiritual lives. This was highlighted in 1977 by the publication of the book *Born Again* by Nixon's former hatchet man, Chuck Colson, and the beginning of Jimmy Carter's presidency. Carter's campaign and presidency made the born-again movement known and accepted to a wide cross-section of Americans who had looked with disfavor on the contemporary Christian culture. It also forced the press to seriously examine the Christian culture. Unfortunately, the secular press—trained to be skeptical— could not really comprehend this movement and initially refused to acknowledge it as an ongoing news story. Instead, they attacked and looked for skeletons in the closet, ignoring a social change that was as radical as the changes of the 1960s which altered the social fabric in American lives.

Christian bookstores moved into malls and away from their former head stop image, Christian books proliferated, and Christian music became widely accepted. The Christian culture became big business as it moved from retail outlets into homes via recordings, books, and assorted trinkets and artifacts worn or hung on walls, in addition to increased church growth. Television evangelists became leading populist figures and magazines by, about, and for Christians delivered their messages straight to the living room.

By 1976 there was an infrastructure in place for contemporary Christian music to grow. A marketing network of Christian bookstores, represented by a trade organization, the Christian Booksellers Association, was firmly in place. The Christian Booksellers Association had begun in 1950 with about 25 stores; in 1976 they represented 2,800 members, who generated $500 million in sales, up from $100 million in 1971. Average annual revenue jumped 17.4 percent per year, almost twice the secular bookstore's growth, which was listed at nine percent per year.

The Christian bookstores were mostly family-owned, changing the view that they were primarily a ministry which offered some religious books for sale to one which recognized them as a family business, concerned deeply with ministry but also aware of the need to institute sound business practices in order to survive.

When the Christian Booksellers Association began, it represented stores which sold Bibles and books; gradually the stock began to diversify with music, Sunday school curriculums, greeting cards, jewelry, and gifts. Their growth came because they provided Christian product unavailable in other outlets.

By 1976 a trade organization for the gospel music industry, the Gospel Music Association, was well-established. The GMA had developed the "Dove Award" for gospel music performers, and these awards would bring recognition and attention to Christian music. The roots for this organization and these awards went back to the previous decade.

In the early 1960s there were several groups of people aware of the need for an association of gospel music performers and business people. The early success of the Country Music Association in Nashville served as a role model. In Memphis the Blackwood Brothers' organization was trying to pull a group together, while in Nashville a group headed by Don Light was also moving in that direction. The Blackwoods and the Statesmen, two Southern gospel groups, had the decided advantage of the National Quartet Convention, which brought together all those involved in Southern gospel music for a weekend of fellowship, fun, showcasing, and business. Later, the event grew into a four-day, then a week, and finally a ten-day event.

The first Quartet Convention was held in October 1956 in Memphis and was a joint venture of the Blackwoods and Statesman quartets, who owned it and viewed it as a business venture. This same group sowed the seeds for the Gospel Music Association and obtained a charter from the state of Tennessee in 1964, joining forces with the group in Nashville to elect the first board of directors. Among the founding fathers were James Blackwood, J.D. Sumner, Cecil Blackwood, and Don Butler; Tennessee Ernie Ford was elected the first president.

The idea of an awards ceremony honoring those in gospel music was first presented by Bill Gaither at a GMA quarterly board meeting in 1968 at the Third National Bank Building offices in Nashville. J.D. Sumner, Bob MacKenzie, and Les Beasley were all enthusiastic and the first ceremony was set for October 10, 1969. The event was held in the penthouse of the Peabody Hotel in Memphis and approximately 665 guests attended. That first Dove Awards was not a lavish affair: the afternoon of the show, members of the Dove Committee had to put on work clothes and mop floors, wash windows, scrub, sweep, and decorate because the penthouse was in disastrous shape. The crew finished in time to shower and dress for the awards show.

The name "Dove" came from Bill Gaither while the design came from Les Beasley, who worked with an artist on the concept. That first year revealed that this was basically a Southern gospel organization, for the winners all came from that field. Among those carrying home those first awards were the Oak Ridge Boys, J.G. Whitfield, Bill Gaither, Vestal Goodman, James Blackwood, the Imperials, the Speers, and "Jesus is Coming Soon" for "Song of the Year."

The next year the Doves were held at the Rivermont Hotel in Memphis and again the winners came from the Southern gospel world. In the third year, 1971, disaster struck when it was discovered the Blackwood Brothers had stuffed the ballot box. The result was that all awards were deemed invalid and that year was wiped off the slate. As a result, the GMA does not count 1971 as a Dove year and the winners do not appear on any of the GMA's official releases of past Dove winners.

The Dove Awards continued to grow and moved to Nashville, where the gospel music business was increasingly centered. In the following years there were awards shows held in a giant tent over the plaza between the Capital Park Inn and Municipal Auditorium, at the War Memorial Auditorium, at several hotels and at the Opry House.

In 1976 writer Tom Wolfe described the 1970s as the "Me Decade," with people turning their attention to jogging, Perrier water, self-help programs, disaster and horror movies, and disco. This trend would continue into the 1980s, which would later be described as the "My Decade" because of the emphasis on material-ism and possessions. For those in the Christian culture, the end of the 1970s became the "We Decade" as Christians flexed their politi-cal muscles, voiced their social concerns to a listening public, saw and heard the gospel message become big-time money-making for the televangelists, and witnessed a market network grow through the expansion of Christian bookstores permeating the land, until Christianity became more than just a faith—it became a "target mar-ket" with demographics, psychographics, and its own vocabulary.

The "we-decade" voiced an "us vs. them" mentality when they fought for issues like prayer in schools, anti-abortion measures, and creationism rather than Darwin's theory of evolution to be taught in schools. It was the beginning of a movement which would market Christianity in a way it had never been marketed before.

Studies of college students at this time showed a pronounced shift towards conservatism in voting registrations (a large number registered as Republicans) but an overall political apathy on cam-puses. There was a continuing trend towards "me-ism" and a lack of concern about political activism: let's stick to the basics, get govern-ment out of individuals' lives (and hence concern about govern-ment), and concentrate on personal success. This was perhaps expressed best in the "average" college student of this time who reg-istered as a Republican, was very materialistic, and wanted less gov-ernment regulation and intrusion while enjoying lots of success and recognition for himself.

The year 1977 marked the end of two eras in music with the deaths of Elvis Presley in August and Bing Crosby in October. But this period was the beginning of a new era in music and religion— the era of Contemporary Christian Music.

The first "star" in contemporary Christian music was Evie Tornquist. A small, blond-haired, blue-eyed young lady from New Jersey, Evie was pert and pretty. Vocally, her style was reminiscent of a trained voice that would fit nicely into a church choir. Evie was the darling of the gospel world both in the United States and in Europe—where she was "discovered." Her album sales were well over the l00,000 mark for each release and many felt she would be the one to carry the banner of contemporary Christian music to the secular world. Gospel music was struggling for recognition and acceptance—and many in the gospel industry felt the key was to find someone who could be a gospel artist yet successful in the pop field.

Evie did not sign with a secular label or stop singing gospel music. Instead, she got married and placed her husband, Pele Karlsson, and (soon afterward) new baby at the center of her life. She stopped recording and touring for awhile, devoted herself to being a wife and mother for a number of years, and when she did "return" to gospel, directed her energies to the church. Pop success never really was a consideration for Evie and when she married, she and her husband wanted a ministry, so they stayed within the gospel community.

B.J. Thomas had a celebrated conversion in the mid-70s which took him away from drug addiction into a born-again experience. Thomas had been a pop star before his conversion (he had reportedly sold 32 million records with hits such as "Raindrops Keep Falling On My Head," "Somebody Done Somebody Wrong Song," and others) and afterwards began recording Christian music for Word Records. He, too, was a bright star in this arena for awhile but soon developed problems with his concerts when two sets of fans showed up—one wanting the old pop hits and the other wanting just gospel. Thomas tried to reconcile the two, singing all of his old hits while closing with his testimony, but the conflict proved too much and he moved out of gospel again. Somehow, the Christian audiences could not accept B.J. Thomas as a Christian entertainer; they wanted him all or nothing, so Thomas stopped recording Christian music on gospel labels and began recording country music.

In 1977 Debby Boone had one of the biggest hits of the year—"You Light Up My Life"—and was on her way to being the star who could bridge the gospel and secular worlds. Debby would bring attention to gospel music because of her overt Christian beliefs and this song, which was not really a "gospel" song but could be interpreted that way. She won a Grammy for "Best New Artist" and followed this up with a number one song on the country music charts but, again, a husband and family took precedence as she withdrew from her performing career to a more low-key life with occasional performances and records. Too, Debby Boone was never really comfortable as a pop star—she was grounded too deeply in the Christian culture and as her Christian records gained a wide acceptance, she realized she was more at home as a gospel artist. Still, she continued to perform in secular venues, such as Las Vegas, and continued receiving some attention from the secular media.

Instead of those leading contenders, Amy Grant would become the first artist to be comfortable as a Christian entertainer who would achieve success in the mainstream secular field. In 1976, when she released her debut album, she was a young high school student.

The daughter of a physician, Amy Grant grew up in Belle Meade, a wealthy suburb of Nashville. She attended private schools and, growing up in a strongly religious family, accepted Christianity at an early age. In the seventh grade, at a Wednesday night church service, Amy "just felt that I needed to make a commitment to the Lord and be baptized so I did, but I really didn't know or understand all that it meant at the time." About two years later, in high school, she became involved in a high school fellowship at her church headed by Brown Bannister. Right after this she began writing songs, and, then, a year later, recording them.

Amy Grant had sung in front of a crowd only once in her life before she was signed to Word Records; that appearance was at a school chapel service when she was 15. She had begun writing songs to share her faith with friends and schoolmates. Unlike many who came along later, she did not dream of bright lights, a record deal, touring to packed concert houses, or hearing her tunes blaring from the radio or stereo speakers. She really did not know enough about the record business to even be aware of such things.

Brown Bannister worked with Chris Christian at Home Sweet Home Productions. They had just begun their association with Word Records producing acts, starting with B.J. Thomas. A family friend of Amy's wanted a tape copy of her songs so she asked Bannister to let her record them in a studio. He had heard her sing some songs once and was impressed by her sincerity and ability to communicate through music.

Once the songs were on tape, Bannister became excited by the results and played them for Chris Christian, who also became excited and called the head of A & R at Word. Word Records had just signed an agreement with Christian whereby he would bring several new acts to the label, so Amy became the first act in that deal. Myrrh Records, a division of Word, signed her to a recording contract when she was 15 years old after hearing a tape played over the phone.

With the release of her first album, her songs—"Old Man's Rubble," "What a Difference You've Made in My Life," and "Beautiful Music"—immediately received radio airplay. The record label was caught by surprise that this high school kid might have a hit on her hands. Amy's father then hired an independent promoter to call radio stations and help the album along.

Before Amy Grant appeared, few if any gospel artists had achieved popularity primarily through radio airplay. The others usually did it through extensive touring over a long period of time. So for Amy Grant to have three hit songs on gospel radio was a remarkable achievement and one that propelled her from oblivion to an almost overnight success. At least the gospel industry sat up and took notice.

With a surprisingly successful first album under Amy's belt, there was demand for a follow-up. Word Records had gotten the hint and was figuring out ways for the album to get maximum support. They made it a priority release and it was named "Album of the Month"— an almost unheard of event for an artist who had only one previous release.

The second album had attractive pictures of Amy on the front and back covers and was filled with excellent songs. Titled *My Father's Eyes*, the album had great production. On the second album, Amy emerged as a songwriter, writing four of the songs herself and co-writing another four with Brown Bannister.

When *My Father's Eyes* was released, Amy was a college student at Furman University in South Carolina. Later, she transferred to Vanderbilt University in Nashville for her last two years, but stopped just short of graduating with a degree in English. While in college she made occasional appearances on weekends, touring full-time only during her summer vacations.

Amy was privileged in several respects. When her first album began to receive attention, her father paid an independent promotion person to help—an advantage many beginning Christian artists could not afford. Later, when she began to tour with a full band, her father again provided financial support—a necessity since her first two major tours lost money. However, they generated a lot of excitement and being a gospel artist touring with a full band putting on a first-class show won her a huge following in the long run. Still, most gospel artists could not afford the initial investment required for this groundbreaking move.

After her second album was released, Amy's brother-in-law, Dan Harrell, joined Mike Blanton, the head of Word's Nashville office and instrumental in orchestrating the marketing of the second album, in forming a management firm with Amy as its first artist.

It was especially rare for a gospel artist to have management. Both Blanton and Harrell were qualified and dedicated and made a mark on Christian music with their management organization. However, they also had the advantage of being underwritten by Dr. Grant, allowing them the money and time to develop as managers— an advantage many such firms don't have.

With strong management and crucial financial backing, Amy was allowed to concentrate on her songwriting, recording, and performing while the details of her business affairs were in trusted hands. Too, the management company pursued additional opportunities for her—such as major TV appearances. Amy was surrounded with what few gospel artists—but most major superstars have: a complete career development team. The direction planned by her management was first for complete exposure in the Christian field, then exposure in the secular field. They wanted her viewed her as a Christian entertainer, rather than a minister. A large degree of her initial success came from making a concentrated and successful effort to reach the youth involved in churches—not by tapping the traditional youth market of rebellious teenagers. That came later.

The NARAS (National Academy of Recording Arts and Sciences) board of directors was beginning to recognize gospel music as a significant style of American music; in 1976 there had only been three categories for gospel music—"Inspirational" (won by Gary S. Paxton for his album, *The Astonishing, Outrageous, Amazing, Incredible, Unbelievable, Different World of Gary S. Paxton*), "Gospel Performance (other than Soul)," which was won by the Oak Ridge Boys, and "Soul Gospel," won by Mahalia Jackson. In 1977 the Grammys would expand to include five awards in gospel.

Also in 1977, *Record World*, a music industry trade magazine, published a special section on gospel music. With this issue, gospel music came to the attention of the secular music business industry. This would lead to long-term changes amongst retailers and other industry personnel which made gospel music more visible in the music industry overall. For the gospel industry itself, this would give it a major boost in self-confidence and begin to make contemporary Christian music a major force both within the gospel world and the pop music world at large.

Also in 1977 the gospel world was all aglow over the first album on a Christian label to be certified "Gold," signifying sales of over 500,000 units. *Alleluia, A Praise Gathering for Believers* by the Bill Gaither Trio on HeartWarming, the Benson Company's record label, achieved this honor. A Gold Album had been an untouchable dream, reserved for secular labels and non-religious artists. Dominating the gospel world, in addition to the Bill Gaither Trio, were B.J. Thomas, Evie Tornquist, Andrae Crouch, Jimmy Swaggart, Reba Rambo Gardner, the Downings, Dallas Holm, Walter Hawkins and the Love Center Choir, James Cleveland, Jessy Dixon, and Danniebelle.

It was a transitional year for gospel music and the Dove Awards reflected that. For the Doves, it would mark the beginning of the end of the dominance of Southern gospel music among the award winners and the beginning rumbles of what would be the major earthquake in gospel music called "contemporary Christian music." The 1977 Doves were held at the Hyatt Regency in Nashville and featured a sit-down dinner as well as a show and awards. Jim and Tammy Bakker created a stir when they appeared and carried home a Dove for "Best Television Show" for the PTL Club—which was only three years old. Other winners that evening were the Cathedrals, the Speers, James Blackwood, Evie Tornquist, Bill Gaither, Henry Slaughter, the Couriers, the Blackwood Brothers, and "Learning to Lean" for "Song of the Year."

Within the Christian music industry, 1977 was the year when Keith Green, who would become one of the most influential artists in contemporary Christian music, released his debut album. More than any other artist, it was Keith Green who provided the example of ministry over everything else in his career and who inspired, encouraged, frustrated, and questioned record executives and recording artists in the field of gospel music.

Keith Green personified radical Christianity; he stood out for his beliefs, even within the Christian culture, and became a light to follow, an inspiration for others involved in gospel music, an example of the Christian as radical. He represented that side of the gospel music industry that says "no time for entertainment—that is frivolity. Here is The Truth! Accept it. Proclaim it. Live it."

A Keith Green concert was really a misnomer; it could hardly be called a "concert" at all. He did perform at his concerts, though it sometimes seemed it was out of a sense of obligation, a drawing card, a warm-up for the audience. In most traveling religious services, it has traditionally been customary to have some singing to start the evening. That is why Dwight Moody had Ira Sankey, why Billy Graham has George Beverly Shea. But Green was Moody and Sankey, Graham and Shea, with the emphasis on preacher, not singer. In a two-and-a-half-hour evening, Green would probably perform ten songs or fewer.

In one concert, Green took the stage after a few opening remarks by Winkie Pratney, a minister who was part of Green's community. When he came on stage and sat at the piano, Keith announced in a tone of urgency, "I'm here because of the broken heart of God and I hope at the end of this evening, His heart will be a little less broken" before playing "How Could They Live Without Jesus." He played several more songs before stopping to talk a while from the piano. The stage held only a grand piano and a lectern. There was no band, no fancy lighting, no wall of speakers. Following a few more songs, Green sang "There Is A Redeemer" and then said, "That is the crux of the whole night."

When "There Is A Redeemer" was finished, Green left the piano bench and walked over to the lectern, opened his Bible, and delivered a full-scale sermon. He spoke from Isaiah 53, a prophetic chapter in the Old Testament that tells in descriptive detail about the coming Messiah for Israel. It was a long, passionate talk, full of warning, rebuke, and exhortation.

Keith Green had come through a long spiritual odyssey that led to his being on that stage in such a setting. It has been said that he "always had a thirst for God." He was born Jewish but raised in Christian Science. He came from a musical family—his mother sang with the Dorsey bands and his grandfather with Eddie Cantor—and Keith showed musical precociousness early. Beginning with the ukulele when he was three, he advanced to the guitar at five and the piano at six, writing his first song at eight and making his first record at ten. He signed a recording contract with Decca when he was eleven.

Green had an early desire to be a star in the record business, and actively pursued that goal during his early years. However, on his 19th birthday, after a bad LSD trip, Keith Green related that he confronted Jesus and finally saw himself as God saw him, "filthy dirty." Later that year, he met Melody Steiner, an orthodox Jew, and the two were married on Christmas Day, 1973. Together they embarked on a spiritual journey, as well as music stardom, signing as writers with the publishing company owned by CBS in 1974. In 1975 Green deepened his Christian faith with a commitment, or "surrender," as he put it, saying "Lord, I'll never play music again unless You give me the words to sing, and You give me the places to play."

The Greens opened up their home for anyone in need and began to witness "compulsively." Living in the Los Angeles area, they eventually had six houses with over 70 people involved, the beginning of their organization called "Last Days Ministries." A few years later, they reduced their number to 25 and moved to Lindale, Texas, where they established a complex that included a division for record sales as well as one for printing tracts and newsletters. The *Last Days Newsletter* was sent to over 100,000 subscribers every six weeks during the time Green was alive.

Keith Green signed a recording contract with Sparrow Records and released his debut album, *For Him Who Has Ears*, which was an immediate, overwhelming success. After his initial success, Green went to the Sparrow executives and told them he did not want to be on the label and in the Christian bookstores—he wanted to distribute the records himself. He said he wanted to make his records available directly to consumers, free if they could not afford to pay. He felt the marketing system did not allow people to receive a free album and wanted his message available to all. Too, Green abhorred the "business" side of the music industry—he felt business people were, on the whole, crooks ripping off musicians.

This startled the gospel industry and some branded Green a "kook" for this attitude. However, his records continued to sell by direct mail and he did indeed give away a number of his albums free. The result was that Green went from rising young star to major influence—a man who practiced what he preached, who had the courage of convictions, who lived what he sang. If the gospel—and salvation—was free, you cannot charge money for an album; at least Keith Green could not.

Throughout his career as a gospel artist, Green was concerned and often repulsed by the gospel music industry. He wrote, "The only music ministers to whom the Lord will say, 'Well done, thou good and faithful servant,' are the ones whose lives prove what their lyrics are saying, and the ones to whom music is the least important part of their life—glorifying the only worthy One has to be the most important!"

Dedicated to proclaiming "truth," it was not unusual for him to lecture the audience, reprimand them, call them "a brood of vipers" and antagonize them. He also challenged them to stop taking Christianity lightly. This was life-or-death stuff and he was on a life-or-death mission—the gospel was the fire escape and he warned that you better get on it.

Chapter 29

CONTEMPORARY CHRISTIAN MUSIC: PART TWO

The 1960s ended in outer space—a man on the moon—but the 1970s were characterized by inner space, a searching for self-respect, a development of self-awareness, and a demand for a positive self-image as the self emerged (often through psychobabble and mellowspeak) to dominate the decade and create a trend of national selfishness with very little counterbalancing self-control.

In 1978 the music world saw the ill-fated American tour of the Sex Pistols. This group would not last but the Punk Movement would have an impact on fashion as well as music and lead another British Invasion into American pop music. At the Grammy Awards on February 15 B.J. Thomas won for "Inspirational Performance," the Happy Goodman Family won for "Traditional Gospel Performance" and Larry Hart took home the Grammy for "Contemporary Gospel Performance."

The Hart win shocked the gospel industry—he was a virtual unknown before the awards ceremony, someone who had recorded a custom album—and his win was the basis for some major changes in the Grammy voting process. Hart's victory came after he had signed the members of the choir in his father's church in Detroit to NARAS membership and bloc-voted for the award. The scandal cast a black cloud over the Grammys but, in the end, gospel music benefitted from the increased attention as the Grammy telecast featured more performances by gospel artists. Overall, though, the musical world of 1978 was dominated by The Bee Gees with "Stayin' Alive" and other songs from the *Saturday Night Fever* soundtrack. By the end of the year, it was estimated they had sold more records during the past twelve months than the entire gospel music field combined.

In July 1978, a new magazine geared to contemporary Christian music appeared. *Contemporary Christian Music* would emerge as the leading voice for and about contemporary Christian music. It began as a tabloid music trade, based in Santa Ana, California and during the first year 12,000 copies of each issue were mailed each month free to those involved in the gospel music industry. On that first cover were The Boone Girls, who had recorded an album for their father, Pat Boone's, label, Lamb & Lion Records. This magazine would dominate the contemporary Christian field, becoming the most popular and influential magazine in that area. Within that first year, in fact, it became for contemporary Christian music what *Rolling Stone* was for rock—the publication which defined a music culture and identified who's in and who's not.

Contemporary Christian Music, or *CCM* as it became known, began as a tabloid paper called *Contemporary Christian Acts* in Orange County, California. The paper was owned primarily by Jim Willems, who also owned the Maranatha Village Christian bookstore, which was responsible for selling more contemporary Christian albums than any other store in the country. The music editor for *Acts* was John Styll, a radio disc jockey who had been the host of the Calvary Chapel Saturday night radio concerts and was doing some syndicated shows. Since the music section of *Acts* was so popular, it was decided to make John Styll editor of the new publication.

The group owning and editing *CCM* all attended Calvary Chapel in southern California so the magazine had a west coast slant. Also, it saw itself geared to contemporary Christian music since that was the stronghold in that area. However, in their charts, they had "Inspirational" and "Southern Gospel" in addition to "Rock."

The charts of *CCM* were a major contribution to contemporary Christian music because no other publication compiled charts from Christian bookstores about music, which is where most of the Christian buyers bought their records. The only other gospel music charts during this time were in *Record World*, and these were compiled primarily from secular distributors who handled some gospel product as part of their normal business. Their charts showed more sales on Southern Gospel, which sold primarily through regular retail outlets, and black gospel, which sold to the record stores in the black sections of a city, rather than the fledgling contemporary Christian music, which had to depend upon the Christian bookstores to reach its core audience.

Those first charts in *CCM* were compiled from about 25 Christian bookstores for albums and from 60-70 radio stations for airplay. The top song on that first chart for contemporary Christian music was "He's Alive" by Don Francisco, followed by "Old Man's Rubble" by Amy Grant, "All Day Dinner" by Reba, "Mansion Builder" by 2nd Chapter of Acts, "What a Difference You've Made in My Life" by Amy Grant, "Now I See The Man" by Chris Christian, "Don't Look Back" by Fireworks, "First Butterfly" by the Boones, "Rise Again" by Dallas Holm, and "Building Block" by Noel Paul Stookey. Other artists on the airplay chart were Scott Wesley Brown, the Bill Gaither Trio, Steve Camp, the Archers, Phil Keaggy Band, Farrell & Farrell, Stephanie Booshada, Karen Lafferty, Evie, and B.J. Thomas.

The top album in the "Contemporary" category was *Mansion Builder* by 2nd Chapter of Acts; followed by *For Him Who Has Ears to Hear* by Keith Green; *Home Where I Belong* by B.J. Thomas; *How the West Was One* by 2nd Chapter of Acts, Phil Keaggy and A Band Called David; *The Lady is a Child* by Reba; *Forgiven* by Don Francisco; *Emerging* by the Phil Keaggy Band; *Fresh Surrender* by the Archers; *Sweet Music* by the Pat Terry Group; and *Chance* by Chris Christian. On the "Inspirational" album chart, the top album was *Mirror* by Evie, followed by two other albums from this young lady—*A Little Song of Joy For My Little Friends* and *Gentle Moments*, then *Live* by Dallas Holm, *Pilgrim's Progress* by the Bill Gaither Trio, *Praise II* by Maranatha! Music, *Praise Strings* by Maranatha! Music, *Come Bless the Lord* by the Continental Singers, *Praise Strings II* by Maranatha! Music, and *The Music Machine* by Candle.

During mid-1978 the top sellers in contemporary Christian music were B.J. Thomas and Evie Tornquist; each was selling over 100,000 units of each release and some albums by these artists reached the 3-400,000 plateau. But for most acts, sales of 20,000 were considered "good" for a first album and 40,000 units was a "hit."

In October *Record World* published its second Gospel Music Special and named the top sellers in "Contemporary and Inspiration" music for the past year. Heading the list was *Mirror* by Evie, followed by *Home Where I Belong* by B.J. Thomas, *Gentle Moments* by Evie, For *Him Who Has Ears to Hear* by Keith Green, *Alleluia* by the Bill Gaither Trio, *Praise II* by Maranatha! Music, *Live* by Dallas Holm and Praise, *This is Not a Dream* by Pam Mark, *Live From Nashville* by Jimmy Swaggart, and *Music Machine* by Candle. Others on the list of top sellers included Mike Warnke, Reba Rambo Gardner, Andrae Crouch, Joe Reed, the Phil Keaggy Band, 2nd Chapter of Acts, Seawind, and J.D. Sumner & the Stamps (with their tribute to Elvis album).

The Dove Awards in 1978 were held Wednesday evening, November 8 at the Opryland Hotel. The affair, hosted by Jerry and Sharalee Lucas, featured a sit-down dinner for 1,200 and performances by Ralph Carmichael and Orchestra, Evie, the Cathedral Quartet, Shirley Caesar, the Mighty Clouds of Joy, and the Couriers. Dallas Holm was the big winner that night, carrying home four Doves, including "Song of the Year" honors for "Rise Again." He also won the "Songwriter of the Year" award and became the first person other than Bill Gaither to win that honor since the inception of the Doves. Evie was "Female Vocalist" for the second year in a row and the Imperials were the top group. Other award winners were Dino Karstonakis, the Cruse Family (for "Contemporary Album of the Year" with their *Transformation* album), the Bill Gaither Trio, the Boones, Andrae Crouch, and the Blackwood Brothers. George Beverly Shea and Mahalia Jackson were inducted into the Gospel Hall of Fame.

This was another critical year for the Gospel Music Association and Dove Awards because new blood had arrived—in the form of Dallas Holm, Evie, and Dino—while some of the old timers were being eased out. In June of that year the GMA had signed an agreement with a Hollywood-based production firm to televise the Doves for the first time, but no deal could be struck and so the show was not televised. That year the GMA also announced plans for a $1.5 million building across from the Country Music Hall of Fame to house the Gospel Music Hall of Fame, offices, and a research center, but the money could not be raised and that area gave rise to the Barbara Mandrell Museum and Store.

In addition to the increased media attention given to the evangelical movement in 1978, there was a growing concern that religion was leading to "cults." This fear was publicized when Jim Jones led his 900 followers to a mass suicide in Guyana.

During the period 1979-1981, the Bill Gaither Trio was performing about 175 concerts a year, mostly on the weekends. It was a massive undertaking because at least 19 people traveled with the show. Most of the musicians and crew traveled in a $170,000 custom-designed bus which allowed them to sleep as it drove through the night while Bill, Gloria, and the female singers usually flew to the concerts in a leased private jet. Gary McSpadden, who was still pastoring a church in Fort Worth, Texas, generally arrived via commercial airline for the concerts.

The Christian Bookseller's 30th Convention was a five-day gathering where the companies that produced Christian books, records, gifts, music, trinkets, and other assorted products gathered to unleash all the might they could muster in order to obtain orders from Christian retailers. Over 8,000 attended this trade show with buyers from over 1,600 Christian bookstores placing orders. Built around the theme, "Making Christ Known," the Convention featured seminars as well as sales pitches, with topics that included "How To Sell the Top Ten Bibles," "Increasing Sales With Specials and Promotions," "Displaying and Selling Music," "Store Personnel Management," and "Cash Flow Controls."

For recording artists, this was the single most important event of their year because of the necessity to establish good relations with Christian bookstore owners. Those who appeared during that convention included Andrae Crouch, Kathie Lee Johnson, Candle, Johnny Zell, Jeremiah People, Christine Wyrtzen, Bridge, Cynthia Clawson, the Bill Gaither Trio, Pat Boone, Dan Peek, Chuck Girard, Rick Foster, David Meece, Truth, Fletch Wiley, Mike Warnke, Honeytree, Gary S. Paxton, Doug Oldham, and a brand new act whose album would be released in October, Sandi Patti. They all came to meet—and be met by—the Christian bookstore personnel who would, they hoped, stock and sell their music. It was a good way to be seen, heard and noticed by the people who count in the Christian retailing industry.

Christians increasingly had their own lingo, or "Christianese," that defined the true Christian in gatherings such as this one. Christians did not just talk, they "shared," did not socialize, they "fellowshiped," did not have drive and ambition, they had a "vision," did not speak of management in finances but of "stewardship," did not have professional or personal urges but a "calling," did not have a career but a "ministry," and were not just pleased or satisfied, but "blessed." This common vocabulary gave a strength to the movement because it united everyone; the Christian culture of the late 1970s showed a unity that was a major factor in gospel music making such a giant leap forward in the late '70s to early '80s period.

There was no Dove Awards show in 1979 because the Gospel Music Association had decided to shift the awards from the fall to the spring of the year, and since this transition would have meant a 1979 Dove Awards just a few months after the 1978 event, it was decided to skip 1979 altogether and hold the next one in 1980, 17 months later.

The move to shift the Dove Awards was the major break with the Quartet Convention. The Southern gospel contingent had begun the GMA and the Doves. The awards had remained part of the Quartet Convention Week activities, although the GMA had sought to include all facets of gospel music and convince the rest of the industry that it was not dominated by the Southern gospel faction. It was decided that the best way to do this was change the time when the Dove Awards was held. With contemporary Christian music coming on strong, and the Gospel Music Association needing the support of that part of the industry, a major move was necessary. The move worked and the Dove Awards increasingly became a showcase for contemporary Christian music in the 1980s. That segment of the gospel pie began to dominate the GMA and the Awards while the Southern gospel influence waned.

During fall, 1979, Evie had three albums on the "Inspirational/MOR" chart in *CCM* while the Bill Gaither Trio had five. Danny Gaither also had an album in the top 25—which meant the little area around Anderson, Indiana grew the talent for almost a fourth of that chart. On the "Contemporary" chart, Keith Green, B.J. Thomas, and Dallas Holm each had two albums in the top ten while Amy Grant's debut album was at number 13. On the "Southern Gospel" charts, Jimmy Swaggart had three of the top eight albums.

Top songs on the "Inspirational/MOR" chart were "I Am Loved," by the Bill Gaither Trio, "Rise Again" by Dallas Holm and three from the Imperials—"Praise the Lord," "Oh, Buddah," and "Sail On." On the "Contemporary" charts, "Blame It On The One I Love" by Kelly Willard was number one; others on the chart included "Cosmic Cowboy" by Barry McGuire, "He's Alive" by Don Francisco, "Never Gonna Serve Anyone Else" by David Meece, "Johnny's Cafe" by John Fischer, and "Old Man's Rubble" by Amy Grant.

Perhaps the most significant event for the gospel music world in 1979 was the arrival of Bob Dylan's Christian album, *Slow Train Coming*. The Christian music industry had long been infatuated with the pop world. The conversion of major celebrities and artists had always been seen as an affirmation of the appeal of Christianity; perhaps the most prized catch of all was Bob Dylan, and his conversion was expected to change American pop music. The theory was that someone of Dylan's magnitude—the "voice of a generation" who had the ears of almost every major rock artist, critic, and follower—would cause massive conversions from the rock 'n' roll world and the gospel fold would be multiplied mightily. Alas, it would not be so.

It is ironic that the Christian world stands against the secular world on one hand, but looks to that same world for affirmation on the other. The Christian media embraced any celebrity from popular culture who was "converted" and put them on magazine covers and TV shows. Further, Christian artists looked at secular acceptance as God's affirmation of their efforts while, at the same time, preaching against success defined in worldly terms.

Dylan's conversion caused more celebration in the gospel world than it did in the rock world, which regarded it primarily as an aberration and viewed it with alarm. Those who would follow wherever Dylan led would find they could not bring themselves to follow him into Christianity and the gospel world came face to face with a reality: the growth of gospel music in the future would not come from acceptance by the secular, or non-gospel, music world, but from better marketing within its own ranks. The infatuation with secular success and the strategies of marketing to the rock 'n' roll world—so much a part of the contemporary Christian mentality at the end of the 1970s—gave way to the realization that gospel music's immediate future was with the true believers. The key to big sales would be saturating the Christian marketplace through the Christian bookstores rather than becoming the darling of the pop music world, which is always looking for "the next big thing."

As the 1970s came to a close, some reflected on the decade where America lost a war and a President and wondered if it was going to lose a lifestyle as well. Rampant runaway inflation, interest rates that reached into the 20s before declining, and massive energy shortages made many wonder if there was an end in sight to the trademark characteristics of most Americans: materialism and optimism. This, combined with apocalyptic forecasts from scientists and economists regarding the supply of natural energy sources, cast a cloud of gloom and doom over the country. The economy was suffering through high inflation, massive unemployment, and a deep recession.

The most famous Christian in the world—Mother Teresa—won the Nobel Prize for Peace. Although she was a beacon of light to the world at large, many in the American evangelical community openly criticized her because she was Catholic and, therefore, not sufficiently "Christian." Her exemplary life and lifetime of work with the poor in India were overlooked because, according to many in the American evangelical community, her "doctrine" wasn't quite right.

The final nail in the coffin for the Carter Presidency came when the American Embassy in Tehran was taken over by Muslim fundamentalists under the leadership of the Ayatolla Khomeini and 52 Americans were taken hostage. Helpless to do anything for her imprisoned citizens, a victim of the Persian Gulf power struggle which would threaten not only citizens traveling abroad but also citizens at home, America had been brought to her knees. Cars lined up at gas pumps because one of the resources the country had always taken for granted—energy—was in danger of being taken away.

Chapter 30

BLACK GOSPEL
AND JAMES CLEVELAND

During the 1970s, James Cleveland became arguably the most important individual in traditional black gospel. He was important because of his influence on other singers, for his help and support of other acts, as an artist whose records had an impact in gospel, and as the founder and president of the Gospel Music Workshop of America. During a period in the late '60s and early '70s, when blacks struggled for self-respect as well as respect from society, Cleveland helped to provide that respect for those who were involved as singers in churches and who attended his convention. With the slogan "Where Everybody is Somebody" and the underlying theology that everyone is someone important in the eyes of God, Cleveland's convention not only helped singers and musicians with their music, it also lifted their hearts, minds, and spirits.

Thomas Dorsey was the first to gather black choir members together for a convention beginning in 1932. However, by the late 1960s there were a number of singers Dorsey was not reaching. Cleveland's first convention was held in Detroit in 1968 and attracted over 3,000 registrants. The next year nearly 5,000 attended the convention in Philadelphia and in 1970 over 5,000 came to St. Louis for the gathering. From there, they held conventions in Dallas, Chicago, Los Angeles, Washington, Kansas City, and New York. At each of the conventions, more classes and seminars were added to help choir members and musicians as well as radio announcers and choir directors. Each night choirs from numerous churches performed and Cleveland often dropped in to perform with a choir or sometimes solo with just a keyboard player (often Billy Preston). He was clearly the center of attention and the magnet that pulled all the disparate forces together. Cleveland's convention managed to speak to the black experience and gratified a desire for significance in a world that often treated African-Americans as second-class citizens. It made Cleveland more than just another gospel singer.

Cleveland said of his workshop, "It was a dream I had. There are a lot of good gospel musicians that need help, you know, like there are a lot of people that play by ear. They don't know where to go to get someone to help them. There are no colleges or schools that actually teach gospel; therefore, the man that has a little knowledge that wants to increase his knowledge doesn't have any place to go. Directors, songwriters, organists, soloists, people who want to learn how to effectively be a lead singer, etc., every phase of gospel music—there is no place they can turn other than to people in the business—so I asked these people to donate a portion of their time each year to help other musicians."

Born in 1932, James Cleveland was raised in Chicago and, as a boy soprano, sang in the church where Thomas Dorsey was minister of music. He heard the piano playing of Roberta Martin and was captivated. Since his family could not afford to buy a piano, he used to practice each night on the window sill where he took the wedges and crevices and made them into black and white keys.

Before he made his mark as a singer, Cleveland made his mark as a piano player, developing a hard, driving style when he played behind Roberta Martin. As a singer, he was influenced by Myrtle Scott of the Roberta Martin Singers and Eugene Smith, also of that group. The flamboyance of Smith was combined with the influences of ballad singer Robert Anderson, jazzman Louis Armstrong, and blues singer Dinah Washington, once the lead singer for Sallie Martin. Washington showed Cleveland the fusion between gospel and blues, and he wove those two musical forms together.

James Cleveland was energetic, bright, and ambitious. He would go anywhere and ask anyone for a chance to sing and play. In the mid-'50s, Cleveland's arrangements caught the ears of the gospel world as he fused some secular blues and jazz influences into black gospel. He was a member of Albertina Walker's legendary Caravans and worked with such greats as Dorothy Norwood, Inez Andrews,

Imogene Green, and Norsalus McKissick. He was the architect of the strong, pushing gospel sound, a sound that drove a song.

Cleveland's gruff vocal style came after his voice changed from soprano and, as he drove himself to sing more and more—fractured his once beautiful voice into a deep growl. He was not a pretty singer, by anyone's standards, but one of the most effective in bringing across a gospel song and pulling emotions out of a crowd.

After recording for several labels with various groups, Cleveland signed with Savoy Records and released records with the Cleveland All-Stars (featuring Billy Preston on keyboards) and the Gospel Chimes (which featured Jessy Dixon). Finally, Fred Mendelsohn, head of Savoy, teamed Cleveland up with the Angelic Choir of Nutley, New Jersey, and he found his niche. Working with this choir, as well as a number of others across the country, Cleveland released records that featured the choirs as a background and on the choruses while he worked with the verses, molding them to his own style.

The 1980s saw Cleveland fall out of vogue with some of the younger black gospel performers and fans. While they moved into the slick, smooth sound influenced by R & B and disco, Cleveland remained with his raw, gutsy, blues-based soul sound. The result was a split in black gospel which resulted in two overlapping factions, referred to as contemporary and traditional.

Cleveland spoke of the importance of music in the gospel world as well as the gulf that often exists between a singer's own spiritual life and the one they sing about. He stated that, "There are a lot of people who have the ability to expound that are not necessarily heavily religious. There are a lot of people who can sing and bring tears to your eyes but are not deeply religious. We have people who can stand up and sing gospel and they have fantastic voices that would impress you if you didn't know anything about their lives. There are folks who don't really care about church and don't really care about the cause but they can still do the job. What we're trying to do is see that person become dedicated to the music, not just be in business for a dollar—see that person becomes dedicated and sing music so it's inspiring to others to come to Christ and the church. More people are drawn to the church through music than what you are preaching. Over the years people have been turned off to preaching so much that they don't want to come to church. But music is one of the most perfect magnets you can use to draw people to church.... I think that any minister of any church of a denomination believing in music should have a well-rounded music department because music softens the heart of the people and the minister can deliver the sermons and effectively a team is going to win souls for Christ."

Cleveland was acutely aware of the problems gospel music—particularly black gospel—had to face in order to be heard by the public. "I would certainly like to reach a wider audience," he said. "Because I find people like gospel as well as anything else, when they get a chance to hear it. My problem, or the problem of most of these singers, is we can't become as big name-wise as the pop singers only because we don't have the exposure. You see, they hear pop 20 hours a day and they hear gospel one hour, and that's usually five or six o'clock in the morning on most radio stations when nobody gets a chance really to hear it. Therefore, the artist can never really be known because they're never exposed at the right time when people can connect with them. But if we had a decent amount of radio time dedicated for gospel in major cities, the artists would become bigger because their popularity would grow as people know who they are. Then record sales would grow and so would public appearances."

The economic panacea of selling black music to white buyers has long been a part of the music industry and began to permeate black gospel in the late 1970s and early 1980. This move towards a smoother, more palatable sound—and away from the rough, raw sound of traditional black gospel—allowed black gospel artists to be stocked in Christian bookstores and sell to the predominantly white contemporary Christian audience.

Cleveland was aware of this and stated in 1978 that, "Andrae Crouch has bridged the gap between black and white audiences and done a very good job. The white artists are very interested in the more soulful type of gospel music. Also, in the contemporary sound of gospel music, many black musicians are now embracing the contemporary sound. There is a great upsurge of white choirs that sing like black choirs and the blacks have always tried to excel and perfect their performances relating to sound, arrangements, and instrumentation. Orchestrations and the like bring us closer to what the white man has been doing all the time. Then the white man is coming more to the soulful side, trying to deal more with the spiritual than the technical aspect. So they're coming our way, and we're going their way. Somewhere in the middle of the road we're bound to run into one another!"

Black gospel was traditionally sold in independently owned record stores (called Mom and Pop stores) in the black sections of town and heard on African-American radio stations, usually during a one-hour program. Christian bookstores were reluctant to stock black gospel, perhaps not trusting black American Christianity as well as not finding a great demand for the distinctive black gospel record. There were, however, a number of African-Americans who became increasingly acceptable to this white market; unfortunately, the gospel performer had to choose his or her own audience and those African-American performers who had whites buying their albums often found they lost their black audience.

James Cleveland kept his black audience and, as a result, few whites bought his recordings. That is probably because Cleveland was a voice for the African-American in America—he spoke to the black experience through his music and preaching—and the white audience had trouble relating. One of James Cleveland's greatest attributes was that he never stepped away from the black church, preferring to give a dignity to the music that comprised the very roots of the black church and its music.

In November 1970 Cleveland became pastor of the Cornerstone Institutional Baptist Church in Los Angeles, where he remained for the rest of his life. In 1972 he recorded an album with Aretha Franklin, *Amazing Grace*, that became a best-seller and won a Grammy. The album was filled with hymns such as "There Is a Fountain Filled With Blood" and "Never Grow Old" as Aretha used her fame in pop and rhythm and blues to return to her roots in the church.

In the mid-1980s the Winans and Tramaine Hawkins took black gospel over into the Christian bookstore market. The albums, *Let My People Go* by the Winans and *Spirit Fall Down* by Tramaine, were embraced by the secular world as well. Released on secular labels, these artists, along with Take 6. the Sounds of Blackness, and the Commodores song "Jesus is Love," brought black gospel to the world at large. The fusion between black gospel and contemporary Christian music that Cleveland dreamed about years earlier came about. In the future religious music would have an appeal in the secular market primarily through African-American performers.

Chapter 31

TELEVANGELISTS AND JIMMY SWAGGART

By the time television arrived in American homes in 1947, the networks had developed the way they would handle religious programming. The problems caused by Father Charles Coughlin during the 1930s and the regulations of the Federal Communications Commission, issued in 1946, set the agenda.

The story of Father Coughlin served as a warning to broadcasters about religious programs for a number of years. After getting pushed off the CBS network, Coughlin purchased time on a number of radio stations, and his programs were extremely popular; he received a tremendous amount of mail each week—many containing money orders or cash.

At the beginning of President Franklin Roosevelt's administration, Coughlin was a supporter; however, he turned against the President and organized a deluge of telegrams to Congress from his followers. He began the National Union for Social Justice and organized rallies in several cities. Coughlin's anti-Semitism put him in sympathy with Hitler and his isolationism put him at odds with the fervor for war after the bombing of Pearl Harbor. By World War II, Father Coughlin was finished, but the memory of his rabble-rousing speeches, his use of religion to launch his political views, and his ability to attract a large audience, then incite them to act on emotional issues, gave national broadcasters a fear of the dangers of putting religion on the air.

In 1926 Father Charles E. Coughlin had been assigned to the Shrine of the Little Flower in Royal Oak, a northern suburb of

Detroit. The church only had 25 families, and in an attempt to build the congregation, Coughlin went to WJR in Detroit to arrange for broadcasts from the church. As Coughlin preached, he began to talk about social and political issues and found that contributions came in when he touched certain "hot button" issues. During the Depression, he castigated those with wealth and power—a popular theme with Depression-era audiences.

Coughlin began an organization, the "Radio League of the Little Flower" (membership was a dollar a year), and then bought time on other stations, including those in Cincinnati and Chicago. At WMAQ in Chicago, a CBS network station, Coughlin purchased time on the CBS network. This increased the flow of contributions as he turned up the emotional heat in his rhetoric; Coughlin attacked President Hoover and bankers, which caused alarm at CBS.

When a CBS executive asked Coughlin to stop the political attacks, Coughlin went on the air—on January 4, 1931—and asked listeners whether he should be muzzled by CBS. The result was over a million letters to CBS protesting their handling of Coughlin. CBS then began a "Church of the Air" series with a rotating group of speakers; this program eased Coughlin off the network in April 1931. From this point forward, CBS produced its own network broadcast of religious programs and did not sell air time to evangelists.

When Congress passed the Communications Act of 1934, which established the Federal Communications Commission to regulate radio and the emerging medium of television, the broadcasters convinced Congress they would provide public groups and churches with free air time if they were not required to do so by law. This led to all stations providing programs "in the public interest" in order to retain their licenses. As radio progressed, it was increasingly criticized for appealing to the lowest common denominator in popular tastes and operating the airwaves for private profit instead of public good.

In 1945 FCC Commissioner Clifford J. Durr began to question station license renewals and demanded to know what kind of programming was being offered to the public. Stations had increasingly declined public-affairs programs in order to program popular programs that listeners preferred. This led to a report issued by the FCC in March 1946 titled *Public Service Responsibility of Broadcast*

Licences, which became known as "the blue book" because its cover was blue. This report directed local broadcasters to provide balanced programming, provide non-commercial programs, serve minority interests, help non-profit groups, and experiment with new techniques in order to have their licenses renewed.

In the end, commercial interests had their way, although each radio station had to show that it had broadcast "in the public interest" before its license would be renewed.

Network television dealt with mainline religious groups through established organizations: The National Council of Catholic Men represented Catholics, the Jewish Seminary of America represented Jews, and the Federal Council of Churches of Christ represented Protestants. During the 1950s the networks produced mainline religious programming: "Lamp Unto My Feet" and "Look Up and Live" were on CBS, "Directions" was on ABC and "Frontiers of Faith" was on NBC. The Southern Baptist Radio and Television Commission had almost 2,500 broadcasts a week donated by local television stations by 1974.

The most popular religious show was done by Bishop Fulton J. Sheen, who began broadcasting over WLWL in New York in 1928 doing "Catholic Hour." When he moved to TV, the production consisted of a speech or classroom lecture on a religious or moral subject; his only "prop" was a blackboard. The show was broadcast in the evening and quite popular; between 1952 and 1957 it drew competitive ratings.

During the 1960s conservative Protestant theology affirmed traditional American culture, including the values of free-enterprise capitalism and the validity of capitalism's monetary rewards. Part of the 1960s rebellion by youth was against this materialist culture that lacked a deeper spirituality.

The growth of independently syndicated evangelical or fundamentalist programs which purchased air time on TV grew from 38 in 1972 to 72 in 1978. The major cause for the change was an FCC ruling in 1960 that opened up the UHF-frequency, allowing new TV stations to go on the air. These new UHF stations did not have a network affiliation, so there were no programs provided to them from the networks; instead, they had to either purchase or create their own programs. Many bought re-runs from the networks or ran syndicated shows that were independently produced and contained time slots where the local station could sell advertisements.

The FCC had also stated, in essence, that there should be no difference in sustaining-time programs—those produced by the station and broadcast free—and commercially sponsored programs when the stations' performance "in the public interest" was evaluated. This allowed stations to meet FCC regulations with religious programs for which air-time was provided as well as programs that paid for their air-time. It did not take television stations long to realize that running programs that paid them was more profitable than running programs that cost them money.

The FCC developed a "hands off" approach to religious stations and programming; it has not enforced the noncommercial requirements of those holding educational or noncommercial licenses when it came to on-air fund-raising, on-air solicitations, or the sale of religious items over the air. In other words, the FCC has ruled that paid-time religious programs are not "commercial," even though these programs actively solicit money from viewers.

The FCC has also not applied the "Fairness Doctrine" to religious television. This doctrine states that when a controversial issue is broadcast, the opposite viewpoint must also be aired. By not enforcing this rule, the FCC has virtually left religious television to do as it pleases.

Because they had to be profitable, the new UHF television stations soon discovered that selling time to religious broadcasters was a good way to fill up time and make money. It was especially appealing during the Sunday morning hours, the "broadcast ghetto" when the fewest number of people watch television. Because Sunday is a traditional day of worship, the reasoning ran, these shows provided a service for those who could not attend church.

As television stations came to know this source of income from paid religious broadcasting, they shifted away from local programming—which cost them money—to paid programming, which made money. In 1959, 53 percent of all religious programs on TV purchased their own air time; in 1977 the percentage was 92 percent. These paid programs virtually eliminated local religious programming. In 1979 this led CBS to cancel "Lamp Unto My Feet" and "Look Up and Live," its two long-running religious shows.

Evangelicals have tended towards a utilitarian view of technology; if the morality of the user and the purpose of the technology was "good," then it was justified. Next, evangelical theology has emphasized the emotional aspects of religious faith; this appeals more to television viewers than the mystical views of Christianity. Finally, conservative theology has tended to affirm traditional American values, especially the values of free enterprise and the validity of financial rewards. This contrasts with liberal mainline religious culture, which is often critical of the capitalist system and consumerism in American life.

Televangelists began appearing in the early 1950s. In 1953 Rex Humbard began his television ministry in Akron, Ohio; from 1953 to 1969 he purchased air-time regularly on 68 stations; in 1970 the show expanded to 110 stations, then over the next two years he added 100 stations each year. Oral Roberts began his television program in 1954, purchasing time on 16 stations; in 1967 he stopped for two years and, when he re-emerged, his show was more like a variety show. In 1956 Jerry Falwell began his church in Lynchburg, Virginia; his television program, "The Old Time Gospel Hour," was an edited version of one of his morning services at the Thomas Road Baptist Church. Pat Robertson graduated from Yale Law School, but could not pass the New York State bar exam; instead he purchased a television station in Virginia Beach in 1960 and began broadcasting in 1961 with his "700 Club." This led to the development of his Christian Broadcasting Network (CBN). In 1955 Robert Schuller, a minster with the Reformed Church of America, was sent to Orange County, California to begin a new congregation; by 1980 his TV program, "Hour of Power," was broadcast from the "Crystal Cathedral," a $15 million glass sanctuary.

Sophisticated computer technology, developed during the 1960s, provided a key element that televangelists needed to have successful programming. This technology allowed evangelical broadcasters to handle a large volume of incoming mail and develop mailing lists to solicit donations from their viewers. It also created money-generating organizations whose views had to be in tune with their audience to keep the funds rolling in. Although these religious broadcasters did not have to depend on Nielson ratings or the decision of network executives to stay on the air, the mail became a polling device and showed audience preferences.

Ten major evangelical programs accounted for over half of all national airings of religious programs in 1979. The National Religious Broadcasters, formed in 1944, were a driving force behind these programs; most independent broadcasters were members of this organization. Their cut-throat purchase of time forced most other religious programs off the air.

The main criteria for what was accepted as the Christian message from these religious broadcasters was one with a popular appeal that viewers responded to. This popular response was then "interpreted" as embracing the inherent truth in the message in addition to having God's blessing. These shows placed a heavy emphasis on personal integrity and good intentions for what was being done; the ends then justified the means.

Televangelists used several methods for on-air solicitation. These included "incentives," or free gifts such as books or records (most of them by the evangelist or a family member), the opportunity for viewers to call for counseling, prayer or conversation, and the recurring "emergency" requiring the viewer's urgent and immediate support. This was usually a religious "horror" story, with the implication that Christianity itself hung in the balance if money was not sent immediately.

These appeals led people to write or call in; the computer technology allowed the broadcaster's organization to compile a mailing list for personalized direct solicitation. To encourage people to give, several tactics were adopted.

First was the theology of "seed faith": if you give something to God, He will take this financial "seed" and multiply it. The believer becomes a venture capitalist with a sure-fire investment: send money to God and it will be multiplied and returned to you. Oral Roberts popularized this concept but it is now practiced by many churches. Pat Robertson espoused "Kingdom Principles," which states that if you give money to "God," you will receive money in return. Jim Bakker and Jerry Falwell promoted the "health and wealth" theology, or that for those who are faithful to God, rewards will come through good health and material success.

The "proof" of God's blessing is in gains and benefits to the believer; consequently, the broadcaster emphasized the miraculous over the mundane, the larger-than-life events in life to create a "Super

Bowl Christianity" for a culture that demands instant gratification.

There is a misperception that more people watched the paid television programs than the network religious shows of the 1950s and 60s. While these network sustaining-time shows did not attract huge audiences, the paid programs attracted even less. In ratings compiled by Nielsen in 1979, only five syndicated religious programs gained a rating of one or better. This means that of all the people in the United States, one percent was watching one of these shows. The top-rated paid program was Oral Roberts, with a two rating. However, the two types of religious programs attracted different audiences; the paid-time program audiences tended to be more vocal and demonstrative while the audiences of the network shows tended to be more passive.

A small, well-organized vocal group will trump a large, scattered, silent audience every time, and that's what happened with paid religious shows. The network shows had large audiences who were not particularly loyal or demonstrative; the paid shows had small, vocal audiences. This played into the hands of the television audience, many of whom view TV as the "real world." The programmers broadcast of affluence, luxury, and entertainment caters to viewers' consumerism and self-interest. The result was an inflated view of the audience and the importance of religious television during the late 1970s and 1980s. In truth, many evangelicals don't watch any of the religious broadcasters' shows, or watch very little, while those who watch tend to watch several shows. Also, the evangelical television shows did not express the religious views of the majority of Americans; their mainline views were not on television. The growth of paid-time religious programs did not increase the audience for religious television, but it changed which religious programs were broadcast.

The largest growth of TV evangelists on paid programs occurred from 1965 to 1975 and went virtually unnoticed; as previously noted, the election of Jimmy Carter to the Presidency in November 1976 brought attention to the "born-again" movement and religion in America. In 1977 the paid programs of televangelists were at their apex; ironically, because of their organizational and fund-raising abilities, and the fact they attracted the attention of the mass media, the period from 1980 to 1988 was the period when people perceived them to have the most power and influence.

In July 1980 the *Wall Street Journal* stated in an article that tele-vangelists were reaching an estimated 128 million viewers each week. That same year, Jerry Falwell was claiming an audience of 20 million people for his show, and began organizing the "Moral Majority." Jim Bakker of "The PTL Club" also claimed 20 million viewers.

But, according to Nielsen ratings, in November 1980 Oral Roberts had 2.275 million viewers; the "Hour of Power" had two million; Rex Humbard had 1.9 million, Jimmy Swaggart had 1.6 million; "Day of Discovery" had 1.24 million; Falwell's "Old Time Gospel Hour" had 1.21 million, "Insight" had 790,000, the PTL Club had 621,000, and Pat Robertson's 700 Club had 447,600 viewers. The Nielsen surveys showed a total combined audience of 19.1 million for all the syndicated shows and, in 1981, only five syndicated programs received a rating of one or better: Oral Roberts, "Hour of Power," Rex Humbard, "Insight," and Jimmy Swaggart.

Ironically, the religious show with the highest rating and largest audience was "Gospel Singing Jubilee," a show hosted by the Florida Boys that featured Southern gospel singing. This show had a 4.2 rating. During 1975 and 1976, "Gospel Singing Jubilee" had the largest audience of any religious program—1.01 million and 1.09 million respectively. During the 1977-1980 period, it was second, behind Falwell's "Old Time Gospel Hour" and in 1981 it was third, behind Falwell and "Insight." But the "Gospel Singing Jubilee" was never on as many stations as the other programs; also, it depended on advertising to stay on the air and subsequently vanished from the airwaves in 1981.

In November 1981, Nielsen estimated the religious programs audience at 21,751,000; other estimates went as high as 36 million but, since most viewers watched several religious programs, it was estimated that the audience for religious broadcasts was actually 10-15 million different people.

According to Peter G. Horsfield in his book, *Religious Television: An American Experience*, which documented these Nielsen numbers, those religious programs were not representative of the religious audience. In 1981 independent evangelical groups accounted for 83.3 percent of the top syndicated religious programs on television; the Roman Catholic Church, which had 37.1 percent of the population in 1979, had only one major syndicated television program, "Insight." The National Council of Churches, which represented 30 percent of the church population in 1979 and 1981, had no major syndicated religious program.

Television in America serves two basic functions: entertainment and killing time. When viewers decide to "kill time" by watching TV, they do not decide whether to watch a specific program; instead, they just decide to watch some TV. The secondary concern is what they will view. Before the popularity of remote controls, the TV tended to stay on one station much longer; with remotes, people regularly click through the whole range of channels. Many people justify their time in front of a TV because of the effort they've expended during the working day; they feel they need this TV viewing to relax and wind down.

The reason that evangelical broadcasters give for using television is "spreading the gospel." However, most of the programs are broadcast on Sunday mornings in regions where church attendance is already high. There are several reasons for this: (1) Sunday morning is the traditional day of worship; (2) time buys on Sunday are cheaper than almost any other time; (3) TV stations prefer selling Sunday morning time slots to religious broadcasters rather than prime time spots (in 1976 there was a potential national audience of 13 million adults on Sunday mornings; during prime time, the number was 70 million); and (4) the religious broadcasters realized that their core audience watched during Sunday mornings. Therefore, in order to raise money, they had to appeal to a core audience—which they tended to find on Sunday mornings in areas that were already populated by church-goers.

A breakdown of the audience watching religious programming showed that women outnumber men about two to one. The "Hour of Power" had 60.9 percent women, Oral Roberts had 59.8 percent, Jimmy Swaggart had 54.6 percent, and the PTL Club had 61.4 percent women. The "Gospel Singing Jubilee" had 55.3 percent women and 44.7 percent men.

The audience also tends to be older—half the regular viewers were over 60 years old. Surveys showed that as people age, particularly women, they tend to watch more religious television, to the point that the core audience for religious programming is women over the age of 50.

The audience tended to have lower incomes, less education, and be employees in blue-collar occupations. Those in white-collar occupations, with higher incomes and more education, tended to watch less religious television. In terms of geography, those in the Southern and Midwestern states—where there was the highest church attendance—watched more than those in the West or East.

While the religious broadcasters claimed that "getting the gospel out" and reaching "the lost" were their primary objectives, in reality the shows were aimed at insiders and they functioned as companionship, inspiration and support for Christians, who wanted uplifting messages.

It is easy to be cynical about religious broadcasters, or claim they're just doing it for the money, but in truth most go into religious broadcasting in order to influence other people towards their own religious stance and view of life. In a way, they are successful in doing this, bringing together scattered people with like-minded views into a core audience. Television's power comes by coalescing an audience around a particular idea, particularly when the audience is leaning towards this idea but has been unable to articulate it. The claim that television can "make" people believe something they haven't thought of before doesn't really hold water; thus the idea that people with no inclination towards religion will somehow watch a religious program and experience a conversion doesn't work to any great degree. Although religious broadcasters will have a story or two like this in their arsenal of "proofs" for their programs, in reality this is an extremely rare occurrence.

There have been preachers on television for as long as television has been a major part of American life, beginning in the 1950s. But from the mid-1970s on, the big news in the Christian world was the TV preachers, who have always been the most visible part of that culture. Those preachers were, in a sense, an aberration from that culture. They were highly emotional, very dramatic, and the money they brought in and lifestyles they lived were not the same as the typical everyday Christian's. In every instance, it was the messenger who dominated.

The world of TV evangelists has always been dominated by a handful of men, eight to ten at most at any given time. Musically, these preachers rarely break any new ground, seeing music in the traditional role of "preparing the way" for the message. As the shows got slicker in the '70s and '80s and began adopting talk-show-type formats, music began to be featured more with some gospel artists appearing on the shows. However, the urge for each preacher to dominate and control his own show prevailed and the preachers all began to develop talent within their own organizations to appear on their programs. They could control these singers, dictate which songs they sang, what music they played, and not have to pay them much. Thus the medium with potentially the greatest influence had little, if any, influence on gospel music.

With the exception of Jimmy Swaggart, none of the televangelists have been particularly musical, most barely able to carry a tune. Instead, they have always seen themselves as preachers and the thrust of their operation was themselves and their messages. Only Swaggart had a strong musical background and he initially built his following on his ability to play and sing, becoming well known through his recordings. Along the way, he became the most successful artist in the Southern gospel, or country gospel vein, dominating the airwaves and selling large numbers of albums outside his own shows.

Swaggart's background is interesting because he came from the Pentecostal tradition and this tradition also provided some performers in the early days of rock 'n' roll. Artists like Elvis Presley, Little Richard, Swaggart's cousin Jerry Lee Lewis, and numerous others came from Pentecostal backgrounds, and the fervid emotionalism of that heritage gave early rock 'n' roll some of its most dramatic qualities. Additionally, Pentecostalism also provided a number of preachers who became successful TV evangelists.

A number of Pentecostal churches sprang up in the early 20th century, including the Four Square Church headed by evangelist Aimee Semple McPherson, and the Assembly of God churches. This latter branch of Pentecostalism came to Ferriday, Louisiana, hometown of Jimmy Swaggart, during the Depression.

Mother Sumrall and her daughter, Leona, came from Mississippi to Ferriday in the spring of 1936. On a vacant lot on Texas Avenue they pulled weeds and cleared the space for some chairs and benches. Lee Calhoun, local big wheel, bootlegger and relative of the Swaggarts, happened to drive by in his truck one afternoon when the

Sumralls were busy fixing up the lot. He asked Mother Sumrall who she was and what she was doing; the evangelist replied that she was making a church. Calhoun replied that the town already had four churches; she countered that there would soon be five. Calhoun, always interested in finances, asked who would be supplying the money for this project. "God" was the answer Mother Sumrall gave. After a few more pleasantries, in which Mother Sumrall made it plain that she was doing the will of God, and invited Lee to her church, Calhoun drove on.

When summer came there was a tent for the services. Mother Sumrall had begun preaching with just her daughter in the chairs, but soon people began stopping by, curious about what was going on. In a short while, there was a small rag-tag congregation from Ferriday and the neighboring area. To them, Mother Sumrall preached the Pentecostal doctrine and through prayer, song, exhortation, and altar calls encouraged them to repent of their sins and give their life to Jesus.

The Swaggarts were not church folk, but Jimmy's father, Willie Leon, was always attracted to music. Pulled like a magnet to the singing in the tent, Willie Leon was soon standing at the front playing his fiddle. His wife, Minnie Bell, played rhythm guitar and Jimmy Lee hung around, close by. It was the first time the family had attended church and they soon became regulars.

The Assembly of God church was built in Ferriday in 1941, financed by Lee Calhoun. It was a small wooden church, painted white with a cross formed from seven panes of glass in each of the two front doors. The Sumrall women left after the church was constructed to begin evangelistic efforts all over again elsewhere. Tom Holcome, a young minister, came to lead the congregation but it was soon obvious the small congregation was too poor to afford to pay their minister full-time. Holcome commuted to Ferriday every week from his day-job in Texas. This was not unusual—many ministers in the rural, poor south had to have regular jobs in addition to their preaching duties. Preaching was a calling, but it didn't always pay well, if at all. Those who went into it did so for God, not for money. It was almost a test of faith.

Brother Holcome's young son died of pneumonia after he was there only a short while, and he gave up the Ferriday ministry after the boy's death. He was replaced by Henry Culbreth, described as a "quiet, brooding" man. It was under his tutelage that the Holy Ghost arrived in full force in Ferriday, Louisiana. The Swaggarts were not there when the first fires occurred because they had moved to Temple, Texas in December 1941. Willie Leon began working in a defense plant after the outbreak of World War II. The family had grown again with the addition of daughter Jeanette, and Temple had grown rapidly because of the high wages paid to defense workers in the plants. The Swaggarts move did not last long because the family was desperately homesick for Ferriday. Jimmy Lee was seven when his family packed all their belongings once again and headed back to Louisiana.

The first Swaggart to manifest the baptism of the Holy Spirit was Jimmy Lee's grandmother, Ada. She had returned from a revival in Snake Ridge speaking in tongues and telling others about her experience. Jimmy Lee was enthralled and entranced by stories of her experience and spent a lot of time at her house on Mississippi Avenue.

Nannie, as young Jimmy Lee called her, had been nearly as wild and woolly as the rest of the Calhoun-Lewis-Swaggart-Gilley clan, enjoying booze, cigarettes, and even some gambling. But when she came back from that Church of God camp meeting all those vices were gone. She was forty-five years old and on fire for the Lord.

Nannie's revelations shocked the family, especially Willie Leon and Minnie Bell, who had never heard tell of such goings on. The 25-member congregation of the Assembly of God church where they attended branded her a fanatic and openly rejected her. Even the family was openly antagonistic and skeptical. All except young Jimmy Lee who admits, "I was thrilled about it." So he kept asking her to tell him the story about "the experience" over and over and again she would tell it.

Swaggart recounts this story in his autobiography, *To Cross a River*. "Jimmy," she'd say. "You know when I went to that camp meeting I was so hungry for the Lord. Those services lasted almost 24 hours a day. When one preacher finished, we'd sing and then another would start. The services never seemed to end. But one day I was standing outside the little tabernacle near a grove of trees praying with my brother John and his wife. The presence of God became so real. Suddenly it seemed as if I had been struck by a bolt of lightning. Lying flat on my back, I raised my hands to praise the Lord. No English came out. Only unknown tongues."

Willie Leon, concerned about the influence of his mother-in-law on the young boy and dubious about her new-found faith, would shake his head openly and say, "Nannie's gone crazy over religion." He told Jimmy Lee, "She's filling your head full of junk" and finally forbade him to go over to Ada's house.

Itinerant evangelist J.M. Cason came to the little Assembly of God church to hold a revival later in that 1943 summer. At the revival were Willie Leon and Minnie Bell, Elmo and Mamie Lewis, and the Gilleys. Jimmy Lee Swaggart and Jerry Lee Lewis were a few blocks away playing with their friends, Mack and Huey P. Stone, when suddenly they heard a piercing scream coming from the church. Jimmy Lee instantly knew it was his mother.

At the church the young boys witnessed a powerful scene—the Holy Spirit had broken loose and was pouring itself out upon the congregation. Brother Cason stood at the front, leading the congregation in singing after giving the altar call, when Minnie Bell Swaggart let loose her howl and bolted from her seat. Mamie Lewis, who was coming back to her seat from the altar where she had answered the call, suddenly leaped in the air and turned back towards the altar. Irene Gilley (Mickey's mother) was kneeling at the altar in front of brother Cason speaking in tongues. The rest of the congregation had begun to dance, yell, sing, and howl in spiritual jubilation. Minnie Bell danced past Mamie, who had fallen to the floor, and both were speaking in tongues. Willie Leon was standing still, a huge smile on his face while his voice shouted at the top of his lungs. The whole church kept getting louder and louder and all the activity kept gathering speed, like a huge ball rolling down a steep hill. Everyone was in his or her own private world, moving, talking in tongues, dancing, running, shouting, waving arms, heads back shaking their hair, their bodies beyond their control. Never had that little church seen such frenzied activity and never again would it be the same.

Thelma Wiggins, a woman preacher from Houston, came to Ferriday for another revival and again the Swaggarts went. Jimmy Lee made trip after trip to the altar, all to no avail. Then, on the final night of the services, something happened. It was like he was being released, like chains were coming off him and he was slipping out of a straitjacket. He began to feel lighter and free—all that pressure built up inside him leaking out, like a steam kettle whose vapor was shooting into the air. He was kneeling down at the altar and praying, just like he had done time and time before, but things were different this time. He became aware of what seemed like a bright shaft of light coming out of heaven. It was like a pinpoint spotlight and it was focused right on him.

Jimmy Lee opened his mouth and a torrent of sounds came out. The language was not the words he spoke everyday but a rushing stream of sound that felt like it was coming right from heaven straight through him. His heart was beating fast and his body was twitching and he was no longer Jimmy Lee Swaggart of Ferriday, Louisiana but an instrument of God which the Lord Almighty was playing fast and furious. His mouth stayed open and the sounds kept coming and Jimmy Lee knew that God had given him His greatest gift, the baptism of the Holy Spirit.

Jimmy Swaggart began his public ministry standing outside a grocery store in a little town on a Saturday and preaching to those who had come into town to do their weekly shopping. The place was Mangham, Louisiana, where his father had been born. It was a small town, only about 500 inhabitants. Then, as always, his wife stood behind him, her strong will a support for him.

Jimmy had married Frances Anderson of Wisner, Alabama when he was 17 years old. By this time Willie Leon was a Pentecostal preacher but Jimmy Lee was a wild teenager. He had quit school because he didn't like it; he had quit church because he didn't like that either. Something about other people telling him what to do just didn't sit well with the hot-headed young man with more than a trace of wild blood running through his veins. He had been doing odd jobs to pick up a dollar here and there but didn't have a steady job. He was cocky and full of fight and figured he'd make a way someway, though he didn't know how.

Jimmy's parents did not want him to get married. They knew their rebellious son would have a hard time making a living, let alone getting along with another human being in an institution such as marriage. The Andersons weren't too keen on the marriage either;

they wanted Frances to finish high school and go to college. Those plans ended when Jimmy and Frances found a Baptist minister to marry them on a Friday night. The ring he slipped on her finger was his mother's, which he had borrowed for the occasion. Willie Leon, who could have married them, refused because he felt they were too young and knew his son to be too wild, reckless, and irresponsible to support a family. It was all wrong but Jimmy was as hard-headed as they come and when he made up his mind to do something he was going to do it even if everybody else was against it.

Before he stood in front of the grocery store and began preaching, Swaggart had asked the town's only policeman for permission. The man just looked at him and shrugged.

Jimmy had his accordion and began playing. Several of the young members of the church had guitars and the rag-tag band began singing, "There Is Power in the Blood." After a few more songs, as 15 or 20 people gathered around, Jimmy began to preach. He told them about Hitler invading Poland. He told them about World War II and how America was dragged into the picture. He covered the years up to the present day, 1953. Then he told them that America was deep in sin and was coming under God's judgment. As he preached he began to sweat. His nerves showed and if you looked close you could see his hands trembling. But they were not trembling because he was nervous—he was talking about the wrath and judgment of God and such things make a body tremble and shake. His knees felt wobbly, his collar was wet with sweat, but he preached on. Louder, faster, the words came out. He knew he had said some of those things before just a few minutes earlier, but he said them again. He drove home his point with his hands chopping the air, his fingers pointing. When he finished, the policeman, who had been watching from the edge of the crowd, came up, shook his hand and said, "Son, you've got the fire." A friendly pat on the back and then a smile. "No question about that," he said. Jimmy Swaggart just stood there, drained.

Jimmy Swaggart had long dreamed of being a traveling evangelist, having been influenced by people such as Jack Coe, William Branham, and Gordon Lindsay (publisher of the *Voice of Healing* magazine) who were prominent in the early 1950s. Since 1954 he had been working as a "swamper" in the Franklin Parish ("oiling and greasing the dragline") and preaching on the weekends. Finally, on

January 1, 1958, he quit his job and began evangelistic work full time.

Swaggart had been approached by several gospel quartets to play piano for them but turned them down. He wanted to preach and be more than just a piano player. By 1960 he had been ordained by the Assembly of God as a preacher and moved to Baton Rouge to be near his father after his mother's death. He was getting a lot of attention and offers to preach revivals because he advertised himself as Jerry Lee Lewis's cousin. Musically, he drew crowds with his honky-tonk style of gospel playing and singing but that style also had its drawbacks and he noted that some in the church "didn't like my piano playing and singing. They thought it wasn't churchy-sounding enough. There seemed to be more rhythm in it than they thought the four walls of the church could stand."

Jerry Lee was a major star in rock 'n' roll, recording on Sun Records in Memphis, the label that had also been home to Elvis Presley, Johnny Cash, Roy Orbison, Carl Perkins, Charlie Rich, and others. Sun had offered Swaggart a chance to record, too, but he turned them down, uncomfortable with the rock 'n' roll atmosphere. Swaggart's other cousin, Mickey Gilley, had been on Dot Records but had not hit like Jerry Lee, so he moved to Houston to begin a night club and try from there.

It was Gilley's connections in Houston that led to Swaggart's first album being recorded there. Swaggart had previously recorded one song, "At the End of the Trail," in the radio station studio in Ferriday, accompanied by his piano, a washtub bass, and three female singers. In Houston he recorded his first album, *Some Golden Daybreak*, which included songs like the title cut, "What a Day That Will Be," "He Bought My Soul," and "Stranger."

The album did well at Swaggart's revivals and he recorded a second album the next year in Memphis at the Sun studios. The engineer for this session was Scotty Moore, who had been Elvis's lead guitar player.

This album also sold well on the sawdust trail and received an added boost from Floyd Miles and Chuck Cossin on WMUZ in Detroit when they began playing "God Took Away My Yesterdays." Orders began coming in for the album and Jimmy and his wife Frances were labeling and shipping the orders out from motel rooms and wherever else they would stop during Swaggart's preaching schedule. Several labels offered him recording deals but Swaggart turned them all down, preferring to keep creative control. Soon stores and distributors began calling him for the album on his custom label and as a result of this exposure, more people began coming to his revivals. He was now preaching revivals four-to-six-weeks long instead of the previous one-or-two week revivals.

"God Took Away My Yesterdays" was the record that opened doors for Swaggart and soon he was preaching at Assembly of God Camp Meetings and recording more albums, which sold well at his revivals.

At the beginning of 1969 Swaggart began his radio program, "The Camp Meeting Hour," on stations in Atlanta, Houston and Minneapolis-St. Paul. Swaggart had purchased some equipment from Houston and set up a small, make-shift studio in his home to record the radio programs. He used the song "Someone to Care," which he had just recorded, as his theme. The initial response was zilch—no cards or letters—but later, after an appeal from one of the stations, Swaggart received 900 letters and $3,000 for the program to continue.

The radio program grew rapidly and soon Swaggart moved the operations out of his home and into an office building he had built in Baton Rouge. The radio program featured a good dose of Swaggart's music, and album sales mushroomed. In 1971 "This Is Just What Heaven Means to Me" topped the charts and in 1972 Swaggart hit with "There Is a River," receiving exposure on radio outside of his program.

Soon "The Camp Meeting Hour" was in most major markets in the United States and Swaggart moved out of churches and into civic auditoriums with his revivals. He added a band and bought a tractor trailer to carry equipment, also expanding his offices in Baton Rouge. In 1973 he began production of his television program.

Swaggart tried to tape the program originally in Baton Rouge and then New Orleans but the facilities did not offer him the quality he wanted. Finally, he settled on Nashville, taping the program in the same studios where "Hee Haw" was taped. The 30-minute format featured about 20 minutes of music, 10 minutes for preaching, and the rest of the time devoted to pitches for albums and announcements about his revival meetings.

By 1976 Swaggart's radio program was on 550 stations, he was selling over a million albums a year, and his operating budget was $35,000 a day. By 1988 Swaggart was on television all over the world, broadcasting from the elaborate studios he had built in Baton Rouge. He was the founder of the Jimmy Swaggart Bible College, planning a Seminary, boss to 1,200 employees, and head of an empire that was bringing in over $150 million annually. He was also the major spokesman against contemporary Christian music.

Early in 1988 Swaggart stated in his magazine, *The Evangelist*, "I definitely feel all contemporary gospel music is inappropriate for the worship of the Lord," adding that "contemporary music" has "a meandering, dislocated melody which means, in everyday terminology, there is no harmony." To those who insisted that contemporary music attracts an audience to hear the gospel message—an argument Swaggart used for his own music in the 1960s—he answered in 1988 that "sacred music was never meant by God to draw the unsaved or to address itself to the unsaved.... *The primary purpose of music is to worship God*" (italics are his). He concluded that contemporary music will lead to "spiritual death" because "the melody is ... discordant; consequently it affects the harmony and it would be totally impossible for people to worship God with it."

In 1988 Jimmy Swaggart achieved national notoriety for "moral failure" (he was caught with a prostitute) and was suspended for three months from preaching. Eventually, he resigned from the Assemblies of God Church to continue his TV shows, crusades, and worldwide evangelism. Later, he suffered an additional moral failure.

More than any other musician and singer in the 1970s and 1980s, Jimmy Swaggart used the media—especially television—to broadcast his music and his message all over the world. He was an important figure in gospel music because he was a musician and a preacher. Unlike the "teams" of Moody-Sankey, Sunday-Rodeheaver, or Graham-Shea, Swaggart has been able to be a musician and a preacher; his success has come because of media exposure of his music as well as because of the man himself, someone who combined the elements of early rock 'n' roll, Southern Gospel, country music, and Pentecostalism to fashion a music that appealed to a number of people. And, through his outspoken views against contemporary Christian music, Swaggart became a controversial figure, opinionated, but influential among those who shared a distaste for contemporary music but did not have the platform or were unable to articulate their views.

For the televangelists in general, the 1980s and early 1990s proved to be their undoing; Swaggart's solicitation of a prostitute, Jim Bakker's extramarital affair, the exhortations of Oral Roberts about raising money or dying, and the "Moral Majority" of Jerry Falwell all caused many among the public to turn a deaf ear to these evangelical leaders.

But three developments have kept two of these televangelists in the public spotlight: Jerry Falwell and Pat Robertson each established a university—Liberty Baptist by Falwell in Lynchburg, Virginia, and Robertson's Regent University in Virginia Beach. Also, the Christian Coalition formed by Pat Robertson has proven to have an impact by raising money and support for Republican candidates.

By the end of the 20th century both men were directing their efforts towards their base constituency of believers. While each still flies the flag of evangelism on his masthead, in reality the televangelists have come to accept that their ministries may wish to speak to outsiders, but are actually speaking to those on the inside.

Chapter 32

CONTEMPORARY CHRISTIAN MUSIC & THE REAGAN REVOLUTION

During the 1980s, a shift occurred in the gospel music industry as contemporary Christian music began to dominate the field. Aimed at young people coming of age during the 1980s, it developed along the lines of pop and rock music, copying the sounds from pop radio and fitting Christian lyrics to them. But while rock fed on the rebellion inherent in the teenage years and directed it to a radical lifestyle away from the "norms" of societal expectations, contemporary Christian music led a generation towards being fans of Christianity. The commercial success of contemporary Christian artists, and the growth in contemporary Christian music, would depend on reaching these young Christians who were enthused about their faith.

In a study conducted by the Cooperative Institutional Research Program of UCLA in the early l980s, there were major differences between students at religious schools and their counterparts. For instance, the religious college student tended to view himself as "conservative," was less likely to drink beer or smoke, and more likely to be against abortion, couples living together outside marriage, premarital sex, and homosexuality. These students tended to be higher achievers than the non-religious college students, more involved with extracurricular activities, and more likely to take tranquilizers.

Overall, these students said that raising a family was more important than influencing social values and that "getting a job" was the primary reason for going to college (as opposed to "preparing graduates for a life of involved and committed citizenship").

The 1980s saw changes in the social fabric of America—the family was not destroyed but it was permanently altered as numerous single parents had to adjust to raising a child alone. In religion there were movements and changes: the Eastern mysticism influence from the 1960s gave way to the cults of the 1970s, that members joined, were kidnapped from, and then deprogrammed from. On one hand there was an incredible amount of religious acceptance as more religions sprang up, but as the Christian movement merged into the right-wing conservative movement of the early 1980s, there was less tolerance for those who believed anything other than fundamental Christianity. Still, the growth of the Christian culture, and the rising fortunes of gospel music in particular, owe a lot to their link with this conservative wave that was pushing towards the American shore during the campaign of Ronald Reagan in 1980.

For contemporary Christian music there were two links to the past: the Jesus Revolution and Bill Gaither. In 1980 Gaither and his group began performing concerts "in the round" because audiences of up to 15,000 wanted to see them. The Gaithers already owned their own light and sound systems (at a cost of $200,000) and invested another $150,000 in light and sound equipment and added another 40-foot semi tractor-trailer to carry this gear—all to help create the "living room" intimacy audiences had come to expect (and Bill wanted to give) at a Bill Gaither Trio concert. Bill Gaither would show how a gospel act could have major success on tour within the Christian world.

The Grammy Awards, held on February 27, 1980 in Los Angeles, featured a lot of gospel music—there were performances by Andrae Crouch and the Mighty Clouds of Joy as well as a tuxedo-clad Bob Dylan singing "Gotta Serve Somebody." Hosted by Andy Williams, the Grammy Awards featured five categories for gospel with B.J. Thomas, the Imperials, the Blackwood Brothers, Andrae Crouch, and the Mighty Clouds of Joy all carrying home awards. Also, Bob Dylan won his first solo Grammy (he had previously been awarded a Grammy for being part of the *Concert for Bangla Desh* album put together by George Harrison in the early 1970s) as "Best Male Vocal Performance" for his "Gotta Serve Somebody" single off the *Slow Train Coming* album. In a *Billboard* article about the awards show, it was noted that "no less than seven times did Grammy recipients thank the Lord or God or Jesus for helping them achieve their coveted awards."

The 11th Dove Awards were held March 26, 1980 at the Opryland Hotel in Nashville. The event was hosted by three couples: Bill and Gloria Gaither, Walter and Tramaine Hawkins, and Paul and Kathie Lee Johnson. Performers that evening included Pat Boone, Cynthia Clawson, James Cleveland, Rusty Goodman, Dallas Holm, Honeytree, Phil Keaggy, the Kingsmen, Tom Netherton, and Grady Nutt. Presenters included Dino and Debbie Kartsonakis, James Blackwood, Shirley Caesar, Bishop Al Hobbs, Pittsburgh Steeler star Terry Bradshaw, "Hee Haw" producer Sam Louvello, and George Beverly Shea. The awards show was preceded by a sit-down dinner.

The Dove Awards were a disappointment in one area for the GMA—they had signed a contract with a Hollywood production firm to televise the event that year and expected this show to be their first national telecast. But the networks gave a thumbs down to gospel music—the market research people couldn't come up with enough "numbers" to placate executives nervous about the appeal of gospel—so the show's success was only covered in the print media.

There was no "Artist of the Year" award yet (the "top" award was for "Male Gospel Group of the Year"—a remnant from the Southern gospel heritage). The top song that year was "He's Alive" and the writer, Don Francisco, captured the "Songwriter of the Year" honor. Other top winners were the Imperials, Bill Gaither Trio, Dallas Holm ("Male Vocalist" and "Contemporary Album"), Cynthia Clawson ("Female Vocalist"), Doug Oldham ("Inspirational Album"), Dino Kartsonakis, and Bob Dylan for "Gospel Album by a Secular Artist," awarded for his album *Slow Train Coming*.

The year 1980 ended on a sad note for those in the music world; John Lennon was shot down outside his apartment building in New York a couple of weeks before Christmas. For many, the prevailing mood was that an era had ended, an era that began on a Sunday night in February 1964 when the Beatles first appeared on the Ed Sullivan Show. But as this era was closed, another era was just beginning: the era of the Reagan Revolution.

The year 1981 was a landmark year for American Christianity in general and gospel music in particular. It is the year when two major secular record labels—CBS and MCA— began gospel divisions, when Bob Dylan released his third gospel-influenced album (*Shot of Love*), and former top pop acts Al Green, Richie Furay, Maria Muldaur, and

Bonnie Bramlett released gospel albums. On television, Barbara Mandrell featured a special segment on gospel (with contemporary Christian artists) on her weekly NBC show.

In the gospel industry, Christian labels were busy announcing they had signed agreements with major secular labels for distribution, while Word, the label that dominated Christian music, celebrated its 30th birthday. The Imperials were the major group in contemporary Christian Music, Word began a video division, gospel artist Andrae Crouch released an album on Warner Brothers, Amy Grant and Gary Chapman announced their engagement, and the contemporary Christian world received another "Gold" album. *Music Machine* by Candle was revolutionary because it showed the Christian market the tremendous appeal of children's music to the Christian culture, which was filled with young born-again parents wanting to raise their children to understand the gospel message. It would be the forerunner for an onslaught of children's albums that Christian labels would release in the 1980s.

Singles were a hot issue in gospel music during the early 1980s. Secular record labels had long sent out 45 rpm singles before an album—in some cases not even releasing an album until or unless a single was a "hit"—but gospel radio was used to getting an entire album, and programming whichever cuts it felt appropriate for its audience. Since gospel radio viewed itself as a "ministry," the programmers felt they should be allowed to choose the cut on an album they would like to program according to "God's will" (i.e., what they deemed appropriate at the time for their audience). The record companies, wanting to sell albums, knew that the success of a song (and album) depended upon people hearing it over and over. As it was, ten different radio stations could program ten different songs and, if a listener heard a song he or she liked, there was no guarantee he/she would hear it again soon or even at all.

Christian companies began to send out singles to focus attention on a particular song on an album and radio stations either had to play the single or refuse the act until the album came along. Since the "Single Airplay" charts were coming into their own, the success of a song could be quickly measured and the success in one radio market meant it would probably be successful in other radio markets. The labels, knowing that radio stations often look to the charts to help make their decisions about which records to program, knew if they could get a song on the charts, the chances would be much better that radio stations would play it and thus there would be a "hit" single to spur sales of the album.

An article in a Christian magazine during this time, subtitled "Are Hits Holy?" sums up the problem well. Radio programmers cited in this article argued that "Christian music is unlike secular music in that nearly all of it has a definite purpose other than entertaining—that of communicating Gospel or moral messages." The programmers asked "What about the other nine cuts on the album?... Can't they be used by the Holy Spirit as well as a 'hit' cut?" The radio programmers argued that "God" would choose which cuts to play on their radio station and which songs would be "hits" if only the record companies would untie His hands by sending albums instead of singles. In the end, the record companies won—the sheer economic factor alone dictated this path—and singles came to increasingly dominate Christian radio airplay.

The other issue contemporary Christian music had to face was the power of the National Religious Broadcasters Association, the most powerful group representing religion on the airwaves. For years, the NRB had represented the "preaching and teaching" programs, the non-profit stations and the programs headed by a preacher whose main thrust was "spreading the gospel" over the airwaves. But as contemporary Christian music came along, and the young listener attracted to this music wanted radio to play music rather than preaching, the NRB looked dangerously out of step.

The Reagan Revolution officially arrived on January 20, 1981 when Ronald Reagan was sworn in as the 40th President of the United States. His election meant a great deal to the Christian culture because, to a large degree, its votes had elected him; too, the conservatism inherent in mainstream Christianity now had a spokesman in Washington at the seat of power. The Reagan Revolution brought religion and politics together and this had an immediate impact on politics (the "born-again" experience became a litmus test for candidates), social issues (such as abortion and school prayer), culture (it was a badge of honor to be considered "Christian" and a mark of disrepute to be labeled "liberal"), and religion (which received major news coverage on a regular basis).

The evangelical community had been disappointed with Jimmy Carter. First, his politics (and the politics of the Democratic party in general) were a little too liberal to suit their tastes; too, they felt he had let them down on issues like school prayer, abortion, and defense. Finally, the problem of inflation seemed out of control and Carter did not seem to have any workable solutions. When Ronald Reagan stepped in, saying the right things while using the right language, the evangelical vote quickly switched. The fact that his conservative politics were basically the same as its own assured the Republican party of a loyal following in the coming years.

Reagan had campaigned with the theme that "Government isn't the solution. Government is the problem" and held the view that less government is better, none is best. This fit perfectly with the evangelical Right, who had an innate distrust of government institutions and generally felt a discomfort with some of the rules that governed them. The Right, led by no less than the President himself, felt that government was not only too big and burdensome but that it was a moral evil infecting American society. They would set about changing it, cleansing it, purifying it, and molding it to their own image. It was a heady time, a time when a feeling of adventure filled the air, a time when God received an open invitation to be a part of politics, government, society, and culture. And the ones doing the inviting were His best friends.

Many of those in gospel music saw a battle raging between good and evil—the righteous and the ungodly—and believed that the force of righteousness would cleanse this country and lead it down the paths of righteousness. As musicians, they saw their position akin to the position of the musicians in Jehosophat's army from the Old Testament—as leaders who would go before the army and win the battle before it could even be fought.

During the Grammy Awards there was a performance of "The Lord's Prayer" which had more major gospel entertainers on stage at one time than in any previous Grammy Show. In addition to composers Dony McGuire and Reba Rambo, there were the Archers, Cynthia Clawson, Andrae Crouch, Walter and Tramaine Hawkins, and B.J. Thomas, who all performed on the album of the same title. This performance received one of the few standing ovations of that evening. That album also won a Grammy. Other Grammy winners were Shirley Caesar, the Blackwood Brothers, James Cleveland, and Debby Boone.

Rev. James Cleveland and James Blackwood served as presenters during the evening while the show's host, Paul Simon, noted that "For years gospel music has been divided into two categories—inspirational and contemporary—which is essentially a euphemism for black gospel and white gospel music." After a brief pause for heavy applause, Simon continued that "Of course, it seems God doesn't make the same distinction."

The Dove Awards, held in Nashville that year at the Roy Acuff Theatre in Opryland on April 15, came in for a bashing. Among the musicians and singers involved in the contemporary Christian movement who had come out of the Jesus Revolution, there had always been a backlash against "awards." The prevailing idea was that all rewards should be "heavenly" and that, somehow, giving awards to Christians from Christians for Christian endeavors was "ungodly." There was also, within the contemporary Christian community, a lack of respect for the Southern gospel community who had paved the way for the Gospel Music Association and the Dove Awards, and a lack of gratitude towards those who had spent years trying to get respect for gospel music and put it in the spotlight.

An editorial in the April 1981 issue of *CCM*, titled "The Doves: What Kind of Strange Birds are They" by Karen Marie Platt, reflected some of these attitudes. Platt begins her editorial by asking, "When the world stands outside in the cold April air, presses its nose against one of the huge antediluvian windows of Nashville's Opryland Hotel and looks in on the 1981 Dove Awards ceremonies, will it perceive the Christian witness beneath all the preened plumage and fancy feathered friends gathered there? Or will the bloodless, critical gaze of the TV cyclops snuff a congregation of faded stars in the murky night?" (NOTE: it had been announced this awards show would be televised.)

The editorial goes on to state that "Anyone who loiters in the hall during and after GMA Week hears and overhears tremulous complaints and whispered dissent among the GMA flock. Humble magpies express discomfort with dispensing achievement awards for doing God's work. Lone eagles worry about the spiritual price of high visibility expansion and mass approvals."

In a "news analysis" article run in the same magazine after the awards, titled "Dove Hunting in Nashville," the writer begins by stating:

FIRST there are those who don't believe Christians should give themselves awards and that any attempt to do so should be met with the reminder that our rewards are heavenly and any rewards or accolades received here on earth cause you to lose brownie points with God. THEN there are those who believe that living in a worldly world the only way to get people to recognize and listen to gospel music is to give awards so they'll sit up and take notice. BUT comes the rejoinder, how can an awards gala filled with people dressed to the nines collecting trophies be spiritual? After all, all that glitters and gleams cannot Shine. WELL, that's not giving much credit to Christian performers comes the answer because if all these people are really Godly people, singing and praising the Creator, how can such a huge gathering of these folks be anything but spiritual?

After all this spiritual preening and proverbial gnashing of teeth about "awards" in general and Christian ones in particular, accompanied by biblical phrases called upon to question such occasions, no one refused a nomination or an award, people dutifully put on tuxedos and evening dresses, and those who won all thanked God for giving His approval to their efforts.

Cynthia Clawson won the "Female Vocalist" award for the second year in a row, Gary Chapman won the "Songwriter of the Year" award, Russ Taff won the "Male Vocalist" award, and album awards were won by the Hemphills, Larnelle Harris, Shirley Caesar, Teddy Huffam & the Gems, the Bill Gaither Trio, Debby Boone, and the ten artists on *The Lord's Prayer*.

The biggest winners that evening were the Imperials, who won three Doves, including the one for the newly instituted "Artist of the Year" award. This award was created to replace the "Associates Award" and gave the Doves one major, overall "Top" award for the event. The GMA has two categories of membership—professional (who work and receive income from gospel music) and the associates (or "fans"). The associates were only allowed to vote on one award, which until 1981 was the "Associates" award and could be given to a person, group, song, or album. But from 1981 on, this group has been allowed to vote (with the professional group) on the "Artist of the Year" honor, so this award reflected the artist who appealed to professionals, amateurs, and fans in the gospel music industry.

The Christian Bookseller's Convention in 1981 was held July 18-21 in Anaheim, California at the convention center. Over 7,000 people attended, with 348 exhibitors manning 1,038 booths—but, overall, attendance was down and the number of stores represented decreased.

There was an economic recession in the country but sales for Christian music were up from previous years. This caused the Christian industry to brag a bit about being "recession-proof" and offer as an explanation that "people turn to the gospel in troubled times." The truth of the matter, however, probably rested in the fact that Christian bookstores were finally accepting contemporary Christian pre-recorded music product as a legitimate part of their inventory.

There had always been a bit of conflict between books and music with retailers, and the name "Christian booksellers" and "Christian bookstores" indicates which side most stores chose to take. However, with sales of music accounting for 17 to 40 percent of a stores' revenue, the owners quickly saw they must get more heavily involved and stock more of this inventory. Too, the growth in the Christian culture had more Christian consumers looking for product, and the growth of the Christian bookstore network meant there were more stores, so it was only logical that more music would be bought because there were more stores and consumers looking for it.

Finally, the early reluctance of Christian bookstores to stock contemporary Christian music was fading away. The store owners had looked on early gospel rock as music from the Devil, unsuitable for their stores, and some customers—mostly older ones—had complained about rock 'n' gospel. The thrust of their argument was "A real Christian wouldn't play OR listen to that stuff!" However, as this segment of the culture grew and mainline Christians realized the sincerity and dedication of those in contemporary Christian music— and when they saw it as a wholesome alternative to real rock 'n' roll for their own children—some of the barriers began to fall away.

The recession of 1981 did not hit the Christian record companies right away because stores and consumers were playing "catch-up" with the product, leaving the impression that gospel music was recession-proof when, in reality, its sales success was a matter of filling a void already created in the market-place, providing a supply for a demand already there. The Christian community would learn in the next year that it was not recession proof.

Chapter 33

CCM COMES AGE TO AGE

The single most important album released in contemporary Christian music during the 1980s was Amy Grant's *Age to Age*. Beginning with her debut album in late 1976, Grant had established herself firmly with Christian audiences, giving herself a strong base from which to attempt such a revolutionary work.

Age to Age, released in 1982, dominated the Christian music industry that year and achieved "Gold" status within a year after its release—which no other Christian album had ever done (*Alleluia* by the Gaithers and *Music Machine* by Candle both took several years to reach the "Gold" plateau in sales).

When Amy, her producer Brown Bannister, and the management team of Mike Blanton and Dan Harrell began planning the *Age to Age* album they decided to attempt a landmark album for the Christian market, akin to *Tapestry* by Carole King in the early '70s, which also set sales records. In essence, they wanted to "define" contemporary Christian music and set the standard for Christian albums. Their marketing strategy was to saturate the Christian culture with Amy Grant—something they had been doing in progressive steps with the albums that came before *Age to Age*. They got youth directors and music ministers involved—bringing kids to concerts and hosting "listening" parties. They wanted the whole church world to know about Amy Grant, and the success they achieved with *Age to Age* is a direct result of their penetration into the Christian market. (Almost 90 percent of the sales on *Age to Age* came through the Christian bookstores.) Ironically, by creating an album that was such a landmark in Christian music, it had an appeal in the pop market from consumers who wanted one contemporary Christian album for their collection, or the curious who wanted to know what all the fuss was about over on the gospel side.

Another irony is that, in the long run, this penetration and saturation of the Christian market helped a new artist who emerged that same year. Sandi Patti became the major artist within the Christian world while Amy Grant increasingly headed in the direction of pop music.

Although Amy Grant still kept her base of support, she ran into a lot of flack because the gospel audience is very demanding—they want their artists to show a total commitment to gospel music at all times. Taking Christianity to the secular marketplace is an anathema in the view of many Christians, who hold that it must keep itself separate to remain "pure." In other words, you don't wear a white dress into a coal mine. But Amy Grant (and her management team) wanted the pop audience to know that Christianity did not have to be stuffy or stale, could be "fun" and relevant to the pop world. They wanted the Christian audience to realize their music could be viable and appealing to the popular culture.

There was no other singer filling that void in 1982 and the marketing of Amy Grant's *Age to Age* album showed the Christian culture how an album and artist could achieve huge sales through exposure and saturation of the Christian marketplace. All the pieces of the puzzle were coming together—the puzzle of contemporary Christian music and how it could create a "star" who would sell lots of records and attract lots of concert-goers but not dilute the Christian message or compromise gospel music.

The effort succeeded with Amy Grant and no other gospel artist because Amy Grant, unlike most other CCM acts, was comfortable as a Christian entertainer. Other CCM acts, while professing to want to reach "the lost," are inherently uncomfortable outside the Christian world, suffering pangs of guilt from achieving mainstream success. Amy Grant alone among the CCM acts at the time was comfortable and secure in both worlds.

At the 1982 Grammy's gospel music took another step forward, featuring a lively performance by Al Green, the Archers, and the Crusaders with Joe Cocker on some gospel songs. Winning Grammys that year were B.J. Thomas, the Imperials, Al Green, Andrae Crouch, and the Masters V (J.D. Sumner, James Blackwood,

Hovie Lister, and Jake Hess). Again, Christian record labels showed a real surge in voting strength as they captured 22 of the 28 nominations in the gospel categories.

NARAS, composed primarily of people from the pop side of the music industry, had always tended to nominate and vote for gospel acts on major secular labels or who were best-known to the secular world, either because they had been around for so long (like the Blackwood Brothers) or because they had been secular stars before going gospel (like B.J. Thomas). But the 1981 gospel Grammy nominations were dominated by all-Christian labels.

The Reagan Revolution, which brought a number of evangelical Christians into the voting booths and got them involved in politics, had a direct influence because people in the gospel music industry, inspired and influenced by the notion of activist voting, began to join NARAS in larger numbers and cast their votes. This represented a major change in attitude within the Christian community. Previously, evangelical Christians had generally shunned the political arena—many not even registering to vote or not voting if they were registered—because it was considered a "worldly" pursuit, had nothing to do with their faith, and was irrelevant to their salvation. A similar view was held in the gospel music community towards secular awards so, until 1980, a very large number of evangelical Christians did not bother joining the National Academy of Recording Arts and Sciences because they felt it was irrelevant to their mission: to spread the gospel through music. That attitude changed dramatically in 1980 and the result was the election of Ronald Reagan as President and a much greater involvement from Christian labels and artists in the Grammy awards.

"Gospel" was a buzz-word on this Grammy night, hosted by John Denver, and numerous acts thanked "the Lord" or expressed an interest in recording gospel albums in the future. Among these were the Pointer Sisters, Ben Vereen, the Oak Ridge Boys, and James Brown.

The Doves were the highlight of Gospel Music Week, held February 28 through March 3 at the Opryland Hotel in Nashville. Host for the Dove evening was Grady Nutt, the popular comedian from "Hee Haw," known as the Prime Minister of Humor, who recorded several comedy albums for Benson. Later that year, he would die in a tragic plane crash.

Competing for "Artist of the Year" honors were Cynthia Clawson, Andrae Crouch, Dallas Holm, the Imperials and a newcomer, Sandi Patti. To the surprise of almost everyone, Sandi Patti won the award. She also won "Female Vocalist of the Year" honors. What had propelled her into the spotlight was her recording of "We Shall Behold Him," written by Dottie Rambo.

Other Dove winners that evening were Joni Eareckson, Edwin Hawkins, Shirley Caesar, Russ Taff, Dino Kartsonakis, Walter Hawkins and Family, the Imperials, and B.J. Thomas. Dottie Rambo won the "Songwriter of the Year" award.

The Christian media had discovered Sandi in a big way in 1982 and there were features, reviews, pictures and column mentions in periodicals such as *CCM*, *Encore*, *Charisma*, *Windstorm*, *In Touch*, *Group*, *Rocking Chair*, *Christian Bookstore Journal*, the *Singing News*, and others. In addition to helping Sandi's career by making her more visible, it also helped the Christian culture get to know her better— and this audience demands that they "know" a performer before they will trust her; she must believe what they believe. This audience feels a need to "test" its celebrities to see if they are in line with the Christian walk—they don't like being fooled by someone who says one thing and believes another. Also, her album *Love Overflowing* and the single "We Shall Behold Him" fit perfectly in the church world.

Sandi Patti was actually Sandi Patty until her first album appeared. It was a custom album (she paid all the production and manufacturing costs herself), entitled *For My Friends*, and the manufacturer made a mistake and printed "Patti" instead of "Patty." Sandi decided to change her name rather than change the album cover or try to explain the mistake.

Shortly after this album was released, a record company executive called Sandi and wanted to talk with her about recording an album for a major label. Because the call came a few days before Sandi's wedding, she had to decline the offer. Several months later the executive called again and this led to her debut album for the Benson company, *Sandi's Songs*, released in 1979.

Sandi Patty received her first music lessons from her mother, who was a piano teacher, and her father, Ron Patty, who was a minister of music. She made her singing debut at age two and a half in an Oklahoma City church choir: a squeaky version of "Jesus Loves

Me." Later, she toured with her parents and two brothers as "The Ron Patty Family," singing in churches. At Anderson College she was preparing to become a music teacher; however, people continued to request concerts and she obliged until she had to choose between teaching and a music ministry. She chose to sing and her music ministry took off.

Sandi's professional singing career actually began in college as a studio singer, recording commercials for Juicy Fruit gum, Steak'n Ale restaurants, and other accounts. Her next big professional step was joining the Bill Gaither Trio as a back-up singer. Later, she stepped into the spotlight as a featured solo performer during the Gaither's tours, singing "We Shall Behold Him." That song soon proved immensely popular. In addition to the Gaither Trio, she also toured with the Gaither Vocal Band, the Imperials, Doug Oldham, Larnelle Harris, and Dino before headlining her own concerts.

Sandi had become a Christian on her eighth birthday and grew up as a believer. As a singer, she personified the great church choir soloist more than the great stylist. Her voice was clear and straightforward. And it is in a church where her voice fits best singing songs of worship and praise that can be heard from any church choir on a Sunday morning.

The music sung by church choirs on Sundays and special programs during the week reaches more people directly than any other outlet for gospel music. Publishing this music has long been a major source of income for the industry; it accounted for about a fourth of the total income of the gospel music world in the mid-1980s. This publishing industry includes not only songs on records and the spin-off songbooks but a whole portfolio of material aimed directly at choirs in the form of octavos, cantatas, musicals, collected works, compilations, instrumental sheet music, and hymnals.

Gospel publishers promote and sell their music primarily through the music ministers of churches. This is a staff position which is responsible for the regular choir as well as specialized choirs—such as children's—and special musical programs at Christmas, Easter, and other times of the year. This individual is also responsible for booking outside musical groups into the church for concerts. For this he often works with a youth minister, whose main function is to involve the church youth with various activities and programs.

The music ministers of churches are reached primarily through workshops staged by different publishing companies for choral readings and the exposure of new material. At these workshops, the music ministers are usually given a sample kit of music as they gather together to sing through some of the works. From this experience, they decide whether they would like to purchase music for their church. Since these ministers purchase large quantities of each work for their choir, these seminars and workshops are an extremely important link between the music minister and the publisher, who will benefit financially if the ministers like the material.

Publishing company representatives also regularly call on the music ministers of large churches to keep them informed of their latest musical offerings. They can also contact the youth minister about new albums for listening parties or artist videos and movies.

Still, the church publishing industry and the gospel music industry are two different worlds. While there is some overlapping—choirs may want to perform a hit song from an album, or a musical may be a successful record as well as a sheet music collection—they generally remain in two distinct camps. Because the church remains the basic foundation for the Christian culture, reaching that audience has been essential for the gospel music industry, which began to turn inward and direct its music more towards the church as it entered the 1980s. This is where the Christian record buying consumers were.

The church openly embraced Sandi Patti during the 1980s when she became the artist most honored within the gospel world. Her concerts (often at large churches) were more like a worship service as she stood on stage, leading the service, accepting that each member of the audience believed what she believed, accepted what she accepted. Sandi Patti did nothing to challenge the faith of her audience; she accepted and encouraged it.

At the end of 1982 contemporary Christian music was dominated by two artists who would continue to dominate the field throughout the 1980s. Amy Grant had the hit singles "Sing Your Praise to the Lord" and "El Shaddai" from her *Age to Age* album, while Sandi Patti's hit singles were "We Shall Behold Him" and "How Majestic is Your Name." This last song was written by another up-and-coming artist/songwriter who would have an immense impact on contemporary Christian music in the coming years.

Michael W. Smith became a teen idol and one-man boy band for many young Christians through his recordings and concerts in the '80s. On stage he ran, danced, jumped, paced, and led the band and audience in concert aerobics, pouring his all into a concert until the audience was raised to a fever pitch. There were a few older people in his audience—probably because the kids were too young to drive and because the older generation wanted to check out all the hullabaloo their children were raving about. But, for the most part, the concert halls were filled with 13 to 20-year olds, some of whom remained standing in front of the stage the entire concert, offering up shrieks and screams throughout the whole performance.

Michael W. Smith grew up in West Virginia in his grandmother's house, where his parents lived from the time they were married. His grandmother was a piano teacher so it was natural he would be attracted to that instrument and at the tender age of four he began to pick out tunes. He began learning how to sight read when he was eight but even at that age he had an aversion to practice.

Smith became a Christian at the age of ten and walked the aisle in the eighth grade to commit himself to full time service. After high school graduation, he suffered a wild hair and ran loose for awhile. He moved to Nashville in 1978 to be part of the music scene and joined the gospel group Higher Ground where he wrote "I Am," his first major song. He was soon signed to a publishing company by Randy Cox and when Cox started his own publishing firm, Michael came along. Before too long, the duo decided to do a pop album with Cox producing. Some tapes were made, they went to Los Angeles, and there was some interest. But Michael began to realize he wasn't cut out to be a pop star, he had to be a Christian artist.

A connection with Mike Blanton and Dan Harrell, managers of Amy Grant, proved crucial and soon they had signed Michael to a management and recording contract with their fledgling Reunion label. Michael's musical prowess had already established his reputation and his writing ability was becoming apparent on albums by a number of Christian artists, including Amy Grant and Gary Chapman. Michael would spend two years working as Amy's keyboard player as well as being a major musical influence on her.

His first album, titled simply *Michael W. Smith*, was geared to young people—high energy techno-pop rock 'n' roll. It was a natural extension of Michael, who enjoyed communicating with high school students and had been part of church groups working with them. Now his music would be another part of his appeal to Christian youth. And they bought it like they'd never bought any other new artist—the first two albums combined to sell almost half a million units. Then there was the tour.

Smith's audience was mostly church-going, clean-cut, well-scrubbed kids who kept the energy but discarded the rebellion of rock 'n' roll; the result was wholesome rock 'n roll. The attitude of gospel is that it is all being done as a ministry—for God—and not just entertainment. There's a message and it needs to be heard, the performers know the Truth and must proclaim it. Smith did a particularly good job of conveying his faith and his message without being overbearing; he let the audience know where he stood and gently prodded and encouraged them to keep the faith while they yelled approvingly.

In the end, it was Gospop—high energy music with a moral message—played by a musician with a mission. It reflected the musical preferences of the kids of the '80s who wanted to hear the timeless message dressed up in the fashion of "now." It was the Old Testament in *Teen Beat*, new wine in new wineskins, played fast but not loose. And it had a whole lot more in common with the Beatles than it did with George Beverly Shea.

It was also a long way from the radical passion of a Keith Green, who died in a plane crash, with two of his children, in July 1982.

Chapter 34
CONTEMPORARY CHRISTIAN MUSIC
& 1984

Research on the Christian market was released in mid-1983 and helped profile the Christian music consumer. The RIAA (Recording Industry Association of America), the organization representing record companies and which certifies gold and platinum albums, reported that gospel sales accounted for six percent of recorded product in the United States, up from the four-percent retail and five-percent direct marketing share reported in 1981.

Gospel industry spokespersons indicated that gospel outsold jazz and classical; however, the RIAA disagreed, saying that classical outsold gospel in direct marketing (sales by mail) and its share of industry sales was larger. An inherent problem in measuring gospel sales against a music like jazz or classical was that the latter reached basically one audience with one kind of music (although there is, obviously, much variety within these musical genres) but gospel reaches a number of different audiences with an extremely wide range of music—from Southern gospel quartets to black gospel choirs to heavy metal gospel and everything in between.

Word Records commissioned a survey of Christian radio, done by students at Baylor University, which showed that contemporary Christian radio was a relatively young industry (about eight years old then) and struggling for a tiny share of the radio audience. Generally, Christian radio stations had smaller antennas and power assignments, making it more difficult to sound good and reach a wide geographical area. Using Arbitron survey results (Arbitron is a broadcasting measurement company which measures ratings and shares of radio stations in markets), this survey found that only five of the top 15 markets in the U. S. had a Christian station with a large enough audience to show up in the ARB's (the name of Arbitron's published results).

Of the contemporary Christian stations which did show up, most had shares in the 1.1 to 1.5 range. (Ratings are based on the percentage of those listening to a particular station measured against the total population of an area, while share indicates the number listening to a particular station measured against the population listening to radio at that time.)

This survey also showed that 83 percent of Christian stations took requests, which meant that since a very narrow segment of the audience ever calls in to request a song, the station was often at the mercy of requestors. Overall, most stations were programmed according to the personal tastes of the music or programming director who believed either that the Lord told him to play a particular song at a particular time or that "the-audience-wants-to-hear-what-I-want-to-hear." About 43 percent of those surveyed had no set rotation of songs with records in "heavy" rotation usually receiving 8 to 16 plays a week and those in "light" rotation receiving plays of one to four times a week.

A major problem at contemporary Christian radio stations was music, or rather the lack of it. The survey reported that the average day at a Christian radio station was 18.2 hours, with music played an average of 8.2 hours and the bulk of the remaining ten hours a day made up of taped programs, or "preaching and teaching" shows.

Another problem with radio, from the record company's point of view, was the issue of singles, coupled with how to prolong the life of an album. The secular marketplace had realized that by having several "hit" singles, the life of an album could be a year in the marketplace with extra sales generated with each hit single. But the Christian programmer wanted albums—and was used to receiving albums—which they aired heavily so the most popular cuts were "burnt-out" after three months, causing demand for another album. In the past, gospel artists had been used to releasing two, three or four albums a year and secular artists were used to releasing two a year (The Beatles used to release an album every six months). Obviously, this was not good for saturating a market and maximizing profits so record companies were looking for ways to prolong the life of an album through singles strategically spaced throughout the year. Christian radio was reluctant to change but was beginning to realize that if they were going to get better ratings and shares in their market to attract "spot" sales (local, regional and national advertising), then they would need to play more music and the hottest songs more often.

The Word report concluded that Christian radio was doing poorly, with about 1.6 percent of the national marketplace, ahead of only "Spanish-language programming, 'solid gold' formats, classical and jazz stations."

Contemporary Christian Music surveyed their readers and discovered a music-loving group, with 59.4 percent of the respondents saying they bought ten or more albums each year and 31.2 percent saying they purchased more than 16 albums a year. 75.8 percent said they listened to music more than ten hours a week, but more (46.9 percent) said what the artist was saying was more important than the quality of the recording (31.6 percent). The *CCM* survey also showed that 94.7 percent of respondents said they attended a concert in the past year, 47.6 percent said they attended more than four, and seven percent attended more than 11. Most (72.8 percent) listened to secular music and attended concerts by secular artists but there was a "hard-core" group of Christian consumers (27.2 percent) who stated they only listened to Christian music. This survey also showed that 94.9 percent of those responding were under 34 with 57.6 percent under 25; 69.9 percent were male and most (61.6 percent) were single. Only 36.3 percent were married and only 56.7 percent of the readers were employed full-time (reflecting a large number of students reading the magazine), although 35.5 percent of the respondents reported a family income exceeding $25,000 a year. Finally, those responding reported that *CCM* was the magazine they read most often (48.2 percent) followed by *Time* (6.8 percent), and *Campus Life* (5.1 percent). All of these facts and figures helped clarify the Christian consumer in the marketplace and pointed out some interesting trends which the Christian music industry would capitalize on in the future. First, there was a sizeable core of young Christians who liked contemporary Christian music and who were active buyers, and second, there was a potential for Christian record companies to achieve big sales figures on albums if only they could convince radio to program singles in high rotation, like their secular counterparts.

The Grammys in 1983 were a disappointment for many contemporary Christian fans, who were getting accustomed to a healthy dose of their favorite music and artists on the network show. Gospel Grammy winners Al Green (with two), Barbara Mandrell, and the Blackwood Brothers were given their awards during the pre-telecast ceremonies and, except for Ricky Skaggs and the Masters V singing "I'll Fly Away" and Little Richard rocking out with "Joy Joy Joy," there were no performances from contemporary Christian artists. Amy Grant picked up a Grammy for her *Age to Age* album.

When the Doves rolled around, on April 13, it was clearly Amy Grant's year as the success of the *Age to Age* album (it was the fastest-selling Christian album ever for Word) led Amy to capture the "Artist of the Year" honor as well as generating three other Dove Awards (including "Song of the Year" for "El Shaddai"). Hosted by Pat Boone, the show was a special evening for Bill Gaither, who was inducted into the Gospel Music Hall of Fame.

At the end of 1983 Sandi Patti and Amy Grant continued to dominate the gospel industry—but there was a noticeable difference in direction for those two ladies who embodied the two directions contemporary Christian music was heading. Amy had just received a gold album for her *Age to Age* album and was beginning to reach towards the pop world, whose media was already beginning to cover her. Sandi was dominating the gospel world—as indicated by her having more songs on the charts at the end of 1983 than any other gospel act—but her sales were not yet in the same league as Amy's. Sandi was intent upon staying with the church audience. Ironically, each lady's decision would pay off handsomely for her, for while each had a base in gospel music as well as a number of other similarities, they were not really competing against each other.

In addition to Amy Grant and Sandi Patti, another Christian act was having a major impact within the industry, but was not receiving any awards or nominations at that time.

The powerhouse Christian band Petra were dedicated evangelistic Christians in a rock band. They began in Fort Wayne, Indiana, at the Christian Training Academy in 1972. Bob Hartman, a young Christian who played the guitar, formed a group consisting of himself, John DeGroff, Bill Glover, and Greg Hough—all students at the Academy—and the four went out to spread the gospel through rock songs to those around Ft. Wayne.

After playing around Ft. Wayne for several years, Petra gradually became more aware of the music business. In late 1973 they drove to Nashville to audition for a major gospel label at a small church. They were being managed by Paul Paino, Honeytree's manager, who had just gotten Honeytree signed to Word through Billy Ray Hearn, a leader in signing contemporary Christian acts to Word's newly formed Myrrh label. Hearn signed the group and then produced Petra's eponymous debut album. It was recorded in South Pekin, Illinois, and marked the first time the band had ever been in a recording studio. Hearn was just learning to be a rock producer as well so the Jesus rock band's first LP suffered some birth pains before being released in early 1974.

The result was less than overwhelming. Christian bookstores were reluctant to stock an album which was so overtly rock because their basically conservative clientele just didn't trust rock music. Getting the album stocked, advertised and promoted was extremely difficult. Suffice it to say it wasn't done very well.

Myrrh was reluctant to do another album with the group, considering the initial problems and reactions to the first release, but finally did record and release *Come and Join Us*. On this album vocalist Greg X. Volz made his Petra debut and this former member of the group "e" would continue to handle the lead vocal chores for the next ten years.

Feeling they should aim for the un-Christian, unchurched, diehard rock fan, Petra recorded loud and powerful. Feeling their competition was the reigning royalty of rock—REO Speedwagon, Rush, Styx—Petra went after a comparable sound. The result was one small step towards rock, one giant leap off the label. The Christian bookstore managers who didn't particularly care for the first Petra album cared even less for the second, and since the distribution system for gospel rock hadn't yet been developed, there was nowhere for Petra to go but home.

Two executives from Word, Darrell Harris and Wayne Donowho, left to form another label, Star Song. These men had a vision of what Petra could do, signed them to Star Song, teamed them with their third producer, George Atwell, and sent them to Bee Jay Studios in Florida for their third album. *Washes Whiter Than*, distributed by a Kansas City-based company, was not serviced properly so the sales were again disappointing. But it did have one thing going for it—a hit single, "Why Should The Father Bother"—which gave them much needed airplay and let people hear them where they had never toured.

Petra's fourth album teamed them with producer Jonathan David Brown, a producer they finally felt comfortable with who allowed them to be themselves and inspired their best work. *Never Say Die* yielded a number one song on Christian radio, "The Coloring Song," a rather mellow song by rock standards, which won them a whole new audience.

The best way for a rock band to break out is through extensive touring. Rock fans don't want just a concert, they want an event that is social, musical and, above all, memorable. Most rock acts become successful because they get on the road and stay there, playing night after night across the country until they have built a large following who demand encore performances, spread the word about the group, and buy their albums. Since radio in general—and Christian radio in particular—has generally been averse to playing hard rock, touring has often been the only way an act like this can break out.

Petra hardly toured during the years they recorded their first four albums, although they wanted to be on the road playing. But nobody was calling them to come play. In 1983 Petra moved to Nashville and broke up. When they did perform, it was Hartman, Volz and whoever they could find for bass and drums. Obviously, another element in a rock band's success is commitment—from all the members. Petra's members were in school, so playing gigs had to be limited to an occasional weekend, and Hartman had a regular job as well, one which he was reluctant to give up what with the vagaries of the music industry.

Hartman met Mark Kelly and John Slick through a Bible study and found they all had the same outlook—they were Christians first, earnestly desiring to communicate the gospel any way possible, and musicians second. Hartman jammed with the two—Slick on keyboard and Kelly on bass—and discovered they were quite good. After rehearsals, and with the addition of drummer Louis Weaver, the new Petra was off and running.

Their fifth album was *Never Say Die* but Petra was still struggling to be heard live. Then, a break came along in the form of another gospel rock band, Servant. Servant was on a national tour and invited Petra to join them. The group blossomed on stage and was finally able to realize their full potential as a gospel rock band.

Surrounding themselves with capable people, Petra launched a series of national tours, often promoting their own concerts so they would have a venue. In 1982 they spent 300 days on the road and in 1983 spent 240 days. Their sixth album, *More Power To Ya*, was released with the support of a full tour that saw the group become an "overnight success" after ten hard years of struggle.

Petra blazed the trail for gospel rock for a number of other acts. Although the group was not the first Christian rock act, they were the first truly successful act to sell large numbers of records and have large, successful tours which attracted thousands of kids to gospel concerts. At first, it was well-behaved church kids at rock concerts, screaming with wild abandon; but increasingly they wanted a heavy dose of entertainment. It is often an uneasy alliance between rock and gospel, ministry and entertainment, but the 1980s saw an increasing number of acts that provided entertainment in a Christian concert setting. And the acts who rocked the best were often the most successful with the kids, whose souls were already saved but whose bodies were still restless.

Chapter 35

THE CHRISTIAN CULTURE IN 1985

The 1984 Dove Awards were the first gospel music awards ceremony to be televised. It aired on cable, over the Christian Broadcasting Network, and came after a number of years of concentrated effort by the Board of the Gospel Music Association. Hosted by Glen Campbell and held March 7 at the Tennessee Performing Arts Center in Nashville, the show achieved a level of notoriety when cue cards were dropped and shuffled, resulting in a series of miscues and mistakes from the presenters and host.

Sandi Patti received "Artist of the Year" honors and two other Doves. Amy Grant, whom many had predicted to be the big winner after her year-long success with her Gold album, *Age to Age*, received only one Dove—for the "Design" of her Christmas album. In May Amy Grant's *Straight Ahead* album debuted at number one on the gospel charts.

An interview with John Bass, executive director of the Christian Bookseller's Association, at their July meeting in Anaheim, California, revealed that, overall, music accounted for 25 percent of gross sales in Christian bookstores. In 1976 music accounted for only nine percent of sales so this eight-year period reflected a tremendous surge in contemporary Christian music's popularity. However, Bass also admitted that "not more than 60 percent of our stores are strong in the music area because they are afraid of it."

The Winter 1984 Arbitron results showed the major markets for Christian radio were Seattle-Tacoma, Baltimore, Houston, Louisville, Boston, Washington, Kansas City, Philadelphia, Dallas, New York, San Diego, Pittsburgh, and St. Louis (in that order) with the Seattle-Tacoma market the definite leader, having stations ranked numbers one and two overall among contemporary Christian stations nationally with shares of 3.2 and 1.7. However, Christian radio was still at the bottom of the heap in overall Arbitrons with most stations having a share of less than one in 23 markets.

When Ronald Reagan captured 59 percent of the popular vote in the 1984 Presidential election against Walter Mondale—capturing every state except Minnesota—the Religious Right looked at the outcome as a mandate for their ideas, views, and programs. Fundamentalists saw homosexuals, the Equal Rights Amendment, the legalization of abortion, sex education in public schools, and the absence of prayer in public schools as threats. These fundamentalists held traditional values, an absolute certainty about things temporal and eternal, and had an infectious enthusiasm for evangelism. They were also united in at least one mission: to rid America of "secular humanism."

White evangelical Protestants accounted for about 20 percent of the U. S. population and, as evangelical leaders pushed voter registrations, 80 percent of these evangelicals voted for Reagan versus 20 percent for Mondale. Blacks and Jews stayed predominantly Democratic in 1984 but mainline church attenders (who accounted for around 30 percent of the electorate) voted overwhelmingly for Reagan.

Coming out of this mid-1980s Christian movement were several views of Jesus. One view held that "Jesus always goes first class." Those who held this view found it easy to adopt the new commandment of the upwardly mobile in the mid-'80s: "Enrich thyself." Christians should not—would not—tolerate being second-class citizens in any way, shape or form. God intended to give Christians the desires of their heart and bless them abundantly with the very best. Another concept was the Warrior/God, or military Jesus. This Jesus would smite those who opposed Him.

The final image of Jesus was one of an easy-going, best friend who was the eternal "nice guy" around Christians. They loved Him and He loved them. On the positive side, this made God personal, interested in the most menial and mundane aspects of a person's life. It encouraged believers to look at God (and Jesus) as some sort of Superman, basically human with supernatural powers. By humanizing God, the believer found Him easier to relate to.

On the negative side, this can trivialize God to the point where the believer loses sight of the big picture and sees God as someone picking at small details. This view tended to lead believers to the conclusion that God had given His stamp of approval to their life; anyone who opposed or disagreed with them is (in this logic) in disagreement with God Himself. In the Christian culture in general, and in contemporary Christian music in particular, these views of God emerged in sermons, books, and songs. The "Jesus is my best friend" theology could be heard in countless songs floating on the airwaves and through stereo speakers.

Music was becoming an increasingly dominant part of the Christian culture. Songs expressed the theology and views of this culture while singers and musicians openly proclaimed allegiance to these Christian-based cultural and social views. There were still reservations from the audience about some music from Christian musicians, particularly gospel rock. Too, as music became as much a matter of style as content—fashion became linked closely with the music—the traditionally conservative Christian culture often found it difficult to support musicians who wore the fashions of pop culture while singing their Christian songs.

The generation of college students who graduated during the 1980s demonstrated a turning away from societal concerns and towards inner, personal concerns. Part of the explanation is that these students witnessed the ravages of an unjust war in Viet Nam, the scandal of Watergate, and resultant loss of prestige for the Presidency caused by the resignation of Richard Nixon, and numerous other scandals which brought dishonor (and even jail sentences) to political leaders. This generation became caught up in a "me-ism" which Arthur Levine, in his book *When Dreams and Heroes Died*, states is "an attitude shared by the lonely" which "separates people." He writes: "In the extreme, it robs them of their ability to see common problems and to work together for common solutions. The problems grow worse, and people feel victimized, coming to view their problems as a form of personal harassment. The feeling of impotence rises and apathy increases."

Many (especially within the Christian culture) considered the rise of "me-ism" to be a major factor in the rise of the Christian movement which swept the country in the mid-1970s to mid-1980s because people saw the church as a way to draw closer together. The conservative movement which developed hand in hand with Christian revivalism provided a new kind of activism for this generation whose overriding concern was personal success and for whom the most asked question was: What's in it for me?

The Grammy Awards, held in Los Angeles and hosted by John Denver, featured a barefoot Amy Grant performing "Angels" and marked the first time a contemporary Christian music song was presented on the show. Approximately 140 million people saw a gospel medley, featuring performances by Andrae Crouch, Denice Williams, the Clark Sisters, Pop Staples, and James Cleveland between lively numbers by Tina Turner and Kenny Loggins. Amy Grant and her song "Angels" won in the "Female" gospel category; other gospel winners included Michael W. Smith, Debby Boone, Phil Driscoll, and Donna Summer.

The l6th annual Dove Awards, again televised nationally over the Christian Broadcasting Network, were held at the Tennessee Performing Arts Center and hosted by Pat Boone and former Miss America, Cheryl Prewitt. Sandi Patti collected three Doves—including the top honor, "Artist of the Year." A fellow Anderson College alumni, Steve Green, received his first Dove that evening. Other Dove winners included Shirley Caesar, the Rex Nelon Singers, Lulu Roman, Michael W. Smith (for "Songwriter of the Year"), Phil Driscoll, Andrae Crouch, and Amy Grant, who received the Dove for "Contemporary" album for her *Straight Ahead* LP.

By 1985 the Christian Bookseller's Association had 3,400 member stores out of a total 5,200-5,500 that sold Christian products. The CBA stores generated $1.269 billion in sales in 1985, which meant the average store generated $235,000 in business, higher than their secular counterparts of the American Bookseller's Association.

The Christian bookstores were mostly family-owned, with about 56 percent in shopping or strip malls and about five percent in regional malls in 1985. The average owner was 37 years old (compared to a 59-year-old average owner in 1965) and often came armed with a degree in business. They saw themselves as retailers and businessmen, although they still acknowledged the "ministry" aspect of their business. This contrasted sharply with the Christian bookstores of the late-'60s, which saw themselves as primarily a ministry which offered some religious books for sale to support that ministry.

When the Christian Bookseller's Association began, it represented stores which sold books. By 1985 book sales accounted for 29 percent of sales while music accounted for 23 percent. Other items included Bibles, which accounted for 16 percent of sales; Sunday school curriculums, which accounted for six percent; greeting cards, four percent; jewelry, two percent; and gifts, ten percent.

A large, strong Christian Culture (or "sub-culture") had emerged by 1985. The cornerstones were the Christian bookstores and the church.

Evangelical Christians were actively involved in their church on a full-time basis. In addition to Sunday services, there might be Bible classes, men's groups, women's groups, outside speakers, seminars and community outreach opportunities during the week. The church may have a softball team, or a gym where children played in a basketball league. The youth minister would have activities planned— from campouts to lock-ins (overnight stays that featured a short sermon along with fun and games)—and so would the music minister, who rehearsed and conducted a choir. There was something going on at an evangelical church almost every night of the week, appealing to the entire family.

During the mid-1980s the Gallup Poll consistently showed that about 96 percent of Americans believed in God; however, for most people, religion was not an all-consuming thing—it might be one day out of seven. Or they may quietly believe in God but would only become vocal about their faith during a crisis. The evangelical Christian, on the other hand, is consumed with God. Religion is the central most important facet of their life. It is not just one day out of seven—it is seven days out of seven. This belief is not just for times of crisis, it is 24 hours a day, each and every day, in good times and bad. If anyone who sees you doesn't see and hear your faith immediately, the reasoning went, then you really aren't a committed Christian.

Evangelical Christians find it hard to accept those who do not view religion with the same consuming urgency. This is life or death for them, and they believe that others who are not consumed with evangelical Christianity are doomed to go to Hell and burn forever. It is not something to be taken lightly.

Christian singers and musicians have to be consumed with God.

They write about Him, sing about Him, talk about Him, and think about Him constantly. Their audience expects nothing less than this total commitment.

Next to church, the other cornerstone in the Christian Culture is the Christian Bookstore. Believers find books, recordings, wall plaques, and gifts that proclaim, support, encourage, and affirm their faith. They also find books, recordings and gifts that will "reach out" to unbelievers as aids for conversions. The atmosphere transmits a shared worldview to evangelical Christians.

The Christian Culture is united nationally by books, recordings and the Christian media. There are Christian television programs, even Christian channels, and Christian radio stations. The Christian culture also includes a number of periodicals, many connected to denominations, but others offering a Christian version of those found on the newsstands. These magazines which reach the Christian culture are generally slanted to the Right politically. They are an important line of communication to Christian consumers as Christian celebrities, authors, and speakers maintain their base of support through exposure in these publications.

In education, there are a large number of Christian colleges, most affiliated with a denomination, which offer students courses in Bible and ministry-related studies as well as degrees in business, the liberal arts, and sciences. This network provides an outlet for speakers, musicians, and authors who wish to penetrate the Christian market. It is not unusual for a youth to be educated in Christian schools his whole life, from kindergarten through post-graduate studies, receive Christian periodicals in the home, buy Christian books at a Christian bookstore, Christian albums to be played on the stereo, and tune into Christian radio and Christian TV regularly. For a job, he/she may work in a Christian organization that markets Christian products or at least be involved in a number of organizations that center their activities and purposes around Christian ideals. The Christian culture is a whole network of like-minded people connected to each other by the church, the Christian bookstores, and the Christian media. It is a culture that is insular and self-perpetuating and has made its influence felt in the political, social, and cultural arena. Those most deeply immersed in the Christian culture only encounter non-believers, or non-evangelical believers, at the grocery store or Wal Mart.

The Christian culture in 1985 was predominantly white. While there were some African-American Christian speakers, authors, and TV personalities, the only real common bond between black and white Christianity was music. Musicians, songwriters and singers from both fields influenced one another. Still, there was a radical difference between black gospel for the black audience and white gospel for the white audience. The end result was that black gospel artists did not benefit from the Christian bookstore network to any great degree.

Black gospel, in the latter part of the 20th century, split into two different camps called "traditional" and "contemporary." The traditional artists had their roots in the church choir and, musically, in blues and the older R & B. Contemporary artists were influenced by the contemporary R & B sound, the Motown influences, jazz, and disco—or dance—music heard on the radio. The contemporary sound generally appealed to younger audiences whose ties to the church were not as strong, while the traditional sound appealed to older audiences and those who grew up with strong ties to the church.

Although those two paths existed in black gospel, they were not two totally separate roads but rather intertwining paths that lay close together. Often played on the same gospel radio programs, often back to back, the two types of black gospel were sold together in record bins at retail outlets. The difference was mostly a matter of attitude, on the part of artists as well as the audiences, which manifested itself in music that either scorned pop (traditional) or embraced it (contemporary).

Within black gospel during the mid-1980s was a move towards a smoother sound that appealed to the white audience. It was this smoother sound that would permeate the white gospel market and provide the initial impetus for traditionally white gospel labels to embrace this music and sell it through the Christian bookstores. Many music marketing executives had picked up the cue from Sam Phillips and his Sun Records of the '50s and Motown of the '60s and sought to market black music to white audiences. It is a tried and proven formula for success and enabled several black gospel acts to enjoy large followings from white audiences during the 1990s.

The term "crossover" generally means a music that appeals to several different audiences and can appear on several different charts—country and pop, R & B and pop, jazz and R&B, rock and easy listening—and therefore can sell in much greater numbers. Within black gospel, the term "crossover" has a two-fold meaning. First, there was the crossover into the pop market and, second, the crossover into the white gospel market. The crossover into the pop market had generally come from artists who went from being black gospel artists to pop artists. These artists had to abandon gospel to cross over. Once these artists switched they were not considered "gospel" anymore. The key factor in the success of a gospel artist was commitment to the gospel and the Christian life, which shuns the trappings of the world. Dedicated fans and audiences want to hear gospel, not pop music. When an artist forsakes gospel music, the audience generally forsakes that artist.

The crossover into the white gospel market became a much more lucrative and viable alternative for the black gospel artist because it allowed them to expand their market while staying true to their Christian commitment. Too, the white audience was generally receptive to African-American artists whose music was smoother and pop-influenced.

Black gospel was generally sold in independently owned retail record stores ("Mom and Pop" stores) or in chain stores located in the black sections of a city. The albums were located in the same bins as R & B, soul, dance, and secular music. It did not sell in huge numbers but, with production costs kept low, promotion limited by the number of radio stations who played it, and tour support and other record company financial amenities virtually non-existent, a label could produce a profit. If artists consistently sold 40-50,000 albums, they were considered highly successful and major stars.

Most black gospel is heard on African-American radio stations that play an hour or two of gospel each day. Programs were generally funded by brokers, who pay for the time and then either sell ads or gain revenue from promoting concerts or other related activities. About 40 percent of black gospel was heard this way. There were only a handful (12 to 15) of radio stations that programmed black gospel full-time. The remainder of radio airplay for this music came from Sunday programs provided by black radio stations and a few white contemporary stations who programmed a black contemporary artist.

Lack of radio airplay was the major problem. There was a limited consistency in radio programming within the ranks of gospel pro- gramming and a general feeling that the black gospel market wasn't large enough or economically viable to support very much radio time. Too, the diversity of artists and records made it impossible— according to critics—to program a commercial sounding station that appealed to all segments of the black gospel audience without offending and turning off others.

The church is still the center of black gospel music, although artists performing in concerts and making studio records have become the center pieces. The black market has created a steady demand for the choirs that record for black gospel labels, although most of these albums sell better regionally than they do nationally.

For their part, black gospel artists are faithful to gospel music, to the church and their audiences. They are rewarded by having audi- ences who are faithful to them for a number of years. The audience and performer are, in a certain sense, married and the only grounds for divorce are a desertion into secular music that induces the per- former to drop their gospel commitment. If a performer leaves pop or soul music for gospel—visibly demonstrating their new commit- ment—they are generally welcomed with open arms by the gospel community.

This commitment is the key to success for an artist in black gospel. The commitment should manifest itself through touring, which continues to provide the bulk of exposure (and therefore record sales) in black gospel and is an integral part of the world of black music with its strong heritage for performers. It also sets black gospel apart from black music, letting it keep its own identity, integrity, and values. It distinguishes itself from white gospel because each of these brands of gospel appeals to a different audience. White gospel has created its own indigenous world while black gospel has remained part of the black culture.

In a world dominated by celebrities and celebrity-consciousness, the Christian culture has generated its own coterie of celebrities who remain basically unknown outside Christian circles. There are Christian super- stars who remain virtually anonymous in the secular culture. There are even circles within circles, and gospel music is an industry similar to the secular music industry in that it produces recordings and gets them played on radio and sold; however, it is vastly different in numerous other ways, including the way recordings are sold, how the artists reach their public, and even why the recordings are made.

Gospel has influenced the pop music world—and is influenced by the pop music world—yet the two remain strangely separate, keeping their distance. There are few instances of musicians functioning in both worlds. For the most part, it is an either/or situation and an artist must chose one side or the other. Gospel is a very jealous music, demanding a total commitment from its artists.

For Christian musicians, the musical world is divided into two segments—gospel and secular. Gospel music is the music that deals lyrically with Jesus Christ and the Christian life. Secular music is everything else.

In one sense, there is really no such thing as gospel music because from heavy metal to light rock, from country to jazz, from dance music to church choirs, gospel encompasses all forms of music. The only really definable gospel music forms are the old hymns, worship and praise songs, and black gospel. The rest changes with the tastes of the times. There are, however, gospel songs, which are defined by the lyrics.

White gospel is divided into several camps. First, there is the inspirational market where choirs and soloists perform primarily for churches. Then there's Southern gospel, which is akin to country music in its sound, and finally there is contemporary Christian music, which is pop music—everything from heavy metal and hard rock to soft rock—with Christian lyrics.

The differences in musical tastes are often differences in the self-image of the consumer. On the whole, gospel music views itself as a ministry rather than entertainment, having a message the world needs to hear, serving God instead of man, representing God's point of view.

This leads to a certain schizophrenia within the gospel world—trying to live in the world but not be of the world—and a certain distrust of those outside this world who wonder how anyone can know what God is thinking or be sure there is only one absolute truth that fits everybody and everything? Contradictions and conflicts abound within the Christian culture but at its core is an absolute certainty that Jesus is the Son of God, the Bible is the Word of God, and that God communicates to man through the Holy Spirit—a silent voice that whispers only to believers.

This mysticism is difficult to accept for the rationalist mind or a scientific society that demands empirical proof as evidence. Still, part of man is a spiritual being and this Christian culture has provided answers and direction for some in their spiritual search. Most of those involved in gospel music are not wealthy and certainly do not do it for money. They do it because they feel called and compelled to do so, for a love that transcends earthly explanations and a commitment to spread the gospel message that defies earthly barriers. It is a mission for those armed with the Answer who seek to convince a questioning world. In the midst of this spiritual quest, it is also the music biz.

Just as the secular music industry produces stars, so does the gospel music industry. The essential difference is that secular stars view themselves as entertainers with music being the most important thing in his/her life while the gospel music stars generally view themselves as a minister with music secondary to their own relationship with God. Their role is to convey the gospel message to those who don't believe or encourage those who do believe to keep the faith.

The gospel artist must be sincere, must truly believe what he/she is singing. He may acknowledge the troubles of life, but never doubt the great truth; he may sometimes question aspects of his faith but never abandon the faith. The gospel artist is more gospel than artist, a conduit for God's voice in the world, a spiritual salesman and a shining example that God is alive and working within an individual's life. The performance is not just a show, it is a service too, and the recordings are not just to listen to—they are to be accepted and agreed with.

There are, of course, a wide range of possibilities and diversions within gospel music. There are those who prefer to be Christian entertainers, or entertainers with a Christian message, or entertainers who serve the saints—providing the church with entertainment that celebrates a total acceptance of the faith. There are also those who preach as much as they sing, who witness to the unbeliever, intent on conversion. It would be foolish to state that all motives are totally pure, but at least it must be acknowledged that at the core of all gospel artists is a firm commitment to live a Godly life and have a close relationship with God.

Those outside the gospel industry often don't see this and cast a jaundiced eye at the gospel world, viewing them as hypocrites or frauds. But that hypocrisy usually comes from trying to serve both man and God and the fraud comes when a gospel artist deceives himself. It is more than a music, it is a way of life, and the gospel artist must live it as well as believe it. It is not an easy life but the gospel artist is driven to use music, making it a function of the gospel. It is this higher calling which sustains him.

The Christian culture cannot be underestimated in America. Its marketing network is responsible for billions of dollars in business each year while the development of its own media (and media stars) allows it to communicate to fellow-believers and affect issues in the world at large. It provides a base of support for those involved in entertainment and has given gospel music in the latter part of the 20th and early 21st centuries the ways and means to reach a like-minded audience, providing entertainment with a message compatible with the audience's beliefs. Although it may be argued that the role of Christian music is to evangelize and attract new believers—and some musicians claim that as their purpose—in reality, the thrust of the gospel industry is "music for the saints" and it provides this service through the church, the Christian bookstores, and the Christian media.

Chapter 36

MARKETING THE MOVEMENT: THE RECORDING LABELS

By the mid-1980s the infra-structure was in place to make contemporary Christian music a major force in the world of music. Three labels dominated the Christian music field—and would continue to dominate it in their various permutations for the rest of the 20th century and into the 21st.

The music industry is made up of three components—the music, the technology, and the business. People hear the music and that is what they remember, but the technology captures this music while the "business" is responsible for getting this music into the market and making it available to consumers. Music by itself is only heard by those within hearing of the performer; it takes technology to make it last. And it takes "business" to make it profitable and thus give an incentive for making it available in the marketplace.

Word Records came to dominate the gospel music industry like no other in the 20th century, becoming a total Christian communications company with book publishing, video tapes, and audio teaching cassettes in addition to its record labels during the 1980s. By the mid-1980s Word owned several labels and distributed a number of others, penetrating the Christian bookstores and the secular marketplace. Musically, they were diverse, recording and presenting Southern gospel, inspirational choirs, black gospel, Jesus rock, contemporary Christian music, and great soloists to the Christian community.

Word Records was begun by a Baylor college student, Jarrell McCracken, in the fall of 1950 when he recorded a spoken word allegory of Christianity and a football game. The recording was "The Game of Life" and this improbable beginning launched the label.

The idea had originated from Ted Nichols, a minister of music at the First Baptist Church in Hearn, Texas, and came from an article written by Jimmy Allen, a student at Howard Payne University. The article was an imaginary play-by-play broadcast of the struggle between Christianity and the forces of evil, broadcast over a station with the call letters WORD.

McCracken was working his way through Baylor as a sports announcer. Nichols was setting up a program for a local youth rally and approached him to give a talk before the rally comparing the Christian life with a football game. McCracken wrote a complete script after reading the magazine article and, with the help of two station engineers, added the sound effects of a football game and recorded "The Game of Life" on two 78-rpm transcriptions.

Nichols played "The Game of Life" at the youth rally and the recording was so popular that about a dozen people requested copies. In December 1950, McCracken placed an order for 100 copies of the two-record set. This cost him $70. One of his friends suggested those first labels bear the name of the mythical radio station, WORD, that broadcast "The Game of Life." That record, the first for Word, is still available.

Although it sounds like a Cinderella story, the basic truth is that sports announcer and young Baylor student Jarrell Franklin McCracken discovered in the two phonograph records the basic element that would change not only his own life, but also Christian music's developing industry.

Reflecting on that time, McCracken stated that, "I really didn't envision much of anything specifically. I felt an inspiration after getting out the first record, which was really not meant to be anything other than a speech, but people started asking me what I was going to do next. I really didn't know, but I wanted to share with people some of the beautiful, inspirational, religious experiences we had on the campus. I kept thinking how great it would be to put these great services on record. That's about as far as my vision went."

Word's first artist was Frank Boggs, a baritone and old friend of McCracken's who was studying at Southwestern Baptist Theological Seminar. Boggs first recorded for Word in 1951. It was also during this time that McCracken incorporated the organization.

The Word offices were, in reality, McCracken's kitchen in his bachelor apartment. McCracken recorded Richard Baker, a song director from Ft. Worth, Billy Pearce, Dick Anthony, the White Sisters, the Melody Four Quartet, J.T. Adams, and some of the choirs at Baylor. The only real success saleswise was from "The Game of Life" and Boggs, who went on to establish a prominent name for himself as a male soloist. (This was the era of the male soloist in gospel music with George Beverly Shea the most prominent.)

Financially, the company was helped along by various friends of McCracken's, who would contribute some cash to the enterprise from time to time. McCracken was supporting himself by teaching some courses at Baylor. That is why this major Christian label became headquartered in Waco, Texas.

Discussing the advantages and disadvantages of establishing a base in Waco instead of New York, Los Angeles, or Nashville, McCracken stated that, "There wasn't anyone around to say 'You can't do that' or 'It won't work.' We just went ahead and did it." McCracken contends that the innovative, pioneering spirit prevalent at the start of Word helped overcome the lack of expertise in the record business. Too, while the company did make and sell records, it was not in the record business as it is known in secular terms, but rather as an extension of the church and religious world.

In May 1952, Marvin Norcross, a young accountant from Dallas, was introduced to McCracken by Ted Snider, one of McCracken's partners at Word and the best man at Norcross's wedding. The two young men (McCracken was 24 and Norcross 23) talked for about three hours and at the end of the conversation McCracken asked if he'd like to be a partner in the organization. Norcross agreed. "I wanted to be in business for myself and I wanted to do something to help further the gospel," he said. "Since I'm not a preacher, I thought this was a good opportunity to help further the gospel."

On the question of how much it would cost to buy into the operation, McCracken added up Word's unpaid bills and came up with the sum of $962. Norcross offered $1,000 so the organization would have $38 in working capital for a fresh start.

By 1954, McCracken realized the company could not survive on the sale of Word's records alone and decided to enter into the wholesale distribution of records. This meant that Word would handle other companies' lines of product and sell them to dealers. Among the products the company took on were a progressive jazz label; classical product from Westminister Records; Cricket Records—a line of 25-cent children's records from Pickwick; and Angel Records, a division of EMI.

Word was in the wholesale distribution business for four years, until 1957, when, according to Norcross, "The distribution business went sour." By that time, because of McCracken's foresight, Word had begun the Family Record Club with a record-of-the-month plan. This was begun in 1957 with the profits from the wholesale distribution business.

The wholesale distribution business taught the Word organization valuable lessons about selling records to stores. The Family Record Club taught them about direct mail and they continued to sell by direct mail, with approximately 100,000 members in their record club.

In 1958, a direct sales division was established selling the Word Audio Library door to door. This library consisted of records, tapes of talks, Bible lessons, and songs and its success lasted about four years, or until around 1962 when it was discontinued.

In 1957, Kurt Kaiser, a brilliant young pianist, composer, arranger and conductor, joined Word as vice president and director of artists and repertoire for Word. He soon became one of the most influential people in sacred music because it was his decision which artists recorded for Word. By 1960, the sale of Word Records was approximately $4 million annually.

The 1960s began for Word with the purchase of Sacred Records, a move which brought Ralph Carmichael into the Word organization. Carmichael was and is a noted West Coast writer, arranger, and producer who had been a pioneer innovator in the Christian music field since the late 1940's when he recorded religious music with the popular big band sound of the day, raising more than a few eyebrows in church circles, which were accustomed to hearing religious music recorded with only an organ or piano.

The purchase of Sacred Records also involved the purchase of half of Lexicon Music, a publishing operation owned and run by Carmichael. This involved Word in a total music publishing operation for the first time. In 1957 Marvin Norcross conceived the idea of

Canaan Records, a label that would feature Southern or country-style gospel music, consisting primarily of male quartets. The idea was ahead of its time at that point but in 1963 the label got underway with Norcross signing the Florida Boys as the first act. Norcross had gotten the idea from John T. Benson, whose Benson Company, based in Nashville, was already recording some Southern gospel groups, beginning with the Speer Family.

In the summer of 1965 Word announced it was starting a book publishing division. The first book was by an obscure Episcopalian layman named Keith Miller entitled *The Taste of New Wine*. It was an immediate best-seller and remained popular in Christian literature.

In the mid-1960's there was turmoil, unrest, and the Vietnam War. There was also the Jesus Revolution, a movement in which large numbers of young people became Christians. At Word, Billy Ray Hearn had been hired in the A & R department. Because of his interest and involvement in contemporary Christian music, he was given the nod to begin Myrrh Records, a division of Word, which would be their contemporary label while the more traditional artists remained on Word.

The first album on Myrrh was by Ray Hildebrand, who had two albums released on Word before his Myrrh release. Hildebrand was known for being the "Paul" of Paul and Paula whose 1962 recording of "Hey, Hey Paula" sold close to three million records. The second album released by Myrrh was by an artist who had also had an album on Word. But Randy Matthews was different; his album on Myrrh, *Wish We'd All Been Ready*, was the first contemporary Christian release (i.e. music that combined rock 'n' roll and gospel) for that label, and he became the first Jesus rock artist to record for Word as Word joined the contemporary market.

A major reason for the success of Word and their different labels was a move it made in 1960 to discontinue its association with wholesale distributors who were handling its product and to assume control of its own distribution. Beginning in 1960 Word sold directly to record outlets and Christian bookstores instead of having its product serviced by wholesale distributors. The reason for the move, according to Norcross, was because Word felt it could not properly promote its own product and offer special price deals through the distributors. Whenever it tried a special sales program, it found the distributor generally benefited with higher profit margins while the individual stores and customers paid the same price.

In 1969 Word purchased the Rodeheaver Company in Winona Lake, Indiana, one of the nation's oldest publishers of sacred music. (They held the copyright to "Rock of Ages" and numerous other classics.) That same year Canaanland Music, a publishing division of Canaan Records, was begun in Nashville by Aaron Brown, giving Word its first offices outside Waco, Texas.

A Christian musical, *Tell It Like It Is*, written by Kurt Kaiser and Ralph Carmichael in 1969, proved to be a landmark in the Christian world. A minister's taped digest was introduced, later evolving into "Catalyst" and "Focus"—a series of teaching cassettes. Word also took over the publication of *Faith/At/Word* magazine. The introduction of Creative Resources saw a whole new line of mixed-media teaching and discussion aids become available for use in churches, homes and small groups. In 1969, Word, Inc. had its first million-selling record. Oddly, it was a comedy album by Southern Gospel artist Wendy Bagwell entitled "The Rattlesnake Remedy," which was a satirical take-off on those who used poison snakes in church services.

The 1970s brought more growth to Word as the Myrrh label grew with the contemporary Christian music field. In fact, sales in all the music fields increased to the point that at the end of 1979, Word, Inc. was grossing approximately $40 million in sales annually and employed 400 people—still based in Waco but with new offices established in Nashville and Los Angeles.

In the mid-'70s Word began to distribute labels again, only this time it was small Christian labels such as Good News, Paragon, Solid Rock, Maranatha, Jim, Lamb and Lion, New Pax, and Image as well as Canaan, Myrrh, and Dayspring, which they owned, and Light, owned in partnership with Ralph Carmichael. This move to distribute other labels was made for several reasons. First, the contemporary Christian music field was growing at a phenomenal pace and these labels had the talent for the market and, second, it increased business for Word and its salesmen, making the organization more profitable and able to employ more people.

Perhaps the biggest event that happened to Word occurred in 1976 when they were purchased by ABC Entertainment Corp., making McCracken one of the principal stockholders in the corporation which owned the ABC television network. With this move, Myrrh was distributed for a short while by ABC Records with the belief that sales would increase. However, the opposite occurred as they found that a secular label did not understand Christian product well enough to sell it effectively. After that lesson, Word retained its autonomy within the ABC organization, and when ABC Records was sold in 1979 to MCA, Word remained with ABC, existing as a separate and independent entity under the corporate umbrella.

As Word entered the 1980s it expanded into black gospel, the only field they had not successfully marketed in the past. Word quickly took black gospel to the Christian bookstores and helped it cross over into the white market, breaking down some of the racial boundaries in Christian music. However, the black gospel they marketed was contemporary, part of the pop sound. They generally avoided the choirs and soloists who reached only a black constituency, leaving that market to the traditional black companies.

Word dominated gospel music from the 1960s and by the 1980s their acts accounted for 60 to 70 percent of all gospel music sold in America. But, as Word increased its dominance of the gospel music industry in the 1980s, some problems developed within the organization. In March 1986, ABC merged with Capital Cities, Inc. and the new organization put new pressures on Word and sought a stronger say in the running of the company. Finally, in September 1986, founder Jarrell McCracken, after 35 years at the helm, left the company. Although official reports stated he left to "pursue other interests," it soon became obvious that he did not leave of his own accord. Still, the company, organized under three divisions—Word Records and Music, Word Publishing, and Word Direct Marketing Services—remained the major Christian company marketing gospel music, with music accounting for about 50 to 60 percent of their $80 million annual income.

The other major Christian label for contemporary Christian music in the early 1980s was the Benson Company with its two record divisions, HeartWarming and Impact. They added Greentree in 1976 just for contemporary music.

Originally founded in 1902 by John T. Benson, his wife Eva, and Rev. J.O. McClurkan as a publishing company, the organization was formed to distribute religious pamphlets in the Nashville area. It published its first songbook, *Living Water Songs*, in 1904 but remained a small, local company until 1935 when John T. Benson, Jr. took over. The younger Benson expanded the company dramatically, and between 1948 and 1951 the company went from $12,000 a year in gross revenues to $100,000 a year.

Bob Benson, the second son of John T. Benson, Jr. and the third generation of Bensons involved with the company, joined the organization in 1960 and soon the company's revenues were over half a million dollars a year and the company's first venture into the record business, HeartWarming Records, was created. John T. Benson III joined the organization in 1969 after the company had been successful with its first artists, which included the Speer Family, the Rambos, and the Bill Gaither Trio, and the company expanded into contemporary Christian music in the 1970s, moving away from the Southern gospel quartet music they had begun with.

The company has remained in Nashville since its inception but was sold to the Zondervan Corporation, a Christian company known for its Bible publishing and chain of Family Bookstores, in 1980 for $3 million, down from the $8-12 million originally asked by the Benson Family.

The first major contemporary Christian music label was Myrrh, begun by Billy Ray Hearn while he was at Word Records. Myrrh, a division of Word, had signed acts like Barry McGuire (who had hit the pop charts with "Eve of Destruction" some years before), the Second Chapter of Acts, and others who were appealing to the youth with the gospel message. This was significant because the major gospel labels had traditionally sought to sell records to consumers in the church world—and those consumers were usually over 25. When Word put its muscle behind Myrrh and contemporary Christian music, this lent it a respectability and assured it shelf space in Christian bookstores, which is where consumers bought most gospel music.

After Myrrh was launched, Billy Ray Hearn received a phone call from Seth Baker with the CHC Corporation in Los Angeles, which owned Los Angeles magazine and a book publishing company, Acton House, wanting to know if he would be interested in starting a new label. A number of sleepless nights later, Hearn moved to Los Angeles and began Sparrow Records. That was January 1976 and, in the ensuing years, Sparrow became a leader in contemporary Christian music through its philosophy of signing acts who were committed to ministry and who used their music as part of that ministry to reach people—young people—with the gospel.

Hearn grew up in Beaumont, Texas where he received music lessons in both the church and school (he played violin at five). He spent two years in the Navy at Pensacola, Florida after graduation and also worked in the music program of a local church. Later, he attended Baylor University in Waco, Texas, where he received a Bachelor of Music degree with a major in church music. He joined Trinity Baptist Church in San Antonio as youth and music director after graduation and stayed there four years, until he joined the Baptist Seminary in Fort Worth, where he taught music ministry and conducting. Hearn became minister of music at the First Baptist Church of Thomasville, Georgia in 1960 and stayed there for eight years, developing a large music program as well as booking contemporary music groups touring in the southeast into his church. Working with young people and contemporary music, he developed the musical, *Good News*, which debuted in 1968. He came to the attention of Word when the musical, a major success, toured throughout the U.S. and Europe. This led Word to invite Hearn to join its staff to help promote musicals that company had developed, including *Tell It Like It Is* by Kurt Kaiser and Ralph Carmichael.

After three years as a contemporary label, Myrrh was coming under increasing fire from Word executives, who did not feel there was any future with contemporary Christian music and believed the new label was costing too much money while not generating enough income. But Jarrell McCracken, head of Word, stood behind Hearn and the label continued. However, Hearn grew increasingly frustrated and by 1975 was looking for ways to begin his own label. That "way" jelled that year when he received a phone call from Seth Baker, head of the CHC Corporation in Los Angeles.

On January 1, 1976 Sparrow opened its doors in Los Angeles with no artists. The first artist signed was Barry McGuire, whose contract was up with Myrrh and who wanted to go with Hearn. Then the Talbot brothers—John Michael and Terry—each signed for an album as did Janny Grein. Second Chapter of Acts—a group Hearn had signed to Myrrh and worked with extensively there—felt they should stay with the Word organization for one more album but one of their members, Annie Herring, signed with Sparrow for a solo project. Those were the first acts with albums released in May 1976, when Sparrow presented its first product to the marketplace.

That first year, Sparrow sold about $700,000 worth of albums, but their big break came when they signed Candle, a group organized by Tony Salerno, who produced children's albums. Hearn was reluctant to sign the group—he did not feel their music fit with Sparrow—but finally became enthused after hearing some of the material; he then created a separate label, Birdwing, just for the group. The first album, *Chief Musician*, sold reasonably well; but the album which would turn the ears of Christian labels to children's music, *The Music Machine*, came out the following year, 1977, after it was previewed at the Christian Bookseller's Convention in July. That album became the biggest seller for Sparrow during their first five years in business and instigated an avalanche of children's product from Christian labels when they realized a huge market was there.

Sparrow became an independent company in August 1977 after the CHC Corporation had been sold to ABC. CHC offered to sell the stock to Hearn so he organized a group of investors who purchased Sparrow on August 31, 1977.

Hearn's philosophy has always been, "We don't sell records—we support artists" and further that, "We don't sign artists unless they can become part of the family—that's a very close knit fellowship of all our artists, who support each other, who love each other, believe in each other."

Sparrow started small but this was an advantage because it was the one-to-one relationship they established with Christian bookstores and distributors in the early days that assured their success. In a 1978 interview, Hearn stated that, "There are four or five thousand book stores but three thousand of them aren't anything at all active in selling records and only about 500 of those sell 80 percent of our product ... so we hired two kids to get on the phones and we called every store and in about three months we had 1,800 accounts direct to stores on the phones and we told them the story ... (the kids) were really into what we are and knew exactly what to say to the bookstore people. I've always hired very dedicated Christian people...they lived the music we were into.... It's better to sell direct and make sure all of your product is in the stores ... and you control your own promotion campaigns, your own in-store advertising dollars." Hearn also knew how to control costs. "I didn't spend any more in production than anyone else was spending," he said. "I had learned how to be very tight with our budgets and I put a lot of the burden of the company on the shoulders of the artists. I was not a big fat company that had money in their eyes, I was the young no-money company that the artist wanted to succeed and so I would give them a very tight budget and they would do everything they could to produce fantastic records with very little money."

Still, Sparrow was very attentive to quality and Hearn states that, "(we) gave the illusion that we spent a lot of money, but really didn't ... it was very close attention to quality. I also believed in the spiritual qualities of the artist. We are very dedicated to spiritual qualities because we feel like people who buy religious records want the spiritual quality, or they wouldn't be into religious records. It takes a person who is totally involved in religious activities to buy religious records. So they need to feel tremendous spiritual quality in the record as well as technical quality."

Perhaps the artist who exemplified the Sparrow philosophy best was Keith Green. Green was also the artist who put Sparrow into the major leagues of gospel music with his early success. When his first album, *For Those Who Have Ears*, was released in 1977, it marked the introduction of an artist who would have a profound affect on contemporary Christian music for the next several years.

Keith Green was not crucified or assassinated for his beliefs—he died in a plane crash—but he personified this radical Christianity. It is sadly appropriate that he died young because he seemed to put his life on the line for his faith.

Chapter 37

CHRISTIAN AND GOSPEL MUSIC IN THE 1990s

The world of Southern Gospel had gone through wrenching changes during the 1960s and 1970s; during the 1980s it was still trying to wrestle with a world that had left them behind. The Brown vs. Board of Education decision in 1954, which integrated schools, angered many Southerners who reacted with belligerence and by digging in their feet for "Southern pride." Concerts featuring black groups like the Golden Gate Quartet singing with southern white groups, which had happened before the ruling, would no longer happen. The South, and Southern gospel, fought against integration by becoming even more segregated. Then, as Southern gospel conservatives slowly came to accept integration, they were hit by the Jesus Revolution and contemporary Christian music, which stole a segment of their audience, then virtually kicked them out of the Gospel Music Association, which they had formed.

At least that's what it seemed like to those involved in Southern gospel. To add insult to injury, the contemporary Christian music crowd looked down their noses at Southern gospel and wouldn't even acknowledge that genre for laying the groundwork for the GMA and Dove Awards with a simple "thank you." They didn't even like the term "gospel," insisting their music was "Christian," therefore implying that neither Southern gospel nor black gospel was really Christian. This also implied that people in other kinds of gospel music weren't really Christian either. It seemed like the epitome of self-righteous arrogance when this young crowd thought they had created the whole industry, that all those who struggled before them did not even exist, much less count.

It was a lot for those Southern gospel folks to swallow. They hunkered down and dug in, but they did not change with the times, even when the times were changing rapidly all around them.

For those groups in Southern gospel whose roots ran back to the Great Depression, gospel music had been a way off the farm and the route to a better life. Though most believed the message of the Christian gospel, it was something they took for granted and they were comfortable with their audiences, who also shared this common set of beliefs.

The idea of evangelism was not the reason this generation got into gospel music. They viewed it as "good, clean entertainment," a better alternative than what was in the popular culture, and a better way to make a living than hard, manual labor. It was a connection to the rural past at a time when the nation was becoming urban centers surrounded by suburbs. It was also a wall built against all the things called "modern" and "progressive" by city intellectuals.

Some members of the Southern gospel community saw their work as a "ministry" and preached a fundamentalist gospel. With the introduction of the Jesus Revolution, when young people were adamant about evangelism, those in Southern gospel found they had to make a choice between ministry and entertainment. Increasingly, those who just wanted to perform "clean, wholesome entertainment" fell out of favor while those preaching a fundamentalist gospel message, rooted in Pentecostalism with evangelical fervor, found an enthusiastic audience.

The 1980s were a low period with a few high points for Southern gospel. In 1985 Tennessee Ernie Ford hosted "The Great American Gospel Sound" for PBS television. This show was so popular that a follow-up, "More of That Great American Gospel," was also produced. But, by and large, the 1980s were a period when Southern gospel music looked like a cultural artifact, a remnant of the past. Groups found it difficult to sell recordings or get bookings and young people, who at one time might have been attracted to Southern gospel, were now attracted to contemporary Christian music.

During the 1980s a number of new Southern gospel groups formed, including the Singing Americans, Gold City, Dixie Melody Boys, Heaven Bound, and Kingdom Heirs as well as family groups such as the Hopper Brothers and Sister Connie, Hemphills, Nelons, Dixie Echoes, Bishops, McKameys, Talleys, Perrys, Greens, Paynes, and Jeff and Sheri Easter. There were even some African-American groups in Southern gospel: Teddy Huffam and the Gems from Richmond, Virginia; Charles Johnson and the Revivers, Don Degarte and Strong Tower, the Gospel Enforcers, Willis Canada, the Scotts, and the Reggie Saddler Family.

The most significant Southern gospel group formed during the 1980s was the Gaither Vocal Band, created by Bill Gaither. With this group, Gaither returned to his first love—Southern gospel. Because of his popularity and guidance, the Gaither Vocal Band was the only Southern gospel group that was able to cross over into the larger world of Contemporary Christian music.

In 1988 Charles Waller held a Grand Ole Gospel Reunion in Greenville, South Carolina, in which he brought together a number of the old-time Southern gospel groups. This event inspired Bill Gaither to begin a video series, called "Homecoming," in which the older Southern gospel performers got together, talked, reminisced, and sang. The videos were sold to Southern gospel fans who had been having a hard time finding their kind of music—and the kind of people—they loved and admired. The series was incredibly successful and made Gaither millions of dollars. But the Southern gospel community was not angry at Gaither for making so much money from these videos; indeed, they were quite thankful. First, Bill Gaither was probably the only person in gospel music who had the finances to fund such a project. And second, this "Homecoming" series almost single-handedly revitalized Southern gospel music and the careers of these Southern gospel performers. Gaither also developed a show on Southern gospel, based on this video series, for The Nashville Network. In short, Bill Gaither "saved" Southern gospel by giving it national exposure and a new sense of pride and elevating it when the field was at its lowest point.

Disenchanted with the direction the Gospel Music Association was headed in, a new organization, the Southern Gospel Music Association, was formed by Charles Waller. But in June 1985 Les Beasley announced that the Gospel Music Association had purchased the SGMA, which would now be under the GMA's umbrella. However, the next year another organization, the Southern Gospel

Music Guild, was organized. Also, Maurice Templeton purchased *The Singing News* from J.G. Whitfield and made a decision that the publication would only cover Southern gospel music. Prior to this time, *The Singing News* was known for its coverage of Southern gospel, but gave space to contemporary Christian music as well.

Disenchanted with the treatment the city of Nashville gave Southern gospel, the National Quartet Convention moved its event to Louisville, Kentucky in the 1990s, then established permanent headquarters in Louisville in 1994. In 1995 Maurice Templeton, owner of *The Singing News*, founded a new Southern Gospel Music Association. The field began to grow again and expanded to a Great Western Quartet Convention in Fresno, California in 1997 and the Canadian Quartet Convention in Red Deer, Alberta, Canada in 1999.

Southern gospel grew during the 1990s by reaching back to its roots in churches. During the 1970s, 17 percent of the concerts put on by Southern gospel groups were in churches; by the mid-1990s, that figure was 65 percent. In their search for an audience through the 1970s and '80s, it seems that they found it right back at home.

For black gospel an era ended while another began during the early 1990s. In February 1991, James Cleveland died; in January 1993, Thomas Dorsey, the "Father of Black Gospel," died. But also in 1993 Kirk Franklin released his debut album, *God's Property*, and it went platinum. The album was released on a label begun by Puff Daddy (Sean Combs) and Russell Simmons, whose Def Jam label had popularized Hip Hop. They knew how to market to the black community in a way that also reached the white community.

Kirk Franklin, along with BeBe and CeCe Winans, Tramaine Hawkins, Yolanda Adams, and others would turn the music industry's head as they proved that gospel music could sell in big numbers. This wasn't contemporary Christian music, but the contemporary Christian audience bought it. Influenced by contemporary Christian music, the singers didn't have the hang-ups of their white counterparts.

By the 1990s there was a new lingo in religious music; "Gospel" referred to black religious music while "Christian" referred to white religious music. Both exploded in growth, but it was "Gospel" that achieved the biggest gains.

There was also a new kind of music—hip hop—which came out

of the African-American community. The Baby Boomers grew up on rock 'n' roll, a music that defined their generation. They had to endure slurs and insults before it came to be accepted. Children of the Baby Boomers had to hear their parents echo an older generation about the new hip hop music—it was music of the Devil, dirty, was all noise and no melody, just a fad, how can anybody stand it—when it came blaring out of speakers. The generation who grew up on rock 'n' roll could not even relate to hip hop as this new music came to dominate the tastes of young music lovers. Contemporary Christian and gospel have followed secular trends, so the trend of hip hop moved into the Christian world during the 1990s.

There were several reasons for the increase in sales in Christian and Gospel music during the 1990s. First, there was consolidation. The Family Bookstore chain was not a series of independently owned stores; consequently, they were not "afraid" of any kind of religious music. Corporate offices demanded they stock what sold—so if it sold, then it was stocked. Next, there was a consolidation of recording labels, usually becoming partners within a much larger organization.

In 1992 Word was sold to Thomas Nelson for $72 million and EMI purchased Sparrow. In 1994 the Music Entertainment Group bought the Benson Music Group, along with Tribute/Diadem. At the end of 1996, Thomas Nelson kept Word's book division and sold the recording label to Gaylord Entertainment, which also owned the Grand Ole Opry and The Nashville Network. Gaylord then purchased Blanton/Harrell Entertainment, which managed Amy Grant and Michael W. Smith.

In 1996 Warner Brothers created Warner Alliance, which marketed to the Christian Booksellers market, then created Warner Resound, which marketed gospel to the secular market. By 1996 Word was using Epic Records and the Sony Music Distribution system to reach the secular market while its own distribution system marketed to Christian bookstores.

In 1997 EMI bought ForeFront, adding to Sparrow and Star Song to create EMI Christian, headed by Bill Hearn. In June 1997 the Zomba Music Group announced the formation of Provident Music Group, by combining Brentwood Music and Reunion—the label begun by Blanton and Harrell which had been sold to BMG before Zomba purchased it. Provident then purchased the Benson Music

Group from the Music Entertainment Group.

By the end of 1997, the major players were no longer Word, Benson and Sparrow—which were the big three a decade earlier—but EMI Christian, Provident and Gaylord. All were headquartered in Nashville, which became the center for contemporary Christian music as well as country music. The corporations that owned these labels had learned some hard lessons in the previous years. First, Christian music needs to be controlled by those who know this business. And so the top executives for these divisions were long-time gospel executives. Next, secular distribution works great for the secular market, but the Christian distribution system that supplies product to Christian bookstores must remain. By having this dual distribution system, and paying careful attention to the core Christian audience in the Christian bookstores, these labels could reach a much larger audience.

The big corporations provided immense capitalization. Those deep pockets helped assure big sales when an artist hit. Small companies usually cannot afford to have a big hit. The costs of manufacturing, marketing and promotion, which are incurred before the label has received income from sales, can break a small company. Worse, they don't allow a smaller company the financial resources to take advantage of big demand from consumers.

Another factor in the success of Gospel and Christian music during the 1990s came from the fact that *Billboard*, the leading trade magazine in the music industry, began to compile its charts based on SoundScan, a computer technology based on bar codes. Bar codes were originally developed to help retailers keep track of inventory and individual stores keep track of sales; SoundScan took these bar codes and developed a system whereby sales numbers could be downloaded each week to reveal what was actually selling and where it was selling.

This computer technology supplied the facts in raw numbers. The charts no longer had to depend upon phone calls to retailers who gave relative rankings. And the industry did not have to be victims of retailers prejudiced against gospel music. If an album sold well—no matter what kind of music—it was reported by the computers. The fact that gospel sold well became a proven fact, thus enticing retailers to expand their selection of gospel and stock more product, which led to more sales. A Kirk Franklin could not have happened as he did without SoundScan technology; the sales numbers could not be denied.

SoundScan also showed the recording labels where their albums were selling and which promotions worked, allowing marketers to make use of this information—which they received week by week—to maximize sales for a hot act.

Gospel and Christian music function better as magnets than as hooks. When the music has sought to reach out to find an audience—to "hook" people, many of them unsuspecting souls who would be caught by "stealth evangelism"—it generally fails. But when the music is allowed to be itself, to stand self-assured and confident, then it is a magnet both for those who love the music already and those outside the field. Gospel and Christian music are powerful attractions when they are allowed to be who they are and do what they do.

One of the most powerful musical trends in both Gospel and Christian music was praise and worship—music in the church for the churched. It is a music sung to God by believers. Both white and black churches increasingly used contemporary music in their services during the late 1980s and throughout the 1990s until it was difficult to find vibrant, growing churches who sang old hymns. The music of Isaac Watts, the Wesleys, and others have been replaced by songs from the albums of contemporary artists, both black and white.

In both the white and African-American communities, conferences, or gatherings of believers, are major events. Promise Keepers and Women of Faith in the white market and the Full Gospel Baptist Church Fellowship Conference and annual COGIC conference, as well as a number of others, draw believers together. Music and musical acts are important parts of these conferences, which serve as a showcase for these performers. These conferences also serve as retailers, as acts bring their tapes and CDs and sell them to attendees at the convention. From the mid-1980s on through the 1990s, these conferences became a key vehicle of exposure for religious music.

During the first half of the 1980s, the biggest "stars" of the white Christian culture were the televangelists; but during the 1990s it was African-American evangelists like Bishop Noel Jones from Los Angeles, Carlton Pearson, Bishop T.D. Jakes from Dallas, and Shirley

Caesar who attracted the most attention.

Finally, the music industry is both hit-driven and star-driven and both Gospel and Christian music produced a number of hits and stars from the late 1980s onward. Amy Grant and Sandi Patti were pioneers in the contemporary Christian field, soon joined by Michael W. Smith, Petra, and the Imperials. In the late 1980s, Steven Curtis Chapman began to dominate the field. The musical trends of rap and hip hop saw dc Talk emerge. Hits by Sixpence None the Richer, Jars of Clay, Bob Carlisle, Audio Adrenaline, Third Day, Point of Grace, Newsboys, and others created consumer demand.

The biggest trailblazer in Gospel has been Kirk Franklin, whose release, *God's Property from Kirk Franklin's Nu Nation*, sold 117,000 units the first week it was released, and, spurred by the hit single, "Stomp," and a video on MTV, landed at number three on Billboard's top album charts. His "Tour of Life" was incredibly successful at selling tickets. This was no ordinary tour—the start-up costs were $250,000 but promoters soon found they could sell out this concert in major cities. Kirk Franklin became the Garth Brooks of Gospel Music during the 1990s.

By 1995 the revenues from the Christian music industry were estimated to be as high as $750 million per year, with sales of recordings accounting for $381 million. In 1985, about 90 percent of all contemporary Christian music was sold in Christian bookstores; by 1995, 64 percent was sold in Christian bookstores, 21 percent in the general market, and 15 percent by direct mail.

Between 1985 and 1995 Christian recordings grew by $298 million, or a 290 percent increase in sales. In 1995 the SoundScan technology began to be used to compile *Billboard*'s religious music charts; the next year, sales of recordings reached $538 million (or a 30 percent increase in one year), placing it sixth in popularity of all music genres, behind rock, country, urban contemporary, pop, and rap, but ahead of classical, jazz, oldies and new age. When concert ticket sales and merchandising were added, religious music generated an estimated $750-900 million in revenue.

In 1996 gospel accounted for 4.3 percent of all music sales; that year there were 33.3 million scans of Christian/Gospel product; in 1997 there were 44 million scans, or a 32 percent growth rate from the previous year. Between 1991 and 1996 Gospel/Christian averaged a 22 percent growth each year while other formats had an average growth rate of around 5 percent. In 1997 Christian/Gospel recordings accounted for $550 million in sales; in 1987 that figure was $160 million.

By 1998 Wal-Mart, Kmart, Blockbuster, MusicLand, Target, and Sam Goody had all increased their stocks of gospel. Wal-Mart, which had 45 linear feet in its total music department, had 8 linear feet for Christian music. This is where the biggest growth in religious music occurred; while the sales at Christian bookstores increased 15-25 percent, the mainstream market for religious music grew 70-80 percent.

By 1997 black gospel was no longer for grandmothers; it was a hip, happening music in the black community. Built on the black church, it was attracting a young audience of record buyers both black and white. Christian music, too, captured a young audience for its young performers. Even the older performers benefitted; sales of James Cleveland's recordings were still strong in the African-American community while acts that had been around two decades, like Amy Grant, Sandi Patti, and Michael W. Smith, were still major forces in the field.

CONCLUSION

There's an old saying about people who are self-righteous, single-minded, and uncompromising, sometimes to the point of being belligerent and obnoxious, that they are "on a mission from God." Well, the entire Christian music industry is "on a mission from God."

Evangelical Christians claim a "personal relationship" with Christ, which often convinces them they have God's perspective on each and every issue or that God agrees with their perspective on each and every issue. Many of those who claim to be "serving God" are doing so in an advisory capacity.

Yet there is a sincerity to their efforts, a total belief their life is part of God's plan, that they are fulfilling God's purpose by living as evangelicals. Evangelicals live with certainties ("Jesus is the Answer") and a firm conviction that their basic beliefs are "right." They are convinced that, while results may not always turn out as envisioned, their motives are good. It is impossible to argue with God so it is impossible to counter this view.

The years 1976 to 1986 are key to understanding the Christian music industry; during this period contemporary Christian music came of age, defined itself, and became the major force in gospel music. Through its commercial success, it influenced Southern gospel and black gospel, making them move towards a more contemporary sound. It also made them see a large, potential market for those singing the gospel. This is proven by a simple fact: Between 1985 and 1995, the sales of Christian recordings grew by $298 million.

The buyers of contemporary Christian music are overwhelmingly white middle-class females in their 30s and 40s living in the suburbs with some college education. Specifically, 76 percent of the music is purchased by females, and 59 percent of the buyers are in their 30s and 40s, with 85 percent of them white. About half of the buyers earn between $30,000 and $60,000 a year, with 77 percent having some college education and 43 percent a college degree.

The deepest fear held by this group is that their children will not be as evangelical as they are. It is a fear grounded in their inherent belief that if their children are not as pious and evangelical, these children will go to hell when they die. There is nothing more traumatic than the death of a child and these evangelicals feel that if their child does not embrace the faith fully, then they are "lost" or "dead." An evangelical cannot live and let live, because to live and let live means to live and let die.

Many of the buyers of contemporary Christian music see it as a tool to help assure their children will also become evangelicals; in addition, they want a music that supports and encourages their own faith. They want to hear artists who embrace their world view, and they want to be with people who share the same values.

There is much hand-wringing and self-absorption in Christian music. It is possibly the most self-centered music in America, constantly agonizing over itself. It constantly questions the roles of entertainment, ministry, performances, capitalism, popular culture and numerous other things.

The question that hovers over all of this hand-wringing is: "Does this music produce results?" Results are defined as the conversion of non-believers, or perceived non-believers, to the criteria evangelists have established that define whether or not someone is a Christian. On the surface, these criteria are: (1) that the Bible is the unerring word of God; (2) belief in the divinity of Jesus Christ; and (3) the belief in Jesus and his resurrection as the salvation of a person's soul.

There are other criteria as well, criteria that are not an outcome of belief, but a precondition to it: the person must not smoke, drink, support abortion, swear, gamble, approve of homosexuality, or be politically "liberal."

Evangelicals, broadly defined, are conservative Protestants who have been "born again," or converted to Christ, believe in the authority of the Bible, and who share their faith with others, hoping to convert them into evangelicals as well.

Early gospel singers did not twist and turn on these issues. For the Southern gospel pioneers, it was often a way to get away from manual labor or off the farm and out of agricultural work. For singers with the traveling evangelists, it was to set up the message, to "prepare the way." For black gospel singers, it was their bulwark against a world that was hard, cruel, unjust and unfair—a source of strength and self-respect. And for country-gospel, it was a simple expression of their faith.

Contemporary Christian music is a demanding music. It differs from secular or non-Gospel music in that Christian artists demand the audience agree with him/her. Further, the audience demands the artist agree with them. No other form of music is like this. In rock or pop or country or R & B, the artist may want the audience to be entertained, or get their money's worth, or leave satisfied, but they are not concerned about the individual beliefs of the members of the audience. The audience for secular music demands music that touches them, demands it be worth the money spent, that the time spent at the show is worthwhile. The artist's personal beliefs are generally irrelevant.

In contemporary Christian music, the song cannot stand alone. What is judged is the writer(s) and/or the performer: Do they truly believe and profess fundamental, evangelical Christianity? That is the major criteria in the world of contemporary Christian music.

Further, in Christian music the artist and the songs must be produced, manufactured, distributed, and sold by a Christian organization. A rigid set of defining criteria must be met. If the song is marketed by a secular organization, it is suspect; if the artist appears before non-Christians—especially if they only sing and do not give a testimony—then they are suspect.

This can become a fault. In the world at large, a song is independent of its writer—it has a life of its own. And a singer may have a great voice—and give a heart-moving, soul-searching performance—so the recording will have a life of its own. But this cannot be enough in contemporary Christian music. Better to have a weak song or a lesser singer whose "heart is in the right place," to use a popular term. One who believes all the "right" things, or sees things "the right way" than to have a great song or great singer. A creative field is known by the works it creates—the creators of those works are secondary. Great songs and great recordings live forever, touching people who never learn anything about the writer or singer. By and large, the contemporary Christian world will not accept this.

If a Christian artist's beliefs are in line with the audience's, there is an acceptance of what is attempted. Granted, this does not assure the artist of commercial success—Christian consumers may not buy an album or attend a concert no matter how much they agree with an artist if the music doesn't particularly "move" them. Still, the artist and the music have the audience's tacit "blessing." However, when the Christian artist moves into the secular arena, they are judged on an entirely different set of criteria: Is the music great? It does not matter what their private, personal beliefs are, their spiritual home, or whatever else—what matters is if they have a great song to deliver and a great voice to deliver it with. It also helps if they are young and physically attractive. But their religious beliefs are irrelevant. They are judged on their work and not their religious faith.

There is criticism within the Christian culture that contemporary Christian music is inherently shallow; ironically, this was the same argument used against the shaped-note songs published by Stamps-Baxter and James D. Vaughan and sung by Southern gospel quartets in the 1920s and 1930s. The issue of whether the vehicle of pop music is fitting and appropriate for religion, or whether the lyrics expressed in a three-minute song contain the depth of full-blown Christianity, ignores the basic fact that recorded music in American culture is primarily geared towards entertainment. It is logical, then, that no three minute song can capture the depth of historical Christianity. The argument about whether a medium geared towards entertainment is appropriate, for religion is more complex than it appears.

Those opposed to contemporary Christian music find it easy to answer "no." One argument against using entertainment or the mass media to further Christianity is that these media do not convey the "brokenness" of Christianity, the concept of sin in everyone. Instead, the lighter, more positive side is emphasized. Further, social action is eschewed in favor of individual action; the need for an individual's salvation is more important, and necessary, than righting the wrongs of society or attacking institutional sin. Evangelicals ignore the problems of society as a whole, arguing that by converting individuals they will reform society.

Those in contemporary Christian music answer that it is imperative to use contemporary culture, and the medium of music, to express a faith that is ageless and, at the same time, forever new. To make Jesus relevant to "today," He must be presented in a form that captures what people today are hearing, seeing and experiencing. If Jesus is relevant to contemporary life, the argument goes, then he must exist in contemporary culture. Contemporary Christian music puts him there.

In their book, *Apostles of Rock: The Splintered World of Contemporary Christian Music*, authors Jay R. Howard and John M. Streck divide contemporary Christian music into three different categories: separational, integrational, and transformational. They add a fourth, "materialist" in their discussion of contemporary Christian music.

"Separational" music is created "to proselytize the nonbeliever, encourage the believer, or praise God." The authors call it "Christian cheerleading" and see it as "music created by and almost exclusively for evangelicals." For separational artists, "whatever their musical abilities, a key talent for these artists was the command of the religious cliche. As long as the lyrics showed the artists to be unequivocally 'gospel' in their approach, a limited amount of musical innovation could be tolerated and occasionally embraced."

Howard and Streck note that "the fundamental unifying force for evangelicals is their common association with the sentimental trappings of the faith: feelings of acceptance, of familiarity and, often, of superiority relative to non-Christians" and that "in the end, God must solve all difficulties, reveal the meaning of suffering, and/or point to some greater good" because "CCM is to be always positive, always hopeful, and apart from some tidy resolution, to never address one's own continuing failures and brokenness."

Another aspect of separational CCM claims that "The worship of God ... is the supreme duty of any Christian" and that "music is to be used primarily for the "praise of God." This "praise and worship music" is the focus for some separational artists while others "respond ... with songs of exhortation." In this role, the music is intended "to keep the Christian on the narrow path."

Howard and Streck conclude that "When the music is intended to evangelize, it is directed at non-Christians; when the music is intended to be used for praise and worship, it is directed at God; and when the music is intended for exhortation, it is directed at fellow believers." It is this last group that comprises CCM's "primary audience" and because they are directing their music to fellow Christians the artists are "now free to rely more heavily on the rhetoric of evangelical Christianity—'Christianese'—without hesitation."

Howard and Streck observe that "by redefining 'ministry' to include praise and worship and exhortation, separational Christian artists [are] able to escape the paradox of attempting to reach the lost while largely playing to the found ... 'ministry' thus becomes a convoluted notion able to incorporate almost any evangelical behavior" that "defines consumption as religion."

Howard and Streck note that "albums with the highest 'Jesus count' are frequently the biggest sellers in the Christian bookstore distribution system" and that "it is Separational CCM that controls the evangelical marketplace."

Integrational music is "opposed to the idea of withdrawing into an isolated Christian subculture" but wants instead to be part of mainstream culture as a "wholesome alternative to mainstream rock." Integrational contemporary Christian music, according to Howard and Streck, "articulate(s) the Christian worldview to those who might not otherwise be exposed to it." It is, in short, "positive pop." Those involved in Integrational CCM "enter the marketplace not as ministers or evangelists but as entertainers" and believe that "it is enough for the music to provide a wholesome alternative to the standard fare of the secular media and to give at least some voice to a Christian worldview within the larger marketplace of ideas."

Transformational CCM, on the other hand, "makes an explicit and self-conscious claim for 'art,' and defines itself explicitly and self-consciously in terms of art." Because of this, Transformational CCM artists "produce music that by its nature, in one way or another, challenges and confronts, making the listener face uncomfortable truths ... it is the effort that is crucial."

Tranformational CCM "brings the claim that the purpose of Christian music is simply to exist; it is valuable because it is, not because it necessarily accomplishes some goal." Howard and Streck conclude that transformational artists "may fancy themselves aesthetically superior, [but] their music generally does not sell."

In terms of the "business" aspect of contemporary Christian music, Howard and Streck note that "profit is acceptable so long as it's not the primary goal."

The idea that popular music can be "art" may be traced back to the Beatles album *Sgt. Pepper's Lonely Hearts Club Band.* With this album, the most popular and influential band in the history of rock 'n' roll stepped beyond mere entertainment into the rarefied world of "art" in their work. But what is overlooked is that the Beatles were entertainers first and foremost before they recorded that album and, afterwards, they were still trying to record commercial albums. But the sheer immensity of their popularity and success elevated them above others in popular music. Still, the Beatles established the fact that pop music can be "art."

It is difficult, if not impossible to define "art" but however "art" is defined, it is something timeless, something that lasts and matters through the ages. By calling their work "art," pop artists are insisting that their work is timeless, that it matters and will last. This desire to matter, to be relevant today and far into the future, is what drives many creative artists. But the answer to whether it is or is not art does not come from self-proclamation; the answer lies in the ages.

Calling oneself an "artist" can be the ultimate in selfish self-centeredness. Many recording artists call their work "art" because it is noncommercial. They use terms like "authentic," "truthful," "honest" and "real" in defining their music. And, to some extent, they are correct in feeling that the creative life is often at odds with capitalism. For recording artists, the problem in the music business has always been how to sell without selling out. It is a problem when "art" meets "commerce," when the "suits" have to work with those who have a need for creative expression and an inherent disdain for the corporate world.

It is difficult to produce "art" in a world that is geared for immediate gratification. But "art" in popular culture has tended to be a by-product of a commercial success—not a reason unto itself. With few exceptions, what has come down to us as great "art" was done originally to satisfy an immediate demand for pleasure and entertainment.

We resemble our culture more than we resemble our parents. Although we may have our looks and some habits from our parents, our culture imparts its "values" (i.e., what is important and what is not) on us. However much we insist on our individuality—and Americans are known for their individualism—we are part of the American culture. The Christian recording artist must accept the basic ground rules in the pop music industry: (1) recordings must attract listeners through the electronic medium; (2) recordings must inspire people to purchase them; and (3) performers must appeal to people paying for tickets to live performances.

Like the secular artist, the Christian artist accepts these rules while, at the same time, is uncomfortable with them. It is a matter of integrity, of personal expression, and of a feeling that the artist should be free to express himself/herself and not be constrained by a marketplace dominated by those with business degrees.

Popular culture is the arts in a market-based, capitalist culture. Works of art are not judged by aesthetic criteria but by commercial criteria: If it sells, it's good. Critics argue that popular culture rewards the "wrong" things, that it seeks the lowest common denominator in presenting works to the public. The public, it is argued, should be given what is "good," i.e., what embraces traditional values.

The idea of Jacksonian Democracy—the wisdom of the common people—is inherent in America. Contemporary Christian music is the God-son and God-daughter of rhythm and blues, country, and rock 'n' roll—which achieved their success by appealing to the masses. During the mid-to-late 1950s and early 1960s, these musics dethroned the "pop" music of the late 1940s and early 1950s because that music didn't speak to youth. The fact that it is now considered "art" or at least "artifact" may be a testament to the wisdom of the masses. But there is a tacit understanding in the commercial music industry that the music must first be commercially viable in its own time before it can last past its time.

Christian music has succeeded in selling recordings because it is music by Christians, for Christians, about Christians and Christianity. Although many claim their intent is to reach the "lost," their commercial success comes by reaching the "found." It is an insular world, distrusting of—and distrusted by—the secular world. It is a sub-culture with its own traditions, language, and rules that has succeeded because it has established an alternative world to the mainstream popular culture. This world is filled with Christian media and marketed by Christian organizations. In many ways, a

CONCLUSION

"Christian" is defined by what he/she buys and the purchase of contemporary Christian music is a "proof" of one's Christianity.

In the end, Contemporary Christian music, while claiming to serve as a tool for evangelism, is really a tool for Christian identity. It is a music that serves Christians in a variety of ways, but the most important is that it is part of the unifying force that holds Christians together, sets them apart, and gives them a music that strengthens, consoles, supports, and affirms their faith. It succeeds in the capitalist, open market system when its success is determined and defined by the capitalist, open market system of popular culture—selling recordings, selling tickets to personal appearances by artists, and acceptance by the mass media. Although Christian music wants to define its "success" in terms of souls saved and individual lives changed, it must incorporate these latter goals with the commercial market.

In the late 20th and early 21st centuries, Christian music has proven itself to be a resounding success in the commercial market. This has allowed it to continue to pursue its goals of saving souls and changing lives. In the future, these last two goals that Christian music sets for itself can only be pursued if it continues to achieve commercial success. Ironically, that commercial success rests on Christian music reaching those whose souls have already been saved and whose lives have already accepted Christianity as a way of life and who demand a music that strengthens, consoles, supports, and affirms that life.

NOTES

Since 1974, I have done countless interviews and written articles on gospel music or gospel performers for *Billboard*, *Record World*, *Contemporary Christian Music*, *Music City News*, *Cashbox*, *Christian Life*, *Christian Review*, *Christian Retailer*, and a number of other publications as well as presented papers on gospel music for the Popular Culture Association and Popular Culture of the South Association meetings. This book is a culmination of all those interviews, articles, conferences, readings and research. This makes it difficult to document many parts of this book, particularly the chapters on contemporary Christian music, because the information has been assimilated, digested, and in many cases recycled until original sources have been lost. Also, my ideas have developed over a long period of time and often I am not sure exactly when or where I came to a particular idea or conclusion except to say that it has been a long, growing process that has come from ideas presented to others, tossed around in conversations, and modified through numerous discussions and articles as well as books I have read. Still, I have tried to name the key individuals and publications that shaped my thinking in each chapter.

Chapter 1: Music in the Bible

The passages from the Bible in this chapter are taken from the New International Version (Grand Rapids, Michigan: The Zondervan Corp., 1978) with the help of *Cruden's Complete Concordance*, also published by Zondervan.

Chapter 2: The Sixteenth Century: Roots of Contemporary Christianity

Sources quoted here are *The Reign of Elizabeth* by J.R. Black; *Henry VIII and Luther* by Erwin Doernberg; and *The Reformation* by Will Durant (Volume 6 of *The Story of Civilization*). Other major sources for this chapter are *The Elizabethan Renaissance* by A.L. Rowse; "The Enduring Relevance of Martin Luther 500 Years After His Birth," by Jaroslav Pelikan in the *New York Times Magazine*, and discussions with Professor William Holland of Middle Tennessee State Univesity.

Chapter 3: John Calvin and the Institutes

Sources quoted here are *The Reformation* by Will Durant, *Calvin: Institutes of the Christian Religion*, John T. McNeill, ed.; and *Calvin Against Himself* by Suzanne Selinger.

Chapter 4: A Mighty Fortress: Martin Luther as Songwriter

Sources quoted in this chapter are "When You Sing Next Sunday, Thank Luther," by Richard D. Dinwiddie; *Luther and Music* by Paul Nettl; *The Handbook to the Lutheran Hymnal* by W. G. Pollack; and *Christian Singers of Germany* by Catherine Winkworth. The songs came from *A Treasury of Hymns,* edited by Marie Leiper and Henry W. Simon. Other sources include *Readings in Luther for Laymen* by Charles S. Anderson; *Music in the History of the Western Church* by Edward Dickinson, *Luther: An Experiment in Biography* by H.G. Haile, and "How One Man's Pen Changed the World," by Henry Zecher.

Chapter 5: First Seeds: Gospel Music in America

Quotes in this chapter come from the two-volume work, *American Hymns Old and New* by Albert Christ-Janer, Charles W. Hughes, and Carleton Sprague; *Early New England Psalmody* by Hamilton C. Macdougal; "Mainstreams and Backwaters in American Psalmody" and "Music of the American Revolution," by Richard Crawford; "White Spirituals from the Sacred Harp," by Allen Lomax; and *Americans and Their Songs* by Frank Luther. Other sources consulted include *The Gospel in Hymns* by Albert Bailey, *The Oxford History of the American People* by Samuel Eliot Morison, and conversations with Professor William Beasley at Middle Tennessee State University.

NOTES

Chapter 6: Isaac Watts

The only source quoted directly in this chapter is *The Gospel in Hymns* by Albert Bailey. Other sources include *Make a Joyful Noise Unto the Lord* by Susan S. Tamke and *A Treasury of Hymns*, edited by Leiper and Simon.

Chapter 7: The Wesleys

Sources quoted here are *The Gospel in Hymns* by Bailey, "Two Brothers..." by Richard Dinwiddie, and *A Treasury of Hymns* edited by Marie Leiper and Henry W. Simon.

Chapter 8: The Secular Influence

Sources quoted here come from *Yesterdays* by Charles Hamm; *Francis Hopkinson and James Lyon* by Oscar G. T. Sonneck; *American Hymns Old and New* by Christ-Janer, Hughes, and Sprague; "Mainstreams and Backwaters in Americand Psalmody" (Jacket notes to *Make a Joyful Noise*, New World Records) and "Music of the American Revolution" (Jacket notes for *The Birth of Liberty*, New World Records) by Richard Crawford; *Early New England Psalmody* by Hamilton C. Macdougal; *Americans and Their Songs* by Frank Luther; "White Spirituals from the Sacred Harp" (Jacket notes for *White Spirituals from the Sacred Harp*, New World) by Alan Lomax; and *Doo-Dah! Stephen Foster and the Rise of American Popular Culture* by Ken Emerson.

Chapter 9: Give Me That Old Time Religion

Quotes are from *White and Negro Spirituals* by George Pullen Jackson and *American Hymns Old and New* by Christ-Janer et. al.

Chapter 10: Black Gospel and the Fisk Jubilee Singers

Important sources for this chapter include *The Story of the Jubilee Singers* by J.B.T. Marsh; *Dark Midnight When I Rise: The Story of the Jubilee Singers Who Introduced the World to the Music of Black America* by Andrew Ward; *Pilgrims in Our Own Land* by Martin Marty; *The Gospel Sound* by Tony Heilbut; *Sing Your Heart Out, Country Boy* by Dorothy Horstman; *Some Aspects of the Religious Music of the United*

States Negro by George R. Ricks; the books by George Pullen Jackson, especially *Spiritual Folk Songs of Early America* and *White and Negro Spirituals*; and *How Sweet the Sound: The Golden Age of Gospel* by Horace Boyer.

Chapter 11: The Great Revival

Sources quoted come from *Pilgrims in Our Own Land* by Martin Marty, *The General Next to God* by Richard Collins, and *My Life and the Story of the Hymns* by Ira Sankey.

Chapter 12: The Pentecostal and Holiness Movements

Major sources include *Vision of the Disinhereited: The Making of American Pentecostalism* by Robert Anderson, *Bright Wind of the Spirit: Pentecostalims Today* by Steve Durasoff, "White Urban Hymnody," by Harry Eskew, and *The Holiness Pentecostal Movement* by Vinson Synan.

Chapter 13: Billy Sunday and Homer Rodeheaver

The source quoted directly here is *Billy Sunday Was His Real Name* by William G. McLoughlin. Other important sources include *Vision of the Disinherited: The Making of American Pentecostalism* by Robert Anderson, *Bright Wind of the Spirit: Pentecostalims Today* by Steve Durasoff, "White Urban Hymnody," by Harry Eskew, and *The Holiness Pentecostal Movement* by Vincson Synan.

Chapter 14: The Rise of Radio and Records

Important sources for this chapter include *The Electric Church* by Ben Armstrong; *American Popular Song* by Alec Wilder; *From Tin Foil to Stereo* by Oliver Read and Walter L. Welch; *Edison: Inventing the Century* by Neil Baldwin; *Empire of the Air* by Tom Lewis; the three volume history of broadcasting by Eric Barnouw; and a number of histories of blues and country music, especially *Country Music U.S.A.* by Bill Malone and books by Paul Oliver.

NOTES

Chapter 15: The Roots of Black Gospel

Critical sources for this chapter include *The Gospel Sound* by Tony Heilbut; *The Rise of Gospel Blues: The Music of Thomas Dorsey in the Urban Church* by Michael W. Harris; *Sing Your Heart Out Country Boy* by Dorothy Horstman; *Some Aspects of the Religious Music of the United States Negro* by George R. Ricks; the books by George Pullen Jackson; *How Sweet the Sound: The Golden Age of Gospel* by Horace Boyer; *Blues Off the Record* by Paul Oliver; and *The History of the Blues* by Francis Davis.

Chpater 16: The Beginnings of Southern Gospel

Sources quoted directly here are "Gospel Boogie: White Southern Gospel Music in Transition" and "Columbia Records and Old-Time Music," both by Charles Woolf. Other major sources include *Wings of a Dove* by Lois Blackwell, conversations with Charles Wolfe, and an unpublished manuscript by James Goff on Southern Gospel music.

Chapter 17: Black Gospel During the 1930s

Sources important for this chapter include *The Gospel Sound* by Tony Heilbut; *The Rise of Gospel Blues: The Music of Thomas Dorsey in the Urban Church* by Michael W. Harris; *Just Mahalia, Baby* by Laurraine Goreau; *Sing Your Heart Out Country Boy* by Dorothy Horstman; *How Sweet the Sound: The Golden Age of Gospel* by Horace Boyer; and *The History of the Blues* by Francis Davis.

Chapter 18: Southern Gospel Music During the Depression

Significant sources used in this chapter include "Gospel Boogie: White Southern Gospel Music in Transition" and "Columbia Records and Old-Time Music," both by Charles Woolf; *Wings of a Dove* by Lois Blackwell and conversations with Charles Wolfe; an unpublished manscript on Southern Gospel by James Goff; *Above All* by Kree Jack Racine; *The James Blackwood Story* by James Blackwood, *Let The Song Go On* by Paula Becker, and conversations with Brock Speer, and James Blackwood.

Chapter 19: Gospel in the Mainstream After World War II

Sources for this chapter include *The Fifties* by David Halberstam; *No Ordinary Time* by Doris Kearns Goodwin; *Rich Relations: The American Occupation of Britain, 1942-1945* by David Reynolds; *In the Time of the Americans: FDR, Truman, Eisenhower, Marshall, MacArthur—The Generation That Changed America's Role in the World* by David Fromkin; and *Then Sings My Soul* by George Beverly Shea and Fred Bauer. I also did an interview with Mr. Shea published in *Music City News* in May 1985.

Chater 20: Southern Gospel After World War II

Sources used in this chapter include *Wings of a Dove* by Lois Blackwell; an unpublished manscript on Southern Gospel by James Goff; *No Ordinary Time* by Doris Kearns Goodwin; *Above All* by Kree Jack Racine; *The James Blackwood Story* by James Blackwood, *Let The Song Go On* by Paula Becker, and conversations with Charles Wolfe, Brock Speer, and James Blackwood.

Chapter 21: Black Gospel After World War II

Sources important for this chapter include *The Gospel Sound* by Tony Heilbut; *The Rise of Gospel Blues: The Music of Thomas Dorsey in the Urban Church* by Michael W. Harris; *Just Mahalia, Baby* by Laurraine Goreau; *How Sweet the Sound: The Golden Age of Gospel* by Horace Boyer; *Sweet Soul Music* by Peter Guralnick as well as the two-volume biography of Elvis Presley that Guralnick authored; *The Fifties* by David Halberstam; *The Way We Never Were: American Families and the Nostalgia Trap* and *The Way We Really Are: Coming To Terms With America's Changing Families* by Stephanie Coontz; *Elvis: The Final Years* by Jerry Hopkins; "Three Chords and a Cloud of Dust" by Bob Terrell in *The Singing News*, and an interview with J.D. Sumner in January 1988 not published previously. Other major sources include an interview with Joe Moscheo done for the article "The Imperials: Building a Musical Bridge."

Chapter 23: Black Gospel and Civil Rights: Fanny Lou Hamer

Sources quoted in this chapter are "Stepping Out Into Freedom: The Life of Fanny Lou Hamer" and "Prophet of Hope for the Sick and Tired," both by Danny Collum, and "Voice of Calm," by Charles McLaurin in *Sojourners* magazine; excerpts from a personal interview conducted with James Cleveland and published as "James Cleveland on Expanding Gospel's Audience" in *Record World*, November 11, 1978. Other major sources include *The Gospel Sound* by Tony Heilbut, *The Greening of America* by Charles Reich, *Parting the Waters* and *Pillar of Fire* by Taylor Branch, *Speak Now Against The Day* by John Egerton, *How Sweet the Sound* by Horace Boyer, books on *Billboard* charts by Joel Whitburn, the article "GMWA: Where 'Everybody is Somebody'" published in *Record World* Oct. 1, 1977, and conversations with Fred Mendelsohn, president of Savoy Records.

Chapter 24: The 1960s: Peace, Love, and Music

The book quoted in this chapter is *The Greening of America* by Charles Reich. Information on the Billboard charts came from Joel Whitburn's *Top Pop Singles 1955-1990* and *The Billboard Book of Top 40 Albums* by Joel Whitburn. Information on Gold and Platinum albums came from *The Billboard Book of Gold and Platinum Records* by Adam White.

Chapter 25: Gospel Music in the 1960s

Major sources for this chapter are *Why Should The Devil Have All the Good Music* by Paul Baker, the books by Joel Whitburn on the *Billboard* charts, "Gold and Platinum Awards" from the RIAA, and an interview with Bill Gaither in June 1986.

Chapter 26: Southern Gospel in the 1960s and 1970s

The quotes from the Cathedrals in this chapter came from a personal interview with Glen Payne and George Younce in 1982 and published in a record company biography for them as well as "The Cathedrals: At the Top of Today's Southern Gospel," in *Rejoice*; I have also used quotes on the Florida Boys from a personal interview with Les Beasley, October 1987, and an interview with Jim Hamill,

September 1987. Other sources quoted are "The Kingsmen ... A Spiritual Explosion" by Jeanne Coffman in *The Singing News* and "Three Chords and a Cloud of Dust: The Jim Hamill Story," by Bob Terrell in *The Singing News*. Other major sources include "Eldridge Fox Receives Norcross Award," by Bob Terrell in *The Singing News* and conversations with Marvin Norcross. The section on the Imperials came from an article I wrote for *Contemporary Christian Music* in February 1980, "The Imperials: Building a Musical Bridge." Also important were the biographies of Elvis Presley by Peter Guralnick and Jerry Hopkins and the interview with J.D. Sumner, *Elvis: The Final Years* by Jerry Hopkins, and an interview with Joe Moscheo done for the article "The Imperials: Building a Musical Bridge."

Chapter 27: The Catholics

Quotes in this chapter are from *Music in the History of the Western Church* by Edward Dickinson. Other sources include *Pilgrims in Their Own Land* by Martin Marty, and a personal interview with Ray Bruno of the North American Litergy Resources published as "The New Movement in Catholic Music" and "St. Louis Jesuits: Music With Mass Appeal," both in *Contemporary Christian Music*.

Chapter 28: Contemporary Christian Music: The Early Years

Major sources for this chapter are *Why Should The Devil Have All the Good Music* by Paul Baker, the books by Joel Whitburn on the *Billboard* charts; "Gold and Platinum Awards" from the RIAA; "The New Rebel Cry: Jesus is Coming!" in *Time*, an interview with Larry Norman conducted in 1978; conversations with Paul Baker, Bill Gaither, and John Styll and my biography on Sandi Patti.

Chapter 29: Contemporary Christian Music: Part Two

The information on Keith Green came from a number of article published in *Contemporary Christian Music*. Particulary helpful was the special issue devoted to Green in September 1982. Other major sources for this chapter are the same as for Chapter 28.

NOTES

Chapter 30: Black Gospel and James Cleveland

Major sources include excerpts from a personal interview conducted with James Cleveland and published as "James Cleveland on Expanding Gospel's Audience," in *Record World*. Other major sources include *The Gospel Sound* by Tony Heilbut; *Gospel Blues* by Michael Harris; the article "GMWA: Where 'Everybody is Somebody'," published in *Record World*; and conversations with Fred Mendelsohn, president of Savoy Records.

Chapter 31: Televangelists and Jimmy Swaggart

Sources quoted in this chapter are *To Cross a River* by Jimmy Swaggart with Robert Paul Lamb; *Hellfire* by Nick Tosches; "Brother Swaggart, Here's My Question," from *The Evangelist* (Feb. 1988 Vol. 20 No. 3: 9-10); "Gospel TV," from *Time* magazine; the Gallup Report and *The Search For America's Faith* by George Gallup, Jr. and David Poling; *Religious Television: An American Experience* by Peter G. Horsfield; and interviews with executives with the Christian Bookseller's Association.

Chapter 32: Contemporary Christian Music & The Reagan Revolution

The major sources for this chapter came from research while doing my biography of Sandi Patti, published by Doubleday in 1988.

Chapter 33: CCM Comes Age to Age

Quotes in this chapter came from several interviews done with Amy Grant and published in "Amy Grant," in *Contemporary Christian Music* in June 1979 and "Amy Grant—Reaching Out," published in *Christian Life* in June 1981. The information on Michael W. Smith came from interviews done with him, and an article by Bill Littleton in *CCM*, "Michael W. Smith." Information on Sandi Patti came from research for the book I did on her, *Sandi Patti: The Voice of Gospel*.

Chapter 34: Contemporary Christian Music & 1984

The information on Petra came from a number of article written about them in *CCM* and from a personal interview I did in 1987.

Chapter 35: The Christian Culture in 1985

Again, the bulk of this information is based on research done for my biography of Sandi Patti. Major sources include the Gallup Report and *The Search For America's Faith* by George Gallup, Jr. and David Poling and interviews with the Christian Bookseller's Association.

Chapter 36: Marketing the Movement: The Recording Labels

Quotes from Jarrell McCracken came from an interview published in *Record World*, "Jarrell McCracken on Spreading the Word." Quotes from Marvin Norcross came from an interview in March, 1982, shortly before he died. Major sources for the Benson Company section came from interviews with John T. Benson III and Bob Benson, both published in *Record World*. Another major source was "The Benson Company: 75 Years of Growth," written by the company and published in *Record World*. Quotes from Billy Ray Hearn came from an interview published in *Record World*, "Billy Ray Hearn on Sparrow's Takeoff." I have also had a number of conversations and interviews with Mr. Hearn in the ensuing years which have been invaluable. Most of the information on the Gospel Music Association in this chapter came from an interview with Don Butler, published in *Record World*.

Chapter 37: Christian and Gospel Music in the 1990s

The information in this chapter came from a number of articles in *Contemporary Christian Music* and *Billboard*, especially the "Spotlights" that *Billboard* does on both Gospel and Christian music. I am also indebted to Bill Hearn, head of EMI Christian for supplying me with a number of W.O.W. CDs that highlight contemporary Christian music.

Conclusion

The book quoted in this chapter is *Apostles of Rock: The Splintered World of Contemporary Christian Music* by Jay Howard and John Streck.

APPENDIX A

DOVE AWARDS

1969: 1st Annual Dove Awards

Song of the Year: "Jesus Is Coming Soon" written by R.E. Winsett; Publisher: R.E. Winsett Music, SESAC

Songwriter of the Year: Bill Gaither

Male Vocalist of the Year: James Blackwood

Female Vocalist of the Year: Vestal Goodman

Male Group of the Year: Imperials

Mixed Group of the Year: Speer Family

Album of the Year: *It's Happening* by The Oak Ridge Boys (Producer: Bob MacKenzie; Label: HeartWarming)

Instrumentalist: Dwayne Friend

Album Jacket: *It's Happening* by Oak Ridge Boys; Label: HeartWarming

Television Program: *Gospel Jubilee* hosted by The Florida Boys

D.J. of the Year: J.G. Whitfield

1970: 2nd Annual Dove Awards

Song of the Year: "The Night Before Easter" written by Don Sumner and Dwayne Friend; Publisher: Gospel Quartet Music, SESAC

Songwriter of the Year: Bill Gaither

Male Vocalist of the Year: James Blackwood

Female Vocalist of the Year: Ann Downing

Male Group of the Year: Oak Ridge Boys

Mixed Group of the Year: Speer Family

Most Promising New Gospel Talent: Four Gallileans

Album of the Year: *Fill My Cup, Lord* by The Blackwood Brothers (Producer: Darol Rice; Label: RCA Victor)

Instrumentalist: Dwayne Friend

Backliner Notes: Mrs. Jake Hess on *Ain't That Beautiful Singin'* by Jake Hess

Cover Photo Or Cover Art: Bill Grine for *This Is My Valley* by The Rambos

Graphic Layout And Design: Jerry Goff for *Thrasher Brothers At Fantastic Caverns* by The Thrasher Brothers

Television Program: *Gospel Jubilee* hosted by The Florida Boys

D.J. of the Year: J.G. Whitfield

1971: 3rd Annual Dove Awards
NO AWARDS

1972: 4th Annual Dove Awards
Song of the Year: "The Lighthouse" written by Ron Hinson; Publisher: Journey Music, BMI

Songwriter of the Year: Bill Gaither

Male Vocalist of the Year: James Blackwood

Female Vocalist of the Year: Sue Chenault

Male Group of the Year: Oak Ridge Boys

Mixed Group of the Year: Speer Family

Most Promising New Gospel Talent: London Paris & The Apostles

Album of the Year: *Light* by The Oak Ridge Boys (Producer: Bob MacKenzie; Label: HeartWarming)

Instrumentalist: Tony Brown

Backliner Notes: Johnny Cash on *Light* by The Oak Ridge Boys

Cover Photo or Cover Art: Bill Grine for *Street Gospel* by The Oak Ridge Boys

Graphic Layout and Design: Ace Lehman for *L-O-V-E Love* by The Blackwood Brothers

Television Program: *Gospel Jubilee* hosted by The Florida Boys

D.J. of the Year: J.G. Whitfield

1973: 5th Annual Dove Awards
Song of the Year: "Why Me, Lord?" written by Kris Kristofferson; Publisher: Resaca Music, BMI

Songwriter of the Year: Bill Gaither

Male Vocalist of the Year: James Blackwood

Female Vocalist of the Year: Sue Chenault

Male Group of the Year: Blackwood Brothers

Mixed Group of the Year: Speer Family

Album of the Year: *Street Gospel* by The Oak Ridge Boys (Producer: Bob MacKenzie; Label: HeartWarming)

Instrumentalist: Henry Slaughter

Backliner Notes: Eddie Miller on *Release Me* by The Blackwood Brothers

Cover Photo or Cover Art: NO AWARD

Graphic Layout and Design: Bob McConnell for *Street Gospel* by The Oak Ridge Boys

Television Program: *Gospel Jubilee* hosted by The Florida Boys

D.J. of the Year: Sid Hughes

1974: 6th Annual Dove Awards

Song of the Year: "Because He Lives" written by Bill Gaither; Publisher: Gaither Music, ASCAP

Songwriter of the Year: Bill Gaither

Male Vocalist of the Year: James Blackwood

Female Vocalist of the Year: Sue Chenault Dodge

Male Group of the Year: Blackwood Brothers

Mixed Group of the Year: Speer Family

Associate Membership Award: Group: Blackwood Brothers

Album of the Year: *Big and Live* by The Kingsmen Quartet (Producer: Marvin Norcross; Label: Canaan)

Instrumentalist: Henry Slaughter

Backliner Notes: Don Butler on *On Stage* by The Blackwood Brothers

Cover Photo Or Cover Art: Hope Powell for *On Stage* by The Blackwood Brothers

Graphic Layout and Design: Charles Hooper for *On Stage* by The Blackwood Brothers

Television Program: *Gospel Jubilee* hosted by The Florida Boys

D.J. of the Year: Jim Black

1975: 7th Annual Dove Awards

Song of the Year: "One Day at a Time" written by Marijohn Wilkin and Kris Kristofferson; Publisher: Buckhorn Music, BMI

Songwriter of the Year: Bill Gaither

Male Vocalist of the Year: James Blackwood

Female Vocalist of the Year: Jeanne Johnson

Male Group of the Year: Imperials

Mixed Group of the Year: Speer Family

Associate Membership Award: Song: "Statue of Liberty" by Neil Enloe (Publisher: Neil Enloe Music, BMI)

Album of the Year: *I Just Feel Like Something Good Is About to Happen* by The Speer Family (Producer: Bob MacKenzie; Label: HeartWarming)

Instrumentalist: Henry Slaughter

Backliner Notes: Wendy Bagwell on *Bust Out Laffin'* by Wendy Bagwell and The Sunliters

Cover Photo or Cover Art: Spears Photo for *There He Goes* by the Blackwood Brothers

Graphic Layout and Design: Bob McConnell for *Praise Him...Live* by The Downings

Album by a Secular Artist: *Sunday Morning with Charley Pride* by Charley Pride (Producer: Jerry Bradley; Label: RCA)

Television Program: *Gospel Jubilee* hosted by The Florida Boys

D.J. of the Year: Jim Black

1976: 8th Annual Dove Awards

Song of the Year: "Statue of Liberty" written by Neil Enloe; Publisher: Enloe Music, BMI

Songwriter of the Year: Bill Gaither

Male Vocalist of the Year: Johnny Cook

Female Vocalist of the Year: Joy McGuire

Male Group of the Year: Imperials

Mixed Group of the Year: Speer Family

Associate Membership Award: Group: Blackwood Brothers

Southern Gospel Album: *Between The Cross and Heaven* by The Speer Family (Producer: Joe Huffman; Label: HeartWarming)

Inspirational Album: *Jesus, We Just Want to Thank You* by The Bill Gaither Trio (Producer: Bob MacKenzie; Label: HeartWarming)

Pop/Contemporary Album: *No Shortage* by The Imperials (Producers: Bob MacKenzie and Gary Paxton; Label: Impact)

Instrumentalist: Henry Slaughter

Backliner Notes: Sylvia Mays on *Just A Little Talk with Jesus* by The Cleavant Derricks Family

Cover Photo or Cover Art: Bill Barnes for *Old Fashion, Down Home, Hand Clappin', Foot Stomping, Southern Style Gospel Quartet* by The Oak Ridge Boys

Graphic Layout and Design: Bob McConnell for *No Shortage* by The Imperials

Album by a Secular Artist: *Home Where I Belong* by B. J. Thomas (Producer: Chris Christian; Label: Myrrh)

Television Program: *PTL Club* hosted by Jim and Tammy Bakker

D.J. of the Year: Sid Hughes

1977: 9th Annual Dove Awards

Song of the Year: "Learning to Lean" written by John Stallings; Publisher: HeartWarming Music, BMI

Songwriter of the Year: Bill Gaither

Male Vocalist of the Year: James Blackwood

Female Vocalist of the Year: Evie Tornquist

Male Group of the Year: Cathedral Quartet

Mixed Group of the Year: Speer Family

Associate Membership Award: Group: Blackwood Brothers

Southern Gospel Album: *Then...and Now* by The Cathedral Quartet
(Producer: Ken Harding; Label: Canaan)

Inspirational Album: *Ovation* by The Couriers (Producer: Jesse Peterson;
Label: Tempo)

Pop/Contemporary Album: *Reba...Lady* by Reba Rambo Gardner
(Producer: Phil Johnson; Label: Greentree)

Soul/Black Gospel Album: *This Is Another Day* by Andrae Crouch and The
Disciples (Producer: Bill Maxwell; Label: Light)

Instrumentalist: Henry Slaughter

Backliner Notes: Joe Huffman on *Cornerstone* by The Speers

Cover Photo or Cover Art: Roy Tremble for *Then...and Now* by The
Cathedral Quartet

Graphic Layout and Design: Dennis Hill for *Then...and Now* by The
Cathedral Quartet

Album by a Secular Artist: *First Class* by The Boones (Producer: Chris
Christian; Label: Lamb & Lion)

Television Program: *Gospel Jubilee* hosted by The Florida Boys

D.J. of the Year: Sid Hughes

1978: 10th Annual Dove Awards

Song of the Year: "Rise Again" written by Dallas Holm; Publisher:
Dimension Music, SESAC

Songwriter of the Year: Dallas Holm

Male Vocalist of the Year: Dallas Holm

Female Vocalist of the Year: Evie Tornquist

Male Group of the Year: Imperials

Mixed Group of the Year: Dallas Holm and Praise

Associate Membership Award: Song: "Rise Again" by Dallas Holm
(Publisher: Dimension Music, SESAC)

Southern Gospel Album: *Kingsmen Live in Chattanooga* by The Kingsmen
(Producers: Joe Huffman and Eldridge Fox; Label: HeartWarming)

Inspirational Album: *Pilgrim's Progress* by The Bill Gaither Trio (Producers:
Bob MacKenzie and John W. Thompson; Label: Impact)

Pop/Contemporary Album: *Transformation* by The Cruse Family
(Producer: Ken Harding; Label: Canaan)

Soul/Black Gospel Album: *Live in London* by Andrae Crouch and The
Disciples (Producers: Bill Maxwell and Andrae Crouch; Label: Light)

Instrumentalist: Dino Kartsonakis

Backliner Notes: Joe and Nancy Cruse on *Transformation* by The Cruse
Family

Cover Photo or Cover Art: Robert August for *Live in London* by Andrae

Crouch & The Disciples

Graphic Layout and Design: Bob McConnell for *Grand Opening* by Andrus, Blackwood & Company

Album by a Secular Artist: *Slow Train Coming* by Bob Dylan (Producers: Jerry Wexler and Barry Beckett; Label: Columbia)

Television Program: *Hemphill Family Time* hosted by The Hemphills

D.J. of the Year: Sid Hughes

1979: NONE

1980: 11th Annual Dove Awards

Song of the Year: "He's Alive" written by Don Francisco; Publisher: New Pax Music, BMI

Songwriter of the Year: Don Francisco

Male Vocalist of the Year: Dallas Holm

Female Vocalist of the Year: Cynthia Clawson

Male Group of the Year: Imperials

Mixed Group of the Year: Bill Gaither Trio

Southern Gospel Album: *From Out of the Past* by The Kingsmen (Producers: Joe Huffman and Eldridge Fox; Label: HeartWarming)

Inspirational Album: *Special Delivery* by Doug Oldham (Producer: Joe Huffman; Label: Impact)

Pop/Contemporary Album: *All That Matters* by Dallas Holm and Praise (Producer: Phil Johnson; Label: Greentree)

Soul/Black Gospel Album: *Love Alive II* by Walter Hawkins and The Love Center Choir (Producer: Walter Hawkins; Label: Light)

Instrumentalist: Dino Kartsonakis

Backliner Notes: Merlin Littlefield on *Breakout* by The Mercy River Boys

Cover Photo or Cover Art: Mike Borum for *You Make It Rain For Me* by Rusty Goodman

Graphic Layout and Design: Bob McConnell for *Special Delivery* by Doug Oldham

Album by a Secular Artist: *With My Song* by Debby Boone (Producer: Brown Bannister; Label: Lamb & Lion)

1981: 12th Annual Dove Awards

Song of the Year: "Praise The Lord" written by Brown Bannister and Mike Hudson; Publishers: Home Sweet Home Music, BMI, and Bug and Bear Music, ASCAP

Songwriter of the Year: Gary Chapman

Male Vocalist of the Year: Russ Taff

Female Vocalist of the Year: Cynthia Clawson

Male Group of the Year: Imperials

Artist of the Year: Imperials

Southern Gospel Album: *Workin'* by The Hemphills (Producer: Jerry Crutchfield; Label: HeartWarming)

Inspirational Album: *You're Welcome Here* by Cynthia Clawson (Producer: JEN Productions; Label: Triangle)

Pop/Contemporary Album: *One More Song for You* by The Imperials (Producer: Michael Omartian; Label: DaySpring)

Inspirational Black Gospel Album: *Rejoice* by Shirley Caesar (Producers: Tony Brown and Ken Harding; Label: Myrrh)

Contemporary Gospel Album: *Give Me More Love In My Heart* by Larnelle Harris (Producers: Howard McCrary and Paul Johnson; Label: Benson)

Traditional Gospel Album: *Incredible* by Teddy Huffam and The Gems (Producer: Ken Harding; Label: Canaan)

Instrumentalist: Dino Kartsonakis

Praise and Worship Album: *The Lord's Prayer* by various artists (Producer: Dony McGuire; Label: Light)

Children's Music Album: *Very Best of the Very Best For Kids* (Producer: Robert MacKenzie; Label: Word)

Musical Album: *The Messiah* by Billy Ray Hearn and Irving Martin (Label: Sparrow)

Recorded Music Packaging: Bill Barnes and Clark Thomas for You're Welcome Here by Cynthia Clawson

Album by a Secular Artist: *Amazing Grace* by B.J. Thomas (Producer: Pete Drake; Label: Myrrh)

1982: 13th Annual Dove Awards

Song of the Year: "We Shall Behold Him" written by Dottie Rambo; Publisher: John T. Benson Publishing, ASCAP

Songwriter of the Year: Dottie Rambo

Male Vocalist of the Year: Russ Taff

Female Vocalist of the Year: Sandi Patti

Group of the Year: Imperials

Artist of the Year: Sandi Patti

Southern Gospel Album: *One Step Closer* by The Rex Nelon Singers (Producer: Ken Harding; Label: Canaan)

Inspirational Album: *Joni's Song* by Joni Eareckson (Producer: Kurt Kaiser; Label: Word)

Pop/Contemporary Album: *Priority* by The Imperials (Producer: Michael Omartian; Label: DaySpring)

Inspirational Black Gospel Album: *Edwin Hawkins Live: Oakland Symphony Orchestra and Edwin Hawkins* (Producer: Gil Askey; Label: Myrrh)

Contemporary Gospel Album: *Walter Hawkins & Family Live* by The

Walter Hawkins Family (Producer: Walter Hawkins; Label: Light)

Traditional Gospel Album: *Go* by Shirley Caesar (Producers: Tony Brown and Shirley Caesar; Label: Myrrh)

Instrumentalist: Dino Kartsonakis

Praise and Worship Album: *Exaltation* (Producer: Ronn Huff; Label: Benson)

Children's Music Album: *Kids Under Construction* (Producers: Robert MacKenzie and Ronn Huff; Label: Paragon)

Musical Album: *The Love Story* by Phil Brower and Don Wyrtzen (Label: New Dawn)

Recorded Music Packaging: Bill Barnes, Matt Barnes, Pat Barnes for Finest Hour by Cynthia Clawson

Album by a Secular Artist: *He Set My Life to Music* by Barbara Mandrell (Producer: Tom Collins; Label: MCA)

1983: 14th Annual Dove Awards

Song of the Year: "El Shaddai" written by Michael Card and John Thompson; Publisher: Whole Armor Publishing, ASCAP

Songwriter of the Year: Michael Card

Male Vocalist of the Year: Larnelle Harris

Female Vocalist of the Year: Sandi Patti

Group of the Year: Imperials

Artist of the Year: Amy Grant

Southern Gospel Album: *Feeling At Home* by The Rex Nelon Singers (Producer: Ken Harding; Label: Canaan)

Inspirational Album: *Lift Up the Lord* by Sandi Patti (Producer: Greg Nelson; Label: Impact)

Pop/Contemporary Album: *Age to Age* by Amy Grant (Producer: Brown Bannister; Label: Myrrh)

Inspirational Black Gospel Album: *Touch Me Lord* by Larnelle Harris (Producer: Greg Nelson; Label: Impact)

Contemporary Gospel Album: *I'll Never Stop Loving You* by Leon Patillo (Producer: Skip Konte; Label: Myrrh)

Traditional Gospel Album: *Precious Lord* by Al Green (Producer: Al Green; Label: Myrrh)

Instrumentalist: Dino Kartsonakis

Praise and Worship Album: *Light Eternal* (Producer: Billy Ray Hearn; Label: Birdwing)

Children's Music Album: *Lullabies and Nursery Rhymes* (Producers: Tony Salerno and Fletch Wiley; Label: Birdwing)

Musical Album: *The Day He Wore My Crown* by David T. Clydesdale (Label: Impact)

Recorded Music Packaging: Dennis Hill and Michael Borum for *Age to Age* by Amy Grant

Album by a Secular Artist: *Surrender* by Debbie Boone (Producer: Brown Bannister; Label: Lamb & Lion)

1984: 15th Annual Dove Awards

Song of the Year: "More than Wonderful" written by Lanny Wolfe; Publisher: Lanny Wolfe Music, ASCAP

Songwriter of the Year: Lanny Wolfe

Male Vocalist of the Year: Russ Taff

Female Vocalist of the Year: Sandi Patti

Group of the Year: NO AWARD

Artist of the Year: Sandi Patti

Southern Gospel Album: *We Shall Behold the King* by The Rex Nelon Singers (Producer: Ken Harding; Label: Canaan)

Inspirational Album: *More Than Wonderful* by Sandi Patti (Producers: David Clydesdale, Greg Nelson, and Sandi Patti Helvering; Label: Impact)

Pop/Contemporary Album: *Side By Side* by The Imperials (Producers: Keith Thomas and Neal Joseph; Label: DaySpring)

Contemporary Gospel Album: *Come Together* by Bobby Jones and New Life (Producer: Tony Brown; Label: Myrrh)

Traditional Gospel Album: *We Sing Praises* by Sandra Crouch (Producer: Sandra Crouch; Label: Light)

Instrumentalist: Phil Driscoll

Praise and Worship Album: *Celebrate the Joy* (Producer: David T. Clydesdale; Label: Impact)

Children's Music Album: *Music Machine II* (Producers: Fletch Wiley, Tony Salerno, and Ron Kreuger; Label: Birdwing)

Musical Album: *Dreamer* by Cam Floria (Label: Christian Artists)

Recorded Music Packaging: Dennis Hill, Bill Farrell, and Michael Borum for *A Christmas Album* by Amy Grant

Album by a Secular Artist: *You Were Loving Me* by Lulu Roman Smith (Producer: Gary McSpadden; Label: Canaan)

1985: 16th Annual Dove Awards

Song of the Year: "Upon This Rock" written by Gloria Gaither and Dony McGuire; Publishers: Gaither Music, It's-N-Me Music, and Lexicon Music; ASCAP

Songwriter of the Year: Michael W. Smith

Male Vocalist of the Year: Steve Green

Female Vocalist of the Year: Sandi Patti

Artist of the Year: Sandi Patti

Southern Gospel Album: *The Best Of and a Whole Lot More* by The Rex Nelon Singers (Producer: Ken Harding; Label: Canaan)

Inspirational Album: *Songs From the Heart* by Sandi Patti (Producers: Greg Nelson and Sandi Patti Helvering; Label: Impact)

Pop/Contemporary Album: *Straight Ahead* by Amy Grant (Producer: Brown Bannister; Label: Myrrh)

Contemporary Gospel Album: *No Time To Lose* by Andrae Crouch (Producer: Bill Maxwell; Label: Light)

Traditional Gospel Album: *Sailin'* by Shirley Caesar (Producers: Sanchez Harley, Shirley Caesar, and David Lehman; Label: Myrrh)

Instrumentalist: Phil Driscoll

Praise and Worship Album: *The Praise in Us* (Producer: Neal Joseph; Label: Myrrh)

Children's Music Album: *Then New Songs With Kids For Kids About Life* (Producer: Ron W. Griffin; Label: Word)

Musical Album: *The Race Is On* by Steve Taylor (Label: Word)

Recorded Music Packaging: Eddie Yip, Stan Evenson, and Don Putnam for *Kingdom of Love* by Scott Wesley Brown

Album by a Secular Artist: *No More Night* by Glen Campbell (Producers: Glen Campbell and Ken Harding; Label: Word)

1986: 17th Annual Dove Awards

Song of the Year: "Via Dolorosa" written by Billy Sprague and Niles Borop; Publishers: Meadowgreen and Word Music, ASCAP

Songwriter of the Year: Gloria Gaither

Male Vocalist of the Year: Larnelle Harris

Female Vocalist of the Year: Sandi Patti

Artist of the Year: Amy Grant

Southern Gospel Album: *Excited* by The Hemphills (Producer: Wayne Hilton and Trent Hemphill; Label: HeartWarming)

Inspirational Album: *I've Just Seen Jesus* by Larnelle Harris (Producer: Greg Nelson; Label: Impact)

Pop/Contemporary Album: *Medals* by Russ Taff (Producers: Russ Taff and Jack Puig; Label: Myrrh)

Contemporary Gospel Album: *Let My People Go* by The Winans; (Producer: Marvin Winans; Label: Qwest)

Traditional Gospel Album: *Celebration* by Shirley Caesar (Producers: Dave Lehman and Shirley Caesar; Label: Rejoice)

Instrumentalist: Dino Kartsonakis

Praise and Worship Album: *I've Just Seen Jesus* by William J. Gaither and Randy Vader (Label: Gaither Music Records)

Children's Music Album: *Bullfrogs & Butterflies Part II* (Producer: Tony Salerno; Label: Birdwing)

Musical Album: *Come Celebrate Jesus* by Neal Joseph and Don Marsh (Label: Word)

Recorded Music Packaging: Thomas Ryan, Kent Hunter, and Mark Tucker for *Unguarded* by Amy Grant

1987: 18th Annual Dove Awards

Song of the Year: "How Excellent Is Thy Name" written by Dick & Melodie Tunney and Paul Smith; Publishers: Word Music, Marquis III, Laurel Press, and Pamela Kay Music, ASCAP

Songwriter of the Year: Dick & Melodie Tunney

Male Vocalist of the Year: Steve Green

Female Vocalist of the Year: Sandi Patti

Group of the Year: First Call

Artist of the Year: Sandi Patti

Southern Gospel Album: *The Master Builder* by The Cathedrals (Producers: Bill Gaither and Gary McSpadden; Label: RiverSong)

Inspirational Album: *Morning Like This* by Sandi Patti (Producers: Greg Nelson and Sandi Patti Helvering; Label: Word)

Pop/Contemporary Album: *The Big Picture* by Michael W. Smith (Producers: Michael W. Smith and John Potoker; Label: Reunion)

Contemporary Gospel Album: *Heart & Soul* by The Clark Sisters (Producers: Norbert Putnam and Twinkie Clark; Label: Rejoice)

Traditional Gospel Album: Christmasing by Shirley Caesar (Producer: Norbert Putnam; Label: Rejoice)

Instrumental Album: *Instrument of Praise* by Phil Driscoll (Producers: Lari Goss, Phil Driscoll, and Ken Pennel; Label: Benson)

Praise and Worship Album: *Hymns* by 2nd Chapter of Acts (Producer: Buck Herring; Label: Live Oak)

Children's Music Album: *God Likes Kids* by Joel and Labreeska Hemphill (Label: Benson)

Musical Album: *A Mighty Fortress* by Steve Green, Dwight Liles, and Niles Borop (Label: Sparrow)

Recorded Music Packaging: Buddy Jackson and Mark Tucker for *Don't Wait For the Movie* by White Heart

Short-Form Music Video: "Famine in Their Land" by The Nelons (Directors: Robert Deaton and George Flanigen; Label: Word)

Long-Form Music Video: "Limelight" by Steve Taylor (Producers and Directors: John Anneman and Steve Taylor; Label: Sparrow)

1988: 19th Annual Dove Awards

Song of the Year: "In the Name of the Lord" written by Phil McHugh, Gloria Gaither, and Sandi Patti Helvering; Publishers: River Oaks Music and Sandi's Songs, BMI, Gaither Music, ASCAP

Songwriter of the Year: Larnelle Harris

Male Vocalist of the Year: Larnelle Harris

Female Vocalist of the Year: Sandi Patti

Group of the Year: First Call

Artist of the Year: Sandi Patti

Southern Gospel Album: *Symphony of Praise* by The Cathedrals (Producer: Lari Goss; Label: RiverSong)

Inspirational Album: *The Father Hath Provided* by Larnelle Harris (Producer: Greg Nelson; Label: Benson)

Pop/Contemporary Album: *Watercolour Ponies* by Wayne Watson (Producers: Wayne Watson and Paul Mills; Label: DaySpring)

Contemporary Gospel Album: *Decisions* by The Winans (Producers: Marvin Winans, Barry Hankerson, Carvin Winans, and Michael Winans; Label: Qwest)

Traditional Gospel Album: *One Lord, One Faith, One Baptism* by Aretha Franklin (Producer: Aretha Franklin; Label: Arista)

Country Album: *An Evening Together* by Steve & Annie Chapman (Producers: Ron Griffin and Steve Chapman; Label: Star Song)

Rock Album: *Crack the Sky* by Mylon LeFevre & Broken Heart (Producers: Joe Hardy and Mylon LeFevre; Label: Myrrh)

Instrumental Album: *The Wind & the Wheat* by Phil Keaggy (Producers: Phil Keaggy and Tom Coomes; Label: Colours)

Praise and Worship Album: *The Final Word* by Michael Card (Producer: Norbert Putnam; Label: Sparrow)

Children's Music Album: *Bullfrogs & Butterflies Part III* by The Agapeland Singers & Candle (Producer: Tony Salerno; Label: Sparrow)

Musical Album: *A Son! A Savior!* by Claire Cloninger, Gary Rhodes, and Bob Krogstad (Label: Word)

Recorded Music Packaging: John Summers and Erick Neuhaus for *Peaceful Meditation* by Greg Buchanan

Short-Form Music Video: "Stay For a While" by Amy Grant (Directors: Marc Ball and Jack Cole; Label: Myrrh)

Long-Form Music Video: "The Big Picture Tour Video" by Michael W. Smith (Directors: Brian Shipley and Stephen Bowlby; Label: Reunion)

1989: 20th Annual Dove Awards

Song of the Year: "Friend of a Wounded Heart" written by Wayne Watson and Claire Cloninger; Publisher: Word, ASCAP

Songwriter of the Year: Steven Curtis Chapman

Male Vocalist of the Year: Wayne Watson

Female Vocalist of the Year: Sandi Patti

Group of the Year: Take 6

Artist of the Year: Amy Grant

New Artist of the Year: Take 6

Southern Gospel Album: *Goin' in Style* by The Cathedrals (Producer: Lari Goss; Label: Homeland)

Southern Gospel Recorded Song: "Champion of Love" (Writers: Phil Cross and Caroly Cross; Recorded by The Cathedrals; Label: RiverSong)

Inspirational Album: *Make His Praise Glorious* by Sandi Patti (Producers: Greg Nelson and Sandi Patti Helvering; Label: Word)

Inspirational Recorded Song: "In Heaven's Eyes" written by Phil McHugh; Recorded by Sandi Patti; Label: Word

Pop/Contemporary Album: *Lead Me On* by Amy Grant (Producer: Brown Bannister; Label: Myrrh)

Pop/Contemporary Recorded Song: "His Eyes" written by Steven Curtis Chapman; Recorded by Steven Curtis Chapman (Label: Sparrow)

Contemporary Gospel Album: *Take 6* by Take 6 (Producers: Mark Kibble, Claude V. McKnight III, and Mervyn E. Warren; Label: Reunion)

Contemporary Gospel Recorded Song: "If We Ever" written by Public Domain; Recorded by Take 6; Label: Reunion

Traditional Gospel Album: *Live...In Chicago* by Shirley Caesar (Producers: Bubba Smith and Shirley Caesar; Label: Rejoice)

Traditional Gospel Recorded Song: "Hold My Mule" written by Shirley Caesar Williams; Recorded by Shirley Caesar (Label: Word)

Country Album: *Richest Man in Town* by Bruce Carroll (Producer: Bubba Smith; Label: New Canaan)

Country Recorded Song: "Above and Beyond" written by Bruce Carroll and Paul Smith; Recorded by Bruce Carroll (Label: Word)

Rock Album: *Russ Taff* by Russ Taff, (Producer: Jack Joseph Puig; Label: Myrrh)

Rock Recorded Song: "Won By One" written by Scott Allen, Trent Arganti, Kenneth Bentley, Ben Hewitt, Paul Joseph, Mylon LeFevre, and Joe Hardy; Recorded by Mylon & Broken Heart (Label: Myrrh)

Hard Music Album: *In God We Trust* by Stryper (Producers: Stryper and Michael Lloyd; Label: Enigma)

Hard Music Recorded Song: "In God We Trust" written by Stryper; Recorded by Stryper (Label: Benson)

Instrumental Album: *A Symphony of Praise* by Sandi Patti (Producer: David T. Clydesdale; Label: Word)

Praise and Worship Album: *Praise 10* by The Maranatha! Singers (Producers: Smitty Price and Tom Coomes; Label: Maranatha!)

Children's Music Album: *Wise Guys and Starry Skies* by Kathie Hill (Producers: Kathie Hill and Randall Dennis; Label: Sparrow)

Musical Album: *In His Presence: The Risen King* by Dick and Melodie Tunney (Label: Genevox)

Choral Collection Album: *Sandi Patti Choral Praise* (Producer: Greg Nelson; Publisher: Word Music)

Recorded Music Packaging: Patrick Pollei, Joan Tankersley, and Phillip Dixon for *Russ Taff* by Russ Taff

Short-Form Music Video: "Lead Me On" by Amy Grant (Directors: Tina Silvey and Andrew Doucette; Label: Myrrh)

Long-Form Music Video: "Carman Live...Radically Saved" by Carman (Producers and Directors: Cindy Dupree, George J. Flanigen IV and Robert Deaton; Label: Benson)

1990: 21st Annual Dove Awards

Song of the Year: "Thank You" written by Ray Boltz; Publishers: Gaither Music and Shepherd Boy Music, ASCAP

Songwriter of the Year: Steven Curtis Chapman

Male Vocalist of the Year: Steven Curtis Chapman

Female Vocalist of the Year: Sandi Patti

Group of the Year: BeBe & CeCe Winans

Artist of the Year: Steven Curtis Chapman

New Artist of the Year: David Mullen

Southern Gospel Album: *I Just Started Living* by The Cathedrals (Producer: Lari Goss; Label: Homeland)

Southern Gospel Recorded Song: "I Can See the Hand of God" written by Steven Curtis Chapman and Jim Chapman III: Recorded by The Cathedrals (Label: Homeland)

Inspirational Album: *The Mission* by Steve Green (Producer: Greg Nelson; Label: Sparrow)

Inspirational Recorded Song: "His Strength is Perfect" written by Steven Curtis Chapman and Jerry Salley; Recorded by Steven Curtis Chapman (Label: Sparrow)

Pop/Contemporary Album: *Heaven* by BeBe and CeCe Winans (Producer: Keith Thomas; Label: Sparrow)

Pop/Contemporary Recorded Song: "Heaven" written by Keith Thomas and Benjamin Winans; Recorded by BeBe & CeCe Winans (Label: Sparrow)

Contemporary Gospel Album: *Will You Be Ready?* by Commissioned (Producers: Fred Hammon and Michael Brooks; Label: Light)

Contemporary Gospel Recorded Song: "With My Whole Heart" written by Patrick Henderson and Louis Brown III; Recorded by BeBe & CeCe Winans (Label: Sparrow)

Traditional Gospel Album: *Saints in Praise* by The West Angeles Church of God in Christ Mass Choir (Producer: Patrick Henderson; Label: Sparrow)

Traditional Gospel Recorded Song: "Wonderful" written by Virginia Davis and Theodore Frye; Recorded by Beau Williams

Country Album: *Heirloom* by Heirloom (Producer: Michael Sykes and Trent Hemphill; Label: Benson)

Country Recorded Song: "'Tis So Sweet to Trust in Jesus" written by Public Domain; Recorded by Amy Grant (Label: Word)

Traditional Gospel Recorded Song: "Wonderful" written by Virginia Davis, Theodore Frye; Recorded by Beau Williams

Rock Album: *The Way Home* by Russ Taff (Producers: Russ Taff and James Hollihan; Label: Myrrh)

Rock Recorded Song: "The River Unbroken" written by Darryl Brown and David Batteau; Recorded by Russ Taff (Label: Myrrh)

Hard Music Album: *Triumphant Return* by White Cross (Producers: Rex Carroll and Joey Powers; Label: Pure Metal)

Hard Music Recorded Song: "In Your Face" written by Ken Tamplin; Recorded by Shout (Label: Intense)

Instrumental Album: *One of Several Possible Musiks* by Kerry Livgren (Producer: Kerry Livgren; Label: Sparrow)

Praise and Worship Album: *Our Hymns* by various artists (Producers: Various; Label: Word)

Children's Music Album: *The Friendship Company* by Sandi Patti (Producer: Sandi Patti; Label: Word)

Musical Album: *Friends Forever/Part 2* by Billy Sprague, Jim Weber, and Nan Gurley (Label: Word; Publisher: Meadowgreen)

Choral Collection Album: *The Acapella Collection* recorded by The Greg Nelson Singers (Producer: Greg Nelson; Label: Wordsong)

Recorded Music Packaging: Buddy Jackson and Mark Tucker for *Petra Praise* by Petra

Short-Form Music Video: "I Miss the Way" by Michael W. Smith (Producer: Stephen Yake; Label: Reunion)

Long-Form Music Video: "On Fire" by Petra (Director: Stephen Yake)

1991: 22nd Annual Dove Awards

Song of the Year: "Another Time, Another Place" written by Gary Driskell; Publisher: Word Music, ASCAP

Songwriter of the Year: Steven Curtis Chapman

Male Vocalist of the Year: Steven Curtis Chapman

Female Vocalist of the Year: Sandi Patti

Group of the Year: Petra

Artist of the Year: Steven Curtis Chapman

New Artist Of the Year: 4Him

Southern Gospel Album: *Climbing Higher & Higher* by The Cathedrals (Producers: Bill Gaither, Mark Trammel, and Lari Goss; Label: Homeland)

Southern Gospel Recorded Song: "He Is Here" written by Kirk Talley; Recorded by The Talleys (Label: Word)

Inspirational Album: *Another Time, Another Place* by Sandi Patti (Producer:

Greg Nelson; Label: Word)

Inspirational Recorded Song: "Who Will Be Jesus?" written by Bruce Carroll and C. Aaron Wilburn; Recorded by Bruce Carroll (Label: Word)

Pop/Contemporary Album: *Go West Young Man* by Michael W. Smith (Producers: Michael W. Smith and Brian Lenox; Label: Reunion)

Pop/Contemporary Recorded Song: "Another Time, Another Place" written by Gary Driskell; Recorded by Sandi Patti (Label: Word)

Contemporary Gospel Album (formerly Contemporary Black Gospel): *So Much 2 Say* by Take 6 (Producer: Take 6; Label: Warner Alliance)

Contemporary Gospel Recorded Songs (formerly Contemporary Black Gospel): "I L-O-V-E You" written by Mervyn Warren and Mark Kibble; Recorded by Take 6 (Label: Warner Alliance)

Country Album: *Sojourner's Song* by Buddy Green (Producer: Bubba Smith; Label: Word)

Country Recorded Song: "Seein' My Father in Me" written by Paul Overstreet and Taylor Dunn; Recorded by Paul Overstreet (Label: Word)

Rock Album: *Beyond Belief* by Petra (Producers: John and Dino Elefante; Label: DaySpring)

Rock Recorded Song: "Beyond Belief" written by Bob Hartman; Recorded by Petra (Label: DaySpring)

Hard Music Album: *Holy Soldier* by Holy Soldier (Producer: David Zaffiro; Label: Myrrh)

Hard Music Recorded Song: "Stranger" written by David Zaffiro; Recorded by Holy Soldier (Label: Myrrh)

Rap/Hip Hop Album: *Nu Thang* by dc Talk (Producers: Toby McKeehan, Mark Heimermann and T.C.; Label: YO! ForeFront)

Rap/Hip Hop Recorded Song: "It's Time" written by: Marvin Winans, Carvin Winans, Teddy Riley and Bernard Bell; Recorded by The Winans (Label: Warner Alliance)

Instrumental Album: *Come Before Him* by Dick Tunney (Producer: Dick Tunney; Label: Word)

Praise and Worship Album: *Strong and Mighty Hands* by Voices of Praise (Producer: John G. Elliott; Label: Reunion)

Children's Music Album: *Hide 'Em in Your Heart Songs* by Steve Green (Producers: Frank and Betsy Hernandez; Label: Sparrow)

Musical Album: *Handel's Young Messiah* by various artists (Producers: Paul Mills, Don Hart and Norman Miller; Label: Word)

Choral Collection Album: *I Call You to Praise* by Steve Green (Producer: Music Sculptures; Label: Sparrow)

Recorded Music Packaging: Buddy Jackson and Mark Tucker for *Beyond Belief* by Petra

Short-Form Music Video: "Revival in the Land" by Carman (Director: Stephen Yake; Label: Benson)

Long-Form Music Video: "Revival in the Land" by Carman (Director: Stephen Yake; Label: Benson)

1992: 23rd Annual Dove Awards

Song of the Year: "Place in This World" written by Amy Grant, Michael W. Smith, and Wayne Kirkpatrick; Publishers: Age to Age Music, O'Ryan, Emily Boothe, ASCAP/BMI

Songwriter of the Year: Steven Curtis Chapman

Male Vocalist of the Year: Michael English

Female Vocalist of the Year: Sandi Patti

Group of the Year: BeBe & CeCe Winans

Artist of the Year: Amy Grant

New Artist of the Year: Michael English

Southern Gospel Album: *Homecoming* by The Gaither Vocal band (Producers: Ken Mansfield and The Gaither Vocal Band; Label: Star Song)

Southern Gospel Recorded Song: "Where Shadows Never Fall" written by Carl Jackson, Jim Weatherly; Recorded by Glen Campbell (Label: New Haven)

Inspirational Album: *Larnelle Live ... Psalms Hymns & Spiritual Songs* by Larnelle Harris (Producer: Lari Goss; Label: Benson)

Inspirational Recorded Song: "For All The World" written by Greg Nelson and Bob Farrell; Recorded by Sandi Patti (Label: Word)

Pop/Contemporary Album: *For the Sake of the Call* by Steven Curtis Chapman (Producer: Phil Naish; Label: Sparrow)

Pop/Contemporary Recorded Song: "Home Free" written by Wayne Watson; Recorded by Wayne Watson; Label: DaySpring

Contemporary Gospel Album (formerly Contemporary Black Gospel): *He is Christmas* by Take 6 (Producer: Take 6; Label: Warner Alliance)

Contemporary Gospel Recorded Song (formerly Contemporary Black Gospel): "Addictive Love" written by Keith Thomas, Benjamin Winans and CeCe Winans; Recorded by BeBe & CeCe Winans (Label: Sparrow)

Traditional Gospel Album (formerly Traditional Black Gospel) *Through the Storm* by Yolanda Adams (Producer V.M. McKay; Label: Tribute)

Traditional Gospel Recorded Song (formerly Traditional Black Gospel): "Through the Storm" written by V.M. McKay; Recorded by Yolanda Adams (Label: Tribute)

Country Album: *Sometimes Miracles Hide* by Bruce Carroll (Producers: Brown Bannister and Tom Hemby; Label: Word)

Country Recorded Song: "Sometimes Miracles Hide" written by Bruce Carroll and C. Aaron Wilburn; Recorded by Bruce Carroll (Label: Word)

Rock Album: *Simple House* by Margaret Becker (Producer: Charlie Peacock; Label: Sparrow)

Rock Recorded Song: "Simple House" written by Margaret Becker and Charlie Peacock; Recorded by Margaret Becker (Label: Sparrow)

Hard Music Album: *In the Kingdom* by Whitecross (Producer: Simon Hanhard; Label: Star Song)

Hard Music Recorded Song: "Everybody Knows My Name" written by Dale Thompson and Troy Thompson; Recorded by Bride (Label: Pure Metal)

Rap/Hip Hop Album: *Mike-E and The G-Rap Crew* by Mike-E (Producers: Mike-E, Jet Penix and Cedric Caldwell; Label: Reunion)

Rap/Hip Hop Recorded Song: "I Love Rap Music" written by Toby McKeehan and Jackie Gore; Recorded by dc Talk (Label: YO! Forefront)

Instrumental Album: *Beyond Nature* by Phil Keaggy (Producer: Phil Keaggy; Label: Myrrh)

Praise and Worship Album: *Sanctuary* by Twila Paris (Producer: Richard Souther; Label: Star Song)

Children's Music Album: *Open For Business* by Sandi Patti & the Friendship Company (Producers: Ron Krueger and Greg Nelson; Label: Everland)

Musical Album: *The Big Picture* by Michael W. Smith (Producers: Andy Stanley and Robert Sterling; Label: Word)

Choral Collection Album: *The Michael W. Smith Collection* (Producers: Robert Sterling and Dennis Worley; Label: Word)

Short-Form Music Video: "Another Time, Another Place" by Sandi Patti and Wayne Watson (Director: Stephen Yake; Label: Word)

Long-Form Music Video: "Rap, Rock & Soul" by dc Talk (Director and Producer: Deaton-Flanigen; Label: Forefront)

Recorded Music Packaging: Mark Tucker, Buddy Jackson and Beth Middleworth for *Brave Heart* by Kim Hill.

1993: 24th Annual Dove Awards

Song of the Year: "The Great Adventure" written by Steven Curtis Chapman and Geoff Moore; Publishers: Sparrow Song, Careers-BMG Music, and Peach Hill Songs, BMI; Starstruck Music, ASCAP

Songwriter of the Year: Steven Curtis Chapman

Male Vocalist of the Year: Michael English

Female Vocalist of the Year: Twila Paris

Group of the Year: 4HIM

Artist of the Year: Steven Curtis Chapman

New Artist of the Year: Cindy Morgan

Southern Gospel Album: *Reunion: A Gospel Homecoming Celebration* by Bill & Gloria Gaither (Producer: Bill Gaither; Label: Star Song)

Southern Gospel Recorded Song: "There Rose a Lamb" written by Kyla Rowland; Recorded by Gold City (Label: RiverSong)

Inspirational Album: *Generation 2 Generation* by Benson artists and their families (Larnelle Harris, Matthew Ward, Glad, Fred Hammond, 4HIM, Dallas Holm, Kelly Nelon Thompson, Billy and Sarah Gaines, Dana Key) (Producers: Don Koch, Ed Nalle, Fred Hammond, Joe Hogue, and Dana Key; Label: Benson)

Inspirational Recorded Song: "In Christ Alone" written by Shawn Craig and Don Koch; Recorded by Michael English (Label: Warner Alliance)

Pop/Contemporary Album: *The Great Adventure* by Steven Curtis Chapman (Producer: Phil Naish; Label: Sparrow)

Pop/Contemporary Recorded Song: "The Great Adventure" written by Steven Curtis Chapman and Geoff Moore; Recorded by Steven Curis Chapman; Label: Sparrow)

Contemporary Gospel Album: *Handel's Messiah—A Soulful Celebration*; by various artists (Mervyn Warren, George Duke, David Pack, Patti Austin, Take 6, Gary Hines, Robert Sadin, Richard Smallwood, The Yellowjackets, Fred Hammon; Label: Warner Alliance)

Contemporary Gospel Recorded Song: "Real" written by Daryl Coley; Recorded by Rev. C. B. Rhone and The Band (Label: Sparrow)

Traditional Gospel Album: *With All of My Heart* by Sandra Crouch and Friends (Producers: Sandra Crouch and Andrae Crouch; Label: Sparrow)

Traditional Gospel Recorded Song: "T'will Be Sweet" written by Richard Smallwood; Recorded by The Richard Smallwood Singers (Label: Sparrow)

Country Album: *Love Is Strong* by Paul Overstreet (Producers: Paul Overstreet and Brown Bannister; Label: Word)

Country Recorded Song: "If We Only Had the Heart" written by Bruce Carroll, Michael Puryear, and Dwight Liles; Recorded by Bruce Carroll (Label: Word)

Rock Album: *Pray For Rain* by Pray For Rain (Producers: Jimmie Lee Sloas and Bobby Blazier; Label: Vireo)

Rock Recorded Song: "Destiny" written by Bob Hartman, John Elefante; Recorded by Petra (Label: DaySpring)

Hard Music Album: NOT ENOUGH ELIGIBLE ENTRIES

Hard Music Recorded Song: "Rattlesnake" written by Dale Thompson, Troy Thompson, Rik Foley, and Jerry McBroom; Recorded by Bride (Label: Star Song)

Rap/Hip Hop Album: *Good News For the Bad Timez* by Mike-E (Producers: Mike E and Jet Penix; Label: Reunion)

Rap/Hip Hop Recorded Song: "Can I Get A Witness?" written by Toby McKeehan; Recorded by DC Talk (Label: YO! ForeFront)

Inspirational Recorded Song: "In Christ Alone" written by Shawn Craig and Don Koch; Recorded by Michael English (Label: Warner Alliance)

Instrumental Album: *Somewhere In Time* by Dino (Producers: Dino Kartsonakis and David T. Clydesdale; Label: Benson)

Praise and Worship Album: *Coram Deo* by Michael Card, Charlie Peacock, Susan Ashton, Michael English, and Out of the Grey (Producer: Charlie Peacock; Label: Sparrow)

Children's Music Album: *YO! KIDZ!* by Carman (Producers: Chris Harris and Ron Krueger; Label: Everland)

Musical Album: *The Majesty and Glory of Christmas* by Billy Ray Hearn and Tom Fettke (Label: Sparrow)

Choral Collection Album: *Steven Curtis Chapman Choral Collection* (Producers: Tom Harley, Randy Smith; Label: Sparrow)

Recorded Music Packaging: Larry Vigon and Denise Milford for *Coram Deo* by Susan Ashton, Michael Card, Michael English, Out of the Grey, and Charlie Peacock (Label: Sparrow)

Short-Form Music Video: "The Great Adventure" by Steven Curtis Chapman (Directors: Nancy Knox; Greg Crutcher; Label: Sparrow)

Long-Form Music Vodeo: "Addicted To Jesus" by Carman (Director: Stephen Yake; Label: Benson)

1994: 25th Annual Dove Awards

Song of the Year: "In Christ Alone" written by Shawn Craig and Don Koch; Publisher: Paragon Music, ASCAP

Songwriter of the Year: Steven Curtis Chapman

Male Vocalist of the Year: Michael English

Female Vocalist of the Year: Twila Paris

Group of the Year: 4HIM

Artist of the Year: Michael English

New Artist of the Year: Point of Grace

Southern Gospel Album: *Southern Classics* by The Gaither Vocal Band (Producers: Bill Gaither, Michael Sykes, and Michael English; Label: Benson)

Southern Gospel Recorded Song: "Satisfied" written by Public Domain; Recorded by The Gaither Vocal Band (Label: Benson)

Inspirational Album: *The Season Of Love* by 4HIM (Producer: Don Koch; Label: Benson)

Inspirational Recorded Song: "Holding Out Hope To You" written by Joe Beck, Brian White, and David Wills; Recorded by Michael English (Label: Warner Alliance)

Pop/Contemporary Album: *Hope* by Michael English (Producer: Brown Bannister; Label: Warner Alliance)

Pop/Contemporary Recorded Song: "Go There With You" written by Steven Curtis Chapman; Recorded by Steven Curtis Chapman (Label: Sparrow)

Contemporary Gospel Album: *Start All Over* by Helen Baylor (Producer: Bill Maxwell; Label: Word)

Contemporary Gospel Recorded Song: "Sold Out" written by Helen Baylor and Logan Reynolds; Recorded by Helen Baylor (Label: Word)

Traditional Gospel Album: *Kirk Franklin & The Family* by Kirk Franklin (Producers: Rodney Fraziere and Arthur Dyer; Label: Gospo Centric)

Traditional Gospel Recorded Song: "Why We Sing" written by Kirk Franklin; Recorded by Kirk Franklin (Label: Gospo Centric)

Country Album: *Walk On* by Bruce Carroll (Producers: Brown Bannister and Tom Hemby; Label: Word)

Country Recorded Song: "There But For the Grace of God" written by Paul Overstreet and Taylor Dunn; Recorded by Paul Overstreet (Label: Word)

Rock Album: *Wake-Up Call* by Petra (Producer: Brown Bannister; Label: DaySpring)

Rock Recorded Song: "Jesus Is Just Alright" written by Arthur Reynolds; Recorded by dc Talk (Label: ForeFront)

Hard Music Album: *Tamplin* by Ken Tamplin (Producer: Ken Tamplin; Label: Benson)

Hard Music Recorded Song: "Psychedelic Super Jesus" written by Troy Thompson, Dale Thompson, Jerry McBroom, Rik Foley; Recorded by Bride (Label: Star Song)

Rap/Hip Hop Album: NOT ENOUGH ELIGIBLE ENTRIES

Rap/Hip Hop Recorded Song: "Socially Acceptable" written by Toby McKeeham and Mark Heimermann; Recorded by dc Talk (Label: ForeFront)

Instrumental Album: *Psalms, Hymns & Spiritual Songs* by Kurt Kaiser (Producer: Kurt Kaiser; Label: Sparrow)

Praise and Worship Album: *Songs From the Loft* by Susan Ashton, Gary Chapman, Ashley Cleveland, Amy Delaine, Amy Grant, Kim Hill, Michael James, Wes King, Donna McElroy, Michael W. Smith (Producers: Gary Chapman and Jim Dineen; Label: Reunion)

Children's Music Album: *Come to the Cradle* by Michael Card (Producer: Phil Naish; Label: Sparrow)

Musical Album: *God with Us* by Don Moen, Tom Fettke, Tom Harley, Jack Hayford, Camp Kirkland (Label: Integrity Music)

Choral Collection Album: *Al Denson Youth Chorus Book, Vol III* (Producers: Dave Spear and Al Denson; Label: Benson)

Recorded Music Packaging: Buddy Jackson, Beth Middleworth, Mark Tucker, and D. Rhodes for *The Wonder Years 1983-1993* by Michael W. Smith (Label: Reunion)

Short-Form Music Video: "Hand On My Shoulder" by Sandi Patti (Director: Stephen Yake; Label: Word)

Long-Form Music Video: "The Live Adventure" by Steven Curtis Chapman (Producers and Directors: Bret Wolcott, Douglas C. Forbes and Michael Solomon; Label: Sparrow)

1995: 26th Annual Dove Awards

Song of the Year: "God Is in Control" written by Twila Paris; Publishers: Ariose Music and Mountain Spring Music, ASCAP

Songwriter of the Year: Steven Curtis Chapman

Male Vocalist of the Year: Steven Curtis Chapman

Female Vocalist of the Year: Twila Paris

Group of the Year: 4HIM

Artist of the Year: Steven Curtis Chapman

New Artist of the Year: Clay Crosse

Southern Gospel Album: *High and Lifted Up* by The Cathedral Quartet (Producer: Lari Goss; Label: Canaan)

Southern Gospel Recorded Song: "I Bowed On My Knees" written by Public Domain; Recorded by Gaither Vocal Band (Label: Benson)

Inspirational Album: *Find It On the Wings* by Sandi Patty (Producers: Greg Nelson and Phil Ramone; Label: Word)

Inspirational Recorded Song: "I Pledge Allegiance to the Lamb" written by Ray Boltz; Recorded by Roy Boltz (Label: Word)

Pop/Contemporary Album: *Heaven in the Real World* by Steven Curtis Chapman (Producers: Phil Naish and Steven Curtis Chapman; Label: Sparrow)

Pop/Contemporary Recorded Song: "Heaven in the Real World" written by Steven Curtis Chapman; Recorded by Steven Curtis Chapman (Label: Sparrow)

Contemporary Gospel Album: *Join the Band* by Take 6 (Producers: Alvin Chea, Cedric Dent, Joel Kibble, Mark Kibble, Claude V. McKnight III, David Thomas, Vincent Herbert, Les Pierce, David Foster, Brian McKnight, and Stevie Wonder; Label: Warner Alliance)

Contemporary Gospel Recorded Song: "God Knows" written by Angelo & Veronica; Recorded by Angelo & Veronica Petrucci (Label: Benson)

Traditional Gospel Album: *Live At GMWA: Shirley Caesar, O'Landa Draper & The Associates, Rev. Milton Brunson & The Thompson Community Singers* (Producers: Bubba Smith and John Stewart; Label: Word)

Country Album: *The Door* by Charlie Daniels (Producer: Ron W. Griffin; Label: Sparrow)

Country Recorded Song: "The Door" written by Ron W. Griffin; Recorded by Charlie Daniels (Label: Sparrow)

Rock Album: *Going Public* by The Newsboys (Producers: Steve Taylor and Peter Furler; Label: Star Song)

Rock Recorded Song: "Shine" written by Peter Furler, Steve Taylor; Recorded by The Newsboys; Label: Star Song

Hard Music Album: *Scarecrow Messiah* by Bride (Producers: John & Dino Elefante; Label: Star Song)

Hard Music Recorded Song: "Come Unto the Light" written by Scott Wenzel, David Zaffiro, Jimmy Lee Sloas; Recorded by Whitecross

(Label: R.E.X.)

Rap/Hip Hop Album: NOT ENOUGH ELIGIBLE ENTRIES

Rap/Hip Hop Recorded Song: "Luv Is a Verb" written by Toby McKeehan, Mark Heimermann, George Cocchini; Recorded by dc Talk (Label: ForeFront)

Instrumental Album: *Strike Up the Band* by Ralph Carmichael's Big Band (Producers: Ralph Carmichael and Paul Stilwell; Label: Brentwood)

Praise and Worship Album: *Coram Deo II: Out of the Grey* by Steve Green, Margaret Becker, Charlie Peacock, Steven Curtis Chapman, CeCe Winans, and Bob Carlisle (Producer: Charlie Peacock; Label: Sparrow)

Children's Music Album: *Y! KIDZ!2: The Armor of God* by Carman (Producers: Chris Harris, Ron Krueger, and David Mullen; Label: Everland)

Musical Album: *Living On the Edge* by Michael W. Smith and Robert Sterling (Label: Word)

Choral Collection Album: *A Christmas Suite* (Producer: David T. Clydesdale; Publisher: David T. Clydesdale Music

Recorded Music Packaging: Karen Philpott, R.J. Lyons, Gerhart Yorkovic and E.J. Carr for *Heaven In the Real World* by Steven Curtis Chapman (Label: Sparrow)

Short-Form Music Video: "I Will Be Free" by Cindy Morgan (Producer and Director: Cindy Montano and Thom Olipahnt; Label: Word)

Long-Form Music Video: "Mouth in Motion" by Mark Lowry (Producers and Directors: Jack Clark, Stephen Yake, and Corey Edwards; Label: Word)

1996: 27th Annual Dove Awards

Song of the Year: "Jesus Freak" written by Mark Heimermann and Toby McKeehan; Publishers: Fun Attic Music ASCAP; Mupin the Mix Music, BMI

Songwriter of the Year: Michael W. Smith

Male Vocalist of the Year: Gary Chapman

Female Vocalist of the Year: CeCe Winans

Group of the Year: Point of Grace

Artist of the Year: DC Talk

New Artist of the Year: Jars of Clay

Producer of the Year: Charlie Peacock

Southern Gospel Album: *The Martins* by The Martins (Producers: Michael Sykes and Michael English; Label: Chapel)

Inspirational Album: *Unbelievable Love* by Larnelle Harris (Producers: Bill Cuomo, Robert White Johnson, and Lari Goss; Label: Benson)

Inspirational Recorded Song: "Man After Your Own Heart" written by Wayne Kirkpatrick, Billy Luz Sprague; Recorded by Gary Chapman (Label: Myrrh/Word)

Pop/Contemporary Album: *The Whole Truth* by Point of Grace (Producer: Robert Sterling; Label: Word)

Pop/Contemporary Recorded Song: "The Great Divide" written by Grant Cunningham, and Matt Huesmann; Recorded by Point of Grace (Label: Word)

Contemporary Gospel Album: *The Call* by Anointed (Producers: Cedric Caldwell, Victor Caldwell, Chris Harris, and Mark Heimermanm; Label: Myrrh)

Contemporary Gospel Recorded Song: "The Call" written by Mary Tiller, Steve Crawford, Nee-C Walls, and Da'Dra Crawford; Recorded by Anointed (Label: Myrrh)

Traditional Gospel Album: *He Will Come: Live* by Shirley Caesar (Producers: Bubba Smith and Shirley Caesar; Label: Word Gospel)

Traditional Gospel Recorded Song: "Great Is Thy Faithfulness" written by Thomas Chisholm; Recorded by CeCe Winans (Label: Sparrow)

Urban Album: *Give Your Life* by Angelo & Veronica (Producers: Fred Hammond, Cliff Branch, Ted Tjornhom, and Angelo Petrucci; Label: Benson)

Urban Recorded Song: "It's in God's Hands Now" written by Madeline Stone and Allen Shamblin; Recorded by Anointed (Label: Myrrh)

Country Album: *Where Loves Runs Deep* by Michael James (Producer: Michael James; Label: Reunion)

Country Recorded Song: "Without You (I Haven't Got a Prayer)" written by Robby McGee, Scott Rath, and Peter Jeffrey; Recorded by MidSouth (Label: Warner Alliance)

Rock Album: *No Doubt* by Petra (Producers: John and Dino Elefante; Label: Word)

Rock Recorded Song: "Jesus Freak" written by Toby McKeehan and Mark Heimermann; Recorded by dc Talk (Label: ForeFront)

Hard Music Album: *Promise Man* by Holy Soldier (Producer: David Zaffiro; Label: ForeFront)

Hard Music Recorded Song: "Promise Man" written by Michael Cutting, Andy Robbins, Scott Soderstrom, Eric Wayne, David Zaffiro, and Michael Anderson; Recorded by Holy Soldier; Label: ForeFront

Rap/Hip Hop Album: *Church of Rhythm* by Church of Rhythm (Producer: Peter Bunetta, Rick Chudacoff; Label: Reunion)

Rap/Hip Hop Recorded Song: "Take Back The Beat" written by Max Hsu, Jason Gregory, Nathan Clair, and Carlton Coleman; Recorded by Church of Rhythm (Label: Reunion)

Rap/Hip Hop Recorded Song: "R.I.O.T (Righteous Invasion of Truth)" written by Carman and Tommy Sims; Recorded by Carman (Label: Sparrow)

Alternative/Modern Rock Album: *This Beautiful Mess* by Sixpence None the Richer (Producer: Armand John Petri; Label: R.E.X.)

Alternative/Modern Rock Recorded Song: "Monkeys At the Zoo" from the album *Everything That's On My Mind* by Charlie Peacock (Producers: Charlie Peacock, Douglas Kaine McKelvey; Label: Sparrow)

Urban Album: *Give Your Life* by Angelo & Veronica (Producers: Fred Hammond, Cliff Branch, Ted Tjornhom, and Angelo Petrucci; Label: Benson)

Instrumental Album: *Classical Peace* by Dino (Producer: Rolin R. Mains; Label: Benson)

Praise and Worship Album: *Promise Keepers: Raise the Standard* by Maranatha! Promise Band (Producer: Bill Schnee; Label: Word Maranatha!)

Children's Music Album: *School Days* (Producers by Mike Gay and Sue Gay; Label: Cedarmont Kids)

Musical Album: *Saviour* by Bob Farrell and Greg Nelson (Label: Word Music)

Youth/Children's Musical of the Year: *Salt & Light (Featuring the Songs from the Loft)* (Producer: Beverly Darnall; Publisher: Word Music)

Choral Collection Album: *Praise Him...Live* recorded by The Brooklyn Tabernacle Choir (Produced by Carol Cymbala; Publisher: Word Music)

Special Event Album: *My Utmost For His Highest* recorded by Amy Grant, Gary Chapman, Michael W. Smith, Point of Grace, 4HIM, Cindy Morgan, Sandi Patty, Bryan Duncan, Steven Curtis Chapman, Twila Paris, Phillips, and Craig & Dean (Producers: Loren Balman and Brown Bannister; Label: Myrrh/Word)

Recorded Music Packaging: Loren Balman, Diana Barnes, Jeff and Lisa Franke and Mathew Barnes for *My Utmost For His Highest* recorded by various artists (Label: Myrrh/Word)

Short-Form Music Video: "Flood" by Jars of Clay (Producers and Directors: Ricky Blair, Michelle Weigle-Brown, Robert Beeson; Label: Essential)

Long-Form Music Video: "Big House" by Audio Adrenaline (Producers and Directors: Clarke Gallivan, Cindy Montano, Kari Reeves; Jeffrey Phillips, Thom Olipahnt; Label: ForeFront)

1997: 28th Annual Dove Awards

Song of the Year: "Butterfly Kisses" written by Bob Carlisle and Randy Thomas; Publishers: DMG Music, SESAC; Polygram International, ASCAP

Songwriter of the Year: Steven Curtis Chapman

Male Vocalist of the Year: Steven Curtis Chapman

Female Vocalist of the Year: CeCe Winans

Group of the Year: Jars of Clay

Artist of the Year: Steven Curtis Chapman

New Artist of the Year: Jaci Velasquez

Southern Gospel Album: *Wherever You Are* by The Martins (Producers: Michael Sykes and Michael English; Label: Spring Hill)

Southern Gospel Recorded Song: "Only God Knows" written by: Joyce Martin McCollough, Harrie McCollough, and Joel Lindsey; Recorded by: The Martins (Label: Spring Hill)

Inspirational Album: *Quiet Prayers (My Utmost For His Highest)* (Producers: Bryan Duncan and Dan Posthuma; Label: Myrrh)

Inspirational Recorded Song: "Butterfly Kisses" written by Bob Carlisle and Randy Thomas; Recorded by Bob Carlisle (Label: Diade)

Pop/Contemporary Album: *Signs of Life* by Steven Curtis Chapman (Producers: Brown Bannister and Steven Curtis Chapman; Label: Sparrow)

Pop/Contemporary Recorded Song: "Between You And Me" written by Toby McKeehan and Mark Heimermann; Recorded by dc Talk (Label: ForeFront)

Contemporary Gospel Album: *Whatcha Lookin' 4* by Kirk Franklin & The Family (Producers: Kirk Franklin, Buster & Shavoni; Label: Gospo Centric)

Contemporary Gospel Recorded Song: "Take Me Back" written by Andrae Crouch; Recorded by CeCe Winans on the album *Tribute—The Songs of Andrae Crouch* (Label: Warner Alliance)

Traditional Gospel Album: *Just a Word* by Shirley Caesar's Outreach Convention Choir (Producers: Bubba Smith, Michael Mathis, and Shirley Caesar; Label: Word Gospel)

Traditional Gospel Recorded Song: "Stop By the Church" written by Sullivan Pugh; Recorded by Babbie Mason (Label: Word)

Urban Album: INSUFFICENT AMOUNT OF ELIGIBLE ENTRIES

Urban Recorded Song: "Under the Influence" written by Mark Heimermann; Recorded by Anointed (Label: Myrrh)

Country Album: *Little Bit of Faith* by Jeff Silvey (Producer: Randy Boudraux; Label: Ranson)

Country Recorded Song: "Somebody Was Prayin' for Me" written by Charlie Daniels; Recorded by Charlie Daniels (Label: Sparrow)

Rock Album: *Jesus Freak* by dc Talk (Producers: Toby McKeehan, Mark Heimermann, and John Painter; Label: ForeFront)

Rock Recorded Song: "Like It, Love It, Need It" written by Toby McKeehan, Mark Heimermann, Kevin Smith, David Soldi, Jason Barrett; Recorded by dc Talk (Label: ForeFront)

Hard Music Album: INSUFFICENT AMOUNT OF ELIGIBLE ENTRIES

Hard Music Recorded Song: INSUFFICENT AMOUNT OF ELIGIBLE ENTRIES

Rap/Hip Hop Album: *Erace* by The Gotee Brothers (Producers: The Gotee Brothers; Label: Gotee)

Alternative/Modern Rock Album: *Free Flying Soul* by The Choir (Producers: Steve Hindalong, and Derry Daugherty; Label: Tatoo)

Alternative/Modern Rock Song: "Epidermis Girl" from the album *Space* by Bleach (Producers: Brad Ford, Dave Baysinger, Matt Gingerich, Sam Barnhart, Todd Kirby; Label: ForeFront)

Instrumental Album: *The Players* by Michael Omartian, Dann Huff, Tommy Sims, Tom Hemby, Terry McMillan, Chris Rodriguez, Shane Keister, Mark Douthit, and Eric Darken (Producers: The Players and Bobby Blazier; Label: Warner Alliance)

Praise and Worship Album: *Welcome Home* by Ron Kenoly (Producer: Tom Brooks; Label: Integrity Music)

Children's Music Album: *A Very Veggie Christmas* by Veggie Tales (Producers: Phil Vischer, Kurt Heinecke, and Mike Nawrocki; Label: Everland)

Musical of the Year: *Make Us One* by Babbie Mason, Kenny Mann, David T. Clydesdale (Publisher: David T. Clydesdale Music

Youth/Children's Musical of the Year: *Candy Cane Lane* (Producers: Celeste and David T. Clydesdale; Publisher: David T. Clydesdale Music)

Choral Collection Album: *My Tribute—Celebrating the Songs of Andrae Crouch* (Producers: Dale Mathews and John DeVries; Publisher: Brentwood Music)

Special Event Album: *Tribute—The Songs of Andrae Crouch* by CeCe Winans, Michael W. Smith, Twila Paris, Bryan Duncan, Wayne Watson, The Winans, Clay Crosse, Take 6, The Brooklyn Tabernacle Choir, First Call, Andrae Crouch, and The All Star Choir (Producers: Norman Miller and Neal Joseph; Label: Warner Alliance)

Short-Form Music Video: "Jesus Freak" by dc Talk (Producer and Director: Steve Strachen and Simon Maxwell; Label: ForeFront)

Long-Form Music Video: "Roadwork" by Geoff Moore & The Distance (Producers and Directors: Dalrene Brock, Gael Van Sant; Tom Bevins; Label: ForeFront)

Recorded Music Packaging: Toni Fitzpenn, Michael Wilson, Norman Roy, George Barris, and Anderson Thomas for *Take Me to Your Leader* by The Newsboys (Label: Star Song)

1998: 29th Annual Dove Awards

Song of the Year: "On My Knees" written by David Mullen, Nicole Colerman-Mullen and Michael Ochs; Publishers: Seat of the Pants Music and Word Music, ASCAP; Ochsongs Music BMI

Songwriter of the Year: Steven Curtis Chapman

Male Vocalist of the Year: Steven Curtis Chapman

Female Vocalist of the Year: Crystal Lewis

Group of the Year: Jars of Clay

Artist of the Year: Rich Mullins

New Artist of the Year: Avalon

Producer of the Year: Brown Bannister

Southern Gospel Album: *Light of the World* by The Martins (Producers: Michael Sykes and Lari Gross; Label: Spring Hill)

Southern Gospel Recorded Song: "Butterfly Kisses" written by Bob Carlisle and Randy Thomas: Recorded by Tim Greene (Label: New Haven)

Inspirational Album: *Artist Of My Soul* by Sandi Patty (Producer: Robbie Buchanan; Label: Word)

Inspirational Recorded Song: "A Baby's Prayer" written by Kathy Troccoli and Scott Brasher; Recorded by Kathy Troccoli (Label: Reunion)

Pop/Contemporary Album: *Behind the Eyes* by Amy Grant (Producers: Keith Thomas and Wayne Kirkpatrick; Label: Myrrh)

Pop/Contemporary Recorded Song: "Let Us Pray" written by Steven Curtis Chapman; Recorded by Steven Curtis Chapman (Label: Sparrow)

Contemporary Gospel Album: *Pray* by Andrae Crouch (Producers: Andrae Crouch and Scott V. Smith; Label: Qwest/Warner Brothers)

Contemporary Gospel Recorded Song: "Up Where I Belong" written by Will Jennings, Jack Nitschi, and Buffy Sainte-Marie; Recorded by BeBe & CeCe Winans (Label: Sparrow)

Traditional Gospel Album: *A Miracle in Harlem* by Shirley Caesar (Producers: Bubba Smith, Shirley Caesar, and Michael Mathis; Label: Word Gospel)

Traditional Gospel Recorded Song: "I Go to the Rock" written by Dottie Rambo; Recorded by Whitney Houston (Label: Arista)

Urban Album: *God's Property From Kirk Franklin's Nu Nation* by God's Property (Producer: Kirk Franklin; Label: B'Rite Music)

Urban Recorded Song: "Stomp" recorded by God's Property; Kirk Franklin, George Clinton, Jr., Gary Shider, Walter Morrison (Label: B'Rite Music)

Country Album: *Hymns From the Ryman* by Gary Chapman (Producer: Gary Chapman, Label: Word Nashville)

Country Recorded Song: "The Gift" written by Tom Douglas and Jim Brickman; Recorded by Collin Raye (Label: Word Nashville)

Rock Album: *Conspiracy No. 5* by Third Day (Producer: Sam Taylor; Label: Reunion)

Rock Recorded Song: "Alien" written by Mark Lee, Tai Anderson, Brad Avery, and David Carr; Recorded by Third Day (Label: Reunion)

Hard Music Album: INSUFFICIENT AMOUNT OF ELIGIBLE ENTRIES

Hard Music Recorded Song: INSUFFICIENT AMOUNT OF ELIGIBLE ENTRIES

Rap/Hip Hop Album: *Revived* by World Wide Message Tribe (Producer: Zarc Porter; Label: Warner Alliance)

Alternative/Modern Rock Album: *Caedmon's Call* by Caedmon's Call (Producer: Don McCollister; Label: Warner Alliance)

Alternative/Modern Rock Recorded Song: "Some Kind of Zombie" written by Mark Stuart, Barry Blair, Will McGinniss, and Bob Herman; Recorded by Audio Adrenaline (Label: ForeFront)

Instrumental Album: *Invention* by Phil Keaggy, Wes King, and Scott Dente (Producer: R. S. Field; Label: Sparrow)

Rap/Hip Hop Recorded Song: "Jumping In the House of God" written by Andy Hawthorne, Zarc Porter, Lee Jackson, Justin Thomas; Recorded by World Wide Message Tribe (Label: Warner Alliance)

Bluegrass Album: *Bridges* by The Isaacs (Producer: Ben Isaacs; Label: Horizon)

Bluegrass Recorded Song of the Year: "Children of the Living God" This Bright Hour; written by: Fernando Ortega, and Alison Krauss; Recorded by Fernado Ortega (Label: Myrrh)

Praise and Worship Album: *Petra Praise 2: We Need Jesus* by Petra (Producers: John & Dino Elefante; Label: Word)

Children's Music Album: *Sing Me To Sleep, Daddy* by Billy Gaines, Michael James, Phil Keaggy, Michael O'Brien, Guy Penrod, Peter Penrose, Angelo Petrucci, Michael W. Smith, Randy Stonehill, and Wayne Watson (Producer: Nathan DiGesare; Label: Brentwood Kids Co.)

Musical of the Year: *My Utmost For His Highest...A Worship Musical* by Gary Ghodes and Claire Cloninger (Publisher: Word Music)

Youth/Children's Musical of the Year: INSUFFICENT AMOUNT OF ELIGIBLE ENTRIES

Choral Collection Album: *Our Savior...Emmanuel* (Producers: Greg Nelson and Bob Farrell; Publisher: Word Music)

Spanish Language Album of the Year: *La Belleze De La Cruz* by Crysal Lewis (Producers: Brian Ray and Dan Posthuma; Label: Word International)

Enhanced CD of the Year: "Live the Life—Maxi Single" by Michael W. Smith (Producer: Craig A. Mason; Label: Reunion)

Special Event Album: *God With Us—A Celebration of Christmas Carols & Classics* by Anointed, Michael W. Smith, Twila Paris, Sandi Patty, Steven Curtis Chapman, Chris Willis, Steve Green, Cheri Keaggy, Avalon, Out of the Grey, Ray Boltz, Clay Crosse, CeCe Winans, and Larnelle Harris (Producer: Norman Miller; Label: Sparrow)

Short-Form Music Video: "Colored People" by dc Talk (Producer and Director: Mars Media and Lawrence Carroll; Label: ForeFront/Virgin)

Long-Form Music Video: "A Very Silly Sing Along" by Veggie Tales (Producers and Directors: Mike Nawrocki, Chris Olsen, Kurt Heinecke; Label: Everland Entertainment)

Recorded Music Packaging: Beth Lee, Gina R. Brinkley, Janice Booker, Ben Pearson, and D.L. Taylor for *Sixpence None the Richer*; Recorded by Sixpence None the Richer (Label: Squint Entertainment)

1999: 30th Annual Dove Awards

Song of the Year: "My Deliverer" written by Rich Mullins and Mitch McVicker; Publishers: Liturgy Legacy Music and Word Music, ASCAP; White Plastic Bag Music, SESAC

Songwriter of the Year: Rich Mullins

Male Vocalist of the Year: Chris Rice

Female Vocalist of the Year: Jaci Velasquez

Group of the Year: Point of the Grace

Artist of the Year: Michael W. Smith

New Artist of the Year: Jennifer Knap

Producer of the Year: Michael W. Smith

Southern Gospel Album: *Still The Greatest Story Ever Told* by The Gaither Vocal Band (Producers: Bill Gaither, Michael Sykes, and Guy Penrod; Label: Spring Hill)

Southern Gospel Recorded Song: "I Believe In a Hill Called Mount Calvery" written by William J. Gaither, and Gloria Gaither; Recorded by Gaither Vocal Band (Label: Spring Hill)

Inspirational Album: *Corner of Eden* by Kathy Troccoli (Producer: Nathan DiGesare; Label: Reunion Records)

Inspirational Recorded Song: "Adonai" written by Stephanie Lewis, Lorraine Ferro and Don Koch; Recorded by Avalon; (Label: Sparrow Records)

Pop/Contemporary Album: *Live the Life* by Michael W. Smith (Producers: Mark Heimermann, Michael W. Smith, and Stephen Lipson; Label: Reunion)

Pop/Contemporary Recorded Song: "Testify To Love" written by Paul Field, Henk Pool, Ralph Van Manen, and Robert Riekerk; Recorded by Avalon (Label: Sparrow Records)

Contemporary Gospel Album: *Nu Nation Project* by Kirk Franklin (Producer: Kirk Franklin; Label: Gospo Centric)

Contemporary Gospel Recorded Song: "Let The Praise Begin" Pages of Life Chapter I & II; written by Fred Hammond; Recorded by Fred Hammond & Radical For Christ (Label: Verity Records)

Traditional Gospel Album: *Christmas with Shirley Caesar* by Shirley Caesar (Producers: Steven Ford and Shirley Caesar; Label: Myrrh Records Black Music Division)

Traditional Gospel Recorded Song: "Is Your All On the Altar?" written by Elisha Hoffman and Percy Bady; Recorded by Yolanda Adams;

Urban Album: INSUFFICIENT AMOUNT OF ELIGIBLE ENTRIES

Urban Recorded Song: "Revolution" written by Kirk Franklin and Rodney Jerkins; Recorded by Nu Nation Project (Label: Gospo Centric)

Country Album: *A Work in Progress* by Jeff and Sheri Easter (Producer: Michael Sykes; Label: Spring Hill)

Country Recorded Song: "Count Your Blessings" written by Kim Patton

Johnston and Joe Johnston; Recorded by The Martins (Label: Spring Hill)

Rock Album: *Anybody Out There?* by Burlap To Cashmere (Producers: Jay Healy and David Rolfe; Label: Squint Entertainment)

Rock Recorded Song: "Undo Me" written by Jennifer Knapp; Recorded by Jennifer Knapp (Label: Gotee Records)

Hard Music Album: *Brightblur* by Massivivid (Producers: Wally Shaw and Mark Nash; Label: Tattoo Records, Benson)

Hard Music Recorded Song: "Awesome God" written by Rich Mullins with additional lyrics by Joe Yerke; Recorded by The Insyderz (Label: Squint Entertainment)

Rap/Hip Hop Album: *Heatseeker* by The World Wide Message Tribe (Producer: Zarc Porter; Label: Warner Resound)

Rap/Hip Hop Recorded Song: "Plagiarism" written by T. Carter, S. Jones, T. Collins, R. Robbins; Recorded by Grits (Label: Gotee Records)

Alternative/Modern Rock Album: *Fourth From the Last* by The W's, Masaki (Producer: 5 Minute Walk; Label: Sarabellum)

Alternative/Modern Rock Recorded Song: "The Devil Is Bad" from the album *Fourth From the Last* by The W's (Producers: Andrew Schar, Todd Gruener, James Carter, Brian Morris, Val Hellman, Bret Barker; Label: Sarabellum)

Bluegrass Album: INSUFFICIENT AMOUNT OF ELIGIBLE ENTRIES

Bluegrass Recorded Song of the Year: "He Still Looks Over Me" written by Mike Richards and Rodney Lay Jr.; Recorded by The Lewis Family (Label: Thoroughbred Records)

Instrumental Album: *Acoustic Sketches* by Phil Keaggy (Producers: Phil Keaggy and John August Schroeter; Label: Sparrow Records)

Praise and Worship Album: *Focus On the Family Presents Renewing The Heart Live Hymns and Songs of Worship* by Kim Hill (Producers: David Zaffiro and Kim Hill; Label: Star Song Records)

Children's Music Album: *Veggie Tunes 2* by Veggie Tales (Producers: Kurt Heinecke and David Mullen; Label: Big Idea Productions)

Musical of the Year: *Mary, Did You Know?* by David Guthrie and Bruce Greer (Publisher: Word Music)

Youth/Children's Musical of the Year: *2 Extreme!* (Producer: Steven V. Taylor; Publisher: Brentwood-Benson Music Publishing)

Choral Collection of the Year: *Peace Speaker* (Producer: Geron Davis; Publisher: Brentwood-Benson Music Publishing)

Spanish Language Album of the Year: (Tie) *Libertad De Mas* by *Sandi Patti* (Producers: Isaac Hernandez and Greg Nelson; Label: Word International) and *ORO* by Crystal Lewis (Producers: Brian Ray and Dan Posthuma; Label: Metro One)

Special Event Album: *Exodus* by dc Talk, Jars of Clay, Sixpence None the Richer, Cindy Morgan, Chris Rice, The Katinas, Third Day, Crystal

Lewis, and Michael W. Smith (Producer: Michael W. Smith; Label: Rocketown Records)

Recorded Music Packaging: Beth Lee, Jimmy Abegg, Ben Pearson, Beth Lee and Ben Pearson for *The Jesus Record*; Recorded by Rich Mullins and a Ragamuffin Band; (Label: Myrrh)

Enhanced CD of the Year: *Stead* on Enhanced CD by Point of Grace (Producers: Denise Niebisch and Rose Irelan; Label: Word Records)

Short-Form Music Video: "Entertaining Angels" by Newsboys (Producers and Directors: Janet Eisner, Joel Newman; Eden, A+R; Label: StarSong, Virgin)

Long-Form Music Video: "My Utmost For His Highest—The Concert" by Cindy Morgan, Avalon, Twila Paris, Bryan Duncan, Sandi Patty, Steven Curtis Chapman, and Nancy Knox (Producers and Directors: Clark Santee and Word Entertainment; Label: Myrrh Records)

2000: 31st Annual Dove Awards

Song of the Year: "This Is Your Time" written by Michael W. Smith and Wes King; Publishers: Milene Music and Deer Valley Music, ASCAP; Sparrow Song and Uncle Ivan Music, BMI

Songwriter of the Year: Michael W. Smith

Male Vocalist of the Year: Steven Curtis Chapman

Female Vocalist of the Year: Jaci Velasquez

Group of the Year: Sixpence None the Richer

Artist of the Year: Steven Curtis Chapman

New Artist of the Year: Ginny Owens

Producer of the Year: Brown Bannister

Southern Gospel Album: *God Is Good* by The Gaither Vocal Band (Producers: Bill Gaither, Michael Sykes, and Guy Penrod; Label: Spring Hill)

Southern Gospel Recorded Song: "Healing" written by Roger Bennett; Recorded by The Cathedrals (Producer: Roger Bennett; Label: Homeland)

Inspirational Album: *Selah* by Selah (Producers: Jason Kyle, Todd Smith, and Allan Hall; Label: Curb)

Inspirational Recorded Song: "I Will Follow Christ" written by Clay Crosse and Steve Siler; Recorded by Clay Crosse (Label: Reunion)

Pop/Contemporary Album: *Speechless* by Steven Curtis Chapman (Producers: Brown Bannister and Steven Curtis Chapman; Label: Sparrow)

Pop/Contemporary Recorded Song: "Dive" written by Steven Curtis Chapman; Recorded by Steven Curtis Chapman (Label: Sparrow)

Contemporary Gospel Album: *Anointed* by Anointed (Producers: Keith Crouch, Tony Rich, Chris Harris, Mark Heimermann, Wayne Tester, and Kern Brantley; Label: Myrrh)

Contemporary Gospel Recorded Song: "Power" written by Fred Hammond and Kim Rutherford; Recorded by Fred Hammond and Radical for Christ on *The Prince of Egypt* Soundtrack (Label: Dreamworks)

Traditional Gospel Album: *Healing—Live in Detroit* by Richard Smallwood with Vision (Producers: Richard Smallwood and Steven Ford; Label: Verity)

Traditional Gospel Recorded Song: "God Can" written by Dottie Peoples; Recorded by Dottie Peoples (Label: AIR Gospel)

Urban Album: INSUFFICIENT NUMBER OF ELIGIBLE ENTRIES

Urban Recorded Song: "Anything Is Possible" written by Nee-c Walls-Allen, Steve Crawford, Da'Dra Crawford Greathouse, Keith Crouch, John Smith, and Sherree Ford Payne; Recorded by Anointed (Label: Myrrh)

Country Album: *A Glen Campbell Christmas* by Glen Campbell (Producers: Barry Beckett and Eddie Bayers; Label: Unison)

Country Recorded Song: "Angel Band" written by Public Domain; Recorded by Vestal Goodman and George Jones (Label: Pamplin)

Rock Album: *Time* by Third Day (Producers: Robert Beeson, Bob Wohler, Blaine Barcus, Monroe Jones, Jim Dineen; Label: Essential)

Rock Recorded Song: "Get Down" written by Mark Stuart, Bob Herdman, Will McGinniss, Ben Cissell, and Tyler Burkum; Recorded by Audio Adrenaline (Label: ForeFront)

Hard Music Album: *Point #1* by Chevelle (Producer: Steve Albini; Label: Squint)

Hard Music Recorded Song: "MIA" written by Pete Loeffler, Joe Loeffler, and Sam Loeffler; Recorded by Chevelle (Label: Squint)

Rap/Hip Hop Album: *Power* by Raze (Producers: Tedd Tjornham, Quinlan, and Zarc Porter; Label: ForeFront)

Rap/Hip Hop Recorded Song: "They All Fall Down" written by T Carter, S. Jones, R. Robbins, and O. Price; Recorded by Grits (Label: Gotee)

Alternative/Modern Rock Album: *Candy Coated Waterdrops* by Plumb (Producers: Bob Wohler, Glenn Rosenstein, and Matt Bronleewe; Label: Essential)

Alternative/Modern Rock Recorded Song: "Unforgetful You" written by Dan Haseltine, Matt Odmark, Steve Mason, and Charlie Lowell; Recorded by Jars of Clay (Label: Essential)

Bluegrass Album: *Kentucky Bluegrass* by The Bishops (Producer: Mark Bishop; Label: Homeland)

Bluegrass Recorded Song of the Year; "So Fine" written by Wayne Haun and Joel Lindsey; Recorded by Lewis Family (Label: Thoroughbred)

Instrumental Album: *Majesty and Wonder* by Phil Keaggy (Producers: Phil Keaggy and David Shober; Label: Myrrh)

Praise and Worship Album: *Sonicflood* by Sonicflood (Producers: Bryan Lenox, Jeff Deyo, Jason Halbert, Dwayne Larring, and Aaron Blanton; Label: Gotee)

Children's Music Album: *Larry Boy: The Soundtrack* by Veggie Tales (Producers: Kurt Heinecke, Mike Nawrocki, Masaki, and David Mullen; Label: Big Idea)

Spanish Language Album of the Year: *Llegar a Ti* by Jaci Velasquez (Producer: Rudy Perez, Mark Heimermann; Label: Myrrh)

Musical of the Year: *A Christmas To Remember* by Claire Cloninger and Gary Rhodes (Publisher: Word Music)

Youth/Children's Musical of the Year: *Lord, I Lift Your Name On High* (Producers: Karla Worley and Steven V. Taylor; Publisher: Word Music)

Choral Collection of the Year: *High & Lifted Up* (Producer: Carol Cymbala; Publisher: Brooklyn Tabernacle Music)

Special Event Album: *Streams* by Cindy Morgan, Maire Brennan, Michael McDonald, Sixpence None the Richer, Chris Rodriguez, Michelle Tumes, 4HIM, Delirious?, Amy Grant, Jaci Velasquez, Burlap to Cashmere, and Point of Grace (Producers: Brent Bourgeois and Loren Balman; Label: Word)

Recorded Music Packaging: Loren Balman, Chuck Hargett, and Robert M. Ascroft II for *Streams*; Recorded by various artists (Label: Word)

Enchanced CD of the Year: *Without Condition* by Ginny Owens (Producer: Craig A. Mason; Label: Rocketown)

Short-Form Music Video: "This is Your Time" Michael W. Smith (Producers and Directors: Amy Marsh; Brandon Dickerson and Ben Pearson; Label: Reunion)

Long-Form Music Video: "The Supernatural Experience" by dc Talk (Producers and Directors: Eric Welch, Dan Pitts and Eric Welch; Label: ForeFront)

2001: 32nd Annual Dove Awards

Song of the Year: "Redeemer" written by Nichole C. Mullen; Publishers: Seat of the Pants Music, ASCAP; Wordspring Music and Lil' Jas' Music, SESAC

Artist of the Year: New Day

New Artist of the Year: Plus One

Male Vocalist of the Year: Steven Curtis Chapman

Female Vocalist: Nichole Nordeman

Group of the Year: Third Day

Songwriter of the Year: Nichole C. Mullen

Producer of the Year: Brown Bannister

Rap/Hip Hop/Dance Recorded Song: "All Around the World" written by Ja'Marc Davis, Zarc Porter and Mark Pennels; Recorded by Raze (Label: ForeFront Records)

Modern Rock/Alternative Recorded Song: "Dive" written by Toby McKeehan, Michael Tait, Kevin Max and Mark Heimermann;

Recorded by dc Talk (Label: Forefront Records)

Hard Music Recorded Song: "Point #1" written by Pete Loeffler, Sam Loeffler, and Joe Loeffler; Recorded by Chevelle (Label: Squint)

Rock Recorded Song: "Sky Falls Down" written by Mac Powell, Mark Lee, Tai Anderson, Brad Avery, and David Carr; Recorded by Third Day (Label: Essential)

Pop/Contemporary Recorded Song: "Redeemer" written by Nicole C. Mullen; Recorded by Nicole C. Mullen (Label: Word)

Inspirational Recorded Song: "Blessed" written by Ginny Owens and Cindy Morgan; Recorded by Rachael Lampa (Label: Word)

Southern Gospel Recorded Song: "God Is Good All the Time" written by Tina Sadler; Recorded by The Gaither Vocal Band (Label: Spring Hill)

Bluegrass Recorded Song: "Are You Afraid To Die?" written by Ira Louvin, Charlie Louvin, and Eddie Hill; Recorded by Ricky Skaggs and Kentucky Thunder (Label: for Skaggs Family)

Country Recorded Song: "Baptism" written by Mickey Cates; Recorded by Randy Travis (Label: Atlantic)

Urban Recorded Song: "Shackles (Praise You)" written by Erica Atkins and Trecina Atkins; Recorded by Mary Mary (Label: Columbia)

Traditional Gospel Recorded Song: "We Fall Down" written by Kyle Matthews; Recorded by Donnie McClurkiny (Label: Verity)

Contemporary Gospel Recorded Song: "Alabaster Box" written by Janice Sjostran; Recorded by CeCe Winans (Label: Wellspring Gospel)

Rap/Hip Hop/Dance Album: *The Plan* by Raze (Producers: Michael Anthony Talyro and Tedd Tjornhom; Label: ForeFront)

Modern Rock/Alternative Album: *Jordan's Sister* by Kendall Payne (Producers: Ron Aniello and Glen Ballard; Label: Sparrow)

Hard Music Album: *Above* by Pillar (Producer: Travis Wyrick; Label: Flickerrecords)

Rock Album: *Tree63* by Tree63 (Producers: Andrew Philip and E.H. Holden; Label: Inpop Records)

Pop/Contemporary Album: *This Is Your Time* by Michael W. Smith (Producers: Michael W. Smith and Bryan Lenox; Label: Reunion)

Inspirational Album: *Home* by Fernando Ortega (Producer: John Andrew Schreiner; Label: Myrrh)

Southern Gospel Album: *I Do Belive* by The Gaither Vocal Band (Producers: Bill Gaither, Guy Penrod and Michael Sykes; Label: Spring Hill)

Bluegrass Album: *Inspirational Journey* by Randy Travis (Producer: Kyle Lehning; Label: Atlantic)

Urban Album: *Thankful* by Mary Mary (Producer: Warryn "Baby Dubb" Campbell; Label: Columbia)

Traditional Gospel Album: *You Can Make It* by Shirley Caesar (Producers: Bubba Smith, Shirley Caesar, and Michael Mathis; Label: Myrrh)

Contemporary Gospel Album: *Purpose By Design* by Fred Hammond & Radical for Christ (Producer: Fred Hammond; Label: Verity)

Instrumental Album: *Lights of Madrid* by Phil Keaggy (Producer: Phil Keaggy; Label: Wordartisan)

Praise & Worship Album: *Offerings: A Worship Album* by Third Day (Producers: Monroe Jones, Mac Powell, Mark Lee, Tai Anderson, Brad Avery, David Carr, and Joey Canady; Label: Essential)

Children's Music Album: *A Queen, A King, and A Very Blue Berry* by Veggie Tunes (Producers: Kurt Heinecke and Mike Nawrocki; Label: Big Idea)

Spanish Language Album: *Solo el Amor* by Miguel Agnel Guerra (Producer: Hal S. Batt; Label: Word Latin)

Special Event Album: *City on a Hill—Songs of Worship and Praise* by Jars of Clay, Sixpence None the Richer, Third Day, Caedmon's Call, FFH, The Choir, Gene Eugene, Sonicflood, and Peter Furler (Producer: Steve Hindalong; Label: Essential)

Musical of the Year: (tie): *2,000 Decembers Ago* by Joel Lindsey, Russell Maultin (Publisher: Brentwood Music) and Redeemer by Claire Cloninger and Robert Sterling (Publisher: Word Music)

Choral Collection of the Year: *God is Working* (Producer: Carol Cymbala; Publisher: Brooklyn Tabernacle Music)

Youth/Children's Musical: *Friends 4Ever* created by Karla Worley, Steven V. Taylor, Seth Worley, Peter Kipley and Michael W. Smith (Publisher: Word Music)

Recorded Music Packaging: art directors Buddy Jackson and Karinne Caulkins/Jackson and Photographer Ben Pearson for *Roaring Lambs* (Label: Squint Records)

Short-Form Music Video: "Rock the Party (Off the Hook)" by P.O.D. (Producers: Angela Jones and Marcos Siega; Label: Atlantic)

Long-Form Music Video: "A Farewell Celebration" by The Cathedrals (Producers and Directors: Bryan Bateman, Bill Gaither and Dennis Glore; Label: Spring House)

APPENDIX B

GOSPEL GRAMMY AWARDS

1958: 1st Grammy Awards
NONE

1959: 2nd Grammy Awards
NONE

1960: 3rd Grammy Awards
NONE

1961: 4th Grammy Awards
Best Gospel or Other Religious Recording
"Everytime I Feel The Spirit" by Mahalia Jackson

1962: 5th Grammy Awards
Best Gospel or Other Religious Recording
Great Songs of Love and Faith by Mahalia Jackson:

1963: 6th Grammy Awards
Best Gospel or Other Religious Recording (Musical)
"Dominique" by Soeur Sourire (The Singing Nun)

1964: 7th Grammy Awards
Best Gospel or Other Religious Recording (Musical)
Great Gospel Songs by Tennessee Ernie Ford

1965: 8th Grammy Awards
Best Gospel or Other Religious Recording (Musical)
Southland Favorites by George Beverly Shea and The Anita Kerr
Singers

1966: 9th Grammy Awards

Best Sacred Recording (Musical)
Grand Old Gospel by Porter Wagoner-Blackwood Brothers

1967: 10th Grammy Awards

Best Gospel Performance
More Grand Old Gospel by Porter Wagoner-Blackwood Brothers Quartet

Best Sacred Performance
"How Great Thou Art" by Elvis Presley

1968: 11th Grammy Awards

Best Gospel Performance
The Happy Gospel of the Happy Goodmans by Happy Goodman Family

Best Sacred Performance
Beautiful Isle of Somewhere by Jake Hess

Best Soul Gospel Performance
The Soul of Me by Dottie Rambo

1969: 12th Grammy Awards

Best Soul Gospel Performance
"Oh Happy Day" by Edwin Hawkins Singers

Best Sacred Performance (Non-Classical)
Ain't That Beautiful Singing by Jake Hess

Best Gospel Performance
In Gospel Country by Porter Wagoner, The Blackwood Brothers

1970: 13th Grammy Awards

Best Soul Gospel Performance
"Every Man Wants to Be Free" by Edwin Hawkins Singers

Best Sacred Performance (Musical)
"Everything Is Beautiful" by Jake Hess

Best Gospel Performance (Other Than Soul Gospel)
Talk About the Good Times by The Oak Ridge Boys

1971: 14th Grammy Awards

Best Soul Gospel Performance
"Put Your Hand in the Hand of the Man from Galilee" by Shirley Caesar

Best Sacred Performance
Did You Think to Pray by Charley Pride

Best Gospel Performance (Other Than Soul Gospel)
"Let Me Live" by Charley Pride

1972: 15th Grammy Awards

Best Gospel Performance
   L-O-V-E by Blackwood Brothers

Best Soul Gospel Performance
   "Amazing Grace" by Aretha Franklin

Best Inspirational Performance
   "He Touched Me" by Elvis Presley

1973: 16th Grammy Awards

Best Gospel Performance
   "Release Me (From My Sin)" by Blackwood Brothers

Best Soul Gospel Performance
   "Love Me Like a Rock" by Dixie Hummingbirds

Best Inspirational Performance
   "Let's Just Praise the Lord" by Bill Gaither Trio

1974: 17th Grammy Awards

Best Gospel Performance
   "The Baptism of Jesse Taylro" by The Oak Ridge Boys

Best Soul Gospel Performance
   "In the Ghetto" by James Cleveland with the Southern California
   Community Choir

Best Inspirational Performance (Non-Classical)
   "How Great Thou Art" by Elvis Presley

1975: 18th Grammy Awards

Best Gospel Performance (Other Than Soul Gospel)
   No Shortage by The Imperials

Best Soul Gospel Performance
   "Take Me Back" by Andrae Crouch and The Disciples

Best Inspirational Performance (Non-Classical)
   "Jesus, We Just Want to Thank You" by Bill Gaither Trio

1976: 19th Grammy Awards

Best Gospel Performance (Other Than Soul Gospel)
   "Where the Soul Never Dies" by The Oak Ridge Boys

Best Soul Gospel Performance
   "How I Got Over" by Mahalia Jackson

Best Inspirational Performance
   The Astonishing, Outrageous, Amazing, Incredible, Unbelievable,
   Different World of Gary S. Paxton by Gary S. Paxton

1977: 20th Grammy Awards

Best Gospel Performance, Contempoary or Inspirational
"Sail On" by The Imperials

Best Soul Gospel Performance, Traditional
James Cleveland Live at Carnegie Hall by James Cleveland

Best Soul Gospel Performance, Contempoary
"Wonderful!" by Edwin Hawkins & the Edwin Hawkins Singers

Best Gospel Performance, Traditional
"Just a Little Talk With Jesus" by The Oak Ridge Boys

Best Inspirational Performance
"Home Where I Belong" by B.J. Thomas

1978: 21st Grammy Awards

Best Gospel Performance, Traditional
"Refreshing" by The Happy Goodman Family

Best Gospel Performance, Contempoary or Inspirational
What a Friend by Larry Hart

Best Soul Gospel Performance, Contemporary
Live in London by Andrae Crouch and The Disciples

Best Soul Gospel Performance, Traditional
Live and Direct by Mighty Clouds of Joy

Best Inspirational Performance
"Happy Man" by B.J. Thomas

1979: 22nd Grammy Awards

Best Gospel Performance, Traditional
Lift Up The Name of Jesus by The Blackwood Brothers

Best Gospel Performance, Contemporary or Inspirational
Heed The Call by The Imperials

Best Soul Gospel Performance, Traditional
Changing Times by Mighty Clouds of Joy

Best Soul Gospel Performance, Contemporary
"I'll Be Thinking of You" by Andrae Crouch

Best Inspirational Performance
"You Gave Me Love (When Nobody Gave Me a Prayer)"
by B.J. Thomas

1980: 23rd Grammy Awards

Best Gospel Performance, Traditional
We Come To Worship by The Blackwood Brothers

Best Gospel Performance, Contemporary or Inspirational
The Lord's Prayer by Reba Rambo, Dony McGuire, B.J. Thomas,
Andrae Crouch, Walter Hawkins, Tremaine Hawkins, Cynthia
Clawson, and The Archers

Best Soul Gospel Performance, Contemporary
  Rejoice by Shirley Caesar
Best Soul Gospel Performance, Traditional
  Lord, Let Me Be An Instrument by James Cleveland and The Charles Fold Singers
Best Inspirational Performance
  With My Song I Will Praise Him by Debby Boone

1981: 24th Grammy Awards

Best Gospel Performance, Traditional
  The Masters V by The Masters V (James Blackwood, J.D. Sumner, Hovie Lister, Rosie Rozell and Jake Hess)
Best Gospel Performance, Contempoary or Inspirational
  Priority by The Imperials
Best Soul Gospel Performance, Contemporary
  Don't Give Up by Andrae Crouch
Best Soul Gospel Performance, Traditional
  The Lord Will Make A Way by Al Green
Best Inspirational Performance
  "Amazing Grace" by B.J. Thomas

1982: 25th Grammy Awards

Best Gospel Performance, Traditional
  "I'm Following You" by The Blackwood Brothers
Best Gospel Performance, Contempoary
  Age to Age by Amy Grant
Best Soul Gospel Performance, Contemporary
  "Higher Plane" by Al Green
Best Soul Gospel Performance, Traditional
  "Precious Lord" by Al Green
Best Inspirational Performance
  He Set My Life To Music by Barbara Mandrell

1983: 26th Grammy Awards

Best Gospel Performance, Female
  "Ageless Medley" by Amy Grant
Best Gospel Performance, Male
  Walls of Glass by Russ Taff
Best Soul Gospel Performance, Male
  "I'll Rise Again" by Al Green
Best Soul Gospel Performance, Female
  "We Sing Praises" by Sandra Crouch

Best Soul Gospel Performance by a Duo or Group
"I'm So Glad I'm Standing Here Today" by Barbara Mandrell and Bobby Jones
Best Gospel Performance By a Duo or Group
"More Than Wonderful" by Sandi Patti, Larnelle Harris
Best Inspirational Performance
"He's A Rebel" by Donna Summer

1984: 27th Grammy Awards

Best Gospel Performance, Female
"Angels" by Amy Grant
Best Gospel Performance, Male
Michael W. Smith by Michael W. Smith
Best Soul Gospel Performance, Male
"Always Remember" by Andrae Crouch
Best Soul Gospel Performance, Female
"Sailin' on the Sea of Your Love" by Shirley Caesar
Best Soul Gospel Performance by a Duo or Group
"Sailin' on the Sea of Your Love" by Shirley Caesar, Al Green
Best Gospel Performance By a Duo or Group
"Keep The Flame Burning" by Debby Boone and Phil Driscoll
Best Inspirational Performance
"Forgive Me" by Donna Summer

1985: 28th Grammy Awards

Best Gospel Performance, Female
Unguarded by Amy Grant
Best Gospel Performance, Male
"How Excellent Is Thy Name" by Larnelle Harris
Best Soul Gospel Performance, Male
"Bring Back The Days of Yea and Nay" by Marvin Winans
Best Soul Gospel Performance, Female
"Martin" by Shirley Caesar
Best Soul Gospel Performance by a Duo or Group, Choir or Chorus
"Tomorrow" by The Winans
Best Gospel Performance by a Duo or Group, Choir or Chorus
"I've Just Seen Jesus" by Sandi Patti, Larnelle Harris
Best Inspirational Performance
"Come Sunday" by Jennifer Holiday

1986: 29th Grammy Awards

Best Gospel Performance, Female
"Morning Like This" by Sandi Patti

Best Gospel Performance, Male
"Triumph" by Philip Bailey

Best Soul Gospel Performance, Male
"Going Away" by Al Green

Best Soul Gospel Performance, Female
"I Surrender All" by Deniece Williams

Best Soul Gospel Performance by a Duo or Group, Choir or Chours
"Let My People Go" by The Winans

Best Gospel Performance by a Duo or Group, Choir or Chorus
"They Say" by Sandi Patti, Deniece Williams

1987: 30th Grammy Awards

Best Gospel Performance, Female
"I Believe In You" by Deniece Williams

Best Gospel Performance, Male
"The Father Hath Provided" by Larnelle Harris

Best Soul Gospel Performance, Male
"Everything's Gonna Be Alright" by Al Green

Best Soul Gospel Performance, Female
"For Always" by CeCe Winans

Best Soul Gospel Performance by a Duo or Group, Choir or Chorus
"Ain't No Need To Worry" by Anita Baker, The Winans

Best Gospel Performance by a Duo or Group, Choir or Chorus
Crack The Sky by Mylon LeFevre and Broken Heart; Producer: Greg Piccolo

1988: 31st Grammy Awards

Best Gospel Performance, Female
Lead Me On by Amy Grant

Best Gospel Performance, Male
Christmas by Larnelle Harris

Best Soul Gospel Performance, Male
Abundant Life by BeBe Winans

Best Soul Gospel Performance, Female
One Lord, One Faith, One Baptism by Aretha Franklin

Best Soul Gospel Performance by a Duo or Group, Choir or Chorus
Take Six by Take 6

Best Gospel Performance by a Duo or Group, Choir or Chorus
The Winans Live At Carnegie Hall by The Winans

1989: 32nd Grammy Awards

Best Gospel Vocal Performance, Female
Don't Cry by CeCe Winans

Best Gospel Vocal Performance, Male
Meantime by BeBe Winans

Best Soul Gospel Performance, Male or Female
As Long As We're Together by Al Green

Best Soul Gospel Performance by a Duo or Group, Choir or Chorus
Let Brotherly Love Continue by Daniel Winans

Best Gospel Performance By a Duo or Group, Choir or Chorus
The Saviour Is Waiting by Take 6

1990: 33rd Grammy Awards

Best Southern Gospel Album
The Great Exchange by Bruce Carroll

Best Gospel Album by a Choir or Chorus
Dr. James Cleveland and The Southern California Community Choir

Best Traditional Soul Gospel Performance
Tramaine Hawkins Live by Tramaine Hawkins

Best Gospel Pop Album
Another Time...Another Place by Sandi Patti

Best Rock/Contemporary Gospel Album
Beyond Belief by Petra

Best Contemporary Soul Gospel Album
So Much 2 Say by Take 6

1991: 34th Grammy Awards

Best Pop Gospel Album
For the Sake of the Call by Steven Curtis Chapman

Best Southern Gospel Album
Homecoming by The Gaither Vocal Band

Best Gospel Album by Choir or Chorus
The Evolution of Gospel by Gary Hines

Best Traditional Soul Gospel Album
Pray For Me by Mighty Clouds of Joy

Best Rock/Contemporary Gospel Album
Under Their Influence by Russ Taff

Best Contempoary Soul Gospel Album
Different Lifestyles by CeCe and BeBe Winans

1992: 35th Grammy Awards

Best Traditional Soul Gospel Album
He's Working It Out for You by Shirley Caesar

Best Southern Gospel Album
Sometimes Miracles Hide by Bruce Carroll

Best Pop Gospel Album
The Great Adventure by Steven Curtis Chapman

Best Gospel Album by a Choir or Chorus
Edwin Hawkins Music & Arts Seminar Mass Choir—Recorded Live in Los Angeles; Director: Edwin Hawkins

Best Rock/Contempoary Gospel Album
Unseen Power by Petra

Best Contemporary Soul Gospel Album
Handel's Messiah—A Soulful Celebration by various artists; Producer: Mervyn E. Warren

1993: 36th Grammy Awards

Best Traditional Soul Gospel Album
Stand Still by Shirley Caesar

Best Pop/Contempoary Gospel Album
The Live Adventure by Steven Curtis Chapman

Best Gospel Album by a Choir or Chorus
Live...We Come Rejoicing by the Brooklyn Tabernacle Choir; Director: Carol Cymbala

Best Rock Gospel Album
Free At Last by dc Talk

Best Southern Gospel, Country Gospel, or Bluegrass Gospel Album
Good News by Kathy Mattea

Best Contemporary Soul Gospel Album
All Out by The Winans

1994: 37th Grammy Awards

Best Gospel Album By a Choir or Chorus
Through God's Eyes by Milton Brunson and Thompson Community Singers

Best Southern Gospel, Country Gospel or Bluegrass Gospel Album
I Know Who Holds Tomorrow by Alison Krauss and The Cox Family

Best Pop/Contemporary Gospel Album
Mercy by Andrae Crouch

Best Rock Gospel Album
Wake-Up Call by Petra

Best Contemporary Soul Gospel Album
Join The Band by Take 6

Best Traditional Soul Gospel Album
Songs Of The Church—Live in Memphis by Albertina Walker
Best Gospel Album by a Choir or Chorus
Live In Atlanta At Morehouse College by The Love Fellowship Crusade Choir, Hezakiah Walker, Director

1995: 38th Grammy Awards

Best Traditional Soul Gospel Album
Shirley Caesar Live..He Will Come by Shirley Caesar
Best Rock Gospel Album
Lesson Of Love by Ashley Cleveland
Best Gospel Album By a Choir or Chorus
Praise Him...Live! by The Brooklyn Tabernacle Choir; Choir Director: Carol Cymbala
Best Southern Gospel, Country Gospel, or Bluegrass Gospel Album
Amazing Grace—A Country Salute to Gospel by various artists; Compilation Producer: Bill Hearn
Best Pop/Contemporary Gospel Album
I'll Lead You Home by Michael W. Smith
Best Contemporary Soul Gospel Album
Alone In His Presence by CeCe Winans

1996: 39th Grammy Awards

Best Gospel Album by a Choir or Chorus
Just A Word by Shirley Caesar's Outreach Convention Choir
Best Rock Gospel Album
Jesus Freak by dc Talk
Best Contemporary Soul Gospel Album
Whatcha Lookin' 4 by Kirk Franklin and The Family
Best Southern Gospel, Country Gospel or Bluegrass Gospel Album
I Love To Tell The Story—25 Timeless Hymns by Andy Griffith
Best Traditional Soul Gospel Album
Face To Face by Cissy Houston
Best Pop/Contemporary Gospel Album
Tribute—The Songs of Andrae Crouch by various artists; Producers: Neal Joseph and Norman Miller

1997: 40th Grammy Awards

Best Gospel Choir or Chorus Album
God's Property From Kirk Franklin's Nu Nation by God's Property; Choir Directors: Kirk Franklin, Myron Butler, and Robert Searight II
Best Southern, Country or Bluegrass Gospel Album
Amazing Grace 2: A Country Salute To Gospel by various artists; Producers: David Corlew and Peter York

Best Rock Gospel Album
Welcome to the Freak Show: dc Talk Live in Concert by dc Talk

Best Traditional Soul Gospel Album
I Couldn't Hear Nobody Pray by The Fairfield Four

Best Pop/Contemporary Gospel Album
Much Afraid by Jars of Clay

Best Contemporary Soul Gospel Album
Brothers by Take 6

1998: 41st Grammy Awards

Best Southern, Country, or Bluegrass Gospel Album
The Apostle—Music from and Inspired by the Motion Picture by various artists; Producers: Peter Afterman, John Huie, and Ken Levitan

Best Rock Gospel Album
You Are There by Ashley Cleveland

Best Gospel Choir or Chorus Album
Reflections by O'Landa Draper and The Associates Choir

Best Contemporary Soul Gospel Album
The Nu Nation Project by Kirk Franklin

Best Traditional Soul Gospel Album
He Leadeth Me by Cissy Houston

Best Pop/Contemporary Gospel Album
This Is My Song by Deniece Williams

1999: 42nd Grammy Awards

Best Contemporary Soul Gospel Album
Mountain High...Valley Low by Yoland Adams

Best Traditional Soul Gospel Album
Christmas With Shirley Caesar by Shirley Caesar

Best Pop/Contemporary Gospel Album
Speechless by Steven Curtis Chapman

Best Gospel Choir or Chorus Album
High and Lifted Up by The Brooklyn Tabernacle Choir; Choir Director Carol Cymbala

Best Southern, Country, or Bluegrass Gospel Album
Kennedy Center Homecoming by Bill and Gloria Gaither and Their Homecoming Friends

Best Rock Gospel Album
Pray by Rebecca St. James

2000: 43rd Grammy Awrds

Rock Gospel Album
Double Take by Petra

Pop/Contemporary Gospel Album
If I Left the Zoo by Jars of Clay

Southern, Country or Bluegrass Gospel Ablum
Soldier of the Cross by Ricky Skaggs and Kentucky Thunder

Traditional Soul Gospel Album
You Can Make It by Shirley Caesar

Contemporary Soul Gospel Album
Thankful by Mary Mary

Gospel Choir or Chorus Album
Live—God is Working by the Brooklyn Tabernacle Choir; Choir Director: Carol Cymbala

BIBLIOGRAPHY

(NOTE: *CCM* is *Contemporary Christian Music*, *RW* is *Record World*, *CB* is *Cashbox*, and *BB* is *Billboard*.

Albertson, Chris. *Bessie*. New York: Stein and Day, 1972.

Anderson, Charles S. *Readings in Luther for Laymen*. Minneapolis: Augsburg, 1967.

Anderson, Robert and Gail North. *Gospel Music Encyclopedia*. New York: Sterling, 1979.

Anderson, Robert Mapes. *Vision of the Disinherited: The Making of American Pentecostalism*. New York: Oxford, 1979.

Anderson, Tim. "The Roots of Rock: Did Gospel Music Give Birth to the Devil's Rock 'n' Roll?" *Contemporary Christian Magazine,* February 1984: 12-14, 42.

Andrews, Edward D. *The Gift To Be Simple*. New York: Dover Pub. 1940.

Appell, Richard G. *The Music of the Bay Psalm Book*. New York: Institute to Studies in American Music, 1975.

Applebome, Peter. *Dixie Rising: How the South is Shaping American Values*, Politics, and Culture. New York: Times Books, 1996.

"Are Hits Holy? Radio Stations, Record Labels Feud Over Use of Singles." *CCM,* Aug/Sept. 1981 Vol. 4 Nos. 2 & 3: 31.

Armstrong, Ben. "How Big is the Religious Radio-TV Audience?" *Religious Broadcasting*, May 1981.

　　　The Electric Church. Nashville: Thomas Nelson, 1979.

Armstrong, Karen. *A History of God*. New York: Alfred A. Knopf, 1994.

"Back to That Old Time Religion." *Time*, 26 December 1977: 52-58.

Baer, Hans A. *The Black Spiritual Movement: A Religious Response to Racism*. Knoxville: University of Tennessee Press, 1974.

Bailey, Albert Edward. *The Gospel in Hymns*. New York: Charles Scribner's Sons, 1950.

Baker, Paul. "Bass Sees Bright Future for Gospel in Christian Market." *CB* 29 March 1980: G-6, G-16.

　　　"Can Gospel Increase Airplay and Climb the Secular Pop Charts?" *CCM,* August 1980 Vol. 3 No. 2: 16-17.

"Jesus Music: A New Dimension in Pop and Gospel." *RW*, 1 October 1977: 12, 88, 98.

"Religious Radio: Ain't What It Used to Be." *BB*, 28 July 1979: R-28, R-43, R-45.

I've Got a New Song. San Diego: Scandinavia, 1983.

Topical Index of Contemporary Christian Music. Pinson, Alabama: Music Helps, 1987.

Why Should The Devil Have All The Good Music. Waco: Word, 1979.

Contemporary Christian Music: Where It Came From, What It is, Where It's Going. Westchester, Ill.: Crossway, 1985

Baldwin, Neil. *Edison: Inventing the Century*. New York: Hyperion, 1995.

Balmer, Randall. *Mine Eyes Have Seen the Glory: A Journey into the Evangelical Subculture of America*. Oxford, England: Oxford University Press, 1989.

Barbour, James. *The Music of William Billings*. New York: Da Capo, 1972.

Barfield, Ray. *Listening to Radio: 1920-1950*. Westport, CT: Praeger, 1996.

Barnouw, Eric. *A History of Broadcasting: Vol I—to 1933*. New York: Oxford University Press, 1966.

Barnouw, Eric. *In Preparation: A History of Broadcasting: Vol III*: New York: Oxford University Press, 1970.

Barnouw, Eric. *The Golden Web: A History of Broadcasting: Vol II—1933-1953*. New York: Oxford University Press, 1968.

Barry, John M. Rising Tide: *The Great Mississippi Flood of 1927 and How It Changed America*. New York: Simon and Schuster, 1997.

Barton, William E. *Old Plantation Hymns*. New York: AMS Press, 1972.

Becker, Paula. *Let The Song Go On*. (Biography of the Speer Family). Nashville: Impact, 1971.

Benson, Louis F. *The English Hymn: Its Development and Use in Worship*. New York: Hodder and Stoughton, 1915.

Benware, David. "Christian Radio in Focus: Part 1." *CCM*, December 1978 Vol. 1 No. 2: 18, 22.

"Christian Radio: Part 2." *CCM*, January 1979 Vol. 1 No. 7: 16, 28.

"Christian Radio: Part 3." *CCM*, Februrary 1979 Vol. 1 No. 8: 18, 25.

"Christian Radio: Part 4." *CCM*, March 1979 Vol. 1 No. 9: 16-21.

"Christian Radio: Part 5." *CCM*, April 1979 Vol. 1 No. 10: 13, 31.

"Christian Radio: Part 6." *CCM*, May 1979 Vol. 1 No. 11: 17, 23.

Berkman, Dave. "Long Before Falwell: Early Radio and Religion—As reported by the Nation's Periodical Press." *Journal of Popular Culture*. Vol. 21 No. 4, Spring 1988. 1-11.

Billings, William. *The Psalm-Singers Amusement*. New York: Da Capo, 1975.

Bisher, Furman. "They Put Rhythm in Religion." *Saturday Evening Post*, c. 1953.

BIBLIOGRAPHY

Blackwell, Lois S. *The Wings of the Dove*. Norfolk, Va.: The Donning Co., 1978.

Blackwood, James, with Dan Martin. *The James Blackwood Story*. Monroeville, Penn.: Whitaker House, 1975.

Bloom, Allan. *The Closing of the American Mind*. New York: Simon & Schuster, 1987.

Bock, Al. *I Saw The Light: The Gospel Life of Hank Williams*. Nashville: Green Valley Record Store, 1977.

Booth, Stanley. *Rhythm Oil: A Journey Through the Music of the American South*. London: Jonathan Cape, 1991.

Boyer, Horace Clarence, text, Lloyd Yearwood, photography. *How Sweet the Sound: The Golden Age of Gospel*. Washington D.C.: Elliott and Clark, 1995.

Bradford, Perry. *Born With The Blues: Perry Bradford's Own Story: The True Story of the Pioneering Blues Singers and Musicians in the Early Days of Jazz*. New York: Oak Publications, 1965.

Branch, Taylor. *Parting the Waters: America in the King Years 1954-63*. New York: Simon & Schuster, 1988.

    Pillar of Fire: America in the King Years 1963-65. New York: Simon & Schuster, 1998.

Bronson, Fred. *The Billboard Book of Number One Hits*. New York: Billboard Books, 1985.

    Billboard's Hottest 100 Hits. New York: Billboard Books, 1991.

Broughton, Viv. *Black Gospel*. Pool, England: Blandford, 1985.

Brown, Theron and Hezekiah Butterworth. *The Story of the Hymns and Tunes*. New York: American Tract Society, 1906.

Bruce, Dickson D. Jr., *And They All Sang Hallelujah*. Knoxville: University of Tennessee Press, 1974.

Burns, Carolyn A. "'83 Grammys" *CCM,* April 1983 Vol. 5 No. 10.

Burt, Jesse and Duane Allen. *The History of Gospel Music*. Nashville: K & S Press, 1971.

Carr, Patrick, ed. *The Illustrated History of Country Music*. Garden City, New York: Dolphin and Doubleday, 1980.

Carter, Dan T. *The Politics of Rage: George Wallace, the Origins of the New Conservatism, and the Transformation of American Politics*. New York: Simon and Schuster, 1995.

Cash, Johnny. *Man in Black*. Grand Rapids, Mich.: Zondervan, 1975.

Cash, June Carter. *Among My Klediments*. Grand Rapids, Mich.: Zondervan, 1979.

"CBA Slights Music Sales." *CCM,* May 1980 Vol. 2 No. 12: 31.

Chanan, Michael. *Repeated Takes: A Short History of Recording and Its Effects on Music*. London: Verso, 1995.

Chandler, Russell. "The Good News in Gospel Music." *Saturday Evening Post*, April 1982: 18-19, 22, 115.

Charters, Samuel. *The Roots of the Blues: An African Search*. Boston: Marion Boyars, 1981.

Chase, Gilbert. *America's Music from the Pilgrims to the Present*. 1955. Revised 2nd ed. New York: McGrawHill, 1966.

Chilton, John. *Let the Good Times Roll: The Story of Louis Jordan and His Music*. Ann Arbor: University of Michigan Press, 1994.

Christ-Janer, Albert, Charles W. Hughes, and Carleton Sprague Smith. *American Hymns Old and New*. New York: Columbia University Press, 1980.

Claghorn, Gene. *Women Composers and Hymnists: A Concise Bibliographical Dictionary*. Metuchen, J. J.: The Scarecrow Press, 1984.

Clarke, Donald. *The Rise and Fall of Popular Music*. New York: St. Martin's, 1995.

Clower, Jerry with Gerry Wood. *Ain't God Good*. Waco: Word, 1975.

Cobb, Buell E., Jr. *The Sacred Harp: A Tradition and It's Music*. Athens, Ga.: University of Georgia Press, 1981.

Coffman, Jeanne. "The Kingsmen ... A Spiritual Explosion." *Singing News*, November 1986.

Collins, Richard. *The General Next To God*. Glasgow: Fantana/Collins, 1965.

Collum, Danny. "Prophet of Hope for the Sick and Tired." (Fanny Lou Hamer) *Sojourners*, Vol. 11 No. 11 December, 1982: 3-4.

> "Stepping Out Into Freedom: The Life of Fanny Lou Hamer." *Sojourners*, Vol. 11 No. 11 December 1982: 11-16.

Cone, James H. *The Spirituals and the Blues: An Interpretation*. New York: Seabury, 1972.

Conn, Charles Paul. *The New Johnny Cash*. Old Tappan, NJ: Spire, 1976.

"Convention Report: National Religious Broadcasters." *CCM,* March 1979 Vol. 1 No. 9: 16.

Coontz, Stephanie. *The Way We Never Were: American Families and the Nostagia Trap*. New York: Basic Books, 1992.

> *The Way We Really Are: Coming To Terms With America's Changing Families*. New York: Basic Books, 1997.

Cooper-Lewter, Nicholas C. and Henry H. Mitchell. *Soul Theology: The Heart of American Black Culture*. San Francisco: Harper & Row, 1986.

Cowen, Tyler. *In Praise of Commerical Culture*. Cambridge, MA: Harvard University Press, 1998.

Crawford, Richard A. *Andrew Law, American Psalmdist*. New York: Da Capo, 1981.

> "Mainstreams and Backwaters in American Psalmody." Jacket notes for *Make a Joyful Noise*. New World Records, NW 255.

> "Music of the American Revolution." Jacket notes for *The Birth of Liberty*. New World Records, NW 276.

> *The Core Repertory of Early American Psalmody*. Madison, Wisc.: A. R. Editions, 1984.

Crosby, Fanny. *Memories of Eighty Hymns*. Boston: James H. Earle & Co., 1906.

Crouch, Andrae with Nina Ball. *Through It All*. Waco: Word, 1974.

BIBLIOGRAPHY

Cullen, Jim. *The Art of Democracy: A Concise History of Popular Culture in the United States*. New York: Monthly Review Press, 1996.

Curtis, J. Scott. "NRB: Can Music Be Plugged Into the Electric Church?" CCM April 1979 Vol. 1 No. 10: 18

Cusic, Don. "A Market Divided." (Black gospel.) *CB* 7 August 1982: G-14.

"Amy Grant—Reaching Out." *Christian Life* June 1981 Vol. 43, No. 2: 18-20.

"Amy Grant." *CCM*, June 1979 Vol. 1 No. 12: 6-7.

"Billy Ray Hearn on Sparrow's Takeoff." *RW* 11 November 1978: 24, 48, 51, 60.

"Bob Benson on Building the Gospel Market." *RW* 1 October 1977: 6, 22, 28.

"The Cathedrals: At the Top of Today's Southern Gospel." *Rejoice*, Winter 1987 Vol. 1 No. 1: 31-32.

"Don Butler: Spreading the Word Through GMA." *RW* 11 November 1978: 22, 52, 60.

"Gospel Faces Important Issues Following Growth of 70s." *CB*, 29 March 1980: G-3, G-12.

"Gospel Music Goes Back to Church With a Return to Tradition." *Rejoice*, Winter 1987 Vol. 1 No. 1: 42-43.

"Gospel Music Seeks Ways to Unite and Publicize Its Various Styles." *RW*, 11 November 1978: 16, 64.

"Gospel Radio at Crossroads Between Music and Message." *CB*, 29 March 1980: G-9.

"Gospel: Music With a Timeless Message." *RW*, 1 October 1977: 4, 99.

"James Cleveland on Expanding Gospel's Audience." *RW*, 11 November 1978: 32, 48.

"Jarrell McCracken on Spreading the Word." *RW*, 1 October 1977: 14, 78, 92, 101.

"John T. Benson III on the Future of the Benson Co." *RW*, 1 October 1977: 4, 31.

"Johnny Cash Carries A Message In Song." *Music City News*, September 1980: Vol. XVII No. 3 16-17.

"Johnny Cash: The First 25 Years." *CB*, 14 June 1980: C-5, 22.

"Shannon Williams Traces the History of Nashboro Records." *CB*, March 29, 1980: G-3, 14.

"Southern Gospel Grows From Rural Roots." *BB*, 28 July 1979: R-16, R-45.

"Southern Gospel: An Historical Review." *Rejoice*, Winter 1987 Vol. 1 No. 1: 29-30.

"St. Louis Jesuits: Music With Mass Appeal." *CCM*, October 1979 Vol. 2 No. 4: 32.

"The Doves Fly Again" *CCM*, April 1982 Vol. 4 No. 10.

"The Imperials: Building a Musical Bridge." *CCM*, February 1980 Vol. 2 No. 8: 6-7.

"The New Movement in Catholic Music." *CCM*, July 1979 Vol. 2 No. 1: 27-28.

"White Christian Market Continues to Grow." *RW*, 1 October 1977: 83.

"Zondervan Corp. Announces Major Record Expansion." *CB*, 29 March 1980: G-19.

Music in the Market. Bowling Green, Ohio: Bowling Green State University Popular Press, 1997.

Sandi Patti: The Voice of Gospel. New York: Dolphin/Doubleday, 1988.

Dabney, Dick. "God's Own Network." *Harper's*, August 1980: 33-52.

Daniel, Ralph T. *The Anthem in New England Before 1800*. New York: Da Capo, 1979.

Darden, Bob. "The World of Gospel Music: Counting Musical Blessings" *Billboard*, 11 October 1986.

"Word Records: A 30-Year Success Story." *CCM*, January 1981 Vol. 3 No. 7: W-4, 5.

"Word's 30 Years Net 70% of Christian Records Sold." *CCM*, January 1981 Vol. 3 No. 7: W-17, 18.

Davis, Francis. *The History of the Blues*. New York: Hyperion, 1995.

Dickinson, Edward. *Music in the History of the Western Church*. New York: Charles Scribner's Sons, 1902 and 1927.

Dinwiddie, Richard D. "Two Brothers...Who Changed the Course of Church Singing." *Christianity Today*, 21 September 1984: 30-34.

"When You Sing Next Sunday, Thank Luther." *Christianity Today*, 21 October 1983: 18-21.

Dorsey, L. C. "A Prophet Who Believed." (Fanny Lou Hamer). *Sojourners*, December 1982 Vol. 11 No. 11: 21.

"Dove and Grammy Awards" *CCM*, February 1982 Vol. 4 No. 8.

Dowley, Tim, ed. *Eerdman's Handbook to the History of Christianity*. Grand Rapids, Mich.: Wm. B. Eerdman's, 1977.

Dumenil, Lynn. *The Modern Temper: American Culture and Society in the 1920s*. New York: Hill and Wang, 1995.

Durasoff, Steve. *Bright Wind of the Spirit: Pentacostalism Today*. Englewood Cliffs: Prentice-Hall, 1972.

Egerton, John. *Speak Now Against the Day: The Generation Before the Civil Rights Movement in the South* New York: Alfred A. Knopf, 1994.

Ellwood, Robert S., Jr. *One Way: The Jesus Movement and Its Meaning*. Englewood Cliffs, NJ: Prentice-Hall, 1973

BIBLIOGRAPHY

Elson, Louis C. *The History of American Music*. New York: MacMillan, 1925.

Emerson, Ken. *Doo-Dah! Stephen Foster and the Rise of American Popular Culture*. New York: Simon & Schuster, 1997.

Enroth, Ronald M., Edward E. Ericson, Jr. and C. Breckinridge Peters. *The Jesus People: Old-Time Religion in the Age of Aquarius*. Grand Rapids, Mich: Eerdmans, 1972.

Epstein, Dena J. *Sinful Tunes and Spirituals*. Urbana: Univesrity of Illinois Press, 1977.

Epstein, Jonathan S. ed. *Adolescents and Their Music: If It's Too Loud, You're Too Old*. New York: Garland, 1995.

Eskew, Harry. "White Urban Hymnody." Jacket notes on *Brighten the Corner Where You Are*. New World, NW 224.

"Facing the Challenges of a Burgeoning Industry." *CCM*, August 1978 Vol. 1 No. 2: 10, 15.

Fernando, S. H., Jr. *The New Beats: Exploring the Music, Culture and Attitudes of Hip-Hop*. New York: Anchor, 1994.

Filene, Benjamin. *Romancing the Folk: Public Memory & American Roots Music*. Chapel Hill, NC: University of North Carolina Press, 2000

Findlay, James F., Jr. *Dwight Moody: American Evangelist, 1837-1899*. Chicago: University of Chicago Press, 1969.

Fishwick, Marshall and Ray B. Browne, ed. *The God Pumpers: Religion in the Electronic Age*. Bowling Green, Ohio: Popular Press, 1987.

Flake, Carol. *Redemptorama: Culture, Politics and the New Evangelism*. Garden City, NY: Anchor and Doubleday, 1984.

Foote, Henry Wilder. *Three Centuries of American Hymnody*. Cambridge: Harvard University Press, 1940.

Ford, Tennessee Ernie. *This is My Story, This is My Song*. Englewood Cliffs: Prentice-Hall, 1963.

Forntale, Peter and Joshua E. Mills. *Radio in the Television Age*. Woodstock, NY: The Overlook Press, 1980.

Franklin, Aretha and David Ritz. *Aretha: From These Roots*. New York: Crown, 1999.

Frazier, E. Franklin. *The Negro Church in America, 1963*. Reprint New York: Schocken Books, 1974.

Friedenthal, Richard. *Luther: His Life and Times*. New York: Harcourt, 1967.

Friedlander, Paul. *Rock and Roll: A Social History*. Boulder, CO: Westview, 1996.

Frith, Simon ed. *Facing the Music: Essays on Pop, Rock, and Culture*. London: Mandarin, 1990.

> *Sound Effects: Youth, Leisure, and the Politics of Rock*. London: Constable and Company Ltd., 1983.

Fromkin, David. *In the Time of the Americans: FDR, Truman, Eisenhower, Marshall, MacArthur—The Generation That Changed America's Role in the World*. New York: Vintage, 1995.

Frum, David. *How We Got Here: The 70's: The Decade That Brought You Modern Life (For Better or Worse)*. New York: Basic Books, 2000.

Gaillard, Frye. *Race, Rock & Religion*. Charlotte, NC: East Woods Press, 1977.

Gaines, Donna. *Teenage Wasteland: Suburbia's Deadend Kids*. New York: Pantheon, 1991.

"Gallup Poll Profiles Christain Market." *CCM*, May 1980 Vol. 2 No. 12: 31.

Gallup Report. "Religion in America." No. 236: May 1985.

Gallup, George Jr. and David Poling. *The Search for America's Faith*. Nashville: Abingdon, 1980.

Gans, Herbert J. *Popular Culture and High Culture*. New York: Baisc, 1974.

Garofalo, Reebee, ed. *Rockin' the Boat: Mass Music & Mass Movements*. Boston: South End, 1992.

Garraty, John A. *The Great Depression*. New York: Harcourt Brace Jovanovich, 1986.

Geer, E. Harold. *Hymnal for Colleges and Schools*. New Haven: Yale, 1956.

Genovese, Eugene D. Roll, Jordan, Roll: *The World the Slaves Made*. 1972. Reprint. New York: Vintage, 1976.

Gentry, Linnell. *A History and Encyclopedia of Country, Western, and Gospel Music*. Nashville: Clairmont Corp, 1969.

George Carol V.R. *Segregated Sabbaths: Richard Allen and the Emergence of Independent Black Churches 1760-1840*. New York: Oxford University Press, 1973.

George, Nelson. *Hip Hop America* New York: Penguin, 1998.

Gillespie, Paul E., ed. *Foxfire 7*. Garden City, NY: Anchor/Doubleday, 1982.

Gillett, Charlie. *The Sound of the City: The Rise of Rock and Roll*. New York: Pantheon, 1983.

Godwin, Jeff. *What's Wrong With Christian Rock?* Chino, CA: Chick, 1990.

Goldberg, Michael. "Amy Grant Wants to Put God on the Charts." *Rolling Stone*. 6 June 1985.

Goodwin, Doris Kearns. *No Ordinary Time: Franklin and Eleanor Roosevelt: The Home Front in World War II*. New York: Touchstone, 1994.

Goreau, Laurraine. *Just Mahalia, Baby: The Mahalia Jackson Story*. Waco, TX: Word Books, 1975.

"Gospel TV: Religion, Politics and Money." *Time*. 17 February 1986: 62-69.

Gould, Nathaniel D. *Church Music In America*. New York: A. N. Johnson, 1853.

Great Songs of the Church (Number Two). Chicago: Great Songs Press, 1965.

Greeley, Andrew. *God in Popular Culture*. Chicago: Thomas More, 1989.

Green, Douglas. *Country Roots*. New York: Hawthorn, 1976.

Green, Keith. "Music or Mission." *CCM*, October 1978 Vol. 1 No. 4: 32.

Green, Melody and David Hazard. *No Compromise: The Life Story of Keith Green*. Chatsworth, CA: Spararow, 1989.

Green, Melody. "A letter from... " *CCM,* September l982 Vol. 5 No. 3: 36-37.

Gubernick, Lisa and Robert LaFranco. "Rocking with God" *Forbes*, 2 January 1995: 49-41.

Guiness, Os. *Fit Bodies, Fat Minds: Why Evangelicals Don't Think and What To Do About It.* Grand Rapids: Baker, 1994.

Guralnick, Peter and Ernst Jorgensen. *Elvis Day By Day: The Definitive Record of His Life and Music.* New York: Ballantine, 1999.

Guralnick, Peter. *Careless Love: The Unmaking of Elvis Presley.* Boston: Little, Brown & Co. 1999.

> *Last Train to Memphis: The Rise of Elvis Presley.* Boston: Little, Brown, 1994.

> *Sweet Soul Music.* New York: Harper & Row, l986.

Hafer, Jack. "A Christian Look at the Arts." *CCM,* July l980 Vol. 3 No. l: 45, 49.

> "Lyrics: Honest, Deep and Christian Too?" *CCM,* November l980 Vol. 3 No. 4: l0, 25.

> "The Importance of Entertainment." *CCM,* September l980 Vol. 3 No 3: 22, 29.

> "The Purpose of Music." *CCM*, Aug. l980 Vol. 3 No. 2: 28, 33.

> "The Spiritual Power of Rock'n'Roll." *CCM,* October l980 Vol. 3 No. 4: 37.

Haile, H. G. *Luther: An Experiment in Biography*. Garden City, NJ: Doubleday, l980.

Halberstam, David. *The Children. New York*: Random House, 1998.

> *The Fifties.* New York: Villard, 1993.

Hall, Sammy with Charles Paul Conn. *Hooked on a Good Thing.* Old Tappan, NJ: Fleming H. Revell, l972.

Hamm, Charles, Bruno Nettl, and Ronald Byrnside. *Contemporary Music and Music Cultures.* Englewood Cliffs: Prentice-Hall, l975.

Hamm, Charles. *Yesterdays: Popular Song in America.* New York: W. W. Norton, l979.

Handy, William C. *Father of the Blues: An Autobiography.* Arna Bontemps, ed. New York: Macmillan, 1941.

Hardy, Phil and Dave Laing. *The Faber Companion to 20th-Century Popular Music.* London: Faber and Faber, 1990.

Harries, Meirion & Susie Harries. *The Last Days of Innocence: World War I.* New York: Random House, 1997.

Harris, Michael W. *The Rise of Gospel Blues: The Music of Thomas Andrew Dorsey in the Urban Church.* New York: Oxford University Press, 1992.

Hartman, Bob. *More Power To Ya.* Ohio: Standard Publishing 1997.

Haynes, Michael K. *The God of Rock: A Christian Perspective of Rock Music.* Lindale, TX: Priority, 1982.

"HeartWarming: First Label." *RW,* 1 October l977: 3, l8, 30.

Heilbut, Anthony. "Black Urban Hymnody." Jacket notes on *Brighten the Corner Where You Are*. New World, NW 224.

Heilbut, Tony. *The Gospel Sound: Good News and Bad Times*. New York: Simon and Schuster, 1971.

Henry, Carl F. *The Uneasy Conscience of Modern Fundamentalism*. Grand Rapids, Mich: Eerdmans, 1947.

Hinchman, Gary J. "Christian Artists: Today's Prophets?" *Contemporary Christian Music,* August 1987: 19.

Hinkle, Sally. "Musical Conversion: From Pop to Praising the Lord." *BB,* 28 July 1979: R-18, 41.

Hirshey, Gerri. *Nowhere to Run: The Story of Soul Music*. New York: Penguin, 1985.

Holm, Dallas with Robert Paul Lamb. *This Is My Story*. Nashville: Impact, 1980.

Hopkins, Jerry. *Elvis: A Biography*. New York: Warner, 1971.

   Elvis: The Final Years. New York: Playboy, 1981.

Horn, Dorothy D. *Sing to Me of Heaven: A Study of Folk and Early American Materials in Three Old Harp Books*. Gainesville, FL: University of Florida Press, 1970.

Horsfield, Peter G. *Religious Television: An American Experience*. New York: Longman, 1984.

Horstman, Dorothy. *Sing Your Heart Out Country Boy*. New York: E. P. Dutton, 1975.

Horton, Michael S. *Made in America: The Shaping of Modern American Evangelicalism*. Grand Rapids, Mich: Baker, 1991.

Howard, Jay R. and John M. Streck. *Apostles of Rock: The Splintered World of Contemporary Christian Music*. Lexington: The University Press of Kentucky 1999.

Howard, John Tasker. *Our American Music: Three Hundred Years of It*. New York: Thomas Y. Crowell, 1930.

Hunter, James Davison. *American Evangelicalism: Conservative Religion and the Quandary of Modernity*. New Brunswick, NJ Rutgers University Press, 1983.

Ingalls, Jeremiah. *The Christian Harmony*. New York: Da Capo, 1981.

Inserra, Lorraine and H. Wiley Hitchcock. *The Music of Ainsworth Psalter*. New York: Institute for Studies in American Music, 1981.

Isserman, Maurice and Michael Kazin. *America Divided: The Civil War of the 1960s*. New York: Oxford University Press, 2000.

Jackson, Clyde Owen. *The Songs of Our Years: A Study of Negro Folk Music*. New York: Exposition, 1968.

Jackson, George Pullen. *Another Sheaf of White Spirituals*. Gainesville: University of Florida Press, 1952.

   ed. *Spiritual Folk-Songs of Early America: Two Hundred and Fifty Tunes and Texts with an Introduction and Notes*. 1937. Reprint. New York: Dover, 1964.

   Down-East Spirituals and Others. New York: J. J. Augustin, 1939.

Spiritual Folk Songs of Early America. New York: J. J. Augustin, 1937.

White and Negro Spirituals. Locust Valley, NY: J. J. Augustin, 1943.

White Spirituals in the Southern Uplands. New York: Dover, 1965.

Jackson, Irene. *Afro-American Religious Music.* Westport, CT: Greenwood Press, 1979.

Jeffrey, Jeff. "Breaking The Chains: Marketing to the Retail Mainstream" *Billboard Spotlight: Gospel* 3 August 1996

Johnson, Guye. *Treasury of Great Hymns and Their Stories.* Greenville, SC: Bob Jones UP, 1986.

Johnson, James Weldon and J. Rosamond Johnson. *American Negro Spirituals.* New York: Viking, 1925.

Johnson, James Weldon. ed. *The Second Book of Negro Spirituals.* New York: Viking, 1926.

Johnson, James Weldon. *God's Trombones.* 1927. Reprint. New York: Viking, 1955.

Johnson, June. "Broken Barriers and Billy Sticks." (Fanny Lou Hamer). *Sojourners,* December 1982 Vol. 11 No. 11: 16-17.

Jorstad, Erling. *Popular Religion in America: The Evangelical Voice.* Westport, CN: Greenwood, 1993.

Julian, John. *Dictionary of Hymnolgy Volume I: A-O.* Grand Rapids, MI.: Kregael, 1985.

   Dictionary of Hymnology Volume II: P-Z. Grand Rapids, MI.: Kregel, 1985.

Katz, Bernard, ed. *The Social Implications of Early Negro Music in the United States.* New York: Arno Press, 1969.

Kay, Jane Holtz. *Asphalt Nation: How the Automobile Took Over America and How We Can Take It Back.* New York: Crown, 1997

Keil, Charles. *Urban Blues.* Chicago: Unversity of Chicago Press, 1966.

"Keith Green" *CCM,* May 1982 Vol. 4 No. 1.

"Keith Green." *CCM,* September 1982 Vol. 5 No. 3: 32-33.

"Keith Green: A Tribute." *CCM,* September 1982 Vol. 5 No. 3: 36-37.

"Keith Green's Musical Journey." *RW,* 1 October 1977: 69.

"Keith Green's Next Album Not to Be Available in Stores." *CCM,* December 1979 Vol. 2 No. 6: 31.

Kenney, William Howland. *Recorded Music in American Life: The Phonograph and Popular Memory, 1890-1945.* New York: Oxford University Press, 1999.

Key, Dana with Steve Rabey. *Don't Stop the Music.* Grand Rapids, Mich: Zondervan, 1989.

King, Edwin. "Go Tell It On The Mountain: A Prophet from the Delta." (Fanny Lou Hamer). *Sojourners,* December 1982 Vol. 11 No. 11: 18-20.

Knaack, Twila. *I Touched a Sparrow: Ethel Waters.* Waco, TX: Word, 1978.

Krasilovsky, M. William and Sidney Shemel. *This Business of Music: The Definitive Guide to the Music Industry, 8th edition.* New York: Billboard Books, 2000.

Krehbiel, Henry E. *Afro-American Folksongs: A Study in Racial and National Music.* New York: G. Schirmer, 1914.

"1982 CBA Convention" *CCM,* September 1982 Vol. 5 No. 3. .

Langdon, Philip. *A Better Place to Live: Reshaping the American Suburb.* Amherst: University of Massachusetts Press, 1994.

"Larry Norman: The Original Christian Street Rocker." *CCM,* March 1981 Vol. 3 No. 9: 8-11, 25.

Larson, Bob. *Hippies, Hindus and Rock & Roll.* McCook, NE: Larson, 1969.

  Rock and Roll: The Devil's Diversion. McCook, NE: Larson, 1967.

  Rock and the Church. Carol Stream, IL: Creation House, 1971.

  Rock. Wheaton, IL.: Tyndale House, 1980.

  The Day the Music Died. Carol Stream, IL: Creation House, 1972.

Lawhead, Steve. "Beyond the Statistics." *CCM,* November 1979 Vol. 2 No. 5: 30, 32.

  "Who is the Consumer?" *CCM,* August 1979 Vol. 2 No. 2: 22.

  "Selling the Message in the Marketplace." *CCM,* May 1980 Vol. 2 No. 12: 21.

  "The Consumer: Christian Music's Most Wanted Person." *CCM,* September 1979 Vol. 2 No. 3: 30, 32.

Leach, MacEdward, ed. *The Ballad Book.* New York: A. S. Barnes, 1955.

Leiper, Maria and Henry W. Simon, eds. *A Treasury of Hymns.* New York: Simon and Schuster, 1953.

Levine, Lawrence W. *Black Culture and Black Consciousness: Afro-American Folk Thought from Slavery to Freedom.* New York: Oxford University Press, 1977.

Lewis, Tom. *Divided Highways: Building the Interstate Highways, Transforming American Life.* New York: Viking, 1997.

Lewis, Tom. *Empire of the Air.* New York: HarperCollins, 1991.

Liesch, Barry. *The New Worship: Straight Talk on Music and the Church.* Grand Rapids, MI: Baker, 1996.

Lomax, Alan. "Baptist Hymns and White Spirituals from the Southern Mountains." Jacket notes for *The Gospel Ship.* New World, NW 294.

  "White Spirituals From the Sacred Harp." Jacket notes for *White Spirituals from the Sacred Harp.* New World, NW 205.

  The Land Where the Blues Began. New York: Pantheon, 1993.

Lorenz, Ellen Jane. *Glory, Hallelujah.* Nashville: Abingdon, 1978.

Lornell, Kip. *Happy in the Service of the Lord: Afro-American Gospel Quartets in Memphis.* Urbana: University of Illinois Press, 1988.

Lovell, John, Jr. *Black Song: The Forge and the Flame: The Story of How the Afro-American Spiritual Was Hammered Out.* New York: Macmillan, 1972.

Luther, Frank. *Americans and Their Songs.* New York: Harper Brothers, 1942.

Lydon, Michael. *Ray Charles: Man and Music.* New York: Riverhead Books, 1998.

BIBLIOGRAPHY

MacDougal, Hamilton C. *Early New England Psalmody*. New York: Da Capo, 1969.

Malone, Bill. *Country Music U.S.A.* Austin: University of Texas Press, 1968.

    Southern Music, American Music. Lexington: University Press of Kentucky, 1979.

Maltin, Leonard. *The Great American Broadcast: A Celebration of Radio's Golden Age*. New York: Dutton, 1997.

Marsden, George M. *Fundamentalism and American Culture: The Shaping of Twentieth-Century Fundamentalism: 1870-1925*. Oxford: Oxford University Press, 1980.

    Marsden, George M. *Reforming Fundamentalism*. Grand Rapids, MI: Eerdmans, 1987.

Marsden, George M. *Understanding Fundamentalism and Evangelicalism*. Grand Rapids, Mich: Eerdmans, 1991.

Marsh, J. B. T. *The Story of the Jubilee Singers*; with their songs Boston: Houghton, Mifflin and Company. 1881.

Marshall, Madeleine Forell and Janet Todd. *Hymns in the Eighteenth Century*. Lexington: University of Kentucky Press, 1982.

Martin, Linda and Kerry Segrave. *Anti-Rock: The Opposition to Rock'n'Roll*. Hamden, CT: Archon Books, 1988.

Martin, Rob. "Keith Green: Sold Out to Jesus." *CCM*, October 1978 Vol. 1, No. 4: 1, 6.

Marty, Martin. *Pilgrims in Their Own Land*. Boston: Little, Brown, 1985.

Marwick, Arthur. *The Sixties*. New York: Oxford University Press, 1998.

Mays, Benjamin E. and Joseph W. Nicholson. *The Negro's Church*. 1933. Reprint. New York: Arno Press, 1969.

McDannell, Colleen. *Material Christianity*. New Haven, CN: Yale University Press, 1995.

McElvaine, Robert S. *The Great Depression: America 1929-1941*. New York: Times Books, 1984.

McGrath, Tom. *MTV: The Making of a Revolution*. Philadelphia: Running Press, 1996.

McKay, David P. and Richard Crawford. *William Billings of Boston*. Princeton: Princeton University Press, 1975.

McLaurin, Charles. "Voice of Calm." (Fanny Lou Hamer). *Sojourners,* December 1982 Vol. 11 No. 11: 12-13.

McLoughlin, William G., Jr. Billy *Sunday Was His Real Name*. Chicago: The University of Chicago Press, 1955.

Medema, Ken with Joyce Norman. *Come and See*. Waco: Word, 1976.

Mellers, Wilfred. *A Darker Shade of Pale: A Backdrop to Bob Dylan*. New York: Oxford University Press, 1985.

Menconi, Al. "What's Wrong with Christian Music?" *CCM*, June 1987: 19-20.

Merrill, Antracia. "The Other Side of Rap: Christian Radio and Fans Believe in the Gospel According to Hip-Hop." *Billboard Spotlight: Gospel* 2 August 1997

Metcalf, Frank. *American Psalmody*. New York: Da Capo, l968.

Miles, Jack. *God: A Biography*. New York: Alfred A. Knopf, 1995.

Millard, Bob. *Amy Grant*. New York: Dolphin/Doubleday, l986.

Miller, Steve. *The Contempoary Christian Music Debate: Worldly Compromise or Agent of Change*. Wheaton, IL: Tyndale House Publishers, Inc. 1993.

Moore, R. Lawrence. *Selling God: American Religion in the Marketplace of Culture*. New York: Oxford University Press, 1994.

"More Major Labels Go For Gospel" *CCM,* October l98l. Vol. 4 No. 4.

Morison, Samuel Eliot. *The Oxford History of the American People*. New York: Oxford, l965.

Morris, Edward. "Oaks Translate Gospel to Secular Success." *BB,* 28 July l979: R-34, R-50.

Muggeridge, Malcom. *Christ and the Media*. Grand Rapids, MI: Eerdmans, 1977.

Murphy, Cullen. "Who Do Men Say That I Am?" *The Atlantic*, December l986: 37-58.

Murrells, Joseph. *Million Selling Records*. New York: Arco, l984.

"Music Companies Actively Pursue Catholic Market." *CCM,* May l980 Vol. 2 No. l2: 9, ll, l4.

Myers, Kenneth A. *All God's Children and Blue Suede Shoes: Christians and Popular Culture*. Wheaton, IL: Crossway, 1989.

Myra, Harold and Dean Merrill. *Rock, Bach and Superschlock*. New York: Holman, 1972.

Nachman, Gerald. *Raised on Radio*. New York: Pantheon, 1998.

Naisbitt, John. *Megatrends*. New York: Warner, l982.

"NALR Institute Revitalizes Worship Music." *CCM,* December l980 Vol. 3 No 6: 31.

"NALR President Ray Bruno." *CCM,* October l980 Vol. 3 No. 4: 12-14.

Nasaw, David. *Going Out: The Rise and Fall of Public Amusements*. New York: Basic Books, 1993.

Nathan, Hans. *William Billings: Data and Documents*. Detroit: The College Music Society, l976.

Nettl, Paul. *Luther and Music*. New York: Russell and Russell, l948.

"The New Rebel Cry: Jesus is Coming!" *Time*. 21 June l97l: 56-63.

Newcomb, Brian Quincy. "Petra: Back to the Rock." *CCM,* October l986 Vol 9 No. 4.

"Petra Wages a New War." *CCM,* October l987 Vol. 10 No. 4.

Nichol, John Thomas. *Pentecostalism*. Plainfield, NJ: Logos, l966.

Nobel, E. Maron. *The Gospel of Music*. Washington, DC: MAR Press, l971.

Noll, Mark A. *The Scandal of the Evangelical Mind*. Grand Rapids, MI: William B. Eerdmans Publishing Co., 1994.

BIBLIOGRAPHY

"NRB Members Restless, Dissatisfied with Gospel Music Industry." *CCM,* August 1980 Vol. 3 No. 2: 35.

Nutt, Grady. *So Good, So Far...* Nashville: Impact, 1979.

Nye, Russel Blaine. *The Cultural Life of the New Nation.* New York: Harper & Brothers, 1960.

    The Unembarrassed Muse: The Popular Arts in America. New York: The Dial Press, 1970).

O'Neil, Thomas. *The Grammy's for the Record.* New York: Penguin, 1993.

O'Neill, Dan. *Troubadour for the Lord: The Story of John Michael Talbot.* New York: Crossroad, 1983.

Oak Ridge Boys with Ellis Widner and Walter Carter. *The Oak Ridge Boys: Our Story.* Chicago: Contemporary, 1987.

Oakley, Giles. *The Devil's Music: A History of the Blues.* New York: Toplinger, 1976.

Odum, Howard W. and Guy B. Johnson. *The Negro and His Songs: A Study of Typical Negro Songs in the South.* Chapel Hill: University of North Carolina Press, 1925.

Oldham, Doug with Fred Bauer. *I Don't Live There Anymore.* Nashville: Impact, 1973.

Oliver, Paul, Max Harrison, and William Bolcom. *The New Grove Gospel, Blues and Jazz.* New York: W. W. Norton, 1986.

Oliver, Paul. *Blues Off the Record.* Kent, England: The Baton Press, 1984.

    Screening the Blues: Aspects of the Blues Tradition. New York: Da Capo, 1968.

    Songsters and Saints: Vocal Traditions on Race Records. Cambridge, England Cambridge University Press, 1984.

Orgill, Michael. *Anchored in Love: The Carter Family.* Old Tappan: Fleming H. Revell, 1975.

Owens, J. Garfield. *All God's Chillun.* New York: Abington, 1971.

Palaosaari, Jim. "The Christian Radio-Record Connection." *CCM* May 1981 Vol. 3 No. 11: 42, 46.

Patterson, Daniel W. *The Shaker Spiritual.* Princeton: Princeton UP, 1979.

Patti, Sandi. *The Book of Words.* Milwaukee, WI.: Hal Leonard, 1986.

Pelikan, Jaroslav. "The Enduring Relevance of Martin Luther 500 Years After His Birth." *New York Times Magazine,* 18 September 1983: 43-45, 99-104.

Pemberton, Carol Ann. *Lowell Mason: His Life and Work.* Ann Arbor, MI: UMI Research P, 1985.

Peters, Dan and Steve Peters with Cher Merrill. *Rock's Hidden Persuader: The Truth About Backmasking.* Minneapolis: Bethany, 1985.

    Why Knock Rock? Minneapolis: Bethany, 1984.

    "Burning Rock's Bottom." *Contemporary Christian Magazine,* November, 1984: 51-53.

What About Christian Rock? Minneapolis: Bethany House, 1986.

"Petra: CCM Focus." *CCM,* November 1982 Vol. 5 No. 5.

"Petra's Story" *CCM,* January 1982. Vol 4 No. 7.

Picardie Justine and Dorothy Wade. *Atlantic and the Godfathers of Rock and Roll.* London: Fourth Estate, 1990.

Pike, G.D. *Jubilee Singers, and their Campaign for Twenty Thousand Dollars.* New York: AMS Press, Inc., 1974, reprinted from edition from Boston: Lee and Shepard, Publishers; New York: Lee, Shepard and Dillingham, 1873.

Platt, Karen Marie. "Catholic Music: Going Into the World." *CCM,* October 1979 Vol. 2 No. 4: 32.

    "Catholic Records Since Vatican II." *CCM,* October 1980 Vol. 3 No. 4: 16, 21, 42.

    "The Doves: What Kind of Strange Birds Are They?" *CCM,* April 1981 Vol. 3 No 10: 29.

Point of Grace and David Seay. *Life, Love & Other Mysteries.* New York: Pocket Books, 1996.

Pollack, W.G. *The Handbook to the Lutheran Hymnal.* St. Louis: Concordia, 1975.

"Power, Glory—And Politics." *Time,* 17 February 1986: 62-69.

Price, Deborah Evans. "A Field in Flux" *Billboard* April 26, 1997 Spotlight: Contemporary Christian Music

    "Industry Hopes Material & Spiritual Prosperity Will Continue After a Year of 'Remarkable Growth'" *Billboard,* 25 April 1998

Quebedeaux, Richard. *The Worldly Evangelicals.* San Francisco: Harper & Row, 1978.

Rabey, Steve. "An Update with John Michael Talbot." *CCM,* October 1980 Vol. 3 No. 4: 14.

    "Keith Green." *CCM.* December, 1987. Vol. 10 No. 6.

    ed. *Rock the Planet.* Grand Rapids, MI: Zondervan, 1989.

    The Heart of Rock'n Roll. Old Tappan, NJ: Fleming H. Revell, 1986.

Racine, Kree Jack. *Above All.* Memphis: Jarodoce, 1967.

Read, Oliver and Walter L. Welch. *From Tin Foil to Stereo.* Indianapolis: Howard W. Sams, 1959 and 1976.

Reagon, Bernice Johnson and Linn Shapiro, eds. *Roberta Martin and the Roberta Martin Singers: The Legacy and The Music.* Washington DC: Smithsonian, 1982.

"Recording Positive Pop in the Secular Market." *CCM,* August 1980 Vol. 3 No. 2: 9.

Reeves, Jeremiah Bascom. *The Hymn as Literature.* New York: The Century Co., 1924.

Reich, Charles A. *The Greening of America.* New York: Bantam, 1970.

"Religious Radio Must Pay." *CCM,* October 1981 Vol. 4 No. 4.

"Religious Right or Religious Wrong?" *CCM,* November 1984 Vol. 7 No. 5 (politics)

BIBLIOGRAPHY

"Remembering 1982" *CCM*, January 1983 Vol. 5 No. 7.

"Rev. James Cleveland." *CCM,* June 1981 Vol. 3 No. 12: 11, 16.

"Rev. James Cleveland: Gospel Artist Extraordinaire." *RW,* October 1, 1977: 103.

Revitt, Paul *The George Pullen Jackson Collection of Southern Hymnody.* Los Angeles: University of California Library, 1964.

Reynolds, David. *Rich Relations: The American Occupation of Britain, 1942-1945.* New York: Random House, 1995.

RIAA. *Gold and Platinum Awards.* New York: Recording Industry Association of America, Inc., 1988.

Ricks, George Robinson. *Some Aspects of the Religious Music of the United States Negro.* New York: Arno Press, 1977.

Roach, Hildred. *Black American Music.* Boston: Crescendo, 1973.

Roell, Craig. *The Piano in America, 1890-1940.* Chapel Hill: University of North Carolina Press, 1989.

Rogal, Samuel J. *Sisters of Sacred Song.* New York: Garland, 1981.

Roland, Tom. *The Billboard Book of Number One Country Hits.* New York: Billboard Books, 1991.

Romanowski, Patricia and Holly George-Warren, eds. *The New Rolling Stone Encyclopedia of Rock & Roll.* New York: Fireside, 1995.

Rookmakker, Hans. *Art Needs No Justification.* Intervarsity Press, 1978.

    The Creative Gift. Cornerstone, 1981.

Ross, Andrew and Tricia Rose, eds. *Microphone Friends: Youth Music and Youth Culture.* New York: Routledge, 1994.

Routley, Erik. *An English Speaking Hymnal Guide.* Collegeville, MN.: The Liturgical P, 1979.

    The Music of Christian Hymns. Chicago: G. I. A. Publications, 1981.

    Words, Music and the Church. Nashville: Abingdon, 1968.

Samuelson, Robert J. *The Good Life and Its Discontents: The American Dream in the Age of Entitlement, 1945-1995.* New York: Times Books, 1995.

Sankey, Ira D. *My Life and The Story of the Gospel Hymns.* Philadelphia: The Sunday School Times, 1907.

Sankey, Ira, James McGranahan, George C. Stebbins, and Phillip Bibbs. *Gospel Hymns Nos. 1 to 6 Complete.* New York: Da Capo, 1972.

Sasson, Diane. *The Shaker Spiritual Narrative.* Knoxville: U of Tennessee P, 1983.

Schaeffer, Franky. *Addicted to Mediocrity: Twentieth Century Christians and the Arts.* Wheaton, IL: Crossway, 1985.

Schalk, Carl. "The Seduction of Church Music: Perspective on the American Scene." *Church Music,* 79: 2-10.

Schipper, Henry. *Broken Record: The Inside Story of the Grammy Awards.* New York: Birch Lane, 1992.

Schultze, Quentin. J. ed. *American Evangelicals and the Mass Media*. Grand Rapids, MI: Zondervan, 1990.

Seay, Davin and Mary Neely. *Stairway to Heaven*. New York: Ballantine, 1986.

Shaw, Arnold. *Honkers and Shouters*. New York: Macmillan, 1978.

    Let's Dance: Popular Music in the 1930s. New York: Oxford University Press, 1998.

    The World of Soul. New York: Paperback Library, 1971.

Shea, George Beverly with Fred Bauer. *Songs That Lift The Heart*. Old Tappan, NJ: Fleming H. Revell, 1972.

Shea, George Beverly with Fred Bauer. *Then Sings My Soul*. Old Tappan, NJ: Fleming H. Revell, 1968.

Shelton, Robert. *No Direction Home: The Life and Music of Bob Dylan*. New York: Beech Tree/William Morrow, 1986.

Sizer, Sandra S. *Gospel Hymns and Social Religion*. Philadelphia: Temple University Press, 1978.

Smith, Anthony, ed. *Television: An International History*. New York: Oxford University Press, 1995.

Smith, Huston. *The Religions of Man*. New York: Harper & Row, 1958.

Smith, Jane Stuard and Betty Carlson. *A Gift of Music*. Cornerstone Books, 1981.

Smith, Kevin. *At the Foot of Heaven*. Nashville: Star Song, 1994.

Smith, Michael S. "Apocalypse Now." *New West*, 12 March 1979: SC 1-3.

Smith, Michael W. and Fritz Ridenour. *Old Enough to Know*. Waco, TX: Word, 1987.

Sonneck, Oscar. G. T. *Francis Hopkinson and James Lyon*. New York: De Capo, 1967.

Sonneck, Oscar George Theodore, and William Treat Upton. *A Bibliography of Early Secular American Music*. Washington DC: Library of Congress, 1945.

Southern, Eileen, ed. *Readings in Black American Music*. No publisher or date listed.

Southern, Eileen. *The Music of Black Americans: A History. 2nd edition*. New York: W. W. Norton, 1983.

St. James, Rebecca. *40 Days with God: A Devotional Journey*. Ohio: Standard Publishing, 1996.

    You're the Voice: Forty More Days with God—A Contemporary Devotional. Nashville: Thomas Nelson Publishers, 1997.

Stevenson, Arthur L. *The Story of Southern Hymnology*. Roanoke: A. L. Stevenson (self-published), 1931.

Stewart-Baxter, Derrick. *Ma Rainey and the Classic Blues Singers*. New York: Stein and Day, 1970.

Styll, John W. "B. J. Thomas' Road Home." *CCM*, December 1978 Vol. 1 No. 6: 1, 24, 28.

    "CBA Convention: A Sense of Purpose." *CCM*, August 1979 Vol. 2 No. 2: 8, 25.

"CBA Fever: Close Encounters of a Profitable Kind." *CCM,* July 1979 Vol. 2 No. 2: 12.

"Christian Music: Who Sets the Standards?" *CCM,* August 1978 Vol. 1, No. 2: 10, 15.

"Christian Rock Wars: Evangelist Jimmy Swaggart tells why he hates today's Christian rock." *CCM,* June 1985 Vol. 7 No. 12: 14-17.

"Good News About Catholic Music." *CCM,* October 1980 Vol. 3 No. 4: 5.

"Keith Green: An Exclusive Interview." *CCM,* March 1980 Vol. 2 No. 9: 6-7.

"Swaggart: One Man's Opinion." *CCM,* September 1980 Vol. 3 No 3: 5.

"The Bill Gaither Trio: Making Concerts in the Round." *CCM,* January 1980 Vol. 2 No. 7: 29, 34.

"The Bill Gaither Trio: Making It Work at Home." *CCM,* May 1979 Vol 1 No. 11: 6-7.

"What Makes Music Christian?" *CCM,* April 1987: 35-36.

Styll, John W. ed. *The Heart of the Matter: The Best of* CCM *Interviews, Volume 1.* Nashville: Star Song, 1991

Swaggart, Jimmy with Robert Paul Lamb. *To Cross a River.* Plainfield, NJ: Logos International, 1977.

"Brother Swaggart, Here is My Question." *The Evangelist,* February 1988, Vol. 20 No. 2: 9-10.

Religious Rock'n'Roll: A Wolf in Sheep's Clothing. Baton Rouge: Jimmy Swaggart Ministries, 1987.

Synan, Vinson. *The Holiness Pentecostal Movement.* Grand Rapids, MI: William B. Eerdmans, 1971.

Tamke, Susan S. *Make a Joyful Noise Unto The Lord.* No Publisher Listed, 1978.

Tepper, Ron. "Retail Witnesses Financial and Distribution Challenges." *BB* 28 July 1979: R-20, 46.

Terrell, Bob. "Three chords and a cloud of dust: The Jim Hamill Story." *Singing News,* February 1988.

"The Benson Company: 75 Years of Growth." *RW,* 1 October 1977: 3, 30.

"The Gospel Boom." *Saturday Evening Post,* April 1979: 34-36, 40, 136.

"The Greatest Story Ever told ... and Retold, and Retold ..." *New Times,* 16 September 1977: 14-15.

Thomas, B. J. *Home Where I Belong.* Waco: Word, YEAR.

Tichi, Cecelia. *Electronic Hearth: Creating an American Television Culture.* New York: Oxford University Press, 1991.

Toffler, Alvin. *The Third Wave.* New York: Bantam, 1980.

Tosches, Nick. *Hellfire: The Jerry Lee Lewis Story.* New York: Delacorte, 1982.

Tribe, Ivan M. *The Stonemans: An Appalachian Family and the Music That Shaped Their Lives.* Urbana and Chicago: University of Illinois Press, 1993.

Underhill, Paco. *Why We Buy: The Science of Shopping.* New York: Simon & Schuster, 1999.

Van West, Carroll, ed. *The Tennessee Encyclopedia of History & Culture.* Nashville: Rutledge Hill, 1998.

Velten, Ron. "The Confessions of John Michael Talbot." *CCM*, October 1979 Vol. 2 No. 4: 6-7, 39.

Walsh, Sheila. *Never Give It Up.* Old Tappan, NJ: Fleming H. Revell, 1986.

Walton, Samuel B. "People Like Honest Sounds." (Bill Gaither Trio). *Saturday Evening Post,* April 1977: 46, 47, 99, 102.

Ward, Andrew. *Dark Midnight When I Rise: The Story of the Jubilee Singers Who Introduced the World to the Music of Black America.* New York: Farrar, Straus and Giroux, 2000.

Ward, Ed, Geoffrey Stokes, and Ken Tucker. *Rock of Ages: The Rolling Stone History of Rock & Roll.* New York: Rolling Stone Press/Summit, 1986.

Warner, Brian. "Why Audiences Aren't Ready For Contemporary Christian Music." *CCM,* January 1980 Vol. 2 No. 7: 18, 24.

Warnke, Mike. *Hitchiking on Hope Street.* Garden City, NY: Doubleday & Co., 1979.

Weber, Max. *The Protestant Ethic and the Spirit of Capitalism.* New York: Scribner, 1958.

Weill, Gus. *You Are My Sunshine: The Jimmie Davis Story.* Waco: Word, 1977.

Whitburn, Joel. *The Billboard Book of Top 40 Albums.* New York: Billboard Books, 1991.

   Top 40 Hits. New York: Billboard Publications, 1987.

   Top Pop Albums 1955-1985. Menomonee Falls, WI: Record Research, 1985.

   Top Pop Singles 1955-1986. Menomonee Falls, WI: Record Research, 1987.

   Pop Memories 1890-1954. Menomonee Falls, WI: Record Research, Inc.: 1986.

White, A. and F. Bronson. *The Billboard Book of Number One Rhythm & Blues Hits.* New York: Billboard Books, 1993.

"Who's Listening to Religious Radio Anyway?" *CCM,* March 1982 Vol. 4 No. 9.

Wilder, Alec. *American Popular Song.* New York: Oxford, 1972.

Willems, Jim and Betty. "Convention Report: National Association of Recording Merchandisers." *CCM,* May 1979 Vol. 1 No. 11: 12.

Willems, Jim. "Christian Retailing: Book Store or Record Store?" *CCM,* April 1979 Vol. 1 No. 10: 8.

   "1980 NARM Convention Faces the Issues." *CCM* May, 1980 Vol. 2 No. 11: 18-19.

Williams, Robert M. *Sing a Sad Song: The Life of Hank Williams.* 2nd ed. Urbana and Chicago: University of Illinois Press, 1981.

BIBLIOGRAPHY

Wills, Garry. *Under God: Religion and American Politics.* New York: Simon and Schuster, 1990.

Winkworth, Catherine. *Christian Singers of Germany.* Freeport, NY: Books for Libraries, 1977.

Witter, Evelyn. *Mahalia Jackson.* Milford, MI.: Mott Media, 1985.

Wolfe, Charles K. "Columbia Records and Old-Time Music." *JEMF Quarterly*: 118-125, 144.

> "Early Gospel Quartets: The Case of The McDonald Brothers." *Rejoice*, Spring 1988 Vol. 1 No. 2: 14-17.

> "Gospel Boogie: White Southern Gospel Music in Transition." *Popular Music.* Cambridge, 1981.

> *Kentucky Country.* Lexington: University of Kentucky Press, 1982.

> *Tennessee Strings.* Knoxville: University of Tennessee Press, YEAR.

"Word Nudges World Awake to Rise of Contemporary Gospel." *CCM*, January 1981 Vol. 3 No. 7: W-7, 12.

Work, John W. ed. *American Negro Songs and Spirituals.* New York: Bonanza, 1940.

Work, John Wesley. *Folk Song of the American Negro.* 1915. Reprint. New York: Negro Univesities Press, 1969.

"The Year in Review" *CCM*, December 1981 Vol. 4 No. 6.

Yergin, Daniel and Joseph Stanislaw. *The Commanding Heights: The Battle Between Government and the Marketplace That is Remaking the Modern World.* New York: Simon & Schuster, 1998.

Zecher, Henry. "How One Man's Pen Changed the World." *Christianity Today,* 21 October 1983: 10-13.

INDEX

INDEX

Apollo 100, 241
Apollo Records, 205, 206
Apostolic Faith Gospel Mission (Houston),
  120. See also Azusa Street Revival
Archers, the, 295, 332, 338
"Are You Ready," 240
Argyll, Duke and Duchess of, 100
Armageddon Experience, The (album), 249
Arminius, 56
Armstrong, Louis, 302
Armstrong, Vanessa Bell, 145
Arne, Thomas, 71–72
Arnold, Eddy, 191
Arnold, Samuel, 73
"Arthur Godfrey Talent Show"
  (television/radio show), 202, 203
Asberry, Richard and Ruth, 120
Asbury, Francis, 92
Assembly of God, 317–20, 324
Astonishing, Outrageous, Amazing, Incredible,
  Unbelievable, Different World of Gary S.
  Paxton, The, 289
"At the End of the Trail," 323
Athens Music Company, 171
Atkins, Chet, 223
Atlantic Records, 206
Atwell, George, 350
Audio Adrenaline, 384
Augustine, Saint, 46
Autry, Gene, 177
Azusa Street Revival, 120, 144–45

Bach, Johann Christian, 71
Bach, Johann Sebastian, 24, 72
Bachelors, the, 238
"Back to God Hour" (radio show), 140
"Back to the Bible" (radio show), 140
Bagwell, Wendy, 370
Bailey, Albert, The Gospel in Hymns, 45–46,
  54, 56
Bainbridge Street Methodist Church
  (Philadelphia), 145–46
Baize, Bill, 266
Baker, Paul, Why Should the Devil Have all
  the Good Music, 247
Baker, Richard, 367
Baker, Seth, 372, 373
Bakker, Jim, 289, 312, 314, 326
Bakker, Tammy Faye, 312
ballad operas, 69
ballads, 65, 69, 82
Ballouw, Silas, 40
Baltimore, George Calvert, Lord, 273

Band Called David, A, 295
Banks Brothers, the, 145
Bannister, Brown, 286–87, 337
"Baptism of Jesse Taylor, The," 260
Baptists, 78, 81–82, 103, 143, 147
  in colonial America, 39, 42
  hymnals, 148
  quartet singing, 146
Barlow, Joel, 39
Barnard, Hilman, 159
Barnard, John, 39
Barnes, Robert, 14
Barnett, Vernon W., 146
Barnhouse, Donald Grey, 140
Barrows, Cliff, 185
Bartlett, Eugene M., 158, 160, 162
Bass, John, 353
bass viol, 37
"Battle Hymn of the Republic, The," 128,
  148, 226
Baxter, Jesse Randall (J.R.), 155, 159–60,
  188
Baxter, Les, 226
Bay Psalm Book, 35, 39
Beasley, Bill, 253–54
Beasley, Les, 252, 253, 254, 283, 379
Beatles, the, 237, 239, 346, 393
beatniks, 221
"Beautiful Dreamer" (Foster), 74
"Beautiful Music," 287
"Because He Lives" (Gaither), 244
Bee Gees, the, 293
Beecher, Henry Ward, 62, 98, 99, 105–6
Beecher, T. K., 98
"Before Jehovah's Awful Throne" (Watts),
  49–50
"Beggar's Opera, The" (Gay), 69
"Begin, My Tongue, Some Heavenly Theme"
  (Watts), 50–51
"Behold the Glories of the Lamb" (Watts),
  44
Beiderwolf, William E., 127
Benson, Bob, 244, 372
Benson, Eva, 371
Benson, John T., 369, 371
Benson, John T., III, 372
Benson Company, 171, 242, 244, 250,
  261–62, 289, 339, 340, 369, 371–72.
  See also HeartWarming label
Benson Music Group, 381–82
Berlin, Irving, 142
Berliner, Emile, 136
Berman, Bess, 205

INDEX

Bossard, Henry, 209
Bostic, Joe, 208
Boyer, Harold, *How Sweet the Sound*, 168
Boyer Brothers, the, 145
Bradford, Alex, 211
Bradford, Perry, 136–37
Bradshaw, Terry, 329
Bradstreet, Anne, 35
Brady, Nicholas, 38, 48
Bramlett, Bonnie, 330
Branham, William, 322
Brentwood Music, 381
Brewster, W. Herbert, 169, 210
Bridge, 297
Bridges, Charles, 149
"Brighten the Corner," 128, 129–30
"Bringing in the Sheaves," 128, 161
Broadcast Music, Inc. (BMI), 139
broadside ballads, 69, 82
Brock, Dwight, 160, 161, 195
Brockman, Polk, 137
Brooklyn Bridge, the, 240
Brown, Aaron, 370
Brown, Colin, 100
Brown, James, 212, 339
Brown, Jonathan David, 350
Brown, R. R., 140
Brown, Scott Wesley, 295
Brownlee, Archie, 208–9
Brownlow, Governor William G., 95, 99
Brumley, Albert E., 160, 162, 188
Brunswick Records, 161
Bryant, Roy, 229
Buffett, Jimmy, 260
"Building Block," 295
Bullet Records, 195, 209
Butler, Don, 283
Butler, Jerry, 212
Byrds, the, 239

Cadence Records, 259
Caesar, Shirley, 211, 329, 383–84
    awards, 296, 333, 334, 340, 356
Cajetan, Cardinal, 11
Calhoun, Lee, 317–18
call-and-response, 80
Calvary Chapel (Costa Mesa), 249–50, 294
Calvin, John, 7–9, 17–22, 43
    The Institutes of Christianity, 7, 17–22
    personality of, 20
Calvinism, 8, 9, 34–35, 40, 43, 45, 46, 48, 50, 56
Camp, Steve, 295

"Camp Meeting Hour, The" (radio show), 324
camp meetings, 78, 79–80, 93–94, 103, 107, 319, 324
Campbell, Billy Joe, 192
Campbell, Glen, 240, 242, 353
Campbell, Lucie, 151
campfire songs, 247
Campus Crusades, 249
Canaan Records, 254, 369, 370
Canaanland Music, 370
Canada, Willis, 379
Canadian Quartet Convention, 380
Candle, 295, 296, 297, 330, 337, 374
Capitol Records, 193, 248, 250
Caravans, the, 302
Carlisle, Bob, 384
Carmichael, Ralph, 247, 248, 296, 368, 370, 373
Carnegie, Andrew, *The Gospel of Wealth*, 104
Carnegie Hall (New York), 168, 206, 208
Carson, Fiddlin' John, 137
Carter, Dave, 173–74
Carter, Jimmy, 242, 280, 281, 300, 313, 332
Carter Family, the, 160–61
Cartwright, Peter, 83–84
Caruso, Enrico, 138
Cash, Johnny, 260
Cason, J. M., 320
Cathedral of Tomorrow (Akron), 254
Cathedral Quartet, 296
Cathedrals, the, 254–56, 289
Catherine of Aragon, 13
"Catholic Hour" (television show), 309
Catholicism, 7, 9, 10–15, 21–22, 27, 28
    chant in, 269–72
    charismatic movement, 277
    in colonial America, 39, 40–41
    radio and television programming, 307–8, 309, 314–15
    Southwestern United States, 33
    Vatican II changes, 269, 274–75
Catledge, Gene, 197–98
CBS Records, 329
Central Music Company, 158, 171
"Chain Gang," 214
Champion Records, 209
Chance (Christian album), 295
"Change Is Gonna Come, A" (Cooke), 214
chant, 33, 269–72
Chapman, Gary, 330, 334, 343
Chapman, J. Wilbur, 126, 127
Chapman, Steven Curtis, 384

INDEX

INDEX

Orioles, the, 213
Orrell, Lloyd, 252
Ott, Doy, 193
"Our Father Thou in Heaven Above" (Luther), 28
"Out of the Depths I Cry to Thee" (Luther), 24
"Out of the Shadow-Land," 116–17
Owens, Fred, 167
Owens, Henry, 148
Owens, Paul, 209
"Ozark Jubilee," 258
Ozman, Agnes, 119–20

Pace, Adger M., 159
Pacific Gas & Electric, the, 240
Page, Emmett Morey, 147
Page, Patti, 177, 222, 226
Page, Ronnie, 259
Paino, Paul, 349
Paragon label, 370
Paramount Records, 149, 150, 161
Parker, Colonel Tom, 223, 263
Parker, Emory, 252
Parks, Barney, 167
Parks, Rosa, 230
Parnham, Charles Fox, 119–20
Pat Terry Group, 295
"Pat That Bread" (Dorsey), 151
Patent Note Publishing Company, 154
patriotic songs, 73, 131
Patterson, Pat, 192
Patti, Sandi, 297, 338, 340–42, 348, 384, 385
        awards, 340, 353, 356
Patti LaBelle & the Blue Belles, 238
Patton, Charlie, 137
Patty, Ron, 340–41
Paul, 4, 8, 9, 10, 46, 271
Paul VI, Pope, 274
Paxton, Gary S., 288–89, 297
Payne, Glen, 254–56
Paynes, the, 379
"Peace in the Valley" (Dorsey), 166, 226
"Peach Pickin' Time in Georgia," 161
Peacock Records, 206
Pearce, Billy, 367
Pearson, Carlton, 383
Peek, Dan, 297
Peer, Ralph, 160
Penn, Governor John, 67
Pentecostalism, 119–23, 145, 148, 157, 163, 169–70, 189, 208, 378

"hard gospel" in, 211
Presley and, 225
Swaggart and, 317–22
"People Get Ready," 239
People (group), 248
Perkins, Percell, 209
Perrys, the, 379
Peter, Paul and Mary, 238
Petra, 348–51, 384
Phil Keaggy Band, 295, 296
Phillips, Sam, 222–23, 225, 359
phonographs. See recordings
piano, 127
        in gospel accompaniment, 147–48, 160, 193, 200, 211
Pickard, "Pee Wee," 211
"Picture of Life's Other Side, A," 162
Pikering and Inglis, Ltd., 185
Pilgrim Baptist Church (Chicago), 149, 151, 164, 166, 302
Pilgrim Travelers, the, 209, 211, 214
Pilgrim's Progress (Gaither album), 295
pitch pipes, 37–38
Platt, Karen Marie, 333
Platters, the, 213
player pianos, 136
Pleasant, W. S., 144
pleasure gardens, 71–72
Plymouth Church (Brooklyn), 62, 98, 105–6
Plymouth colony, 33, 34, 35
Plymouth Congregational Church (Chicago), 106
Point of Grace, 384
Pointer Sisters, the, 339
polygamy, 14
popular music
        "art" and, 393–95
        early American, 71–75
        early twentieth century, 129–31, 136, 141–42
        gospel and, 189, 191, 206–7, 211–15, 238–39, 247–50, 260–64, 280–81, 299, 390
Port Royal colony, 34
Porter, Maggie L., 97, 99
positivism, 29–30
Praise, This Is Not a Dream (Mark), 296
praise and worship genre, 341–42, 362, 383, 391–92
Praise II (Maranatha album), 295, 296
Praise Strings (Maranatha album), 295
Praise Strings II (Maranatha album), 295
"Praise the Lord," 298